The Wolf at the Door

The Wolf at the Door

THE MENACE OF ECONOMIC INSECURITY AND HOW TO FIGHT IT

Michael J. Graetz and Ian Shapiro

Harvard University Press

Cambridge, Massachusetts

London, England

2020

Library of Congress Cataloging-in-Publication Data

Names: Graetz, Michael J., author. | Shapiro, Ian, author.
Title: The wolf at the door : the menace of economic insecurity and
how to fight it / Michael J. Graetz and Ian Shapiro.
Description: Cambridge, Massachusetts : Harvard University Press, 2020. |
Includes bibliographical references and index.
Identifiers: LCCN 2019031718 | ISBN 9780674980884 (cloth)
Subjects: LCSH: Economic security—United States. | United States—
Economic conditions—1945– | United States—Economic policy.
Classification: LCC HC103 .G73 2020 | DDC 330.973—dc23
LC record available at https://lccn.loc.gov/2019031718

For Brett Dignam and Frances McCall Rosenbluth

CONTENTS

The Wolf at the Door

It is not news that inequality has been growing for decades. Since the mid-1970s, working- and middle-class incomes and wealth have stagnated, while the rich have grown steadily richer. This is true across much of the developed world, but the trend has been especially pronounced in the United States. People disagree about the causes and extent of these changes. They also debate whether the greater equality that prevailed during World War II and its aftermath was normal, with our current circumstances being aberrational, or the other way around. But there is no doubt that today's levels of inequality have not been seen since the Gilded Age.

According to Federal Reserve economists, in 2018 the wealthiest 10 percent of US households owned 70 percent of the country's wealth and nearly two-thirds of its assets.[1] We are living in a world, as Vermont Senator Bernie Sanders has complained, in which the wealthiest 400 Americans own more than the bottom half of the population—some 150 million people—and the twenty-five best-paid hedge fund managers earn more than the combined salaries of 425,000 public school teachers.[2]

If anyone seemed less likely to mount a serious challenge to Hillary Clinton's presidential aspirations than a first-term African American senator from Illinois, it was surely Sanders, a seventy-four-year-old independent socialist who had not even joined the Democratic Party. Yet his presidential candidacy caught fire in 2016 by tapping into the discontent that had burst onto the political scene in New York's Zuccotti Park in September 2011. For months, Zucotti and town greens and other parks across the country were overtaken by the Occupy movement. It was a grass-roots mobilization against an economic and political regime that seemed rigged to benefit a tiny, privileged minority that taxpayers had bailed out of the financial collapse they had caused. By then they were resuming business as usual: the rebounding stock market was replenishing the missing millions in their brokerage and re-tirement accounts, their depleted home values were recovering, and it had become clear that none of these financiers would face criminal prosecution for the egregious malfeasance that cost tens of millions of vulnerable Americans their homes and jobs and brought the world economy to the brink of catastrophe. "We are the 99 percent!" had been the Zuccotti protestors' furious refrain. For them, the injustice was palpable.

The Sanders campaign wasn't linked to the Occupy movement, which had opposed all institutionalized forms of political action. But his supporters were motivated by the same rage at an Amer-ica in which the top 1 percent had come to own 38 percent of the wealth and was receiving 95 percent of all new income, while the wages of the bottom 60 percent were stagnant or declining.[3] Sanders belted out these kinds of statistics at rally after rally, winning caucuses and primaries across New England, the Rust Belt, and much of the West. Bellwether electoral states such as Wisconsin, Indiana, and West Virginia broke for Sanders. Hillary Clinton and her strategists, who had not taken Sanders seriously and expected to have the nomination wrapped up early in 2016, found themselves fighting for the Democratic mantle.

Clinton ultimately survived with strong support from the Democratic Party establishment and 55 percent of votes in the nominating contests. But she was wounded and forced to make substantial concessions to the Sanders campaign. Pressed to establish her bona fides with Sanders and his supporters, she embraced proposals for a $15-per-hour federal minimum wage and free college tuition for families making under $85,000 per year. She also promised to remove the US from the Trans-Pacific Partnership, which she had championed as secretary of state in the Obama administration.[4]

The improbable populist who did triumph in November 2016 echoed Sanders's focus on job loss and restoring middle- and working-class incomes. Like Sanders, Donald Trump railed against elites—especially bankers and other financiers—and against the political class that had championed globalization and free trade. Trump also shared Sanders's view that the US should replace existing trade agreements, including the Trans-Pacific Partnership, with protectionist measures that he claimed would not only stanch the hemorrhaging of jobs offshore but even reverse it.

To be sure, there were major differences between Trump and Sanders. Sanders championed Medicare and free college education for all. Trump made no such commitments. Sanders never mimicked Trump's racist appeals to mobilize supporters. Although, like Trump, Sanders had trouble connecting with minority voters—and so ran poorly in most Southern Democratic primaries—he did not demonize them. The villains in Sanders's world were domestic elites who used and threatened outsourcing to exploit American workers, not the foreign workers to whom the jobs were outsourced. Trump, by contrast, attacked foreign workers with a vengeance, whether beneficiaries of offshoring by US corporations or immigrants alleged to be taking American jobs at home. Both campaigns were populist, but they differed dramatically in message and tone.

There was another major and widely overlooked difference. Even though both candidates focused on alienated working- and middle-class voters, the inequalities that Sanders never stopped railing against played no role in Trump's campaign. Trump never mentioned the growing wealth gap; nor did he even hint that some people might have too much income or wealth. While Sanders portrayed the small elite hoarding the nation's wealth and attendant advantages as the main cause of working- and middle-class anger, Trump bragged constantly about his membership in that elite. He went on at length about his wealth—perhaps exaggerated—and boasted of paying few or no taxes.

Yet Trump won almost 63 million votes. Many came from people who had been suffering in relative and even absolute terms for decades. He earned their support without proposing to do anything about unequal incomes or to limit, let alone reduce, massive accumulations of wealth. When Trump insisted that he was "really, really rich!" he was not even affirming Ronald Reagan's aspirational message about an America in which people can become rich.[5] Trump's claims about his wealth were deployed instead to demonstrate his incorruptibility by special interests wielding campaign contributions. Only someone in his position could, he said, "drain the swamp." Trump assured his supporters that they would no longer be the suckers that successive Democratic and Republican administrations had made them. He promised to bring back their mining and industrial jobs. But he didn't say that they would get rich—or that someone else would be taken down.

Fear, not outrage at inequality, was at the heart of Trump's rallying cry: fear of bomb-carrying Muslim terrorists and of brown-skinned immigrants crossing the southern border. Fear of jobs fleeing to Mexico and Asia and of job losses to Chinese imports. Fear, to borrow Arlie Hochschild's phrase, of losing out to others who were "cutting in line."[6]

Trump was shrewd to ignore inequality in favor of a relentless focus on the insecurities wrought by wage and job loss. For one thing, equality, however important to Sanders and the Occupy movement, is a tough sell to Americans beyond the left flank of the Democratic Party. For another, Trump's stance signaled to the Republican establishment that he had no plans to tax away their incomes and wealth. This helped defuse potential establishment coalitions that might otherwise oppose his unorthodox campaign. Resistance to tax increases has been the holy grail of Republican politics since California enacted its tax-limiting Proposition 13 in 1978 and has been a nonnegotiable Republican position since 1992, when George H. W. Bush paid a heavy price for violating his "Read my lips: no new taxes" pledge. Trump's fidelity to Republican tax orthodoxy meant that, however much the party establishment disliked him, few Republicans running for office would risk an open rift with him once he became assured of the nomination.

Trump targeted working- and, increasingly, middle-class Americans where they hurt most. He made brilliant use of a truth that social psychologists and political economists have known for decades: people are more powerfully motivated by the losses they experience or anticipate than by the prospect of gain.[7] "America's best days are yet to come" was an effective slogan for Ronald Reagan in the early 1980s, but Hillary Clinton's deployment of it in 2016 was tone-deaf to the effects of decades of stagnation capped by the financial crisis and its aftermath. Consciously or not, Trump was wiser to coopt a different Reagan slogan, insisting that he would "Make America Great Again." This signaled that his agenda was to restore something that had been taken away from millions of Americans. It fueled what Katherine Cramer has described as a politics of resentment, as Trump directed his ire at supposed villains at home and abroad whom he alleged were responsible for the decline.[8] The racist and chauvinistic element of this message fed the anger of people who had come to feel, as Hochschild put it, like strangers in their own land.

Twenty-sixteen was a watershed year not only in the United States, but also—as Adam Tooze has noted—across most of the established democracies.[9] Repeatedly, voters backed parties and positions that emphasized their perceived losses. In June the British shocked the world—and many of themselves—by voting in a referendum to leave the European Union. Furious voters in declining industrial cities and neglected rural regions in England and Wales vented their rage at the prosperous City of London and immigrants who they believed were taking their jobs. In the next few years, resurgent anti-immigrant parties would rattle establishments from Italy to the Netherlands, Austria, Germany, and even famously placid Nordic democracies—as well as in the European Parliament.[10] Aberrational as the Trump campaign had seemed at the time, it exemplified this larger pattern.

In the midterm elections two years later, both Republicans and Democrats employed fear to motivate their voters. Trump echoed some of the themes of his 2016 campaign, telling supporters that Democratic control of Congress threatened the economic gains that had occurred since his election. More pointedly, he emphasized xenophobic fear of immigrants. The coincidental march to the border of a "caravan" of refugees fleeing violence in their Central American homelands provided an occasion for Trump to stoke fear of an immigrant invasion. He claimed, without evidence, that Middle Eastern terrorists had joined the few thousand migrants, and he deployed troops to the border in an ostentatious, perhaps illegal, display of his resistance.

Democrats emphasized different fears: the fear that Trump's race-baiting enabled potentially violent white-nationalists, fear that he debased the office of the presidency, and, most importantly, fear that two more years of unified Republican government would bring cuts to health care and Social Security. Both parties' appeals to fear worked, yielding a split decision with Democrats capturing a thirty-six-seat majority in the House, while Republicans expanded their slim Senate majority by two seats.

Whether Trump's proposals held any realistic prospect of addressing the anger and insecurity he had tapped into is another matter. In the chapters that follow we maintain that they did not and do not. Still, an essential lesson to draw from these recent elections—one that too few analysts have appreciated—is that addressing voters' insecurity is vital to the success of any future political program. That is the central message of this book.

Fighting insecurity might involve attending to some aspects of the growth of inequality, but the primary focus must be on mitigating sources of economic insecurity. We can glean a sense of just how complex the relations between inequality and insecurity are from the fact that 75 percent of all venture capital in the US is invested in New York, Massachusetts, and California, yet these are among the most unequal states in the nation.[11] At the least this suggests that adopting policies to expand employment and wage growth might live in some tension with an agenda of reducing inequality. And when we think about the political coalitions needed to implement policies that reduce insecurity, these tensions often become more complex.

These complexities must be engaged, not ignored or wished away. Trumpeting desirable polices in a political vacuum is pointless; they inevitably fall by the wayside. But while policy without politics might be empty, politics without policy is blind. Focusing on what is politically salable, without informed attention to whether it can be effective, lures people into strategies that will not only fail but also can make things worse. Sometimes that results from cynicism or opportunism, but it can also happen despite the best of intentions: misdiagnosed problems lead reformers to converge on counterproductive policies, as we will see. Our goal here is not only to draw attention to Americans' concerns with insecurity, but also to set out elements of a politically feasible agenda to combat it. This means attending to the realities of policy and politics and to the ways in which they interact.

Our central focus is on legislative rather than electoral politics. Vital as elections are to the enterprise of policymaking, they are only part of the story. James Curry and Frances Lee remind us that, even in today's polarized era, the vast majority of legislation needs bipartisan support in at least one chamber of Congress to be enacted. This is true even when one party controls both houses.[12] And America's chronically weak political parties—whose leaders face severe constraints in their efforts to compel members to support bills—make coalition-building within parties as important as garnering support across the aisle.[13] Individual senators and representatives must respond to local constituencies and outside interests that fund their campaigns.[14] The resulting challenges can be addressed only by keeping one unblinking eye on building and sustaining effective coalitions that support policies that will work. That is what we do here.

This is not to gainsay the importance of electoral politics, which obviously enable and constrain what politicians can do. Indeed, failing to build effective coalitions to fight economic insecurity has fueled the destructive electoral politics that we have been witnessing since 2016. Blaming others—whether immigrants, global elites, or the wealthy—is often the path of least resistance for power-seeking populists because it's like catnip for potential supporters. Nepetalactone, the active ingredient in catnip, induces euphoria in most felines for about ten minutes, after which they become inured to it for a few hours until it can seduce them once again.[15] The bliss of populist scapegoating lasts longer, even though it is no more nourishing. And whereas catnip is harmless, populist scapegoating breeds destructive policies along with ugly politics.

Insecurity is the heart of the matter. Middle- and low-income families have shockingly few resources to fall back on, with millions just one emergency away from economic disaster. In 2018 fully a third of all families with incomes between $40,000 and $85,000 per year reported that they could not pay for an emergency expense of $400 with cash or with a credit card they could pay off by the end of the month.[16] Only about 40 percent of families had liquid assets equivalent to three months of expenses, and fewer than 30 percent had liquid assets equivalent to six months of expenses.[17] Insecurity is by no means the only source of the nativism, racism, and tribalism that feed many populist agendas. They have long been features of the American political landscape.[18] But the chronic insecurity that is creeping up the income ladder makes them more potent politically. This is a book about feasible—indeed vital—ways of addressing that insecurity. We ignore that challenge at our peril.

CHAPTER ONE

Then and Now

Fortune smiled, grinned even, if you were lucky enough to be a white male in America in the decade or so following World War II. For starters, the United States had all the money. Europe and Japan were a shambles; China was embarking on a dark, destructive communist experiment; much of the developing world was consumed with battles for national independence; Eastern Europe was under the Soviet Union's thumb; and the Soviet leadership cared more about its hegemonic worldwide ambitions than the well-being of its people. The US economy was poised to expand at a sustained pace for nearly a generation—an economic expansion fulfilling the nation's promise as the land of exceptional opportunity.

For young men just back from the war—in which virtually every able-bodied American participated—the federal government offered free college education through the GI bill. Those who didn't go to college, even unskilled workers, usually had good jobs—jobs that paid a living wage and could last a lifetime. Or they started small businesses, which had excellent chances to succeed given the years of robust economic growth on the horizon.

American social institutions were strong. Stable family life was commonplace. Granted, families were never so problem-free as the Nelsons, of the popular, long-running sitcom *The Adventures of Ozzie and Harriet*.[1] For the Nelsons—Ozzie puttering around the house in his cardigan sweater; his wife Harriet, always in the kitchen; and their two sons, David and the rock-star Ricky—a serious problem consisted of having two chairs delivered to their house by mistake. This sugarcoated caricature of a comfortable, worry-free middle-class family life has come to symbolize the 1950s and early 1960s. But even if Hollywood wasn't portraying reality, one income, typically the husband's, often financed the family's everyday living expenses and the purchase of a home, which was frequently supported by a federally subsidized and guaranteed fixed-rate mortgage. Paying for housing and health insurance consumed only a modest portion of the family's income, as did college—a stark contrast with today, when good health insurance coverage and housing are shockingly expensive, and many private colleges and universities charge more than most American families earn annually.[2] Divorce was quite rare in the postwar years, as were single-parent households. Mothers of young children seldom worked outside the home. Family dinners were routine.

Like the family, other public and private institutions were strong. Public education offered ladders up for white children all over the country. Labor unions represented more than one-third of all private-sector workers and were often powerful enough to negotiate good wages and benefits, including health insurance and lifetime pensions that paid retired workers a substantial fraction of their preretirement wages. Unions also played a major role representing middle-class workers' interests in federal and state elections and legislatures. Pluralistic secular and religious organizations offered important social support, confirming Alexis de Tocqueville's observation more than a century earlier that "Americans of all ages, all stations of life and all types of dispositions are forever forming associations."[3] Many of these associations depended on families that could thrive economically with one breadwinning parent. It was a far cry from the isolation and individualism depicted in Robert Putnam's 2000 book *Bowling Alone*.[4]

In 1972 US gross domestic product was more than twice as great in real terms as it had been in 1945, and during the postwar period robust economic growth had become a widespread expectation.[5] When in 1971 Richard Nixon repeated Milton Friedman's quip that "we are all Keynesians now," Nixon was referring to Keynes's claim that, with the right policies, economists could end economic insecurity in the "Western world." Indeed, the consensus among economists was that, by fiddling with taxation and public spending, the government could ensure widely distributed economic growth.[6]

Together, these conditions—growth and confidence in government—produced a sense of economic security and inculcated a faith that upward mobility was available to most. People were confident that their children's lives would be better than theirs.

The happy portrait of American middle-class life painted here was dominated by the color white. African Americans were ghettoized in both Northern and Southern cities. In the South, Jim Crow reigned. Public schools rarely served as pathways up for black children. And any woman who needed or wanted to work outside the home found limited opportunities: for most, only "pink collar" jobs such as teaching, secretarial work, and nursing were available. Black women faced even fewer options. When Adlai Stevenson campaigned for the 1952 Democratic presidential nomination with the slogan "You never had it so good!" he was appealing to voters who were insulated from these realities, never suspecting that irresistible pressure for change was around the corner.[7]

There are many ways to date the turning points. Serious efforts to remedy the immense injustices experienced by minorities and women had just begun paying dividends by the mid-1960s.[8] The Civil Rights Act of 1964 and the Voting Rights Act of 1965 expanded economic and political opportunities for African Americans. The Equal Rights Amendment (ERA), which would have enhanced women's rights, passed both houses of Congress in 1972 but was never ratified. Nevertheless, Supreme Court decisions of the 1970s, along with a bevy of new federal laws, provided women with comparable guarantees—a "de facto ERA."[9]

The Immigration and Naturalization Act of 1965 transformed America's immigration policy. Since the 1920s the US had used immigration quotas based on national origin, which strongly favored immigrants from Northern and Western Europe. By 1965 a political consensus had emerged to eliminate this discriminatory immigration policy, and Congress made family unification an immigration priority. Massachusetts Senator Edward Kennedy assured his Senate colleagues that under the new legislation the level of immigration would remain "substantially the same" and that "the ethnic mix of this country will not be upset."[10] This prediction could hardly have been more wrong. In the 1950s more than 70 percent of US immigrants came from Europe and Canada, with less than 30 percent from Latin America, the Caribbean, and Asia. In the 1980s only 11 percent of US immigrants came from Europe and Canada; more than 85 percent were from Latin America, the Caribbean, and Asia.[11] Along with the civil rights revolution, this unintended—and unexpected—transformation of immigration policy would profoundly affect the workforce and national politics.[12]

Few foresaw the impending political realignment, but one who did was the prescient and controversial Republican political strategist Kevin Phillips. In his late twenties, the Bronx native became an architect of Richard Nixon's Southern strategy. Phillips predicted much of what would happen in his 1969 book *The Emerging Republican Majority*.[13] "Liberalism," he wrote, "has turned away from the common people and become institutionalized into an establishment, its spokesmen are driven around in limousines and supported by rich foundations, the television networks and publishing houses, the knowledge industry, the billion dollar universities and the urban consulting firms which profiteer from poverty." He added that all "the talk about Republicans making inroads into the Negro vote is persiflage. . . . The more Negroes who register as Democrats in the South, the sooner the Negrophobe whites will quit the Democrats and become Republicans. That's where the votes are." Phillips concluded, "For a long time, the liberal-conservative split was on economic issues. That favored the Democrats until the focus shifted from programs which taxed the few for the many to things like 'welfare' that taxed the many for the few."[14]

As Thomas and Mary Edsall have shown, this last sentiment—with race lurking in the background and rising housing prices and property taxes in the foreground—became the wedge for enacting California's Proposition 13, the June 1978 referendum that added property-tax limits to the state's constitution. The vote ushered in a national anti-government and anti-tax movement in the Republican Party.[15] This movement has had such success and staying power that, a generation later, the Republican activist Grover Norquist described the anti-tax issue as the glue that holds the Republican coalition together.[16]

In the mid-1970s economic growth began leveling off and most incomes started to flatten. Nineteen-seventy-three was the year of the first oil embargo, when oil prices spiked and Americans were forced to pay Middle Eastern oil-producing nations enormous sums just to keep their homes lit and their gas tanks full, a dramatic signal that the postwar economic boom was over. Since then, middle-income families have struggled—often without success—to increase take-home pay to keep pace with rising prices. During the middle and late 1970s, stagflation—a toxic mix of high inflation and low growth—afflicted the American economy. In 1979, when the revolution led by Ayatollah Khomeini replaced the Shah of Iran, a second oil price spike and a failed attempt to rescue Americans held hostage by the Iranians further shook Americans' confidence.[17] A new age of economic limits had arrived.

From Steel Valley to Rust Belt

"If misery loves company, misery has company enough." Henry David Thoreau was ruminating on the reality that, in nature, beauty is routinely destroyed by disease.[18] The same is true of industrial centers. Misery and decay have certainly been the fate of Youngstown, Ohio, the once-thriving manufacturing center that straddles the Mahoning River in the foothills of the Appalachian Mountains, roughly equidistant from Cleveland and Pittsburgh and midway between New York and Chicago. It is hard to find a city that more fully embodies industrial decline and the insecurities of American workers. Youngstown shows how extensive, geographically concentrated job losses can reverberate through communities with devastating cumulative effect.

Len Ballack has lived this reality. He was drinking coffee on the golf course after eighteen holes with his friends when he heard that Campbell Works, formerly the Youngstown Sheet and Tube Company, was shutting down and eliminating 5,000 jobs. "I was 48 years old. I had two teenage kids. I had a good job, and I was making halfway decent money. I had security," he told the *Washington Post*. "I was fortunate because a year after the shutdown my wife, who had been a school teacher ... got a contract. . . . It helps quite a lot. But it still doesn't give me anything to do as far as work goes. . . . It makes me sad because of what used to be here." He continued, "It's time the government started taking care of its own here. . . . It makes me mad that we can turn around and spend millions and millions of dollars—billions!—to help people overseas that spit on us yet we can't seem to help people here that need it the most."

Ballack lost his job on the day that everyone in Youngstown still calls Black Monday, September 19, 1977. Other local steel mills closed soon after, laying off 1,500 workers in one, 2,500 in another, and 1,700 in the last to shut its doors. Three years later, in September 1980—when Ronald Reagan and Jimmy Carter both campaigned in Youngstown—unemployment there was nearly 14 percent.[19] In 1995 Bruce Springsteen released an iconic, nostalgic ode to the steel mills: "Here in Youngstown/ . . . Taconite, coke, and limestone/Fed my children and made my pay/Them smokestacks reachin' like the arms of God/Into a beautiful sky of soot and clay." Listen to his refrain to Jeanette, the old furnace at Youngstown Sheet and Tube: "In Youngstown/Here in Youngstown/My sweet Jenny, I'm sinkin' down/Here darlin' in Youngstown."[20]

Visiting Youngstown is a longstanding tradition for US presidential candidates. George W. Bush visited during his 2000 campaign. Bill Clinton apparently holds the record, having traveled to Youngstown eight times.[21] Barack Obama and Donald Trump agreed on little, but both went to Youngstown to demonstrate their commitments to restoring manufacturing jobs to the local economy. Obama visited Youngstown seven times, four before he was elected president. During a May 2010 appearance he described how an expenditure on a Youngstown rail spur during his presidency had prompted a $600 million investment from Vallourec Star, a subsidiary of a French company, for a new plant to produce steel tubing for the oil and gas industry.[22] The plant, which is highly mechanized, ultimately employed about 350 workers.[23]

Seven years later, on a sweltering July evening in 2017, President Trump, who had visited Youngstown three times as a candidate, went back for one of his signature campaign-style rallies. He told a crowd of several thousand, "I was looking at some of those big, once-incredible, job-producing factories. And my wife, Melania, said, 'What happened?' I said, 'Those jobs have left Ohio.'" Trump then promised, "They are all coming back. . . . We're going to fill up those factories or rip 'em down and build new ones. That's what's going to happen."[24] How it would happen, Trump left unsaid.

Youngstown's unemployment rate was 6.7 percent in 1970. It has been above 15 percent at every decennial census since, except in 2000 when it hit a low of 11.3 percent after the economic boom of the late 1990s. Its population in 2015 was less than 66,000, just over half its level in 1980. About 23,000 of these 2015 residents were employed locally. The median per capita income was $17,280, as compared to a national median of $47,669. The population had been three-quarters white in 1970; by 2015 it was 48 percent black and 9.3 percent Latino. Nearly 20 percent of Youngstown's housing units were vacant; the median home price was about $45,000.[25] During the depths of the Great Recession in 2010, only 2,300 workers were employed in manufacturing jobs. By 2015 the number had increased to 3,600, which still was less than 20 percent of the total in 1970. Nearly as many Youngstown residents were employed in the retail, arts, entertainment, and recreation industries, and almost twice as many worked in education and health care. The institutional, political, and social changes wrought by Youngstown's collapse are profound.

Bob Vansickle, appointed to direct the new mental health center three years after the Youngstown Steel and Tube plant closed, described the social problems in 1980: "You see it manifested in child abuse. You see it manifested in alcohol and drug abuse. . . . They're hanging around bars, telling each other war stories, and when they get enough juice in them, to use the vernacular, they come home and beat up on the wife and the kids or find some other mechanisms to avoid their responsibilities."[26] Now, nearly four decades later, the opioid crisis is rampant. The health challenges remain daunting. And the tax base to support these costs has shrunken dramatically. To work at today's high-tech steel plants, one almost always needs a college education. The private labor unions that once protected large workforces are also gone. The 350 workers managing the huge industrial machines at the Vallourec Star mill are well paid, but when you ask them whether they have any interest in unionizing, they scoff. Well-paying, unionized steel-mill jobs for high school graduates are a thing of the past.

Despite all of Youngstown's problems and its long decline, residents and many of its diaspora remain committed to improving the community. Many are surprisingly optimistic. But the insistence of US political leaders—indeed of both Barack Obama and Donald Trump—that the future of Youngstown lies in a renaissance of American manufacturing is Pollyannaish. Youngstown's decline and efforts at recovery now span more than forty years. Politicians throughout that period have promised that the clock might run backwards—restoring the city's vitality as a center of steel and other manufacturing jobs. But this nostalgic yearning ignores the realities of lower-cost production abroad and of the technological transformations that now enable steel to be produced with a fraction of the workers once required. Building four more Vallourec-type plants in Youngstown would cost more than $6 billion, yet—even assuming no increase in the use of robots or other mechanization—this would provide fewer than 1,600 full-time jobs.

Slower Growth

As the steel industry well illustrates, the economy is now global and the United States no longer dominates it. In 1960, with less than 6 percent of the world's population, the US produced nearly 40 percent of the world's output. The US now accounts for less than one-quarter, and given a slower growth rate than countries like China and India, that number seems certain to decline.[27] Global trade in goods and services has risen exponentially, while the US share of merchandise exports has fallen from nearly 15 percent in the 1960s to less than 9 percent in the 2010s.[28] In the 1960s 90 percent of the world's largest twenty companies were headquartered in the US; in the 2010s fewer than half were.[29] Manufacturing and selling products depends on global supply chains: international networks of companies that produce and distribute goods. Capital moves around the world with the click of a mouse. As Gareth Jones has written, "Fundamental to the power of capital . . . is its geographic mobility, to shape-shift from being something fixed to being a flow."[30] This mobility limits any nation's ability to tax capital or business income at the kinds of high rates of the postwar period.

The composition of US economic output has also shifted dramatically. Technology now allows companies headquartered in Seattle, Peoria, or San Jose to monitor production of their products anywhere in the world, enabling them to vary output in response to worldwide fluctuations in demand. Meanwhile, dramatic decreases in transportation costs allow these products to be sold profitably anywhere. Firms can produce only as much as they need to, and they can do so wherever they choose. This has had a negative impact on US manufacturing employment. Manufacturing accounted for 18.2 million jobs in 1974 but supplied only about

12 million in 2016, despite the substantial growth in the US population. In stark contrast, the number of private-sector employees in service industries grew from just over 40 million to nearly 104 million.[31] Men can no longer afford to allow traditional masculine pride to let them to shun service jobs, such as in health care, in the hope that high-wage factory jobs will soon spring up in their hometowns.[32] Political leaders like to talk about reviving and expanding US manufacturing, but the public would be better served by ensuring that service jobs produce a living wage. Returning to the postwar era is not an option.

Jobs are less secure than ever. Artificial intelligence and automation, including robotics, pose new threats to American workers. One study of the deployment of robots in nineteen industries between 1990 and 2007 found large negative effects on both employment and wages, particularly for men and for workers with less than a college degree, although that conclusion and the timing of the robot threat are controversial.[33] But no one doubts that technological advances in the years ahead will pose large risks, especially to workers who perform relatively routine tasks.[34] The greatest costs might ultimately be imposed on workers in developing countries, but the impact will be felt everywhere. Analysts debate how often someone entering the workforce today should expect to change employment, but the prospect for lifetime job security—once a natural expectation of American high school graduates—is disappearing. The technological revolution has shifted the best-paying jobs to workers with at least a college education, and many of them no longer enjoy any real job security.

Economists disagree over the extent to which imports, especially from China, and offshoring of jobs are mainly responsible for job insecurity or whether technology is the main culprit. For workers who lose their jobs, it hardly matters. But blaming globalization is tempting politically. It yields identifiable villains in the form of avaricious foreigners, and it invites muscular protectionism, even if the benefits are often mainly symbolic and costly to overall domestic employment and welfare. Donald Trump illustrated as much both on the campaign trail and in office. Many more workers applauded his 2018 tariffs on steel and aluminum than gained economic security by this action, which inevitably cost more jobs than it saved.[35]

It is difficult, in contrast, to find politicians who indulge in antediluvian ranting against technology. Doing that risks being lambasted as a quixotic opponent of progress, a latter-day version of the Luddites who fought the innovations of the industrial revolution. Nor does technology offer up politically defenseless targets to demonize. There is no point in attacking artificial intelligence, driverless vehicles, 3-D printing, and sophisticated robotics. The people who create and use them vote, lobby, and donate to campaigns and politicians. Many of them would resist efforts to limit innovation. So it is not surprising that most of the political rhetoric and action around threats to job loss focuses on trade.

Political geography reinforces this tendency. Job losses from offshoring and imports are often concentrated in particular industries and localities. This plays into the "all politics is local" dynamic in constituency-based political systems like the US, because politicians must respond to developments in their states and districts or risk losing to opponents who will attack them for failing to do so. So when expanding Chinese furniture imports in the late 1990s had a devastating impact on furniture manufacturing jobs in Western North Carolina and Eastern Tennessee, trade was bound to become electorally charged in these states.[36] In such circumstances, politicians are often tempted to run on protectionist platforms that show them responding to their constituents' pain and determined to hold culprits to account.

The jobs lost to technology have less to do with location. Historically technological advances have mostly replaced workers with no more than a high school education who perform routine tasks and less frequently college-educated workers who perform more complex ones.[37] This can happen anywhere, though it has particularly aggravated job loss in agricultural, rust belt, and mining states, leaving employees in information-heavy fields like engineering, computer software, information technology, and financial services—often concentrated in states like California and New York—more secure. But this might be changing, increasing the vulnerability of the exam-passing classes. Greater reliance on big data and computing power in fields like finance and investment banking, and growing use of off-the-shelf software to handle mortgages, consumer finance, and tasks that used to be performed by middle managers, means that deskilling and concomitant job loss are spreading out geographically and creeping up the socioeconomic ladder. Technology gets less political attention than trade and globalization, but it is at least as large a looming challenge.

The Human Impact of Job Loss

In July 2018 the Trump administration announced $12 billion in government relief for farmers who had been harmed by the escalating trade war with China, and in 2019 the White House added another $16 billion. The president no doubt expected gratitude, but instead he ran into a buzz saw of criticism from many intended beneficiaries who objected that, as Missouri soybean farmer Neal Bredehoeft put it, "We, as farmers, don't want handouts."[38] Bredehoeft was giving voice to an outlook that dates at least to the debates about unemployment during the Depression: that being paid not to work is profoundly dispiriting and corrosive of self-esteem. As one of countless jobless interviewees said to an investigator in the early 1930s, "During the depression, I lost something. Maybe you call it self-respect, but in losing it I also lost the respect of my children, and I am afraid that I am losing my wife."[39] Like Bredehoeft eight decades later, he was looking to the government to restore and protect his capacity to work, and with it his dignity.

This marks a signal difference between American ideologies of social protection and social democracy as it is typically understood in Europe. Perhaps because of historical association with debates about the "parliamentary road to socialism" or perhaps for other reasons, European social democracy has always been linked to egalitarian commitments and the redistribution of income and wealth.[40] That cannot be said of the US. To be sure, there have been radical socialist groups with varying support in American history. It is also true that elite acquiescence in the New Deal was partly motivated by felt imperatives—however warranted—to forestall an increased appeal of communism to millions of unemployed American workers during the Depression. But none of this translated into meaningful demands for egalitarian redistribution. Rather, as David Kennedy points out in his history of the Depression, the New Deal's defining focus was instead on eliminating the sources of insecurity so that people could provide for themselves.

Kennedy notes that there was no encompassing ideology behind the New Deal. Roosevelt made up his "bewildering array of sometimes contradictory policies" as he went along in response to shifting coalitions, conflicting expert advice, and changing political and economic circumstances. Deficit spending to create employment and stimulate demand was undermined by pressures to balance budgets as FDR tacked back and forth among hard-money bankers and proponents of inflation, trust-busters and regulators, Southern racists and Northern liberals, and collective bargaining advocates and proponents of managed prices and wages.[41] FDR had to navigate the resulting crosscurrents while battling stubborn unemployment, which stood at almost 25 percent when he took office and remained above 20 percent for much of the 1930s.[42]

Notably absent, however, were significant demands for egalitarian redistribution. Even the populist senator and former governor of Louisiana Huey Long, who abandoned FDR when he concluded that the New Deal did not go far enough, focused mainly on lifting people at the bottom. True, he proposed a capital levy on accumulations of wealth above $1 million ($18.6 million in 2018) and limits on personal accumulations to between $5 and $8 million ($93 and $149 million in 2018), but that policy, had it been implemented, would have affected tiny numbers of people. For those at the bottom, he pushed a guaranteed family income of between $2,000 and $2,500 ($37,375 to $46,700 in 2018 dollars), old-age pensions, and publicly funded education for all.[43] Long was in any case an outlier. His proposals never stood a serious chance of being adopted by the Senate, let alone becoming law.

Long is sometimes credited with pressuring FDR to enact some of the more far-reaching elements of his Second New Deal in 1935.[44] The only one of these that was explicitly, if mildly, targeted at the top was that year's Revenue Act. All the others were geared, like the Works Progress Administration, to creating employment or, like the Social Security Act and Aid to Dependent Children, to reducing poverty and economic insecurity. Insuring people against the prospect of having their lives ravaged as they had been by the economy's collapse was the New Deal's central motif and motivation. As FDR put it in his message to Congress in June 1934, "I place the *security* of the men, women, and children of the nation first." People had a right, he went on, to three sources of security: decent housing, productive work, and social insurance. The last would provide "security against the hazards and vicissitudes of life." In the past, this had been attained "through the interdependence of members of families upon each other and of families within a small community upon each other." But "the complexities of great communities and of organized industry make less real these simple means of security." In the future this task would fall to the government.[45]

If New Deal protections were aimed at—and justified by—reducing insecurity, they nonetheless had redistributive effects. Social Security's contribution and payout schedules, for example, mean that well-paid workers subsidize the retirement of those paid less. This makes such a program inevitably redistributive. However, Americans have tended not to think of Social Security in these terms. Longstanding ideology emphasizes the government's role in enabling people to provide for themselves and their families through work, maintaining their self-respect in the process. Thus the redistribution label was absent from FDR's proposals. This distinguishes the New Deal approach to social insurance from European social democracy's, not to mention socialism's. And because the New Deal has been the most successful and far-reaching model of legislation to combat economic insecurity in American history, it should not be dismissed lightly.

Stubborn Depression-era unemployment was eventually vanquished by the war economy and then by the postwar rising tide that lifted the fortunes of the great majority of middle-class families during the next three decades. The changes in labor markets since the mid-1970s, however, present different and more enduring challenges. Many manufacturing jobs that have not migrated abroad will continue disappearing to technology, and the service sector has been divided into well-paying jobs for those on the right side of the information revolution and insecure low-paying ones for the rest. This combination of wage stagnation and employment insecurity feeds the alienation that accompanies fears of downward mobility and diminished options for one's children, which has been well documented by Katherine Cramer and Arlie Hochschild, among others.[46]

Today, guaranteed lifetime job security is available to few other than federal judges and tenured professors. Most Americans live with levels of employment insecurity that would have been unimaginable in the post–World War II generation. People born in the later years of the baby boom, who joined the labor market as wage stagnation was setting in during the 1970s, held an average of 11.9 jobs between the ages of eighteen and fifty—more than half after age twenty-five.[47]

Only recently have researchers begun cataloging the costs of involuntary job loss.[48] The psychological damage to unemployed workers and their families is often less serious when there is widespread unemployment due to an economic downturn or when there is someone else to blame: an employer who has closed a plant, Wall Street bankers and subprime mortgage borrowers during the Great Recession, importers, or immigrants who are thought to keep wages down. But the problems faced by the involuntarily unemployed have become less episodic and more dispiriting. Losing a job is often followed by long periods of unemployment, part-time employment, and lower earnings in the next job, even when job search and retraining services are available. In the short run, people lose on average a third of their earnings; over their lifetime, they lose a fifth of their cumulative earnings.[49] These losses are greatest for older and less-educated workers. They form a new "precariat" whose existence and vulnerability are obscured by data that show the economy operating at near-full employment. Today's low-income workers find themselves working fewer hours for lower pay than those of a generation ago. Eight years after the financial crisis, twelve percent of households with at least one employed worker were living in poverty.[50]

The economic costs of involuntary job loss are often compounded by physical, psychological, and social costs, including declines in well-being that often show up as anxiety, insecurity, depression, and loss of self-esteem. One measure of this toll has been the sharp rise in Social Security disability claims. In 1985 2.2 percent of the workforce lodged disability claims; two decades later, that figure had nearly doubled to over 4 percent.[51] Job loss also debilitates families, sometimes resulting in divorce, and a parent's job loss often produces intergenerational costs as their children call into question the value of hard work and education. When the next job involves a step down in money and status, reemployment only partly mitigates these costs. It is no coincidence that a national opioid crisis has emerged as job insecurity has become more widespread, or that deaths from drug overdoses—including of synthetic opioids—reached all-time highs in West Virginia, Ohio, and Pennsylvania in 2017.[52]

A Zero-Sum Society?

At the end of the 1970s, MIT economist Lester Thurow insisted in his best seller, *The Zero-Sum Society*, that the only significant economic question for government had become: To whom should the nation's limited output be distributed?[53] Thurow believed that people would inevitably turn to politics for answers, but the Watergate debacle and the failures in Vietnam had made Americans gloomy about politics at a time when economic insecurity had increased to levels not seen since the Depression. Even Ronald

Reagan's sunny optimism failed to persuade most Americans that their economic well-being was assured.

Reagan's election as president in 1980 made it undeniable that the working-class Democratic coalition—which had dominated US politics from Franklin Roosevelt's New Deal through Lyndon Johnson's Great Society—had split apart. Issues of race and immigration performed crucial supporting roles in this transformation, but by the time of Reagan's election, economic insecurity had come to play the lead. Reagan insisted that "government is the problem"—the source of economic malaise and insecurity—and that vigorous individualism operating in an unregulated market economy would be the solution.[54] But, in spite of deregulation and tax cuts, economic insecurity has continued to haunt the populace. Although there were periods of respite, especially during the information technology boom of the late 1990s, subsequent decades did little to dispel the public's fears. Instead the economic forces of the twenty-first century have exacerbated Americans' economic challenges.

Given the concentration of the gains at the top of the income scale and the low levels of economic growth since the Great Financial Crisis of 2007–2009, it is not surprising that economists, political scientists, and politicians have turned their spotlights on the top 1 percent. Economists who have focused on data concerning inequality of income—especially the share of income going to the top 1 percent—labelled the postwar period the "egalitarian era" in an effort to draw a sharp contrast with the present.[55] But the focus on the top 1 percent diverts attention from critical differences between today's economy and that of the postwar period, and deflects us from devising viable responses to the challenges we now face. Obsessing about the very top is a distraction from the more pressing problems of economic stagnation and insecurity among increasing numbers of the middle class as well as the poor.

The big problem is not that the top 1 percent—or even the top 0.1 percent—has thrived during this transformation of the economy. That is an injustice, and their tendency to avoid taxes and lobby against tax increases adds insult to injury. But the fundamental problem, arising from many causes, is the insecurity facing the hollowed-out middle class and those living in or near poverty. It typically takes two working parents to provide an adequate family income, but single-parent households abound, especially among women with less than a college education. Life expectancy for both men and women at the middle of the income distribution has dropped in recent years. There is an epidemic of drug abuse and even suicide among working-class white men in America. In 2018 one-fourth of middle-income adults said they skipped some kind of medical care because of its cost.[56] Total US household debt is now $13.7 trillion, surpassing the 2008 peak, with most of the increase since then having gone to pay for cars and colleges.[57] Defined-benefit retirement pensions are a relic, leaving retirees vulnerable to the vicissitudes of business cycles and financial markets. Labor unions now represent just over 10 percent of workers, with the majority of those in the public sector. Rising costs have put adequate housing out of reach for millions of Americans. In 2017 a worker had to earn $17.14 an hour—nearly 2.5 times the federal minimum-wage—to afford a one-bedroom rental home without spending more than 30 percent of his or her income.[58] Middle-class fathers and mothers, struggling to make a living, now fear—with good reason—that their children will be worse off than they are.

There is even greater economic stress among the poor and near poor. One in every five children in the US lives in poverty, more than in 1970. The number of children living with a single parent with only a high school education or less has reached new highs. Nearly a fifth of American have less than *half* the median income, even taking government transfers into account. Similar, if less dramatic, stories could be told about all the advanced capitalist democracies.

Some commentators brush this dismal picture aside by insisting that America is the land of great opportunity for all. Reality demurs. Perhaps the United States once led the world in upward mobility, but today it is in the middle of the pack of rich economies—behind many European countries that American politicians routinely dismiss as hostile to our more muscular bootstrapping ethos. The rank of American children on income and wealth ladders overlaps remarkably with that of their parents. The likelihood of attaining a college degree in the US turns more heavily on parents' income than ever before.[59]

It is not surprising that these economic fears and frustrations erupted in the Occupy movement. Their impact in the US presidential election of 2016 was, however, a surprise to many. While lambasting bankers and other elites—many of whom would later be appointed to his administration—Trump skillfully pounded his nativist and xenophobic ideology to parlay Americans' fears of downward mobility and economic insecurity into a pathway to the presidency.[60]

Echoing Reagan's promises of a generation earlier, Trump also saw the solution to the economic insecurities of poor and middle-class Americans in market forces augmented by deregulation and tax cuts—but with two important exceptions. One was his opposition to immigration. The other was his intention to threaten, cajole, and subsidize companies to keep manufacturing jobs in America, along with new tariffs on imported goods. On the free-market side of the ledger, he proposed massive tax cuts, especially for businesses; eliminating many environmental regulations; and dismantling of much of the Dodd-Frank regulation of financial institutions adopted following the financial crisis. He also sought to repeal the Affordable Care Act, also known as Obamacare, which Republicans had blasted since its enactment as a government takeover of health care. Congressional Republicans failed to repeal Obamacare, but in 2017 they enacted major tax cuts, especially for businesses and the wealthy—legislation that also repealed Obamacare's requirement that everyone have health insurance, a change that threatened to wipe out affordable health insurance for millions of Americans.

Just how such a recipe was going to make America more prosperous or Americans economically more secure was never spelled out, prompting widespread skepticism from experts on both the left and the right. But the voters who sent Trump to the White House didn't seem to care. "What have you got to lose?" he had demanded of African Americans to whom he offered nothing concrete to improve their lots. Millions of other voters took that rhetorical question to heart and acted on it.

After Trump's election, pundits debated whether it was his populist message, leavened by relentless attacks on elites, or his appeals to racial and nativist prejudice that had carried him into the White House. But this question hardly seems worth resolving. Even Kevin Phillips did not foresee the political toxicity for white male voters of the combination of a massive increase in Latino immigration and the expansion of civil rights for African Americans and women.[61] Nor need we decide whether economic or cultural issues are motivating his middle-class white voters. Both are obviously at play. Economic insecurity has upended US politics.

The data reveal why white men without college degrees feel especially aggrieved. In 1960 white men with no more than a high school diploma earned more than African Americans or white women *with* a college degree. Half of the US workforce in 1960 had not even finished high school, and only 10 percent had college degrees or more. White men with no college degree composed more than half of the workforce and served in 55 percent of the top-paying US managerial and professional jobs. Eight of every nine workers was white, about 9.5 percent were African Americans, and less than 2.4 percent were Latinos or Asians. Since then, the racial and educational composition of the American workforce has changed dramatically, and the educational attainment of African Americans and women has grown markedly. In 2014 only two-thirds of the US workforce was white, and half of these were women. The share of workers without a college degree had declined from 90 to 65 percent. The annual wage gap between white male workers and blacks or women with the same education was still typically about $10,000, but white men had to compete with other groups for jobs.[62] The economic insecurity of white working-class men, therefore, can be at least partially explained by a combination of the declining barriers to job opportunities based on race, ethnicity, and sex; and the increasing necessity of a college degree for those wishing more secure well-paying jobs.

These changes supply the beginnings of an answer to the great political mystery: if we are the 99 percent—or, as *New York Times* columnist Paul Krugman insists, even the 99.9 percent—why don't "we" win? The short answer is that "we are the 99 percent" is a rallying cry, not the basis for an effective coalition for electoral or legislative change.[63] And, as we explain in chapter 2, effective coalitions are essential for successful political action.

It has become common to think this might be impossible because American politics are so polarized. But perhaps we give polarization too much credit for preventing formation of the coalitions we need. For one thing the salient differences among voters are far too numerous and cross-cutting to be captured by bipolar imagery, even if recent presidential elections have tended to split nearly fifty-fifty for the Republican and Democratic candidates. (Recent presidential elections have been so close that two of the first three twenty-first-century presidents lost the popular vote while winning in the Electoral College.) Like the meme of the 99 percent, the narrow margins in presidential contests obscure much about American disunities. Voters are divided by race and ethnic or national origin; by religious beliefs and practices; by sex, age, and education; by the nature and status of their work or the lack thereof; by income and wealth; and by geography: whether they live on coasts or in the plains, in the South or North, in cities or rural areas. These divisions are hardly new; what is new is the nature of the political difficulties in bridging them.

The toxic combination of economic distress and dysfunctional politics has produced the conundrum that impels this book. Market solutions or unregulated markets, whether coupled with trade and immigration barriers or not, will not usher in a new era of robust, widely distributed economic growth. Nor will they alleviate the inescapable economic insecurities of middle-class or poor Americans. Some popular proposals are simply bad policy. Protectionism and hostility to immigration might be politically rewarding, but they are sideshows when it comes to saving middle-class jobs or reversing diminished prospects for upward mobility. Much job destruction is due to technological innovation, and restricting trade increases the prices of many consumer goods, eroding the purchasing power of American wages. It is hardly surprising, therefore, that no political candidate advocating these measures ever explains in any detail how such measures might be expected actually to improve Americans' lives.

Indeed, some legislation, notably from Republicans, would exacerbate both economic insecurity and inequality. Notoriously, health insurance legislation enacted in 2017 helped to finance tax cuts for businesses and the wealthy by reducing health insurance options for poor and middle-class Americans.[64] Trump and most congressional Republicans would have gone further by cutting federal subsidies for Medicaid, but they failed to muster the necessary majorities. The 2017 tax cuts also reduced America's most progressive tax: the tax on large accumulations of wealth transmitted by gifts or by inheritance. This will bring additional millions to heirs and other ultra-rich citizens. The ink was hardly dry on the 2017 tax cuts before Majority Leader McConnell began suggesting that Social Security, Medicaid, and Medicare would have to be cut in order to contain the spiraling public debt unleashed by the cuts. How can it be that so-called populists like Donald Trump can get away with policies that will skew the distribution of income and wealth even more toward America's wealthiest, while failing to redress the stagnation and insecurity of everyone else?

This puzzle is much older than the recent acceleration in economic insecurity and inequality. Yet the United States has not always been inept at fighting economic insecurity. There were strikingly effective policies enacted from the New Deal into the 1970s. Social Security and Medicare took millions of elderly Americans out of poverty for good. Food stamps, Medicaid, Aid to Families with Dependent Children, and the earned income tax credit have kept large numbers of parents and their children out of poverty and improved the lots of both the unemployed and the poor. Why have such successes been so difficult to replicate?

Answers abound. Commentators point to the political polarization that erodes consensus on social policy. They look to gerrymandering and to blue state–red state sorting, which reinforce this polarization. They lament money's deleterious role in politics, authorized by the Supreme Court's 1976 decision in *Buckley v. Valeo* and exacerbated three decades later by protections for unlimited, secret political spending in *Citizens United* (2010) and its progeny.[65] They point to the decline of unions, the emergence of the powerful anti-tax and anti-government movement, and the rightward shift of both major political parties following the disintegration of the Soviet Union and the collapse of communism in Europe. They blame gridlock—in institutions that the founders deliberately designed to impede change—for feeding government impotence in the face of the new insecurities wrought by technological advances and the global economy. They despair at Americans' abiding hostility to egalitarianism. And they point to shifts in the social and political culture, to racism, and to the rise of single-parent families, all of which inhibit possibilities for upward mobility.

There is truth, or at least some truth, in many of these diagnoses. But they ignore the underlying dynamics that shape distributive politics. Some of today's prevailing conditions—such as polarization, unregulated money, weak unions, racism, and hostility to taxation—have coexisted with notably less political resistance to addressing threats to economic security in earlier eras. Some obstacles to protecting middle- and lower-income families are indeed new or have taken on novel forms that compound the challenges. In any event, these barriers, old or new, are part of the landscape on which today's distributive battles must be fought. They are not going away, so they must be factored into any political strategies to fight economic insecurity.

At the heart of our book is a framework for doing just that. In the next chapter, we identify six features of successful distributive politics and explain how they account for past failures and successes. We show how they can help sort through the plethora of proposals that have emanated from political candidates, academic analysts, and the chattering classes, and reveal the most viable avenues for change. Our analysis confirms how challenging it is to make significant inroads redressing economic insecurity and removing barriers to upward mobility, but it also demonstrates that the cause is far from hopeless. We show that while many touted proposals would be ineffective, and others that might work are unlikely to be adopted, there exists a feasible agenda that is both potentially effective and politically viable.

CHAPTER TWO

Building Blocks of Distributive Politics

At the start of *The Little Prince,* Antoine de Saint-Exupéry recalls his dispiriting experience as a six-year-old aspiring artist who failed in his quest to frighten the grown-ups by drawing a picture of a boa constrictor digesting an elephant. They mistook his masterpiece for a picture of a hat. He had to make a second drawing of a transparent boa constrictor to compensate for the adult mind's lack of imagination and get his point across. But this did not frighten them either, prompting him to abandon his artistic ambitions for an alternative career as a pilot.[1]

We can be confident that the grown-ups in de Saint-Exupéry's story were not economists. If they had been, they would instead have mistaken his drawing for a diagram of inequality. The boa constrictor—with its long neck stretching to the right of an engorged middle and a short tail on the left—maps the reality that most people in capitalist systems are considerably poorer than the average person. They earn less income and they own less wealth. Economists call this a Pareto distribution, named for the famous Italian economist Vilfredo Pareto.[2] The exact shape of a Pareto distribution varies over time and from country to country, but most people are always below the average. As economists put it, the median is always below the mean.

The reason is that wealthy people skew the distribution at the top. For most people to enjoy average amounts of income and wealth, there would have to be a counterbalance at the bottom, as distant from the mean as the rich are at the top. But that would push the poorest people so far into negative territory that they would die of starvation and therefore could not be counted in the distributive calculus. Given this, the only way to bring the median in line with the mean would be to institute a confiscatory tax system, one that continually shifts downward the gains that accumulate at the top. Even the most progressive tax systems in history have fallen well short of that. Pareto's claim about distribution is not an immutable law, but it comes close.

This does not make capitalist democracies immune from efforts to reduce inequality by redistributing from the rich to people who have less. In fact, even though modern economists would likely have gotten the boa constrictor drawing as wrong as the grown-ups who exasperated the young de Saint-Exupéry, he might at least have succeeded in frightening the economists. After all, contemplating the Pareto distribution suggests the possibility that most voters, who enjoy less-than-average income and wealth, will likely support politicians who promise to do something about it. Indeed, it was exactly the prospect that the poor might fleece the rich that led nineteenth-century elites to resist expanding the voting franchise.

Nor was this prospect lost on more radical commentators. Karl Marx invoked the same logic toward the end of his life, after Europe's working classes had repeatedly disappointed him by failing to radicalize the democratic uprisings of 1830 and 1848. He had hoped, and predicted, that these revolutions would become vehicles for socialist transformations that had not occurred. Pondering his disappointment from the Reading Room of London's British Museum in 1871 while toiling over his magnum opus, *Das Kapital*, Marx lent his support to the formation of a workers party that would pursue socialism by parliamentary means.[3] He hoped that workers would do through the ballot box what they had not done at the barricades—exactly what wealthy elites feared.

Such hopes and fears are not relics of a bygone era. Twentieth-century political economists formalized these expectations into the median-voter theorem, which predicts that democratic governments will tax the rich and redistribute the proceeds downward.[4] To be sure, not every politician pursues the median voter single-mindedly and come what may. Ideologies render some politicians inflexible, while others respond to the pull of principled commitments, and still others are in the sway of donors or other powerful figures in their constituencies. But politicians who stray too far from the median voter risk losing to more responsive opponents. Like the thief Willie Sutton, who explained that he robbed banks "because that's where the money is," politicians make it their business to find out where the votes are, and they know that their adversaries do as well.[5]

One great puzzle of modern political economy is that voters routinely defy the median-voter theorem. This is not to deny that there is plenty of redistribution in capitalist democracies. Sometimes there is redistribution to favored sectors or even companies in the form of subsidies, such as for energy and agriculture. Often there is regional redistribution. A puzzling anomaly of American politics is that there is a net flow of federal tax receipts from blue states like New York and California, where public opinion is relatively friendly to redistribution, to red states like Louisiana and Mississippi, where the public is strongly antagonistic. Sometimes there is even upward redistribution, as with repeals of taxes on large inheritances and large estates and, less obviously, with Georgia's Hope Scholarships, which use lottery proceeds provided predominately by lower-income Georgians to fund colleges attended for free by many middle- and upper-class children.[6]

Upward redistribution is in line with recent findings showing that the preferences of low- and middle-income voters in the US are rarely reflected in policy, which typically favors the well-to-do.[7] The question is why? Some commentators point to institutional factors, notably the separation of powers, which makes change hard to achieve. Others focus on the leverage that the wealthy enjoy, both in funding politicians who are then beholden to them and in threatening to move heavily taxed assets offshore. Still others invoke voters' beliefs and ideologies. Many voters oppose redistribution, misunderstand the sources and extent of economic inequality, or care more about other things: race, guns, and abortion are common candidates. Richard Nixon's Southern strategy took advantage of this reality. Nixon assumed—correctly, as it turned out—that white working-class resentment of the 1960s civil rights legislation was intense enough to create an opening for the Republicans in the traditionally Democratic South, even when Democrats favored economic policies that would benefit many of those white working-class voters. When ethnic, racial, or religious identities matter more to people than bread-and-butter distributive issues, the median voter might be anywhere in the income distribution.[8]

Institutional stickiness, money, beliefs, values, and ideological commitments all play their roles, but more fundamental dynamics also militate against downwardly redistributive politics. There are good reasons to think that even if none of these was a factor—so that politicians needed only to consider one-dimensional voters who cared exclusively about getting the biggest possible slice of the economic pie—we still wouldn't get the policies predicted by the median-voter theorem. It would still lead analysts to ask the wrong questions and look for answers in many of the wrong places.

Consider this insight from game theory: all distributive outcomes can be upset by majority rule. A simple divide-a-dollar game illustrates the point. Ann, Beth, and Cleo must vote to divide a dollar by majority rule. If Ann and Beth agree to split the dollar equally, giving Cleo nothing, she can upset this arrangement by offering a different split, say 60-40, to Ann or Beth. This creates an opportunity to build a new majority supporting a new split. But there is no reason for the rearranging to stop there. In fact, it might go on ad infinitum. Even if all three agreed on an equal split, any two could form a majority coalition to upend that result and divide the dollar among themselves at the expense of the third.

Notice that this instability does not require us to assume that the three women are selfish. Perhaps Ann is acting on behalf of Save the Whales, Beth wants her share to go to AIDS research, and Cleo is pushing for funds for the National Rifle Association. The result holds so long as each wants to maximize her slice of the pie, regardless of motivation. Nor does it depend on a "wedge issue" of the kind that made Nixon's Southern strategy successful. We are dealing here only with money, or indeed any divisible good. Other concerns—be they race, religion, guns, women's rights, or anything else—might often motivate people, but the instability of the distributional system in no way depends on those other concerns. Only agreement among all participants about what counts as a fair division—and a commitment to adhere to that view—will preclude any possible distribution from being upset by a new majority.

In the real world, institutional arrangements and ideological, political, and moral commitments limit this inherent instability. In the US, for example, the separation of powers privileges the status quo, and federal arrangements often alter the possibilities for distributive change. Nevertheless, viewing distributive politics through the divide-a-dollar lens usefully redirects our attention away from the flawed median-voter theorem and toward six building blocks that lie at the core of effective distributive politics. To be sure, attending to these factors does not guarantee success, which often turns on contingencies. The British campaign to abolish the Atlantic slave trade turned decisively on the fortuitous existence of an abolitionist faction of Dissenting MPs that held the balance of power in Parliament between the mid-1830s and mid-1850s. They used their leverage to force successive governments to abolish the trade and then enforce that abolition at the cost of tens of millions of pounds to the British Treasury and the nation's economy.[9] But while the Dissenters took good advantage of their power, their success would not have been possible without attending to the factors we discuss here—all of which are vital to success in distributive legislative politics.

Build Coalitions

The divide-a-dollar lens on distributive politics shifts the focus from median voters to successful coalitions. Perhaps those in the middle of the boa constrictor's belly will join with everyone with less income, but there are many other possibilities. Monarchs have sometimes supported the poor against the aristocracy, as when Frederick William III abolished serfdom in Prussia in 1807 and Czar Alexander II did the same in Russia in 1861, despite strong aristocratic resistance in both cases. In a democracy the rich might buy off working-class discontent by taxing the middle class. And bread-and-circus strategies are as old as the hills.

At times the wealthy have supported middle-class tax breaks at the expense of the poor. This becomes more likely in an era, like ours, when middle-class incomes have been stagnant for decades, and there is no longer a potentially disruptive anti-capitalist ideology competing for the hearts and minds of the poorest workers.

In these circumstances, punitive attitudes toward people at the bottom can become attractive politically, or at least less risky.

Median voters might also become skittish about redistribution to the poor when structural unemployment is high, preferring instead to ally with business interests to protect their own jobs and wages. This has happened in South Africa, where both the top marginal tax rate and the most common measure of inequality—which remains one of the highest in the world—have not changed since the end of apartheid. In 2019 the unemployment rate was 25 percent and youth unemployment was over 55 percent, despite more than a quarter-century of rule by the avowedly redistributive African National Congress. The ANC has retained considerable middle-class support and fostered creation of a black millionaire class, but most poor South Africans have gained little.[10]

The divide-a-dollar logic makes these outcomes unsurprising. Fundamentally, what the game tells us is that there are no natural coalitions in democratic politics, as the fizzling of the Occupy Wall Street movement demonstrated. Occupy activists believed otherwise; hence their table-thumping declaration that "we are the 99 percent!" Michael Moore embodied this view, insisting in *The Nation* six months after the occupations began that "the hardest part of this or any movement—building a majority—has already happened. The people are with us."[11] But as David Runciman has noted, a coalition of the 99 percent will prove ineffective because there is little or nothing on which so many people will agree.[12]

Politicians and political activists have long known that such large coalitions can easily be pulled apart. Indeed, they will likely destroy themselves. In 1807, following the virtual collapse of the Federalists, Thomas Jefferson predicted that if his Democratic-Republican Party continued to lack any effective opposition its members would "schismatize among themselves" to the point of dissolution. That is exactly what happened in the mid-1820s, when Andrew Jackson split the Democratic-Republicans, yielding the Democrats and the National Republicans, who would eventually become the Whigs.[13]

If coalitions can be too big, does that mean there is an optimal size? That question cannot be answered in the abstract. But we can say that because all coalitions have the potential to splinter, the larger they are, the more ways there are for them to fall apart. This means that the most effective coalition might be the smallest coalition that is big enough to do its job. However, a just-large-enough coalition is also maximally vulnerable to the risk of defection, which increases the leverage of any coalition member: anyone can threaten to defect unless she gets what she wants. But changing the terms of the coalition to please one member may upset other members and thereby undermine unity.[14] It takes ongoing work to hold coalitions together and head off their centrifugal tendencies, not to mention the predictable efforts by opponents to create and take advantage of internal fissures. How big is big enough depends on the organizational skills of leaders, the commitment level of members, the power and organization of the forces arrayed against the coalition, and—above all—what the coalition is trying to achieve.

Advance Moral Commitments

A central lesson of the divide-a-dollar game is that self-interest is not enough to drive successful distributive politics. A coalition whose members' only aim is to maximize their own slice of the pie will break apart when some of them are offered better deals at the expense of others. Moral and ideological commitments matter.

They help motivate people to do what is needed to organize coalitions and hold them together.

At least since Mancur Olson published *The Logic of Collective Action* in 1965, political economists have been aware that self-interested people have no reason to contribute to collective goods that will be provided regardless of their financial support; they might as well free ride on the efforts of others. Olson conjectured that this is why organizations often offer people additional incentives—he called them selective benefits—to support the collective cause. If seniors will benefit from the lobbying activities of the AARP regardless of whether they pay dues, they had better get something else for the dues as well, such as eligibility for cheap group-term life insurance.[15]

Yet, plausible as this might sound, it betrays a certain obtuseness over what really motivates people to fight for effective causes: believing in them. To see the limits of Olson's logic, imagine someone walking down a street on which there is a pro-choice demonstration on one side and a pro-life demonstration on the other. Our pedestrian is not going to become an ardent supporter of one or the other based on which offers better refreshments.[16] People who are going to spend time, energy, and effort on collective causes need to be committed to them. Moral and ideological commitments reflect and reinforce their motivations.

Self-interest might sunder coalitions, but moral and ideological commitments can hold them together. This is why dedicated activists are essential to effective political action. They will resist being bought off by adversaries and will keep working when the chips are down, waiting for the moment—which might never come—when the contingencies line up and they can push through to victory. If motivating moral commitments are lacking, coalitions will have little staying power and small likelihood of success. The Moral Majority exemplifies the success that comes to passionate advocacy. Its longstanding influence on the right of the Republican Party is due to its activists' intense commitments to their brand of family and religious values and to their vision in which arrogant secular elites threaten those values. They are not just well organized; they are motivated and willing to fight. Strategy matters, but it cannot substitute for commitment.

Vital as moral commitments are to building coalitions, they are also essential for holding them together. In 2001 liberal Democrats tried to split the coalition working to repeal the estate tax by offering to exempt farmers and small business owners from the tax forever. This was an appealing offer, because the law they were working on would repeal the tax only for ten years—an obvious limitation in view of the fact that most people do not know when they are going to die and certainly are not going to accelerate that event to save on taxes.

What foiled this destabilizing effort was the intense belief among coalition members and President George W. Bush that the estate tax was an immoral form of double taxation, one that unfairly burdened those who had undertaken a lifetime of hard work and thrift. As with all effective coalitions, the repeal coalition had committed, hard-working activists who resisted being bought off by their adversaries. They made sure that coalition members would not settle for a large increase in the level of tax-exempt bequests, even when the proposed exemption was large enough to protect most families from the tax. These activists routinely explained their commitment by appealing to morality. Representatives of small business and farmers told us that they would not have been able to look at themselves in the mirror or admit to their children that they had sold out the repeal cause for personal gain. To be sure, they were sorely tempted, and some of the stormiest meetings of the coalition were held over these issues. But in the end, their commitment to the cause was strong enough to keep everyone on board fighting for full—even if temporary—repeal.[17]

Several years later, in 2005, President Bush got a taste of the same medicine. He tried to divide the constituencies that favored keeping Social Security as a government-funded retirement benefit by offering to exclude people older than fifty from his proposals to restructure the program into one heavily reliant on private retirement accounts. This ploy failed, however, because most elderly people—even though personally protected from any loss—believed in preserving Social Security for future generations. A commitment to an ideal other than their individual interests turned out to be strong enough to hold the blocking coalition together, despite massive expenditures of effort and resources by the Bush administration to break it apart.[18] Partisans of such commitments will describe them as moral, while their opponents may call them ideological. Whatever the label, the key is that people believe in them. These commitments bind winning coalitions together and destroy losing ones.

To see how easily coalitions fracture when such commitments are missing, consider the fate of the Republican effort to repeal the Affordable Care Act in 2017. Despite having campaigned virtually nonstop for repeal since the law's adoption in 2010, Republicans never made a moral or ideological case to themselves or their constituencies for an alternative. When they took full control of the government after the 2016 election, they had no proposal that their members and supporters would get behind. This failure came home to roost once they were faced with writing a law for which they were unable to articulate an affirmative moral defense. Nor was there any help on this score from the White House. As Daniel Henninger complained in the *Wall Street Journal*, President Trump was an "unideological" figure—at least on this issue—who repeatedly signaled that he did not care what

House and Senate Republicans replaced Obamacare with. Indeed, on some occasions, he seemed unconcerned as to whether they replaced it with anything at all. His indifference made Congress's task harder. Lacking "an ideological North Star," Henninger noted, "they divided—first with the Freedom Caucus's rebellion from the right in the House and then with the moderate Republicans' spending demands in the Senate."[19]

Indispensable as moral commitments are for motivating supporters, they also serve to repel adversaries. Bill Clinton's strategy of "triangulation"—his penchant for adopting policies to the right of most Democrats in an effort to peel off centrist Republicans—illustrates the costs of ignoring this. Triangulation may yield short-term victories, but once your adversaries realize what you are doing, they discover powerful incentives to keep moving the goalposts—secure in the knowledge that your lack of a moral commitment will enable them to drag you ever further in their direction. This is how progressive features were stripped out of Clinton's 1996 welfare reform as it worked its way through Congress. Similarly, Clinton's willingness to give ground after the 1994 midterms enabled Newt Gingrich and congressional Republicans to move the center of political gravity on the estate tax well to the right of anything that Democrats would have believed possible in the early 1990s.[20] Triangulation also demoralizes principled supporters, who become increasingly difficult to mobilize as disappointing results accumulate. Triangulation, in short, might be good tactics, but it is bad strategy.

Compelling moral arguments are essential to effective political action, but this does not mean that everyone in a coalition must embrace the same ones. Anti-slavery activists in the nineteenth century were motivated by various religious and secular arguments.[21] Indeed, while some American opponents of the Atlantic slave trade were moved by moral opposition to racism and bondage, others held the racist belief that there were too many nonwhites in the US, and still others wanted to protect the domestic slave trade from foreign competition.[22] Likewise, while some stalwarts of the estate tax repeal coalition were moved by arguments about unjust double taxation and unfair burdens on thrifty entrepreneurs, others had different moral concerns. LGBT groups saw the estate tax as discriminatory because at that time they were denied deductions available to married couples under the subsequently invalidated federal Defense of Marriage Act. African American supporters of repeal, led by Black Entertainment Television billionaire Bob Johnson, saw the tax as discriminatory for a different reason: it inhibited capital formation and accumulation in black communities. These and other arguments moved people with relatively little in common to support the repeal cause. What they shared was not merely the belief that the tax was against their interests, but that it was, from their different perspectives, unfair.

Pursue Proximate Goals

A third implication of the divide-a-dollar logic is that, in legislative politics, single-minded pursuit of a proximate goal is often vital for success to endure. Proximate goals provide focal points around which to organize coalitions and incite political movements whose members might well disagree on many other matters. Proximate goals also create benchmarks for success that can help to motivate people when the going gets tough.

Abolishing the North Atlantic slave trade in the 1830s was a well-chosen waystation on the road to outlawing slavery altogether. This was partly because essential American cooperation in enforcement would not otherwise have been forthcoming and partly because focusing on the slave trade rather than slavery it-self defused potentially powerful opposition from British com-mercial interests—most importantly those aligned with the Man-chester textile industry dependent on cheap cotton from the American South. When the American Civil War erupted in 1860, some of these business interests tried to pressure the British gov-ernment into supporting the secessionist South, but British public opinion had by then shifted against slavery so that this was im-possible.[23] Britain remained guardedly neutral for much of the war but eventually supported the Union once its victory seemed likely.[24]

Coalitions that lack well-defined proximate goals are destined for political oblivion. Consider one of the many differences be-tween Occupy Wall Street and the Tea Party movement that emerged in response to Barack Obama's election to the US presi-dency. The Tea Party focused intensively on hobbling Obama's legislative agenda and getting their favored candidates elected in Republican primaries, while Occupy activists made it a point of pride not to have a program, strategy, or even an organization. As one occupier said, "There is no one unified message for the pro-testers, but that doesn't mean these protests are not real. . . . From students protesting against tuition hikes to union leaders speaking out against the death of the middle class, people are angry and disillusioned with the economy and political process."[25] Another echoed this sentiment, insisting that "making a list of three or four demands would have ended the conversation before it started."[26]

Perhaps, but the price of eschewing proximate goals was impo-tence. Some might disagree, characterizing the Bernie Sanders campaigns for the Democratic nomination or the enactment of $15 an hour minimum wages in some states and cities as wins for Occupy. There is no evidence, however, of any organizational link between Occupy and these developments. More likely, the same dynamics produced them all. By contrast, the Tea Party has had an indelible impact on legislation that might persist for decades.

To be sure, focusing on proximate goals often poses difficult political choices. In the American battle against slavery, radicals like Thaddeus Stevens had to repudiate any defense of racial equality in order to corral the votes to secure passage of the Thirteenth Amendment by the House in January of 1865.[27] The American battle for women's suffrage was won by explicit dissociation from issues of racial discrimination, even though this caused painful soul searching among many feminists.[28] The Civil Rights revolution, contrariwise, virtually ignored women. Indeed, the most important mention of sex discrimination in the Civil Rights Act was inserted into Title VII of the legislation at the last minute by Congressman Howard Smith of Virginia, a vigorous foe of integration who hoped to turn women's rights into a wedge issue and derail the legislation. Smith's amendment provoked jokes on the Senate Floor, and sex discrimination was not included in the implementing legislation creating the Equal Employment Opportunity Commission.[29]

The women's movement had to wait until the 1970s before systematic gains would become possible, helped along by increased demand for female labor with the rise of the service economy. The Equal Rights Amendment adopted by Congress in 1972 failed to win ratification by the states, but women notched a series of proximate advances in education, employment, and politics that few in earlier decades would have dreamed possible. Also in 1972 Title IX of the Education Amendments Act guaranteed equal access to education programs and resources receiving federal financial aid, regardless of gender. The following year *Roe v. Wade* guaranteed women substantial reproductive freedom. Five years later, the Pregnancy Discrimination Act forbade workplace discrimination based on the possibility of pregnancy and mandated that employers provide women unable to work because of pregnancy with benefits similar to those of other workers with temporary disabling conditions. In 1993 the Family and Medical Leave Act guaranteed unpaid leave for personal and family illness, family military leave, pregnancy, adoption, and foster-care placement of children. The Lily Ledbetter Equal Pay Act of 2009 made it easier to file equal-pay lawsuits. This is to say nothing of the successful battle through state legislatures and courts to eliminate the marital rape exception that had shielded husbands from prosecution for raping their wives and comparable protections that had been afforded by interspousal tort immunity.[30] The Equal Rights Amendment was never ratified, but many of its goals were achieved, piece by piece.[31]

The exceptional success of Social Security was also achieved by pursuing proximate goals. In 1930, before the law was in place, at least 40 percent of the elderly population in the US had less than $300 in annual income and less than $1,000 in assets and therefore had to depend on family, friends, or charity to survive. The states provided limited cash relief to the elderly, and public almshouses were common. Social Security dramatically changed this picture, but slowly. In 1960, twenty-five years after Social Security's enactment, the elderly poverty rate was still nearly double that of the rest of the population. By the early 1990s, however, the elderly had the lowest poverty rate of any demographic group in the United States. More than half of elderly Americans would have incomes below the poverty level without their Social Security benefits, and nearly 60 percent of Social Security recipients get more than half of their income from the program.

In the 1930s neither the enactment nor the durability of Social Security was a foregone conclusion. Along with other New Deal legislation, it constituted a major transformation of the role and responsibility of the federal government to provide for the well-being of the citizenry. Powerful established interests opposed this change, often virulently. The coalitions that produced (and subsequently expanded) Social Security included a wide variety of groups whose interests conflicted on many matters. Notably, to succeed, these coalitions had to attract Southern members of Congress who were committed to racial apartheid. Excluding agricultural and domestic workers from Social Security's coverage helped achieve this goal, a de facto exclusion of African Americans that took decades to remedy.

Barring domestic and agricultural workers from Social Security was as morally obnoxious to some New Dealers as excluding the elimination of slavery itself from the early battles over the slave trade had been to abolitionists a century earlier. But FDR had no illusions about the chances for enacting Social Security without making concessions to racist Southern Democrats in Congress. He refused even to support anti-lynching legislation for fear of antagonizing them.[32] Civil Rights for racial minorities had to wait until the 1960s.

Entrench Proximate Gains

If disciplined pursuit of proximate goals is the key to advancing distributive agendas, how do their champions ensure that these goals indeed prove to be steps on the path to a better future? In light of the opportunity costs and difficult tradeoffs we have been discussing, how can advocates be sure that they are at least taking two steps forward for every one step backward? Fears of reversal are understandable and commonplace. Following Donald Trump's victory in November 2016, President Obama tried to comfort disconsolate supporters by telling them that "history doesn't move in a straight line. It zigs and zags."[33] This was a less eloquent expression of Martin Luther King's insistence half a century earlier that "the arc of the moral universe is long, but it bends toward justice."[34] But does it? How can we know whether a change is a mere zig-zag rather than a long-lasting reversal?

The truth is that progress is not guaranteed and advances can be undone. The failure of Reconstruction after the Civil War and the rise of Jim Crow offer a dramatic illustration. The Civil War constitutional amendments outlawed slavery, guaranteed equal citizenship and equality before the law, and banned discrimination in voting rights on the basis of "race, color, or previous condition of servitude." The Reconstruction Acts of 1867 and 1868 empowered the federal government to reshape the South to ensure racial integration. But by the time the last of these amendments was ratified in 1870, Reconstruction was already in retreat. President Ulysses S. Grant's appetite for enforcing the Reconstruction laws was waning as his administration was consumed by scandals and the 1873 depression. Then his Republican Party suffered major losses in the 1874 midterm elections, giving Democrats control of the House and large gains in the Senate. In the *Slaughter-House Cases* (1873) and *United States v. Cruikshank* (1876), a hostile Supreme Court led by Chief Justice Morrison Waite read the Reconstruction amendments narrowly to defeat their purpose of protecting blacks from racist intimidation. The Republicans began splintering in the South, losing control of state legislatures one by one. It soon became evident that Southern whites, who had never accepted their loss in the Civil War, were far more committed to resisting racial integration than were Northern whites to enforcing it.[35] Politicians and courts responded accordingly, ushering in decades of black disenfranchisement and the full panoply of racist Jim Crow legislation that would not be seriously challenged until the Supreme Court's 1954 decision in *Brown v. Board of Education* and the civil rights legislation of the 1960s.

Nothing short of extending military reconstruction indefinitely would likely have prevented this outcome, but the reason why it occurred is instructive. It is vital to build constituencies for the cause for it to survive, particularly given the inevitable opposition from those with the capacity to derail it. Essential to this effort is empowering beneficiaries of new policies to defend them. Sometimes, as with Southern blacks, the need of empowerment is great. Their adversaries were highly motivated and locally powerful. Even if most Southern whites had not owned slaves, they were profoundly humiliated by defeat. Many were also ill-equipped to do well in the postwar economy and believed, accurately, that their way of life was threatened. They were strongly motivated to restore the prewar order. Empowering blacks successfully would also have required massive investments in the Southern economy: something resembling the combination of the Marshall Plan and the US military presence in West Germany after World War II. Even if that had been possible politically, it might have failed.

Usually democratic politics do not collapse into war, but it is still essential to build powerful constituencies to secure proximate gains as staging grounds for future advances. When Ronald Reagan and Margaret Thatcher came to power in the 1980s, they were credited with strong electoral mandates to roll back the frontiers of government. Yet they ran into well-organized interests that had grown up with the benefits of Britain's postwar welfare state and, in the US, those provided by New Deal and Great Society legislation. These entrenched interests blocked many aspects of Thatcher's and Reagan's retrenchment agendas.[36] When President Trump and the congressional Republicans set about to repeal Obamacare in 2017, they ran into similar obstacles. Millions of people had grown accustomed to the benefits of the legislation, especially the requirement that family policies insure children up to age twenty-six, the expansions in most states of coverage under

Medicaid, and the requirement that insurers cover people with preexisting medical conditions without charging higher premiums.

The popularity of these benefits compounded the basic challenge Republicans faced: lack of a moral case to hold their coalition together in support of an alternative. Despite multiple electoral mandates for Republicans to repeal Obamacare, the reality was that millions of constituents stood to lose coverage, and powerful interests in the medical, hospital, and insurance establishments opposed the repeal efforts. In December 2017 Republicans finally managed to get rid of the less popular requirement that everyone purchase insurance—the so-called individual mandate—to help fund their tax cut, but the rest of Obamacare remained intact. Republicans found themselves caught in a bind between hard-core supporters—often primary voters—who wanted the law repealed and the frightening prospect of widespread public backlash if they stripped coverage from millions of Americans.

One of the best ways to entrench proximate gains is to get them embedded in a major political party's program. Both the civil rights and women's rights agendas secured longer-term traction through their inclusion in Democratic Party platforms. The politics of coalition building prevented these planks from being added at the same time, but most Democratic constituencies now see them as compatible. On the Republican side, repealing the estate tax was a fringe issue as recently as 1994. Yet it has become a staple of platforms and campaigns to such an extent that Republicans running for national office consistently affirm allegiance to it. This remains true even though, after the 2017 changes, the tax is paid only by a small fraction of the wealthiest 1 percent of estates—those with assets of more than $11.2 million, or $22.4 million for married couples. By embedding the goal of repeal in the GOP platform, activists succeeded in decreasing the bite of the tax step-by-step. It is a clear success story for the program of entrenching proximate gains.

Better even than embedding proximate goals in one major-party platform is to embed them in both major-party platforms. The National Health Service has achieved this standing in the United Kingdom. Labour and the Tories compete around the edges over the scope of coverage and sources of funding, but the program for all practical purposes has become bulletproof. Social Security and Medicare have achieved comparable status in US politics. Neither Democrats nor Republicans can abandon them, even if they fight over exactly who and what they cover and how to fund the benefits. This reflects the powerful constituencies that have been built up to support the programs since their inception. As FDR recalled in 1941, talking about Social Security, "We put those payroll contributions there so as to give the contributors a legal, moral, and political right to collect their pensions . . . With those taxes in there, no damn politician can ever scrap my Social Security program."[37] By making coverage nearly universal over time and characterizing Social Security as insurance protected by a government trust fund, rather than as a kind of transfer payment or redistribution, FDR made it difficult for opponents, regardless of party, to find a rallying point around which their opposition could coalesce.

Beyond party platforms, it is sometimes possible to craft other institutional mechanisms to entrench proximate achievements. Here again FDR's structuring of the Social Security trust fund is the gold standard. He devised an intergenerational funding mechanism whereby payments by the current working generation support current retirees. Apart from the obvious advantages of creating an immediate constituency for the program, this means that any replacement requires the financing of two systems for an entire cohort of beneficiaries—both current retirees and current workers. That is a tall order for any would-be reformer, as President Bush discovered in 2005 when he sought partially to privatize the program by having employees and employers pay their contributions into private accounts that they would invest in the stock market for themselves. The cost was prohibitive, and he eventually gave up. This was fortunate for him. Bush left office in January of 2009 amidst the global financial crisis and his failed Middle East wars with a final approval rating of 22 percent, the lowest of any American president since Gallup began polling seventy years earlier.[38] Imagine how low his rating would have gone if millions of retirees had lost half of their Social Security savings in the stock market collapse during his final six months in office.

Deploy Resources

Creating effective distributive coalitions takes resources, as does disrupting them. The Tea Party is a case in point. In many respects the Tea Party was a bottom-up, grassroots movement, but, as Jane Mayer has documented, its agenda was bankrolled to the tune of millions of dollars by the Koch organization and other conservative billionaires. These donors funded meetings, candidacies, and advertising campaigns. Although the Tea Party now receives less attention than during the Obama years, all of that funding continues to keep their candidates in business during primary campaigns and has sustained one legislative effort after another.[39]

The estate tax–repeal coalition's success also underscores the importance of resources. The Policy and Taxation Group—founded in 1995 by Patricia Soldano, an Orange County advisor to wealthy families—operated as a conduit for financial support from the billionaires who funded the coalition. Another part of the story was substantial investment by groups such as the Heritage Foundation, which poured personnel and money into the effort at key junctures. This was in stark contrast to the repeal opponents, who ran shoestring operations perpetually on the edge of insolvency.[40]

The funds that successful coalitions have been able to count on set them apart from the Occupy movement, which was largely bereft of resources other than the sweat equity of the activists. Most US mayors ignored their encampments on local greens in the fall of 2011, knowing that, if need of income didn't drive them away, the approaching winter weather would. That is what happened. Despite a limited continuing virtual presence on social media and a handful of demonstrations at international trade meetings, Occupy had ceased to be much of a visible presence by the winter's end.

These examples remind us that money means more in politics than campaign contributions. Particularly since the Supreme Court's decision in *Citizens United*, debates about money in politics have centered on the resources that well-heeled individuals and corporations spend on candidates and campaigns.[41] But, as the estate tax–repeal effort makes clear, money plays many other roles in distributive politics. In that case, money was spent on organizing meetings and efforts, cleverly designed push polls, and grassroots advertising. Resources were deployed to finance the "research" of friendly think tanks and other advocacy organizations and to bring repeal advocates to speak to congressional committees and members. All such expenditures are protected by the free speech guarantees of the First Amendment. That will continue to be true regardless of any rollback of the current protections afforded campaign contributions. Resources will always matter for effective distributive politics.

Most building blocks of distributive politics are symmetrical between progressive and regressive agendas, but any cause that is favored by business interests or the wealthy is more likely to attract the resources needed to sustain a long-term commitment. The estate tax–repeal coalition and the Tea Party are latter-day offspring of the tax revolt that began with the property-tax ceiling created by Proposition 13 in California. Resources to support such efforts are bound to be more abundant than those available to their opponents or to fund downwardly redistributive causes. This is why it is often wise to embed the latter in larger strategic agendas in which politicians will become invested and around which institutions and supportive interest groups can develop.

Yet the divide-a-dollar lens also points to strategies for including business interests and wealthy individuals in coalitions to help those at the bottom. The median-voter story builds on the nineteenth-century expectation that the poor would soak the rich by assuming that the median voter will ally with those below her in the income distribution against those above her. Understanding that this is not necessarily so raises the possibility of engaging the rich as part of a coalition to reduce the insecurity of those lower down the income scale.

Find Effective Leaders

Occupy's failure was overdetermined. Its poorly delineated coalition, few resources, lack of proximate goals, and failure to develop strategies to entrench gains against future assaults all ensured that its political impact would be limited. To be sure, Occupy was organized around a claim of moral outrage—"We are the 99 percent!"—but there was no effort to connect that outrage to effective political action. And unlike the anti–Vietnam War protesters of the 1960s—who marched on Washington besieging the

White House with daily chants of "Hey! Hey! LBJ! How many kids have you killed today?"—Occupy protesters set up their encampments on city and town greens, as if local governments were in a position to redress their major grievances. Yet the obstacles didn't end there. Occupy also lacked a final building block of effective distributive politics: capable leadership.[42]

"Usually when we think of leadership, we think of authority, but nobody has authority here." So said Nicole Carty, a twenty-three-year-old Occupy facilitator in New York City, in November of 2011. She was articulating the antihierarchical philosophy that the movement had embraced from the outset, as it rejected the goals, priorities, and other ingredients of traditional political organizing.[43] On one of the few occasions when a protest was organized by people who could be mistaken for conventional leaders, angry purists broke away, declaring that they would have nothing to do with events organized by "verticals." Their activities would be run by "horizontals."[44]

But leaders are essential in distributive fights. They choose how and where to deploy resources, enlist allies for the cause, and shape the moral arguments that promote and nurture coalitions to achieve proximate goals that are hard to reverse. Leaders must be willing to take risks for causes larger than themselves, and they need to know how to move supporters. This was well illustrated in the battles over Obamacare and attempts to repeal it. Unlike President Obama, who barnstormed the country and the airwaves with speech after speech during the congressional fights over the legislation, President Trump's intermittent, conflicting, ad hoc interventions in 2017 revealed his indifference to the real stakes for people who would be affected by the repeal legislation. His repeated declarations that he would sign anything Congress would pass and call it a "win" signaled unambiguously that, to him, this contest was all about desire for a victory, regardless of the consequences for people's health care.

Because every distributive coalition is potentially unstable, every such coalition needs effective leaders to bring and hold it together in the face of defections and opposition. Leaders must be effective strategists, who can judge when adversaries can be coopted—or, even better, convinced to join—and when they must instead be marginalized or defeated. Sometimes leaders stride forward to shape the moral argument, as President Truman did when he issued Executive Order 9981 on July 26, 1948, desegregating the military in the face of much hostile public opinion. His announcement that he would accept the immediate resignation of any general who refused to comply lent force and gravitas to his case. At other times, leaders quietly build consensus. That is what Chief Justice Earl Warren did when he engaged in months of diplomacy to achieve a unanimous Supreme Court in the *Brown v. Board* desegregation decision. Doing so was necessary, he believed, if the country was to accept such a controversial ruling.[45]

The 1964 Civil Rights Act might well not have passed without President Johnson's leadership. The Kennedy administration had sent civil rights legislation to the Congress the previous summer, but it was languishing in committees—stifled by opponents who understood the intricacies of congressional politics better than anyone in JFK's White House. That changed when LBJ ascended to the presidency and made civil rights his signature undertaking in the run-up to the 1964 elections. He had been a formidable majority leader in the Senate, famous for his unmatched skill at legislative politics. He outmaneuvered the committee chairmen who had frustrated Kennedy's efforts, and he campaigned across the country with civil rights leaders to build public support.[46]

The building blocks we describe here are essential to successful distributive politics to fight economic insecurity. But they are not enough. Effective leaders might emerge at the right time. They might advance moral commitments that move people to sustained political action. They might build and sustain coalitions. These coalitions might secure the resources to win proximate battles. Well-organized and well-run coalitions might get lucky when contingencies break their way at vital moments, creating opportunities to achieve their goals and entrench them for the longer run. But all will be for naught if they have chosen the wrong policies. That is the subject we take up next.

CHAPTER THREE

Good Politics, Wrong Policy

"One of the great successes of the United States in this century has been the partnership forged by the national government and the private sector to steadily expand the dream of home owner-ship to all Americans." It was June 5, 1995, and President Bill Clinton was speaking in the East Room of the White House. He and his Secretary of Housing and Urban Development, Henry Cisneros, were celebrating "The National Homeownership Strategy: Partners in the American Dream," which HUD had published the previous month. Its goal was "to achieve an all-time high level of homeownership in America within the next 6 years through an unprecedented collaboration of public and private housing industry organizations." Describing the strategy as "the new way home for the American middle class," the president trumpeted his aspiration "to increase security for people who are doing the right thing."

Candidate Bill Clinton had revived his faltering primary cam-paign in February 1992 by zeroing in on the devastating effects of globalization on America's middle class.[1] On this day three years later, he reiterated that theme. "No person, not even the Pres-ident," can tell you that you "will always have the job you have today, and you'll make more money next year than you did this year. . . . That's not the way the world works anymore." Yet Clinton insisted that his housing strategy "can guarantee to people that we are going to empower them to help themselves. We'll make home ownership more accessible." This would give people, he said, "some permanence and stability in their lives even as they deal with all the changing forces that are out there in this global economy."[2]

Promoting home ownership as a path to prosperity was not a new idea in 1995. During the New Deal, the National Housing Act of 1934—which created HUD's predecessor, the Federal Housing Association—helped extend home ownership to millions of middle- and low-income workers by limiting the interest rates that banks could charge and by providing cheap mortgage insurance for loans, which could be secured by down payments as low as 3.5 percent of a property's value. A decade later the GI Bill ushered in the Veterans Administration's Home Loan Guarantee program which, as President Clinton noted, extended the American dream to another generation. "For four decades after that, in the greatest period of expansion of middle class dreams any country has ever seen anywhere in human history, home ownership expanded as incomes rose, jobs increased, the educational level of the American people improved." This was not strictly accurate, as middle-class incomes began stagnating in the mid-1970s, but Clinton was correct that until then both home ownership and real incomes had been stable and increasing.

Clinton was also right that by the 1980s the American dream of home ownership had begun slipping away, though he was not the first American politician to notice—and register alarm—about this change. In 1989 President George H. W. Bush's HUD Secretary, Jack Kemp, began a pilot program selling public housing tenants their homes in a bid to create new "urban homesteaders." Kemp declared that his HOPE (Homeownership and Opportunity for People Everywhere) program would be "one of the most dynamic movements in America since Rosa Parks moved to the front of the bus."[3] By freeing public housing tenants from government dependency, HOPE, he said, would "tear down the walls that come between people and their self-respect" and prevent them from "exercising their talents and reaching their potential."[4] Kemp's effort soon ran into logistical difficulties and a buzz saw of resistance in the Bush White House, when it became clear that renovation costs would exceed $100,000 per unit. The program fizzled.[5]

Clinton and Cisneros were determined to do better. By working through the Federal National Mortgage Association, better known as Fannie Mae, the federal government did indeed reverse the declining trend in home ownership. Created in 1938, Fannie expands the home mortgage market by buying mortgages from the lenders and then reselling those mortgages as securities to investors. This adds liquidity to the market by enabling lenders to reinvest in new loans. Fannie became publicly traded in 1968, but it remained a government-sponsored enterprise (GSE), whose policies and agenda were set by the administration. By signaling a preference for loans favoring low-income buyers, Fannie lured financial institutions further into the mortgage market than they would otherwise have gone—secure in the knowledge that Fannie would take risky loans off their books.

Fannie became an enabler of the subprime mortgage market in the 1990s under the leadership of James A. Johnson, who became its chairman and CEO in the last year of the George H. W. Bush administration. Johnson was a longtime Democrat, who had worked on Eugene McCarthy's and George McGovern's campaigns and was Vice President Walter Mondale's executive assistant and then his presidential campaign manager in 1984. Johnson had also earned a reputation as an aggressive competitor in financial consulting and investment banking, eventually rising to become managing director of Lehman Brothers in 1985. He brought his hard-charging style to the sleepy GSE, transforming Fannie into one of the world's largest financial institutions and a highly effective lobbying machine on Capitol Hill. By linking Fannie's executive compensation to the volume of its business, he created powerful incentives to grow Fannie into the behemoth it eventually became. He did this by relaxing Fannie's underwriting criteria and pressuring private lenders to follow suit, greasing the wheels for the "National Homeownership Strategy" that Clinton and Cisneros were celebrating.

During his rollout of the strategy, Clinton crowed that, since he had entered office, the number of owner-occupied homes in the US had increased by 2.8 million, doubling the growth rate of the previous two years. "But we have to do a lot better." His goal was to boost home ownership to 67.5 percent in the year 2000, taking it to an all-time high by helping as many as 8 million American families buy homes. The administration achieved this goal: by the time Clinton left office, 68.1 percent of homes were owner-occupied.[6]

The quest for more homeowners did not end there. Home ownership rates fell off when Clinton left office, and in the second year of his first term, George W. Bush declared that "we can put light where there's darkness, and hope where there's despondency in this country. And part of it is working together as a nation to encourage folks to own their own home."[7] Like Clinton and Kemp before him, Bush wanted to spread the American dream of home ownership to lower-income Americans, especially to minorities, by pressuring and partnering with the private sector.

Bush succeeded. By 2004 the home ownership rate had reached an all-time high of 69.2 percent, and it was still above 67 percent when financial disaster struck three years later. Young and minority households had seen the largest increases in homeownership rates, sucked into a ballooning real-estate bubble by ever more liberal lending practices: low teaser interest rates that would soon increase and become unaffordable; drive-by appraisals; minimal down payments; discounted bad credit histories; and, most importantly, indifference to whether borrowers had the income and employment security to pay their loans if confronted with even minor adverse developments. Subprime borrowers enjoyed unprecedented access to credit. Unsurprisingly they took the biggest losses when the bubble exploded.[8]

Expanding household debt has tracked the growth in inequality since the 1980s. The millions who lost their homes and savings after 2007 were disproportionately younger, poorer, and disadvantaged minorities.[9] Between 2007 and 2009, African Americans were 80 percent more likely than whites to lose homes, and Latinos were 70 percent likelier, reflecting their greater economic insecurity.[10] During the first two years of the recovery, median white household wealth was restored to pre-recession levels, while African American households continued bleeding, losing an additional 13 percent. Overall they lost home equity at two-and-a-half times the rate of whites. To add insult to injury, minorities have also been disproportionately harmed by foreclosures on reverse mortgages. These loans serve as annuities for the elderly and are secured against the equity in their homes, but they can be called if the homeowner misses a tax or insurance payment or some other deadline.[11] Long-term projections suggest that the racial disparity in the loss of home equity might persist for decades.[12] A policy that was intended to reduce racial disparities in wealth and to increase minority home ownership had backfired spectacularly, compounding the insecurities it had been meant to redress.

A Perfect Political Storm

All of the building blocks of effective politics were present. The coalition to increase low-income and minority home ownership was diverse and included many powerful players. Along with strong support from successive Republican and Democratic administrations dating back to the 1980s, the goal enjoyed bipartisan advocacy on Capitol Hill from liberal Democrats like Barney Frank of Massachusetts and Maxine Waters of California, moderates like Bruce Vento of Minnesota, centrist Republicans like Missouri Senator Christopher Bond, and conservatives like Georgia Congressman and House Speaker Newt Gingrich.[13] Johnson was an effective leader of Fannie Mae, marshalling supporters in Washington and across the country.

His efforts were buttressed by many advocates outside the Beltway, all of whom had incentives to boost investment in the subprime mortgage market. There were the loan originators, who would sell mortgages within days of issuing them, leaving themselves without capital at risk—no "skin in the game"—on loans that might sour. There were the appraisers and ratings agencies, whose profits depended on reputations for issuing appraisals and credit ratings that would facilitate loan-making. There were the investment banks and other companies that followed Fannie into the securitization business, and for which a steady supply of new loans provided large amounts of income. There were Johnson and his associates, whose compensation depended on the size of Fannie Mae's portfolio. And there were financial-sector lobbyists pressing for broader financial deregulation that would let banks become badly exposed in the subprime mortgage market without the capital to weather a serious downturn.

Extending home ownership to low-income and minority families was supported by two moral claims that are powerfully resonant in American politics: that home ownership is fundamental to realizing the American dream and that extending home ownership to minorities and other disadvantaged groups is an important way to fulfill the civil rights agenda of inclusive equality. This is one reason why the home ownership agenda seduced politicians of so many different stripes. They could affirm the traditional

American values of private property and middle-class stability while also standing on the right side of the civil rights agenda.

If this was not enough, there was the added incentive of not wanting to risk being tarred as a racist. In 1992 the Federal Reserve Bank of Boston produced a widely disseminated study of racial discrimination in mortgage markets. The authors concluded that African Americans and Latinos were rejected for mortgages at substantially higher rates than whites, at least in part because "race played a significant role in the mortgage lending decision." This was true despite the lack of evidence that race is "an accurate signal for loan performance."[14] Aspects of the study would later be questioned, but when published it created added pressure to liberalize lending standards. In 1993, in the wake of this study, the Boston Fed published *Closing the Gap*, a set of guidelines for nondiscriminatory lending that urged loan officers to consider extenuating circumstances of atypical borrowers.[15] In a like spirit, Fannie joined with several lenders in the private mortgage market to pilot "alternative qualifying" lending programs, which dispensed with accepted loan-to-income ratios.

There was no opposing coalition with an incentive to resist. Originating banks that had sold their mortgages to Fannie Mae and elsewhere in the secondary markets had nothing at stake. The vast majority of those holding worthless paper didn't know it until too late, because the junk nature of their holdings was obscured by the inflated ratings of securitized mortgages. The slicing and dicing of individual loans into tradeable securities also foreclosed coordination among the owners of securities. Shareholders of financial institutions lacked the information and the wherewithal to second-guess the trading in mortgage-backed securities by the banks. When investment bankers did realize that their securities would decline in value, they found it easier to sell them (sometimes to their own clients) than to sound an alarm. Eventually the major investment banks would pay billions in fines and restitution for misleading investors about the value of subprime products, but this lay many years in the future.[16]

One might expect that opposition would emanate from government watchdogs and public interest groups, concerned about the moral hazards created by the taxpayer guarantees that had to be paid in the 1980s and early 1990s. That would have been a reasonable expectation in light of the then-recent savings and loans crisis, which cost taxpayers $153 billion for cleaning up $512 billion of loan failures.[17]

In fact, by the early 1990s there was considerable pressure among concerned lawmakers to privatize Fannie and other GSEs so that their liabilities wouldn't fall to the taxpayer. If that wasn't possible, then at least the GSEs could be regulated more stringently. But this pressure was circumscribed by Johnson and his lobbyists, who argued that privatization or increased regulation would undermine their ability to extend home ownership to low-income borrowers.[18] When the Federal Housing Enterprises Financial Safety and Soundness Act was enacted in the waning days of the George H. W. Bush administration, it enshrined conflicting mandates. It was designed to protect taxpayers from potential losses if Fannie and other GSEs became overextended, but also to give preference to low- and moderate-income families, inner-city borrowers, and other underserved populations when buying and reselling loans. Meeting these goals required relaxing down-payment, credit-worthiness, and other conventional underwriting criteria. As Barney Frank put it at a hearing on the bill, "The focus on safety and soundness to the exclusion of any concern about their mission suggests to me that what we're going to get is a result where safety and soundness become, not the primary but the exclusive focus."[19] Safety and soundness receded into the background.[20]

Politicians found the home ownership agenda especially attractive because they didn't have to raise any taxes to pay for it. The funds came from private lenders, obscuring the ways in which taxpayers had in effect guaranteed the risks of the ever-expanding subprime mortgage market. This made the program seem—almost magically—costless. Banks were investing their own funds but then selling the loans, and Fannie and other GSEs were buying and repackaging those loans as securitized mortgages, using the proceeds to buy additional loans and repeat the process. As the bubble expanded, banks began securitizing loans and selling them on their own, accelerating the cycle's pace.

When the house of cards finally collapsed in 2008–2009, $187 billion in taxpayer funds was needed to keep Fannie and the other GSEs afloat. An additional $68 billion was infused into American Insurance Group (AIG) in exchange for an 80 percent ownership stake to pay off insurance claims on mortgage-backed securities. Taxpayers also ponied up tens of billions more to bail out the major financial institutions and the automobile industry. These funds ultimately came back to the Treasury, in some cases even netting a profit for taxpayers, and the government eventually sold its interests in AIG stock. Seven years after the collapse, taxpayers had been made whole for these outlays.[21] The enduring losses were borne mainly by borrowers who lost their homes and savings. Among the worst hit were African Americans and Latinos. In effect, the government had subsidized predatory lending.

Could this outcome have been avoided? Hindsight is often said to be 20/20, but in this case the risks were known in real time. Credible individuals and organizations tried to sound alarm bells well before the bubble burst. Some were troubled by the distortion of the mortgage market through the lack of underwriting oversight and low capital requirements along with the taxpayers' guarantees of debt. But the heavily lobbied congressional committees ignored arguments about fully privatizing Fannie and other GSEs and instead went along with various schemes Johnson initiated to weaken efforts to rein them in. The ineffective oversight continued until disaster struck, and even then none of the policy's advocates took responsibility or was held accountable for what they had done. By then, Johnson had retired with a multimillion-dollar pension, and the program's congressional champions, such as Frank, had developed convenient amnesia about their previous advocacy.[22]

One outside-the-Beltway voice urging a different outcome was Wall Street analyst Joshua Rosner. He began warning as early as June of 2001 that focusing on low-income borrowers, dropping and even eliminating down-payment requirements, reducing private mortgage insurance on high loan-to-value mortgages, and accepting widespread excessive appraisals would keep fueling the housing boom but also make housing markets vulnerable to adverse developments in employment markets. If a recession struck, substantial numbers of people—having no equity to draw on and few resources or incentives to avoid defaulting—would be pushed into the red. Rosner's pithy summation: "A home without equity is just a rental with debt."[23]

Perhaps the best known of those sounding alarms was future Nobel laureate Robert Shiller, whose book *Irrational Exuberance* became a best seller for identifying the dot-com bubble just as it was about to burst. Shiller published a second edition in 2006, updated to include data on the housing bubble he had begun warning about three years earlier.[24] Noting that median home prices in some markets had risen to between six and nine times more than median incomes, Shiller identified the serious risks of falling prices, rising default rates, foreclosures, and a major recession.[25] He continued publishing these warnings in the *Wall Street Journal* and elsewhere until disaster finally struck.[26]

When the bubble burst, some experts argued that, rather than simply bail out the banks, the government should induce them to reduce the amounts owed on underwater mortgages, so that the principal would no longer exceed the home's market value. Securitization made this difficult, but a number of investors and bankers made this case to Congress and the Federal Reserve and proposed various implementation programs. They reasoned that writing down the principal owed on the loans would mitigate losses as compared to the costs of foreclosing on properties, evicting homeowners, and then reselling what would likely be dilapidated properties subject to accumulated liens. The better course, they argued, would be to write down principal to the point where the mortgage was no longer underwater, giving homeowners an incentive to continue making payments on their loans and keep their homes.[27]

These entreaties fell on deaf ears. The Obama administration did institute the modest Home Affordable Modification Program that reduced interest rates in an effort to make it easier for homeowners to pay their mortgages. But with negative equity in their homes, incentives to keep paying were slight, so it is not surprising that large numbers of defaulting homeowners who benefitted from this program redefaulted within twelve months.[28] As economist John Geanakoplos, among others, explained, the only way to create the right incentives was to write down the loan principal.[29] The Obama administration and some banks flirted with this possibility but never moved effectively in this direction.[30]

Economically sensible as such a policy might have been, it was dead on arrival politically. The reason is that most people don't think in terms of the absolute gains and losses embedded in economic models. They make comparisons. Writing down the principal on underwater loans would have mitigated lenders' losses while protecting subprime owners, but it would also have provoked fury from voters who had not defaulted on their loans. Any doubt about that was scotched in the second month of the Obama presidency when CNBC commentator Rick Santelli delivered a frontal assault on the new administration's plan to supply temporary relief to underwater homeowners by giving banks $75 billion to rewrite delinquent loans along the lines economists were proposing. In a clip that soon went viral because of its culminating demand for a new Tea Party, Santelli called on the administration to sponsor an online referendum "to see if we really want to subsidize the losers' mortgages," or whether we should prefer to reward people who "carry the water instead of drink the water." That was just his warm-up. Continuing what he would later describe as "the best five minutes of my life," Santelli bellowed at the traders on the floor of the Chicago Mercantile Exchange where he was broadcasting: "This is America! How many of you people want to pay for your neighbor's mortgage that has an extra bathroom and can't pay their bills? Raise your hand!" This produced a chorus of groans and boos, amplified by Santelli yelling at the top of his voice, "President Obama are you listening?"[31]

How important Santelli's tirade was in galvanizing the Tea Party movement into existence or action is debatable.[32] But the instant celebrity caused by his comments made clear that the policies that would work were not feasible politically. A July 2009 Boston Federal Reserve study showed that banks had been reluctant to write down loans—or were incapable of doing so—to reduce borrowers' monthly payments, and that this was unlikely to change despite government financial inducements.[33] One of the study's authors said that the government would do better by giving the money directly to the struggling borrowers, but even a Democratic Congress and administration could not contemplate weathering the political storm that would have erupted had they tried to do that.[34] The voices of Geanakoplos and others who advocated substantial homeowner mortgage relief were ignored, and decades of efforts to move home ownership down the socioeconomic ladder proved tragically self-defeating. The consequences are still playing out many years after the bubble burst.

Why Pushing Homeownership Was the Wrong Policy

The question arises: How could so many people have believed that this episode would not end badly? In the run-up to the 2008 financial crisis, some influential economists had come to believe that improved tools of macroeconomic management had produced, if not a repeal of the business cycle, a "great moderation," as future Federal Reserve Chairman Ben Bernanke put it in a 2004 speech.[35] But even such benign assumptions do not justify a conclusion of continuously increasing housing prices. To convince yourself that giving loans to low-income borrowers who have no meaningful savings to cushion a downturn is a good idea, you have to believe that real estate prices always go up, so that house values will grow their owners into prosperity. Some people might believe that, but economists know that bad times follow good, that recessions come and go, that bubbles expand and eventually burst.

Some might also be fooled by changes in nominal prices, but Shiller showed decisively that, adjusted for inflation, real estate prices do not change much over the long run, and there is little reason to expect that they will. Indeed, Shiller pointed out that owner-occupied housing offers practically no gains for long-term investors, making it a bad long-term investment relative to the stock market. The popular idea that real estate prices always go up is a myth.[36]

There are other reasons why enthusiasm for home ownership persists. One hearkens back to the fact that owning property, along with being a white male, was a requirement to vote in most American states in the early years of the Republic. This might carry a lingering whiff that people without property have not fully arrived as citizens, that they are not living the American dream—unlike in countries like Germany and Switzerland where home ownership is not widely valued and fewer than half of the population own their own homes.[37] There is also the idea that real estate has often been a desirable hedge against stock market fluctuations. This suggests that home ownership might be a prudent way of diversifying risk. Securitization and the linking of regional and even global mortgage markets has rendered this assumption anachronistic, but many people did not realize this until after the crash came. Going forward, however, this rationale is best seen for the relic that it is.

Yet another reason is that Americans are notoriously poor savers, and paying off a mortgage is a means of forced savings to create a nest egg for retirement, along with frequently inadequate 401(k)s, now-rare employer pensions, and Social Security. That rationale also belongs to a bygone era, when people spent their working lives paying off a thirty-year mortgage. This would leave them with a valuable asset that they could depend on in their twilight years for shelter or income, or both, and perhaps pass on to their children. These personal savings comprised one leg of a three-legged-stool, a post-New Deal metaphor for retirement planning often mistakenly attributed to President Roosevelt. The other two were social security and employer-provided pensions.[38]

The advent of perpetual refinancing to cash out any increases in home equity has largely obliterated the scenario in which people build up savings by paying off a mortgage, particularly when decades of stagnant real incomes have created strong incentives to borrow to pay for current consumption. In an effort to reduce consumer debt, in 1986 the federal income tax law was reformed to eliminate the deduction for interest on consumer debt while retaining it for home equity loans. (The home-equity deduction was finally eliminated in 2017). To believe that this would reduce high levels of consumer debt is to ignore the fact that water flows around a rock. Homeowners looked for ways to shift their consumer debt from their credit cards to their homes, a shift that financial institutions advertised and encouraged. The 1990s and 2000s saw increased use of home-equity lines of credit, cash-out refinancings of first mortgages, and other ways for people to treat their homes as ongoing sources of consumer credit.

When the growth in consumer installment debt slowed after the 1986 reform, home-equity borrowing increased dramatically—the bulk for debt consolidation or to finance spending on goods and services. Total home-equity lending increased by 75 percent from 1988 to 1992, with increases of 110 percent in open-ended lines of credit and 60 percent for closed-end loans.[39] This helped fuel the housing bubble, and it meant that many mortgages that had not originally been subprime were held on properties that went underwater when the bubble burst. This, too, was predictable and predicted.[40]

The growing reliance on home-equity borrowing to fund consumption diluted the forced-savings aspect of home ownership, as people depended on increased nominal values to borrow for tax-favored spending. How much of the decline in savings rates in the US is due to home-equity withdrawals continues to be debated among economists, but it is clear that home ownership as the third leg of the three-legged retirement income stool makes for a wobbly piece of furniture.[41] People dislike having a landlord who can ignore you or even throw you out; it did not occur to them that their lenders could do the same.

The most damaging misconception behind the policy to greatly expand home ownership was the misguided idea that enabling subprime borrowers to buy homes would increase their economic security. When President Clinton said that the goal was "to increase security for people who are doing the right thing" and insisted that extending home ownership would give low-income families "permanence and stability in their lives," he and other ownership proponents missed the reality that if there is a relationship between home ownership and economic security, the causal arrows operate in the opposite direction. As George W. Bush's Treasury Secretary John Snow later lamented, "What we forgot in the process was that it has to be done in the context of people being able to afford their house. We now realize there was a high cost."[42]

Ironically it was Clinton who had identified middle-class economic insecurity as the inescapable challenge of an integrated world economy and who made greater security a centerpiece of his 1992 campaign. Once in office, however, he supplied leadership for a policy that ultimately made this problem worse for millions of the most vulnerable. He and the other champions of extending home ownership to low-income borrowers pursued it with alacrity, setting out proximate goals that entrenched the most disastrous results in ways that would prove impossible politically to remedy. The coalition that supported his home ownership policy consisted of strange bedfellows spanning from the left of the Democratic Party to deregulatory Republican libertarians, along with Fannie Mae executives, subprime lenders, realtors, investment bankers, and their lobbyists. Opponents were marginalized or unwittingly bought off. The program was propelled by two moral agendas—fulfilling the American dream and delivering on the civil rights agenda. The resources needed to expand subprime mortgages came from the private sector, lured by the prospect of a quick sale of the mortgages to a GSE or private securitizer.

It was not until after the music stopped—as Alan Blinder, former vice-chairman of the Federal Reserve Board of Governors, later put it—that it became obvious that this policy had indeed created losers.[43] The people hurt most were largely the policy's intended beneficiaries: the subprime borrowers for whom a home without equity turned out to be much worse than a rental with debt. Millions found their homes foreclosed and their credit ratings ruined as they struggled to salvage an economic future during the worst recession and slowest recovery since the Great Depression. They had become the victims of self-defeating policies that had reduced their economic security. The better, if more difficult, focus for Clinton and his successors would have been efforts to address the long-term employment challenge that he had presciently identified in his 1992 New Hampshire primary campaign. Without secure employment, home ownership based on unsustainable mortgages gave people illusions of security rather than genuine and realistic prospects for a better future. Responding to job losses and making work pay are the inescapable heart of the matter, and the subjects we take up in subsequent chapters. But as a prelude to that, we turn first to the role of business. In today's world—and tomorrow's—it is idle to speculate about policies for creating secure employment without attending to the unique place of business in our politics and the economy.

CHAPTER FOUR

The Essential Role of Business

Improving economic security for the vast majority of Americans and strengthening the government's ability to respond to wage stagnation and job loss requires robust economic growth. A healthy economy has long been the main source of employment and government revenue. Even the relatively anemic economic growth in the decade following the Great Recession produced sizable gains in employment and eventually increases in wages.[1] The crucial role of economic growth will endure.

Continued prosperity depends on a thriving business sector, but this does not require business profits to continue taking historically unprecedented shares of the nation's income.[2] What is required for business to thrive changes over time and is bound to provoke disagreement. Once it was widely claimed that "what's good for General Motors is good for America."[3] Today most politicians and economists looking for growth would focus elsewhere in the economy: information technology; health, education, and other services; and construction.[4]

Attending to business interests is also vital because of their outsized influence on politics. This has always been substantial, but today business is more powerful than ever, as there is no effective counterweight to offset its political clout. Countervailing coalitions, notably those led by private-sector labor unions, have all but disappeared as consequential legislative forces. Moreover, as the political power of business interests has grown, they have focused less on the public good and more on the impact of laws and regulations on profitability. It wasn't always so.

A Bit of History

Business does not always fight redistributive spending for social protection. Indeed, the political scientist Peter Swenson has shown that even in Europe welfare-state expansion has usually occurred with support from substantial business interests—often in a tacit coalition with organized labor. Likewise, during the New Deal, important US business interests supported expanding unemployment insurance and the creation of Social Security's retirement benefits. This came in stark contrast to business's virulent hostility to the Wagner Act of 1935, which had strengthened labor unions. To be sure, business interests did not speak with one voice during the New Deal, and some—notably the National Association of Manufacturers—were hostile. But NAM was generally unrepresentative of business leaders on this subject.[5] Figures like Alfred du Pont and Marion Folsom of Eastman Kodak welcomed expansions of social protection, and many others actively resisted subsequent efforts at retrenchment.[6]

This business support did not necessarily reflect altruism. Some leaders of large businesses wanted to eliminate advantages enjoyed by smaller businesses, which generally paid fewer benefits to their workers—particularly in industries like oil. Some business leaders also endorsed the view that government should spend to stimulate employment and consumption. This view, soon to be immortalized in John Maynard Keynes's *The General Theory of Unemployment, Interest, and Money* published in 1936, had currency from the start of FDR's first term.[7] The existence of a rival economic model in the USSR, along with a frightening communist ideology competing for the hearts and minds of American workers, also influenced attitudes of business elites during and after the Depression. The prospect that American capitalism might collapse was not fanciful at the time; well into the 1940s, major unions—particularly in the CIO—were led by communists or closely allied with them.[8] Important business leaders, like the banking and railroad executive Averell Harriman, supported the New Deal partly out of concern for these threats.[9]

Consequential as the New Deal was for social protection, it failed to end the Depression, which persisted into the late 1930s and deepened during the sharp recession of 1937–1938. Only after the United States entered World War II did the nation's economy return to a solid footing with robust economic growth. American business leaders had been divided over the merits of US entry into World War II. Many, including 1940 Republican presidential candidate Wendell Willkie, favored going to war. But many did not. These included the staunch isolationist Joseph Kennedy and the anti-Semitic Henry Ford, who did business with Nazi Germany throughout the 1930s. But once war came to the US in December 1941, most business leaders made substantial contributions to the war effort. Some created new business organizations to promote both commercial and national interests.

One important group was the Committee for Economic Development (CED), convened by executives of large businesses in 1941. The CED supported "intelligent planning" by the government to help produce a strong postwar economy and thereby avoid repeating the economic troubles of the 1930s. The organization had the potentially contradictory goals of promoting "commerce after the war" while seeking "to avoid assiduously any tendency towards promoting the special interests of business, itself, as such." The CED's leaders came almost exclusively from large businesses across a broad array of industries.[10] Most were Republicans. During its heyday, which lasted from the end of World War II into the early 1970s, the CED promoted policy proposals similar to those that we argue for later in this book: a negative income tax and infrastructure spending using public-private partnerships to take advantage of the government's financial capacity and business-management skills. The CED also pushed a tax increase in the late 1960s to reduce deficits and help finance the Vietnam War.

In June 1971, in a short book entitled *Social Responsibilities of Business Corporations,* the CED published what proved for nearly a half century to be the last hurrah of business organizations' focus on their responsibilities to their employees, the community, and the nation. The report declared that, as corporations have grown, "they also have developed sizable constituencies of people whose interests and welfare are inexorably linked with the company and whose support is vital to its success." Their constituencies included not only employees and stockholders, but also customers, consumers more generally, suppliers, and "community neighbors." Declaring that "in a democratic society, power sooner or later begets equivalent accountability," the report argued that the "great growth of corporations in size, market power, and impact on society has brought with it a commensurate growth in responsibilities." The CED also applauded the creation of laws and regulations "to ensure that *all* corporations conduct business ethically, compete vigorously, treat employees fairly, [and] advertise honestly," insisting that corporations are expected "to behave in accordance with social customs, high moral standards, and humane values."

This report staked out a rousing moral agenda for business. "Current profitability, once regarded as the dominant if not exclusive objective, is now often seen more as a vital means and powerful motivating force for achieving broader ends, rather than as an end in itself." The goal was to develop "a clearer view of the business enterprise as an integral part of our pluralistic society and as a full and responsible participant in the national community." If business "is to continue to receive public confidence and support," then its leaders must demonstrate the vision and leadership "to develop a broader social role for the corporation."[11] This emphasis by an organization of major corporate leaders on the social responsibilities of business, putting employees before stockholders, prioritizing long-term goals and responsibilities above short-term profits, and insisting on corporations' role in promoting the "national community" sounds archaic to our twenty-first-century ears. Why the change?

When the CED report was published in June 1971, confidence in the government's capacity to solve the nation's economic problems and public support for government regulation of business were robust. Median income had doubled since the end of World War II. Economic growth averaged 5 nearly percent between 1965 and 1968; after a downturn in 1970, growth rebounded to almost 6 percent in 1972.[12] In July 1969 Neil Armstrong redeemed John Kennedy's 1961 promise to put a man on the moon within a decade. Many business leaders believed that Lyndon Johnson's civil rights and Great Society legislation of the 1960s heralded the end of racism and promised success in his war on poverty. In 1971 the Clean Air Act, the National Environmental Protection Act, and the Occupational Health and Safety Act were all less than a year old, and the costs of complying with them had not yet hit businesses' bottom lines. Richard Nixon's disastrous wage and price controls of August 1971 were not yet in view.

When the CED report was issued, no one knew the United States was at an inflection point in terms of citizens' and business's trust in government's abilities. The authors could not foretell the loss of confidence in government that would soon follow from the abuses of power of Watergate; the costs and ultimate failure of the Vietnam War; the debilitating energy crises of 1973–1979; the stagflation that began in the mid-1970s; and the 1979 Iranian hostage crisis, complete with Jimmy Carter's botched rescue effort in April 1980. When Ronald Reagan gave his first inaugural address in January 1981, nearly a decade after the CED Report was published, no one was surprised when he declared, "Government is not the solution to our problem; government is the problem."[13]

By that time, businesses had become far more adept at legislative politics than they had been in the early 1970s, when they had suffered major setbacks in Congress. The long period of robust postwar economic growth that lasted into the early 1970s had freed members of Congress from having to kowtow to business interests. Large segments of the prosperous middle class were scornful of corporate America; they supported the newly active environmental organizations and consumer advocacy groups seeking greater regulation of accountability from businesses— especially of big businesses—for the benefit of public health and safety. Revelations of illegal corporate contributions to Nixon's 1972 reelection campaign had engendered public disdain for and distrust of large corporations. Until stagflation set in in the mid-1970s, many business leaders were also complacent, apparently believing that robust economic growth and growing profitability were inevitable. That would soon change.

Throughout the 1970s, business interests became more politically active, better coordinated, more creative in mustering support for their positions, and much more effective. By the end of 1974, only eighty-nine companies had created political action committees (PACs), despite a Supreme Court decision blessing them. Then in the 1976 election, corporate and business trade association PACs outspent labor unions for the first time. Business contributions doubled again by 1980. By July 1980 there were 1,204 corporate and business PACs.[14]

The Business Roundtable, an organization of chief executive officers of large companies, was formed in 1974 and instantly garnered sway with members of Congress. There's nothing many representatives or senators like better than a tête-à-tête with an important CEO.[15] By 1975 the Roundtable comprised 160 members, including 70 representing the largest 100 of the Fortune 500 companies.[16] Unlike the CED, which had emphasized improving national outcomes, the Roundtable was formed to lobby on behalf of the parochial interests of large corporations. The Roundtable quickly demonstrated its effectiveness by thwarting the ability of state attorneys general to bring antitrust lawsuits and convincing Gerald Ford to veto legislation creating a consumer protection agency. The CED soon took a backseat to the Business Roundtable and then disappeared. By the end of the 1970s, business groups had begun forming ad hoc coalitions to support or oppose particular legislation, a practice that has continued ever since. These coalitions typically dissolve once the legislation's fate is resolved.

Business's political influence is not confined to Fortune 500 companies. Small businesses operate differently than large ones, but they are enormously effective in Congress. Their trade associations enlist owners or executives who have personal relationships with senators or representatives to garner support for their legislative agendas. Although often outspent by other businesses and industry trade groups, the National Federation of Independent Businesses, the main small business trade association, is routinely ranked among the three most effective lobbying organizations, along with the National Rifle Association and the American Association of Retired Persons.[17]

The effectiveness of business interests was enhanced by a dispersion of power in Congress in the mid-1970s. Before that, legislation was controlled by a handful of powerful committee chairs—mostly conservative Southern Democrats—all with enough seniority and clout not to worry much about their reelection prospects. These committee chairs were especially powerful in the House, deciding the details of legislation behind closed doors, blocking the ability of members to amend legislation on the House floor, and selecting the members who would represent their chamber in final negotiations with the Senate. The chairs also had cordial and constructive relationships with the ranking Republican members of their committees. But this system broke down in January 1975 when seventy-five new Democratic representatives were elected to the House following Nixon's resignation. The legendary lobbyist Tommy Boggs (son of Hale Boggs, a powerful Louisiana congressman) described the changes: "Instead of 10 committee chairmen, you now have 70 people running the House and a hundred people running the Senate. In the past, a lobbyist needed to know only about 10 people on the House side. . . . All that has changed as power has dispersed."[18] Weakening party discipline in the House enhanced businesses' ability to stymie regulatory enforcement and block legislation adverse to their interests, and to push legislation they wanted by cultivating relationships with individual representatives and senators. Congress's ability to say "no" to business interests diminished.

Of all the changes that have benefitted business interests, however, the most important is that they no longer confront effective opposing coalitions, unless there are business coalitions on the other side. The demise of organized labor—especially unions representing private-sector employees—has fundamentally altered the political landscape on which business operates.

The Decline of Union Power

In 1935 Congress enacted the National Labor Relations Act, also known as the Wagner Act after its sponsor Senator Robert F. Wagner of New York. A linchpin of the New Deal, this law created the legal foundation for workers' rights to organize and bargain collectively. It also prohibited employers from interfering with the rights of workers to organize or choose representatives who would bargain with employers. The act aimed to promote "a just relationship among the respective forces in modern economic society" by strengthening labor in the hope of forging more equitable and effective labor-management partnerships.[19] In 1937, after the Supreme Court in a 5–4 vote upheld the legislation as constitutional, Senator Wagner trumpeted his law; it facilitated, he said, "a partnership between industry and labor" that was the "indispensable complement of political democracy." The right to collective bargaining was "at the bottom of social justice for the workers, as well as the sensible conduct of business affairs." He added, "The denial or observance of this right means the difference between despotism and democracy."[20]

For a while, the Wagner Act seemed likely to accomplish its goals. Private-sector union membership grew steadily, peaking at 39.2 percent of the workforce in 1954.[21] But there has subsequently been a steep decline: in 2016 only about 6.5 percent of private-sector workers belonged to a union—the level that prevailed in 1932, before the Wagner Act became law.[22] In the twenty-first century, public-sector unions are stronger than those representing private-sector workers, but their membership has also begun shrinking.

The seeds of union decline were planted shortly after World War II ended. In 1945 and 1946, the return of 10 million US military personnel to the civilian labor force led to declining wages and, in response, widespread strikes in the oil, steel, auto, railroad, mining, coal, and electric-power industries. About 5 million workers walked off their jobs. The wage gains that followed stimulated double-digit inflation and a strong political backlash against the Truman administration. In the 1946 congressional election, Republicans picked up fifty-five House seats and regained control of that chamber for the first time since 1930.

In 1947 Congress enacted the Labor Management Relations Act, also known as the Taft-Hartley Act, over President Truman's veto. That law, which remains in force, sharply curtailed the Wagner Act's protections for workers. Complaining that "certain practices by some labor organizations . . . have the intent or the necessary effect of burdening commerce . . . through strikes and other forms of industrial unrest," the new law created a list of unfair union practices subject to restraint by the National Labor Relations Board. Taft-Harley also made illegal the closed shop, which had required newly hired workers to join existing unions.[23] The law empowered employers to oppose unionization and granted the president new powers to halt strikes deemed inimical to national health or safety. Taft-Hartley also affirmed that states could enact "right to work" laws that allow workers to refuse to pay union dues even when the union is obliged to bargain on their behalf. In general the law opened the door to vigorous anti-union campaigns by employers. Organized labor called it the "Slave Labor Act."[24]

Taft-Hartley was the first of a series of legal setbacks for unions. In 1959 Congress enacted the Labor-Management Reporting and Disclosure Act, better known as the Landrum-Griffin Act, in response to Senate hearings that had uncovered penetration by organized crime into the management and financial control of several unions, notably the International Brotherhood of Teamsters. This legislation further limited unions' rights to boycott and picket, increased the rights of workers who permanently replace striking union workers, and created a code of conduct protecting industrial workers from certain union practices and procedures.

In 1978 the Senate fell just one vote short of breaking a filibuster that defeated pro-union legislation. This would have improved the likelihood of successful collective bargaining by limiting employers' ability to engage in anti-union activities and increasing sanctions for doing so. That near miss was the curtain call for union rights in Congress.[25]

Republican administrations have long treated unions with disfavor. In August 1981 Reagan incited widespread public hostility to unions, especially public-sector unions, by firing more than 11,000 air traffic controllers two days after they walked off their jobs in an illegal strike. It was the first time since an 1894 nationwide railroad strike that the federal government had broken a union. The historian Joseph McCartin calls it "the most significant strike of the late twentieth century."[26] Alan Greenspan, later appointed by Reagan to head the Federal Reserve, described the destruction of the air controllers' union as "perhaps the most important" of Reagan's domestic achievements.[27] Reagan's action emboldened large numbers of private and public employers to take advantage of Taft-Hartley by firing striking workers and replacing them permanently.

Unions also suffered setbacks in the courts. Since the 1970s business interests have enjoyed great success in litigation before the Supreme Court. The National Chamber Litigation Center—the litigation arm of the Chamber of Commerce, the largest organization representing businesses—routinely files friend-of-the-Court briefs in cases involving issues important to business interests, and it has had great influence over which cases the Court decides to hear and how it decides them. According to Bloomberg News, the Chamber of Commerce might be second only to the solicitor general's office in its influence at the Supreme Court.[28]

The Court has frequently upheld employers' prerogatives in confrontations with unions. In 1984 the Court declared that a business may shed collective bargaining agreements when all or part of the business is sold or merged into a new business, or when the business goes into bankruptcy.[29] Airline companies have been the most notorious beneficiaries of the bankruptcy rule, using it to void union contracts.[30] Perhaps the Court's most significant blow against union organizers was its 5-4 decision in 1974 allowing employers to reject cards signed by a majority of employees authorizing representation by a union. Instead employers were permitted to insist on a secret ballot, even if proof of majority union support was forthcoming.[31] Unions have long attempted to get Congress to overturn that decision. In 2009, at the urging of President Obama, the Democratic majority in the House of Representatives passed such "card-check" legislation, but it failed in the Senate.[32]

In two cases decided in May and June 2018, employers' interests again prevailed over employees' collective and union rights. Both cases were decided by votes of 5-4, with the Court's conservative members in the majority and its more liberal members in dissent. In *Epic Systems Corp. v. Lewis*, the Court concluded that the Wagner Act's protections for employees from their employers' interference with joint, collective, and class actions relating to their conditions of employment do not apply to employees who have agreed to arbitrate individual disputes over issues like overtime pay and work hours—even if the employees face threats of being fired if they do not agree to arbitration.[33] Responding to the majority's decision that the Federal Arbitration Act of 1925 trumps the Wagner Act, and writing for the four dissenters, Justice Ruth Bader Ginsburg countered, "Employees' rights to band together to meet their employers' superior strength would be worth precious little if employers could condition employment on workers signing away those rights."[34]

A month later in *Janus v. American Federation of State, County, and Municipal Employers,* the Court, by the same 5-4 vote, overruled a forty-year-old precedent that had allowed government entities to require all employees to pay a share of a public-sector union's costs in negotiating on all workers' behalf over the terms of employment, as long as the nonunion employee was not required to pay for any of the union's political or ideological activities.[35] The Court's decision meant that such a requirement violates nonunion employees' free-speech rights under the First Amendment, striking down such requirements in twenty-two states, the District of Columbia, and Puerto Rico and requiring revisions of "thousands of contracts covering millions of workers." The First Amendment, Justice Elena Kagan wrote in dissent, "was meant not to undermine but to protect democratic governance—including over the role of public-sector workers."[36] This decision weakens public-sector unions.

In addition to defeats suffered in Congress, the White House, and the courts, economic changes since the mid-1970s have contributed to the decline of union power. The increased ability of businesses to outsource jobs to lower-paid foreign workers has been important, as has the relocation of manufacturing to the nonunionized South. Since the 1980s automobile manufacturing, along with much other industrial production, moved to Southern states that are notoriously hostile to unions.[37] The shift in the composition of US jobs from manufacturing to the service sector has also contributed to the decline of unions, service industries being notoriously harder to organize.

Finally, the fact that workers in public-sector jobs now account for half of all union workers has diminished support for unions. When unions enhance private-sector workers' wages and benefits—especially when the unionized employees work for large multinational corporations—the public tends to support their efforts. In contrast, when wages and benefits are increased for public-sector workers, other workers tend to object because they know that they will have to pay for these increases through higher taxes. And when teachers, police officers, or firefighters go on strike, it is the community—not some faceless multinational corporation and its shareholders—that suffers the consequences. So it is hardly surprising that as unions have come more and more to represent government rather than private employees, support for unions has waned.

This decline has diminished union's political sway, freeing business interests to dominate the legislative process on economic matters. When business organizations coalesce behind a policy, such as the 2017 business tax cuts, they usually walk through open doors in Congress. And as the political strength of business interests increased, the willingness of businesses to promote national rather than narrow interests deteriorated.

The Rise of Owner and Investor Power

Business's retreat from attending to the national interest took hold in the 1980s, as economists and lawyers solidified the role of corporate managers to act as agents of the business's owners. No longer seen as properly attentive to broad societal interests, now they were hands hired to increase financial returns to shareholders.[38] Writing in the *New York Times Magazine* in 1970, Milton Friedman said that the only legitimate "social responsibility" of a corporation is "to increase its profits ... without deception or fraud." A company pursuing any other objective, including trying "to take seriously ... providing employment" was, Friedman said, "preaching pure and unadulterated socialism."[39] As Rakesh Khurana recounts in *From Higher Aims to Hired Hands,* this change in focus was reflected in the standard American business school curriculum. Agency theory displaced stakeholder theory, as if managers' sole responsibility was to act as agents of shareholders.[40] Emblematic of the new attitude, when Khurana asked an American CEO after a lecture at Harvard Business School whether he was concerned about the country's floundering public education system, the CEO replied that he wasn't, as he could just hire workers from other countries with better systems.[41]

In order to better align the personal financial incentives of upper-echelon managers with their owners' goals, executive compensation was tied to the performance of company stock. Often, due to accounting advantages, this compensation took the form of stock options that become more valuable as the company's stock price increases.[42] In 1993 Congress gave a significant, if unfortunate, boost to this kind of compensation by disallowing business deductions for the compensation of top executives in excess of $1 million unless the compensation depended on performance.[43] Congress did not, however, require companies to perform well relative to peers—for example, by insisting that their stock gains outperform an index such as the S&P 500. The compensation packages of top-level mangers that have prevailed since the early 1990s have allowed them to reap greater pay as the company's stock rises, even when the entire stock market is rising.

If a company's profits can be increased by limiting the compensation of employees, such as by avoiding wage increases or by decreasing or outsourcing labor, managers and shareholders are rewarded. Wages are just like any other business expense—a cost to be trimmed whenever possible.[44] In 1965 CEOs at large companies made 20 times the pay of the average worker; in 2000 they made 375 times as much.[45] To take one prominent example, "Neutron" Jack Welch, the renowned CEO of General Electric from 1981 to 2001, eliminated more than 118,000 employees by the end of 1985, 81,000 of whom were simply fired.[46] When Welch retired, he collected a severance package estimated to be worth $417 million.[47] Between 1980 and 1990, the number of US employees at Fortune 500 companies dropped from 16 million to fewer than 12.5 million.[48]

Rising executive compensation linked to stock performance only partly explains why corporate managers now pay little heed to the needs of employees, community, or the nation. The 1980s also ushered in an era of business acquisitions and novel financing techniques that threatened executives' job security if they failed to maximize their companies' share prices. During the second half of the 1980s, an unprecedented wave of corporate takeovers transpired as potential buyers found ways to make large profits by buying businesses and then selling off parts of them. Between 1980 and 1990, more than a quarter of Fortune 500 companies were targets of hostile takeovers, and by 1990 more than one-third of Fortune 500 companies had been restructured, mostly through hostile takeovers. The average tenure of Fortune 500 CEOs declined from 9.2 years in 1982 to 6.8 years three decades later.[49]

In a 1981 policy statement, the Business Roundtable was still maintaining that "more than ever corporate managers are expected to serve the public interest as well as private profit," but by the late 1990s the Roundtable had changed its tune. Corporate social responsibility had fallen by the wayside: "The paramount duty of management and boards of directors is to the corporation's shareholders," the Roundtable now insisted. "The notion that the board must somehow balance the interests of other stakeholders fundamentally misconstrues the role of directors."[50] Owners' interests in business managers' decision-making, and managers' obsession with shareholder returns and profitability, continue at the price of enduring wage stagnation for many employees.

Business lobbying now routinely serves the narrow interests of businesses and their owners. In 2013, after a comprehensive analysis of the long decline in the social responsibility of corporate leaders, sociologist Mark Mizruchi described the consequences:

> The corporate elite has lost its ability to restrain the most insidious elements of American political life, contributing to an extremism in politics that the country has not seen in nearly a century if not longer.... This is an elite that, rather than leading, has retreated into narrow self-interest, its individual elements increasingly able to get what they want in the form of favors from the state but unable collectively to address any of the problems whose solution is necessary for their own survival.[51]

This retreat has created new political obstacles to addressing the economic insecurity now plaguing millions of Americans.

Business Interests in Congress

Businesses are not monolithic. One force that can beat a business coalition—other than a crisis that demands a congressional response—is an opposing business coalition. Small business interests sometimes prevail in contests with large multinational corporations, and on a number of important legislative issues, business interests will split, leading to victory for one side or forcing a compromise.

Consider the fate of climate change legislation in 2010. In 2009 Congressman Henry Waxman of California, the Democratic chair of the House Energy and Commerce Committee, and his colleague Edward J. Markey of Massachusetts introduced the American Clean Energy and Security Act. This legislation would have limited carbon emissions through a cap-and-trade system under which the government would put a ceiling (a cap) on the total permissible annual emissions of greenhouse gasses, and companies would be issued permits to emit specified quantities of those gases that they could then buy or sell with other companies (trade). President Obama's budget director, Peter Orszag, told a House committee that the government should auction the permits to the highest bidders—that failure to do so "would represent the largest corporate welfare program that has ever been enacted in the United States."[52] But Waxman's committee, in a historic giveaway intended to buy off opposition to the bill from producers and users of coal and other fossil fuels, approved legislation that would have turned over more than 80 percent of the permits at no cost.

The House cap-and-trade proposal energized unlikely coalitions of business and environmental organizations on both sides. The most influential coalition in support of cap and trade was the United States Climate Action Partnership (USCAP), composed of twenty-five large US businesses and five environmental groups. The coalition included Exelon Energy, a Midwestern electricity supplier; Duke Energy Corporation, an electric utility serving 11 million customers in the South and Midwest, and at the time the third-largest emitter of greenhouse gases among US corporations; Florida Power and Light; and General Electric, a manufacturer of natural gas–fired electric power turbines and wind-power towers.[53] The Nature Conservancy and the Natural Resources Defense Council were the most prominent environmentalist members of USCAP. Waxman said that USCAP's "Blueprint for Legislative Action," which proposed that emission permits be given away rather than auctioned, "became the model" for his legislation. Other businesses—including a group of 150 called BICEP (Business for Innovative Climate and Energy Policy) and led by Levi Strauss, Nike, Starbucks, Sun Microsystems, and Timberland—were also active in trying to shape the legislation. So were financial institutions anxious to create and serve the new financial markets necessary to facilitate trades of the emissions permits.

Opposing the bill was a coalition that included the Heritage Foundation, the Tea Party, the Chamber of Commerce, coal industry representatives, the National Association of Manufacturers, the American Council for Capital Formation, and other environmental organizations. (The Business Roundtable had members on both sides and claimed to be neutral but offered no real support for the legislation.) Business opponents claimed that the Waxman-Markey bill was too intrusive. Many environmental organizations opposed the bill for not going far enough. In June 2009 Greenpeace announced its opposition, claiming that the proposed "giveaways and preferences . . . will actually spur a new generation of nuclear and coal-fired power plants to the detriment of real energy solutions." Friends of the Earth said that the House bill "will lock us into a system that rewards polluters with massive giveaways and can be gamed by Wall Street." The Climate Justice Leadership Forum, representing twenty-eight organizations, said that cap-and-trade legislation is "designed to benefit corporate interests—not communities or the climate." These environmental groups called for a carbon tax instead.[54]

The Waxman-Markey bill passed the House of Representatives in June 2009 by a vote of 219 to 212. Eight Republicans voted for the legislation, and forty-four Democrats, mostly from states that produced coal or used electricity produced by coal, opposed the bill. But a few liberal Democrats, such as Pete Stark of California and Dennis Kucinich of Ohio, also voted against the bill, which they viewed as too weak.

In the Senate, despite the efforts of a bipartisan leadership coalition of Democrat John Kerry of Massachusetts, independent Joe Lieberman of Connecticut, and Republican Lindsey Graham of South Carolina, the House bill did not even come to a vote. The bill collapsed in the Senate despite additional payoffs: $8 billion for highway construction in South Carolina plus another $1 billion in free emissions permits to electric utilities. This was not enough for the American Trucking Association, which said it wanted double the highway construction money in order to support the bill. In an effort to muster business support for the House bill, President Obama agreed to support more oil drilling in the Gulf of Mexico, the Atlantic Ocean, and in the Arctic Ocean. But this was of no avail after the Deepwater Horizon oil rig began spilling about 60,000 barrels of oil daily into the Gulf that April.[55]

The failure of climate change legislation was overdetermined. Poor economic conditions, along with fears that they might get much worse, made 2009 a bad time to enact legislation that would raise energy prices, at least in the short run. The Obama administration was consumed with efforts to enact an economic stimulus bill, financial reforms, and health care legislation. Benefits to the businesses that favored the bill were substantially less than the losses for its business opponents, especially those in coal and coal-based electricity industries. Divisions among the environmental organizations strengthened the hand of the opposing business coalitions. The oil spill in the Gulf of Mexico undermined the government's promise to the oil industry of more offshore drilling and exacerbated fears of a spike in energy prices. The financial crisis heightened doubts about the banking industry's ability to implement a fair and transparent system for emissions-permit trading. The public was generally indifferent; a 2009 Pew Research Poll found Americans ranked climate change last in importance out of twenty-one issues. Neither the president nor the Senate majority leader worked to secure the necessary votes. Congressional leaders who pushed for the legislation—especially Kerry and Lieberman in the Senate—had insufficient sway. Senate Republicans' refusal to support the legislation weakened its prospects for enactment. Ultimately climate change legislation could not surmount a blocking coalition of opponents from the right who thought that the legislation went too far and from the left who complained that it did not go far enough.

Efforts to enact transformative health insurance legislation, in contrast, overcame similar obstacles during the same period. What explains the different result?

Before World War II, there was little health insurance coverage in the United States. Only 9 percent of the population had such coverage in 1940. A decade later, half of the US population was covered by private employer-based health insurance. This expansion occurred largely because of an exemption for health coverage from wartime wage controls, which gave businesses facing a tight labor market a way to deliver increased compensation to workers that would otherwise have been prohibited. Since then, employer-provided health insurance, exempt from both income and payroll taxes, has become the main source of health coverage for US workers.[56]

This employer-based system is, however, far from perfect. It results in large gaps in coverage and inadequate cost controls. Presidents of both parties have long tried to move the country toward universal coverage and to control costs, which in the US are roughly double those of other OECD countries. In 1950 Harry Truman's effort to enact national health insurance failed, as did

Dwight Eisenhower's in 1953, John Kennedy's in 1962, Richard Nixon's in 1973, Jimmy Carter's in 1977, and Bill Clinton's in 1993. The sole successes—limited to seniors age sixty-five and older and to poor families—were Medicare and Medicaid, signed into law by Lyndon Johnson in 1965. Medicare is a national program for the elderly run by the federal government; Medicaid is a joint federal-state program for lower-income families with wide variations in eligibility among the states. Given the long history of failures, the enactment in 2010 of the Patient Protection and Affordable Care Act (ACA), also known as Obamacare, was a notable accomplishment.[57]

The tax exemptions for employer-provided health insurance cost the government more than $250 billion annually in foregone revenues, and large increases in health care costs have accounted for a disproportionate share of increases in total compensation. As a result, employers have strong incentive to cut coverage, and this has become worse over time: in 1979 82 percent of full-time civilian employees were covered; by 2017 only 55 percent were. Part-time and temporary workers and small-business employees are less likely to be insured by their employers than are full-time workers, as are workers in risky industries. Workers have also faced significant growth in their shares of health insurance costs: in the early 1980s, 44 percent of workers had the full cost of their health insurance coverage paid by their employers; by 1998 only 28 percent did.[58] Increased contributions for health insurance completely eliminated the gains in wages for the bottom 60 percent of workers between 1980 and 2015.[59] John Castellani, president of the Business Roundtable, complained in 2007 that health care costs were "the single largest cost pressure that employers face—far exceeding energy, labor, material, even litigation." Forty-seven million Americans then lacked health insurance coverage.[60]

On Christmas Eve 2009, by a vote of 60 to 39—the minimum necessary to overcome a filibuster—the Senate passed the Obamacare legislation. No Republican senator voted for the legislation. All Senate Democrats and two independents supported it. There was no room for defections; every senator therefore enjoyed enormous power to shape the legislation, giving parochial interests great sway. Senators from Florida, Louisiana, and Michigan secured amendments favoring their states, but two deals stood out: one for Nebraska, the other for Connecticut. In the former, Senator Ben Nelson secured the "Cornhusker Kickback," a commitment by the federal government permanently to finance Nebraska's expansion of Medicaid coverage.

Lieberman, who caucused with the Democrats, ultimately refused to vote for the legislation unless a proposed public option, which would have allowed individuals and families to buy health insurance coverage from the federal government, was dropped. The public option was considered essential to control costs and to guarantee that all individuals could secure health coverage at a reasonable price. Eliminating it was a costly amendment that benefited private insurers, many headquartered in Lieberman's home state of Connecticut. The senator, who had received millions in financial support from the insurance industry, threatened to filibuster the legislation as long as it contained a federal alternative to private insurance.[61] The bill's sponsors relented, and the insurance companies got a huge gift: expanded coverage through an individual mandate requiring that everyone purchase health coverage, while keeping the public option out of the bill. The nation got less stable and less effective health insurance legislation.

Private insurers were not the only business beneficiaries of the Obamacare legislation. Pharmaceutical companies had achieved a major legislative victory in 2003 when a law expanding Medicare

to cover prescription drugs prohibited the government from negotiating over the prices of those drugs. In his campaign for
president, Obama promised to repeal this prohibition and use the
cost savings to expand coverage for uninsured Americans. However, in seeking the pharmaceutical industry's support for the
ACA, which he deemed essential for enactment, Obama dropped
his proposal to repeal the prohibition on drug-price negotiations.
Instead the pharmaceutical companies promised $80 billion in
Medicare price savings over a ten-year period. This agreement
was estimated to save the pharmaceutical companies between
$151 billion and $360 billion, a large net gain.[62]

With their prerogatives assured, the insurance and pharmaceutical industries agreed to support the Senate bill, and in
March 2010 it passed the House. President Obama then signed
it into law. The ACA extended health insurance coverage to millions of Americans, but it lacked a public insurance option, and
the government still could not negotiate drug prices. Health insurance costs and drug prices continued to rise, threatening the
long-term viability of the new system.[63]

One reason that Obamacare fared better than climate change
legislation was that the pharmaceutical and insurance interests
managed to strip the former of objectionable content, neutralizing
any effective business opposition. Moreover, the main proximate
goal of the healthcare legislation—covering more uninsured
Americans—had better prospects of success than the cap-and-
trade legislation's goal to curb greenhouse gas emissions. Even
cap-and-trade advocates understood that limiting climate change
required a sustained global effort to which US action would be
one contributor; the law could never achieve that global effort on
its own. Moreover, while the widespread lack of health insurance
coverage was undeniable, the existence of manmade climate
change was contested by many Republicans in the face of strong

scientific evidence. This gave the advocates of health insurance legislation a more effective moral argument, even though the threat of climate change implies far greater existential risks. And while both pieces of legislation benefitted from committed leaders in the Congress, President Obama was a more determined and effective advocate for Obamacare than for the cap-and-trade bill. Ironically, achieving the business quiescence that became essential for the ACA's enactment deprived the legislation of two important components—the public option and the ability of the government to negotiate drug prices—that would have given it much better traction going forward.

Harbingers of Change?

The rise in the political power of business interests in Congress makes it virtually impossible to enact legislation over unified business opposition. This means that across-the-board tax increases on business income to pay for more robust social insurance are unlikely to succeed. As we argue in chapter 9, it is both better policy and better politics to focus tax increases on high-income investors than on businesses. A handful of wealthy individuals have great sway with Congress because of the baleful role of money in US political campaigns, but their interests and political preferences often diverge, limiting their effectiveness.

While it is Pollyannaish to think that business forces will not unite in opposition to a general tax increase on business income, there is at least some good news: the grip of shareholder returns as the sole focus of business leaders may be waning. That is the lesson of a recent letter by Larry Fink, one of the most important representatives of shareholders. Fink is the chairman and CEO of Blackrock, the world's largest money-management firm, with more than $6.3 trillion of investments, including 5 percent or more of the stock of more than half of all US publicly traded companies.[64] His 2018 annual letter to the CEOs of companies in which Blackrock invests, titled "A Sense of Purpose," says:

> We are seeing a paradox of high returns and high anxiety. Since the financial crisis, those with capital have reaped enormous benefits. At the same time, many individuals across the world are facing a combination of low rates, low wage growth, and inadequate retirement systems. Many don't have the financial capacity, the resources, or the tools to save effectively . . . For millions, the prospect of a secure retirement is slipping further and further away—especially among workers with less education, whose job security is increasingly tenuous. I believe that these trends are a major source of the anxiety and polarization that we see across the world today.
>
> We also see many governments failing to prepare for the future, on issues ranging from retirement and infrastructure to automation and worker retraining. As a result, society increasingly is turning to the private sector and asking that companies respond to broader societal challenges. Indeed, the public expectations of your company have never been greater. Society is demanding that companies, both public and private, serve a social purpose. To prosper over time, every company must not only deliver financial performance, but also show how it makes a positive contribution to society. *Companies must benefit all of their stakeholders, including shareholders, employees, customers, and the communities in which they operate.*[65]

The next year Fink repeated his emphasis on companies' responsibilities to workers. He pointed out that, when asked what the primary purpose of business should be, 63 percent more millennials—who in 2019 comprised 35 percent of the workforce—answered "improving society" than "generating profit." "This phenomenon," Fink observed, "will only grow as millennials and even younger generations occupy increasingly senior positions in business."[66]

Fink reported that 90 percent of the CEOs who received his 2018 letter responded positively, but he admitted that a vocal minority hated it. David Abney, CEO of UPS, the parcel delivery company, corroborated Fink's assessment: "I can tell you not everybody agreed with Larry's letter, but I'd say there's more people leaning in Larry's direction, or at least they say they are."[67]

In his influential 2019 book *Prosperity: Better Business Makes the Greater Good,* Colin Mayer, former dean of the Saïd Business School at Oxford, rejects Friedman's argument that companies' sole purpose is to maximize shareholder value. He describes Friedman's position as "hopelessly naïve," being grounded in "simple elegant economic models that simply do not hold in practice." Mayer laments that the past half century has witnessed "the retreat of the multi-purposed, publicly oriented corporation into a single-focused, self-interested entity," and he insists that corporations have the unique potential and power to promote economic and social well-being. The failure to do so, he claims, will likely usher in a new era of government regulations and perhaps a transformation of the rules of corporate governance. "We are on the border," Mayer says, "between creation and cataclysm."[68]

In a *Harvard Business Review* article, Joseph Bower and Lynn Paine detail the kinds of changes in corporate boardrooms necessary to take "the corporation seriously as an institution in society," achieve ethical standards for interventions with "society at large," and create value for customers, employees, and their communities as well as for shareholders. They, like Mayer, reject Friedman's paradigm, arguing that all companies "are embedded in a political and socioeconomic system whose health is vital to their sustainability."[69]

One influential business leader who takes these issues seriously is JPMorgan Chase Chairman and CEO Jamie Dimon. In a long letter to shareholders in April 2019, after forty pages detailing his assessment of the health and risks to his company and the American economy, Dimon spent his final ten pages on pressing issues of public policy. After a short "paean" to US prosperity, resources, and principles, he turned to challenges facing middle-class Americans, including stagnant incomes, low wages, meager savings, inadequate or no health insurance, limited educational opportunities, and relatively slow economic and productivity growth. These shortcomings, Dimon said, "clearly have impeded the prosperity of the U.S. economy and have failed many of our fellow citizens over the past two decades or so." After describing capitalism as the "most successful economic system the world has ever seen," one that "has helped lift billions of people out of poverty," Dimon turned to the "flaws" of capitalism and how it is "leaving people behind." "It's essential," he said, "to have a strong social safety net." Blaming both Democrats and Republicans, he recommended a number of specific policies, such as infrastructure and education improvements, observing that many companies have been able "to avoid—almost literally drive by—many of society's problems." "Now," he concluded, "they are being called upon to do more—and they should."[70] Dimon might not, however, be the best advocate for change. In a congressional hearing after this letter was sent, Representative Katie Porter (D-California) excoriated him for the company's low wages.[71]

The week Dimon's letter was released, Ray Dalio—the billionaire founder of Bridgewater Associates, the world's largest hedge fund—issued a foreboding warning: capitalism, he said, is at a "juncture." It "isn't working well for most Americans." It must "evolve or die." "My big worry," he said, "is that the sides will be intransigent in their positions so that capitalism will either a) be abandoned or b) not reformed because those on the right will fight for keeping it as it is and those on the left will fight against it."[72] "Americans will reform capitalism together," he told the *60 Minutes* television audience, "or we will do it in conflict."[73]

Then, in August 2019, the Business Roundtable revised its "Principles of Governance," which for nearly a half century had emphasized shareholder primacy, and revamped its conception of corporate responsibility "to promote an economy that serves all Americans." The new principles describe a fundamental commitment to five categories of stakeholders: customers, employees, suppliers, communities, and shareholders. The Roundtable now says that firms should not only compensate workers fairly, but also support them "through training and education that help develop new skills for a rapidly changing world."[74] The revised principles were signed by the CEOs of 181 companies that generate a total of about $7 trillion in revenue each year. Not surprisingly this restatement of corporate priorities was met with considerable skepticism. Larry Summers worried that it was simply a diversion, "part of a strategy for holding off necessary tax and regulatory reform." And a spokesman for the liberal Center for American Progress said he would wait "to see if they put their money where their mouth is."[75]

Morris Pearl, a former colleague of Fink's at Blackrock and chair of an organization called Patriotic Millionaires, says that these kinds of messages have begun attracting attention because "a lot of smart people suddenly realized that there are a lot of people in the middle parts of the country that have just sort of had enough. Capitalism, if it's going to survive, is going to have to address that." He added, "Given the choice between pitchforks and taxes, I'm choosing taxes."[76]

Going forward—as the Roundtable's discarding of its long-standing shareholder-first dogma suggests—it will become difficult for business leaders to continue just to "drive by" the economic insecurities now haunting millions of Americans, including many of their employees and their families. Potential challenges to business autonomy will not be restricted to proposals to increase business taxes or to restructure corporate governance, which may unite the business community in opposition. Opponents are likely also to try to seize opportunities to divide business interests to limit their ability to block changes. This occurred in 2009 with climate change legislation, and it may happen again with tax or antitrust proposals targeted at particular industries, such as financial institutions or digital companies. Greater economic security for low- and middle-income workers depends on business leaders abandoning their exclusive focus on returns to investors and adopting a genuine concern for the well-being of their employees, their customers, their communities, and the nation.

We saw earlier that business support for the New Deal was partly motivated by fear—fear of the economy's collapse and of a socialist or communist takeover of business ownership. The demise of the USSR after 1991, coupled with the collapse of organized labor as a political force, might temporarily have extinguished the basis for that fear. Parties on the left either lost power or moved so far to the center that they ceased to threaten business and other elites. Complacency became the path of least resistance. But the populist explosions since 2016 offer a sobering corrective. To date, successful populist political movements in the

US have taken a right-wing form supportive of business interests. The Trump business tax cuts of 2017 are a prominent example of that support. But this may not last: populism from the left is also on the rise, as business luminaries such as Dalio, Dimon, Fink, and Pearl are clearly aware. But they need to move beyond shareholder reports and opinion pieces and begin organizing in active support of legislation to address the economic insecurities of American families—changes like those we propose in the coming chapters. Otherwise, they will likely reap the consequences of their refusals to sow.

CHAPTER FIVE

Making Work Pay

Spring weekends in 2018 saw people gathering in meeting halls and churches across the United States to plan six weeks of marches on state capitals and Washington, DC. They would begin on May 14, Mothers' Day. The organizers strived to echo the gathering on the Washington Mall on a hot August day fifty-five years earlier, when Martin Luther King, Jr., delivered his renowned "I Have a Dream" speech. Few remember that King was the last speaker that day before a large audience that had marched on Washington for "Jobs and Freedom." The first speaker had been A. Philip Randolph, one of the main organizers of the march, a seventy-four-year-old black labor activist who had spent decades battling racial barriers in American unions.[1]

The Mother's Day march of 2018 was the opening salvo by the Poor People's Campaign: A National Call for Moral Revival, which was pushing a broad agenda for change.[2] The group was modeled after the Poor People's Campaign organized by Martin Luther King and Ralph Abernathy of the Southern Christian Leadership Conference a half-century earlier. On Mother's Day in 1968, Coretta Scott King had led the protest, which culminated with thousands of protesters living for six weeks in a muddy tent city on the National Mall. Like its predecessor, the 2018 campaign set multiple goals, but, like its forerunner, its main mission was to shine a light on workers who, despite holding jobs, are living near or in poverty.

On a Saturday morning in late April, one of those workers, Ashley Cathey, stood up to tell her story to a large group crowded into the basement meeting room of the First Congregational Church in Memphis, a fifteen-minute drive from the Lorraine Motel, where Martin Luther King had been assassinated five decades earlier. Cathey, a twenty-eight-year-old African American, was wearing a black shirt urging, "Fight poverty, not the poor." She said that since her mother died two years earlier, she had been working a hundred hours a week to support her younger siblings. During the week, she worked the maximum number of hours for part-time workers at both Church's Chicken and the Crown Plaza Hotel. On weekends she worked—mostly for tips—at a Memphis nightclub called Paradise. "At Church's I only make $7.35. At the hotel, I make $10.50. And at Paradise I make $2.23," she said. "I'm still struggling even though I work three jobs, so I'm poor." Cathey has no health insurance and no savings. "I'm still working hard today, so why haven't [*sic*] it paid off?" she asked.[3]

Nick Mason, a thirty-four-year-old father of two, dropped out of the University of Tennessee, Chattanooga, when his marriage dissolved. In Chattanooga 27 percent of residents and 42 percent of children live in poverty. When Volkswagen opened an automobile assembly plant there in 2011, 80,000 people applied for 2,000 jobs that paid $19.50 an hour. So when Mason left school and moved himself and his children in with his parents, he was facing an economy that offered him few options. He took a full-time job earning $9 an hour at Domino's, where he supervised six employees who made even less. People tell him to go back to school so that he can find a more remunerative job, but he says, "They haven't been in my shoes. I already don't get to see my kids enough. I doubt I'll be able to afford school and I don't know where I would find the time." He was hoping instead to run a Domino's, which would pay $15 an hour.[4]

Cathey's and Mason's stories underscore that the most important problem in the American economy, as in most others, is not that the top 1 percent is thriving. The most important problem is the economic insecurity of low- and middle-income workers and their families. Their difficulties also demonstrate that it is foolish to think of the bottom 99 percent as in the same boat, either economically or politically. Political slogans drawing attention to the top 1 percent might produce electoral advantages and rhetorical satisfaction, but at the cost of distracting people from our most pressing economic challenge: addressing the economic insecurity that plagues people who are nowhere near the top tier and never will be.

Trump's election, the Brexit vote in the UK, and the rise of the populist movements and parties across Europe, Brazil, and elsewhere since 2016 have turned the spotlight on this insecurity, but the two Poor People's Campaigns a half-century apart make it clear that the problem is longstanding. Indeed, for some time now, it has been apparent that insecurity has been on the rise. Toward the end of the most recent great economic boom, in 1997, Wharton management professor Peter Cappelli published an article entitled "Career Jobs are Dead." Cappelli defined "good jobs" as "full time jobs that last reasonably long, pay reasonably well . . . and provide the means to prevent economic hardships." He lamented that the working poor "have not participated to the same extent as other segments of the workforce in the economic expansion" and called this "perhaps the most important point about rising inequality." At the same time, white-collar workers had begun facing "much the same increased insecurity and instability as production workers."[5] His prescient explanation was that stable product markets and collective bargaining were fast disappearing. Stable, secure long-term careers with the same employer might have helped solve the economic insecurities of the 1950s and

1960s, but in the twenty-first century they have become a mirage for just about everyone.

Commentators point to an extensive list of underlying culprits, including not only technological change and globalization, but also greater pressures on companies to increase shareholder returns, downsize, outsource, and employ more contingent and part-time workers. The unavoidable fact is that the good old days of well-paying, long-lasting employment are behind us, and they are not coming back. Bill Clinton might have been wrongheaded to propose extensive low-income home ownership as a solution, but he was right about the employment problem.

The great challenge of our time is to provide economic security and adequate opportunities to workers and their families. No one will get far in politics without plausibly claiming to know how to do that, but finding viable answers is easier said than done. In this chapter and the next two, we examine three important aspects of the challenge: making work pay; sustaining a productive and competitive workforce for a world in which skills atrophy more rapidly than they used to; and creating more good jobs, especially through infrastructure investments. Here we begin by examining three prominent ideas for increasing take-home pay: a universal basic income, expanding earned income tax credits now granted by states and the federal government, and increasing the minimum wage to $15 an hour.

Adopting a Universal Basic Income

One demand of the 1968 Poor People's Campaign was for a guaranteed income. In his final book *Where Do We Go from Here: Chaos or Community?*, published in 1967, Martin Luther King urged that the US guarantee all citizens a level of income "pegged to the median of society" that, as a later writer put it, would "rise automatically along with the U.S. standard of living." King insisted that "the simplest approach will prove to be the most effective—the solution to poverty is to abolish it directly by a now widely discussed measure: the guaranteed income."[6]

King relied on the nineteenth-century populist philosopher Henry George in support of his guaranteed income proposal, but he also had an unlikely twentieth-century ally in the conservative economist Milton Friedman. In his 1962 book *Capitalism and Freedom*, Friedman advocated a negative income tax. Whatever its drawbacks, the negative income tax is unquestionably elegant. The government sets a threshold level, such as the poverty rate. Those earning more pay income tax. Those earning less receive a payment as determined by the negative income tax rate. If, for example, the threshold were $20,000 and the negative income tax rate 25 percent, a family with income of $16,000 would receive $1,000 from the government (25 percent of the $4,000 below the income tax threshold). A family with no income would receive $5,000 (25 percent of $20,000). The negative income tax thereby guarantees a minimum income and imposes taxes on those with incomes above the threshold.

Notwithstanding the elegance of its design, the negative income tax has never been adopted anywhere. And only a few nations have experimented with other forms of universal guaranteed income. The closest the United States ever came was in the early 1970s.

On August 6, 1969, President Nixon proposed his Family Assistance Plan (FAP) urging "that the Federal Government build a foundation under the income of every American family with dependent children." The plan, which had its origins in Friedman's book, had been developed by Daniel Patrick Moynihan, Nixon's urban affairs counselor, who would subsequently serve as New York's Democratic senator from 1977 until 2001, when he would be succeeded by Hillary Clinton. For a family of four, Nixon's FAP would have provided a maximum benefit of $1,600 (more than $10,000 in today's dollars). This grant would have been available only to parents, including single parents. Like the negative income tax, FAP would have required parents considered "employable" to work unless they had small children. Most of its benefits would have gone to the working poor.

Despite opposition from some conservatives, FAP was supported by Wilbur Mills, the powerful Democratic chairman of the Ways and Means Committee. It passed easily in the House. But, due to the opposition of an unlikely coalition of conservative and very liberal senators, it died in the Senate.

Unlike Roosevelt, who had fought cleverly and vigorously for Social Security and other New Deal legislation a generation earlier, Nixon took a half-hearted approach to enacting his FAP proposal. He never invested in leadership efforts to get it through Congress, and public support remained tepid. The blocking coalition in the Senate included numerous conservatives who naturally opposed such an expansion of federal spending, and many who thought FAP did not eliminate enough other federal programs for the poor. Friedman himself opposed the House version of FAP, complaining that its work requirements were inadequate. But the Senate was much more liberal than the House, so pundits predicted the law still would easily pass. Surprisingly, however, key liberal Senate Democrats also opposed FAP—on the ground that its benefits were too small.

These Senate Democrats were responding to outside pressure. The National Welfare Rights Organization (NWRO)—a group of more than 500 local welfare rights organizations with a membership of nearly 25,000 mostly poor, African American women dedicated to improving the lives of women and children—provided important, successful, and surprising opposition to FAP in the

Senate. The NWRO insisted that the $1,600 ceiling on payments was too low and instead urged a minimum base income of $5,500 a year, more than $33,000 in today's dollars.[7] That goal was hardly realistic: in 1970 a full-time minimum-wage worker earned only $3,200 a year, and the poverty level was $3,968 for a family of four.[8]

Liberal Democrats on the Senate Finance Committee—including Fred Harris of Oklahoma and Connecticut's Abe Ribicoff, who were among the most liberal members of the chamber as a whole—opposed the work requirements of FAP, attempted to tie the FAP legislation to a significant increase in the minimum wage, and joined the NWRO in insisting that the amount of the benefit was much too low. At the behest of the NWRO, they refused to accept FAP as the only realistic proximate goal. Compounding the irony, it was the Committee's conservative senators who pointed out that many millions of families would benefit from the program and described the $1,600 FAP benefit as just a "start." The Nixon administration responded to the liberal senators' requests for additional benefits by proposing cutbacks to the House bill to appease Senate conservatives. Ultimately, in November of 1970, a coalition of conservatives and liberals on the Senate Finance Committee voted not even to send the FAP legislation to the full Senate for debate. The proposal was dead. In March 1975 the NWRO dissolved in bankruptcy.[9]

The unlikely coalition that killed FAP included conservatives willing to support only a much smaller benefit and liberals insisting on much more. Together they scuttled a rare opportunity to put in place a federal program for a minimum guaranteed income, at least for parents who work. Failing to recognize that putting such a structure in place and subsequently pushing for increases in benefits and coverage over time was a realistic proximate goal, advocates for its beneficiaries insisted on more and got nothing. Yet as Christopher Howard subsequently pointed out in *The Hidden Welfare State*, tax expenditures of the sort envisaged in FAP often start small. Once embedded in the tax law, however, they often persist and grow.[10]

After FAP, the most notable call for a universal transfer payment in US politics was by George McGovern in his failed 1972 presidential campaign. He pushed for a "demogrant" of $1,000 ($6,000 in 2018) per person. No similar proposal has come close to being enacted in the decades since FAP's demise.

Recently—in response to growing income inequality, wage stagnation, and threats to job security—the idea of a universal cash transfer has been resurrected. Calls for a "universal basic income (UBI) that would not be conditioned on a work requirement have emanated from both the left and the right."[11] Writing in *The Nation*, Michelle Chen describes UBI advocates on the left as hoping that it "would foster a more harmonious, cooperative post-work society simply by countering scarcity and selfishness."[12] In his campaigns for the presidency, Bernie Sanders endorsed a UBI, as has Mark Zuckerberg of Facebook, along with several other entrepreneurs—not to say titans—such as Elon Musk, Richard Branson, Andrew Yang, Sam Altman, and Bill Gross. Altman and others have funded a $10 million, two-year project to study UBI's feasibility.[13] Andy Stern, the influential former head of the Service Employees International Union, who built the union into the largest member of the AFL-CIO, has urged that a UBI could return to workers the kind of bargaining power lost due to the decline of private-sector labor unions.[14]

While UBI support is more robust on the left, on the right the libertarian Charles Murray has advocated the UBI as a substitute for all existing social welfare programs. Murray's proposal would eliminate not only welfare programs such as Temporary Assistance for Needy Families, food stamps, Social Security, and

Medicare but also other federal expenditures such as subsidies for farmers. He suggests using the $2 trillion a year saved on these programs to provide every American over age twenty-one a guaranteed $13,000 income. In doing so the federal government would still save more than $200 billion annually.[15]

Do not be deceived by this apparent bipartisanship, however. Even though a 2018 poll showed 48 percent of Americans support a UBI, and even though pilot programs exist in Alaska and Canada, the prospect of an emerging left-right coalition to enact a UBI is illusory. Conservatives will support a substantial UBI only if it substitutes for welfare and social insurance programs that are sacrosanct on the American left. Moreover, if Social Security or other payments for retirees were threatened, the AARP—whose lobbying effectiveness is matched only by the NRA—would pour substantial resources into a blocking coalition. They would likely be joined by associations of physicians, hospitals, and pharmaceutical companies if government subsidies for health care were on the chopping block. It is not surprising that one of the most effective political advocates for low-income Americans, Center on Budget and Policy Priorities President Robert Greenstein, concludes that the UBI "is a beautiful pie-in-the-sky idea. But I don't ever see it getting beyond pie-in-the-sky." Greenstein estimates that it would cost more than $3 trillion annually to provide all Americans $10,000 a year, an amount that could not make up for the loss of Social Security and Medicare. Replacing those with a $10,000 UBI would be more likely to increase poverty than reduce it.[16]

Moreover, the UBI idea is not backed by a moral argument that is compelling to most American voters. The case for providing health care and food to families too poor to afford them is obvious and widely embraced. In sharp contrast, and despite careful and creative arguments that a guaranteed income is an essential element of freedom, acceptance of UBI is lacking. The idea that surfers and other nonworking able adults, or the rich (think Mark Zuckerberg or Charles Koch), should receive a substantial sum annually from public coffers remains unpersuasive to most Americans.[17] It also has failed to gain traction in Europe, which is traditionally much friendlier to income support than the US. In 2016 voters in a Swiss referendum rejected introduction of a UBI by 77 to 23 percent.[18] Two years later Finland abandoned its pilot exploration of a UBI.[19] Unlike the FAP in the early 1970s, today the UBI is not a viable proximate goal.

The UBI might be unpopular partly because it requires nothing of recipients. Yet the great transformation of US social welfare policy, beginning with the Clinton administration and a Republican Congress in the mid-1990s, underscores the political importance of conditioning federal and state benefits on work. Under the law as amended in 1996, even mothers with young children have to at least try to gain employment in order to obtain benefits.[20] Efforts to enter the labor force—and, if necessary, develop the skills to do so—have become an essential element of any entitlement to government support. Working is the decisive attribute that majorities on both the left and right insist divides the deserving from the undeserving poor. This is reflected in public opinion: most Americans even favor allowing states to condition Medicaid eligibility on work.[21]

Given the widespread commitment to the importance of work, proposals to expand the minimum wage and the Earned Income Tax Credit (EITC) enjoy better political purchase in the US than does the UBI. Unlike the UBI, which exists mostly in theory, federal and state EITCs have long served to make low-wage jobs pay better.

Enhancing Earned Income Tax Credits

Russell Billiu Long, son of the legendary Louisiana populist Huey P. Long, served as that state's Democratic senator from 1948 until 1981. He was voluble, charming, caring, and charismatic, and he shared some of his father's populist views, especially for employee ownership of their employers' stock. But Russell did not share Huey's distaste for wealth and power. Whereas Huey railed against the power of petroleum interests, especially Standard Oil, Russell regarded protecting Louisiana's oil and gas interests as an essential aspect of his senatorial mission—particularly during in 1965–1981, when he chaired the Senate Finance Committee. And Russell was a notably more effective lawmaker than his father, having been described by Ronald Reagan as "one of the most skilled legislators in history." The *Wall Street Journal* called him "the fourth branch of government."[22]

When Nixon proposed FAP, Russell Long became one of its staunchest and most important opponents, claiming that "it provided its largest benefits to those *without* earnings."[23] As an alternative, Long in 1972 proposed a "work bonus plan," which he said would be "a dignified way" to help poor workers because "the more he works the more he gets."[24] Long aimed to cut the welfare rolls by reducing the barriers to work imposed by Social Security taxes. A work bonus plan passed the Senate in 1972, 1973, and 1974 but could not pass the House. Long's work bonus plan was then renamed the Earned Income Tax Credit and enacted on a temporary basis in the Tax Reduction Act of 1975, tax-cut legislation that had been proposed by President Ford in an effort to stimulate a stagnant economy.

The EITC signed into law by President Ford was quite modest: the credit was equal to 10 percent of the first $4,000 of earnings, for a maximum of $400, and it was phased out so that no credit was available for workers whose earnings exceeded $8,000. If an individual's EITC exceeded her tax liability, she received a check for the difference. In tax jargon, the credit was refundable. Because the EITC was originally designed to substitute for federal welfare payments, eligibility was limited essentially to the same population: single mothers with children.

Over the nearly half century since its enactment, the EITC was made permanent. Its maximum benefits also were increased—rather modestly during the presidencies of Jimmy Carter and Ronald Reagan, then more robustly when George H. W. Bush and Bill Clinton occupied the White House. During the Reagan administration, Congress also indexed the EITC to inflation, and in the 1990s the credit was extended, albeit at very modest levels, to childless workers.

Writing for the *Wall Street Journal* in 1989, David Wessel remarked that the EITC had emerged "as the antipoverty tool of choice among poverty experts and politicians as ideologically far apart as [Republican] Vice President Dan Quayle and Rep. Tom Downey, a liberal New York Democrat."[25] By 2017 the EITC provided more than $70 billion in wage subsidies—or, to echo Russell Long, work bonuses—to more than 25 million families. It is the fourth-largest transfer program for low-income families after Medicaid, food stamps, and Supplemental Security Income. According to the Census Bureau, only Social Security has lifted more people out of poverty than the combination of the EITC and refundable child tax credits.

The precise numbers change annually with inflation, but in 2017 a married couple with two children was eligible for a credit of 40 percent of earned income up to a maximum value of $5,616. The credit did not phase out completely until earned income reached about $50,600. The maximum credit is a bit more for parents with three children and a bit less for workers with only one child. But the EITC is less than 10 percent as great for individuals without children—a maximum of $510 in 2017—and it is phased out completely when their earnings reach $20,600.

More than four decades ago, Russell Long provided the essential leadership to put the EITC in place, and subsequently other leaders have emerged in both the White House and on Capitol Hill to expand the credit. Unlike the UBI, advocates of which struggle to find a moral argument that garners widespread public support, the EITC manifests a compelling moral claim. The effort to lift working parents out of poverty and ensure that full-time workers with children receive a living wage has won support, especially as wages have stagnated for so many American workers.

However, the EITC seems unique in its continual expansion, given that it hasn't benefited from the substantial financial resources that we typically find behind other tax breaks. It helps that no separate bureaucracy is needed to operate the EITC. It is paid as a tax refund and administered by the Internal Revenue Service. That makes it cheap to administer and reduces the likelihood of it becoming a target for critics of government bloat. And the EITC has enjoyed the ongoing attention and support of a group of effective advocates. Perhaps the most notable is the Center for Budget and Policy Priorities (CBPP), led by the very able Robert Greenstein.

Since its founding in 1981, CBPP has made the expansion of the federal EITC and refundable child credits a priority. And since the 1990s, it has worked tirelessly in state capitals to create state-based EITCs to supplement the federal credit. Coordinating more than forty state-based advocacy organizations, CBPP and its allies have been remarkably successful in extending the EITC into state laws. These effective advocates have provided both the leadership and the resources—often predominately their time and energy—to expand the reach and benefits of federal and state EITCs.

In 2017 twenty-nine states and the District of Columbia provided EITCs that supplement the federal credits. Again reflecting widespread bipartisan support, these states span the political spectrum and the country. They include, for example, Democratic New York, California, and all of New England except New Hampshire; Republican Midwest and prairie states such as Indiana, Nebraska, Kansas, and Oklahoma; and purple states, such as Minnesota, Michigan, Wisconsin, and Ohio. The regions with the fewest state EITCs are the South—where only Virginia, South Carolina, and Louisiana have such credits—and the West, where Idaho, Wyoming, Utah, and Arizona do not have EITCs. But enactment and expansion of state EITCs continues with Hawaii, Montana, and South Carolina having all enacted such measures in 2017.

State EITCs are simple to administer because they can piggyback on the federal program. Their coverage varies. Louisiana and Washington State provide a credit equal to less than 5 percent of the federal EITC's, while California provides 85 percent equivalent, and the District of Columbia 100 percent. In 2017 state EITCs added $4 billion to the after-tax wages of low- and moderate-income workers.

State EITCs offer an important counterpoint to claims that federalism is an obstacle to redistributive politics, enabling race-to-the-bottom logic. States that adopt protections for workers might frighten capital away to states where it is cheaper to do business. Right-to-work states have become magnets for employers, driving them from the once-union-dominated Rust Belt to the South. Minimum wages, discussed below, court a similar danger when enforced at the state or local level. To be sure, businesses sometimes support increases in local minimum wages if they believe the new income will be spent in their establishments. But most employers seek, or threaten to seek, greener pastures to keep wages down.

But state-level EITCs encourage the opposite: a race to the top. The subsidies they offer attract firms by potentially reducing their labor costs and increasing the take-home pay of their workers. States that are the most generous will be the most attractive. The challenge they face is to avoid the moral hazard whereby firms have an incentive to pay below-market wages knowing that the state EITC will make up the difference. States therefore need to stipulate that market wages must be paid in order to qualify for their EITC. There are other creative possibilities. States might agree to offset at least part of the cost of raises and productivity bonuses with enhanced EITC payments, supplying firms with incentives to increase what workers actually receive.

A great advantage of the EITC is that, although in part a subsidy to a firm, it is paid directly by the government to the worker. This restricts opportunities for firms to absorb payments as overhead or other forms of shareholder benefit. Moreover the benefits to workers are not speculative, which is the case where indirect incentives to create employment—such as corporate tax cuts—are concerned. Businesses cannot use the EITC to buy back shares or reward managers; workers must be hired and paid for the benefit to be available.

A policy instituting or increasing a wage subsidy such as the EITC must be sold to the voters who will pay for it as taxpayers. This is challenging, partly because of conservative resistance to redistribution. As the refundable portion of the credit has grown, support for the EITC has indeed waned among conservative Republicans. But here too the obstacles are less forbidding than with many other forms of redistribution. Howard notes that tax expenditures are not widely seen as redistributive in the way that direct transfer payments are—one reason why they garner less opposition. Powerful lobbies do not invest resources in opposing it. The fact that the EITC is linked to employment shields it from being derided as a handout, and the employment it supports generates positive externalities: more spending and employment.

The EITC was an American invention, but its benefits have become widely known, and similar wage subsidies delivered through the tax code are now found elsewhere. In the United Kingdom, for example, the comparable credit, known as the Working Tax Credit, is about twice as generous as the EITC. Canada offers a similar refundable tax credit for low-income workers and their families.[26]

Despite the EITC's expansion over the years, the work to improve the policy remains unfinished: there remain important opportunities to take advantage of the longstanding bipartisan coalitions that support the credits. Expanding the EITC phase-in range and providing a more gradual phase-out would increase the take-home pay of workers who earn only moderate wages. Such changes could also reduce or even eliminate the significant tax increases that occur when lower-income parents marry, buttressing recent congressional efforts to reduce marriage penalties in the tax law. Such changes would also offer greater potential to increase the well-being of children from low-income, single-parent families. Each of these changes could garner bipartisan support if the necessary leadership came forward.

Millions more low- and moderate-income workers would greatly benefit if Congress would replace the pittance that the EITC pays to unmarried childless workers with the kind of substantial "work bonus" available to single parents.[27] Currently, credits for childless workers amount to about three percent of all federal EITC benefits. A 2019 Urban Institute study showed that tripling this benefit (to about half that of the credit for workers with one child), and better aligning phase-in and phase-out rules with those for workers with children, would boost the incomes of over 24 million individuals and married couples by an average of $1,000. In twenty-two states there would be an additional increase in take-home pay from state-level EITCs, calculated as a percentage of the federal credit—at a combined net annual state and federal cost of about $25 billion. Given the advantages to employers and workers, narrowing the disparity between single parents and unmarried childless workers could well constitute low-hanging fruit in EITC's next phase.[28]

Donald Trump and congressional Republicans passed up a significant opportunity in 2017 to improve the economic security of American workers by deciding to spend $1 trillion of federal revenues on doubling the standard deduction instead of increasing the EITC. By cutting back on the inflation measure for indexing income-tax provisions, the 2017 legislation will also erode the purchasing power of both federal and state EITCs over time.

Increasing the Minimum Wage

Instead of focusing their efforts on increasing the EITC, recently liberal Democrats more often have been urging an increase in the federal minimum wage. Like much US domestic policy, a minimum wage mandated by the federal government was a product of the Depression. In 1933, soon after he took office, Franklin Roosevelt secured enactment of the National Industrial Recovery Act, which suspended antitrust laws and allowed businesses to form cartels and jointly set prices. The resulting price increases spurred Roosevelt to institute the President's Reemployment Agreements, designed to stimulate employment and raise wages. More than 2.3 million agreements were signed by employers of more than 16 million workers. These employers agreed to avoid child labor, limit weekly work hours, and pay a minimum wage of $12 to $15 a week.[29] A number of industries also adopted complementary voluntary agreements: the Cotton Textile Code, for example, established a minimum weekly wage of $13 in the North and $12 in the South.

But on May 27, 1935, sometimes referred to as Black Monday, the Supreme Court unanimously struck down the National Recovery Act as unconstitutional and invalidated the agreements and codes allowed by the Act.[30] The following year the Court struck down a New York minimum wage law as an unconstitutional violation of freedom of contract.[31] The Court's refusal to uphold New Deal legislation inspired Roosevelt's 1936 reelection campaign to castigate the Court and promise to find a constitutional way to protect workers by barring child labor, limiting maximum work hours, and requiring a minimum wage. After he won reelection by a landslide—523 to 8 in the electoral college—Roosevelt famously proposed packing the Court by adding up to six new justices, who he believed would be sympathetic to his legislative goals. This provoked outrage, but some historians credit the court-packing threat with the "switch in time that saved nine." In a March 1937 case, the conservative justice Owen Roberts joined four liberals on the Court to award back pay to a Washington chambermaid whose employer had paid her less than the state-mandated minimum. In doing so, the majority overruled prior decisions and upheld as constitutional Washington State's minimum wage.[32]

Two months later FDR proposed legislation that called for a federal minimum wage of forty cents an hour, a maximum workweek of forty hours, and a minimum working age of sixteen years old (with some exceptions)—protections that would apply to any firms involved in interstate commerce. This was blocked in the House by a coalition of business-backing Republicans and Southern Democrats looking out for agricultural interests. The Southern Democrats also refused to support any legislation that might mandate an increase in the pay of black workers. This coalition successfully blocked the legislation again in a special session of Congress called by Roosevelt that November.

Roosevelt was unbowed. On January 3, 1938, he told Congress that he was once again seeking "legislation to end starvation wages and intolerable hours."[33] The coalition of House Republicans and Southern Democrats remained unmoved. But a few months after that, political winds shifted. Congressman Claude Pepper, a Roosevelt ally, defeated J. Mark Wilcox, a vigorous opponent of the New Deal, by a large margin in the Florida Senate primary. Thereafter a majority of the House pushed the legislation to a floor vote, where it passed 314 to 97 after a series of compromises that weakened the bill. The Senate approved the legislation on a voice vote, and on June 25, 1938, Roosevelt signed a whittled-down Fair Labor Standards Act, which provided for a minimum wage of 25 cents an hour. It had taken FDR five years since his first inauguration to get Congress to enact minimum wage legislation that would withstand Supreme Court scrutiny.

Since adoption, the federal minimum wage has routinely been increased, though it has never been indexed for inflation. Increases were enacted under nine presidents—five Democrats and four Republicans—with large bipartisan majorities in Congress. Most recently, in 2009, the minimum wage was raised to $7.25 an hour.

Over the past three-quarters of a century, the moral case for a minimum wage has remained essentially unchanged. As Roosevelt said in May 1938, "Our nation so richly endowed with natural resources and with a capable and industrious population should be able to devise ways and means of insuring to all our able-bodied working men and women a fair day's pay for a fair day's work."[34] Roosevelt's secretary of labor, Frances Perkins, the first woman to hold that job, added, "On the ability of the common man to support himself hung the prosperity of everyone in the country."[35] "Without question," said FDR in 1938, the minimum wage "starts us toward a better standard of living and increases purchasing power to buy the products of farm and factory."[36]

But Roosevelt also advanced a more contentious moral claim, reflecting the temptation, ubiquitous among politicians, to find a villain to blame: "It seems to me to be . . . plain that no business which depends for existence on paying less than living wages to its workers has any right to continue in this country."[37]

By the time the minimum wage reached its peak purchasing power in 1968, FDR's insistence that employers fulfill obligations to the public—a constituency much broader than their shareholders—was generally discarded as a political rallying cry. It surely had fallen into desuetude by the 1980s, when Ronald Reagan's reverence for deregulation and the free market took firm hold not only among Republicans but also among triangulating Democrats who were shaping Bill Clinton's Democratic Leadership Council. Increasingly, leaders of both parties—but especially Republicans—have treated employers as the "makers" in the US economy. Small businesses, in particular, have been held in the greatest esteem by US lawmakers.

In the 2016 presidential campaign, both Bernie Sanders and Hillary Clinton endorsed a $15 an hour federal minimum wage. This "fight for fifteen" was subsequently joined by many in Congress, including Senate Minority Leader Chuck Schumer and twenty-nine other Senate Democrats.[38] They proposed both the higher minimum and an automatic increase whenever the national median wage rises. A comprehensive Congressional Budget Office assessment of economic evidence in 2019 concluded that, at $15 an hour, the minimum wage would be at its highest point relative to overall wages since 1973 and would result in an average wage increase of 21 percent. Millions of workers would see their salaries rise. But a $15 minimum also would produce some job loss, as employers would substitute other inputs—either capital (such as robots) or more productive higher-wage workers—to offset the increased costs of wages at the bottom. The researchers also noted that the cost of higher wages tends to be passed on to consumers through higher prices and to reduce business profits somewhat.[39] Economists debate the extent to which higher minimum wages drives down employment and drives up prices, but there is little dispute that these effects dominate any impact on profits, especially over the long term. Thus, to the extent that higher minimum wages inflict pain, they tend to do so on certain workers and consumers, not just employers.

After more than doubling the federal minimum wage became a key feature of Democratic presidential and congressional campaigns, bipartisan support for an increase largely disappeared. These days it can be hard to remember that Republicans once supported minimum wage hikes. President George W. Bush signed the most recent increase into law in 2007. The legislation, which passed both houses of Congress by a very large margin, raised the $5.15 minimum wage in three increments. It topped out in July 2009 at $7.25, where it remained through 2019.[40] Barack Obama proposed phasing in another increase to $9.00 an hour in 2013, and in his 2014 State of the Union Address he upped his request to a $10.10 minimum. But it didn't matter how high he was bidding. Republicans in Congress—supporting Senator McConnell's explicit determination to thwart Obama's policies at every turn—refused to act. Recognizing that his proposed legislation was dead, Obama issued an executive order, "Minimum Wage for Contractors," establishing as of January 1, 2015 a minimum wage of $10.10 an hour for most individuals working under new contracts with the federal government.[41] The Republican blocking coalition to thwart any increase in the federal minimum wage has now stood firm for more than a decade.

But some states have acted, often with bipartisan support. On January 1, 2018, nineteen states saw increases in their minimum wages. Eight of these expansions were due to automatic cost of living increases already provided by the states' laws, but eleven states increased their minimum wages via legislation or ballot initiatives. Most states that have enacted higher minimum wage laws in recent years, such as California, New York, and Washington, are Democratic strongholds. But some, including Arizona, Arkansas, Colorado, and Maine, are either purple states or dominated by Republicans. In these states voters increased minimum wages through ballot initiatives.[42] By 2016 three years of state minimum wage increases had raised the pay of more than 7 million workers.[43]

Local governments also have taken action. In the 1990s Baltimore was the earliest city to respond when labor leaders, public employees, service workers' collectives and unions, and churches came together to support a minimum wage increase. Since 2013 more than twenty-five local governments have raised their minimum wage requirements and about thirty more have raised the minimum wage for their employees or employees of contractors doing public business. Opponents have challenged these actions in state courts as exceeding the powers of local government, and twenty-one states—the vast majority controlled by Republicans— have enacted laws prohibiting localities from enacting minimum wage laws.[44]

Tennessee is one of only five states that has no state minimum wage law. In 2014 nearly 7.5 percent of the state's workforce worked at or below the federal minimum of $7.25 an hour, the highest share in the US. (The national number was 4.3 percent, about 3.3 million workers.) That year the Tennessee legislature rejected a proposal to increase the minimum wage by $1 an hour for workers not offered health insurance by their employers.[45]

Unlike the EITC, increasing the minimum wage—which is much easier to describe on a campaign stump—has developed into a partisan issue. The moral argument for a minimum wage that would increase take-home pay and protect full-time workers from poverty remains strong, however. The employment declines or price increases that would likely result remain invisible to the public. Higher minimum wages enjoy broad public backing, evinced by successful ballot initiatives even in red states. Polls routinely show public support hovering around 70 percent.[46]

What has changed is the nature of the opposition. Republican opponents of a higher federal minimum wage have come to insist that the minimum be left to the states, the stance eventually adopted by President Trump after much waffling as a candidate. We have seen that coalitions for raising state or local minimum wages are strong in some states. In others, however, deregulation supporters, often bolstered by the substitution of private contractors for government workers, have joined together with antitax advocates and business owners to create effective blocking coalitions. Similar blocking coalitions have been successful in Congress since the last increase took effect in 2009, often bolstered by the contention that minimum wages lead to higher prices, greater unemployment, and perhaps the exodus of jobs abroad.

Despite success in some states and localities, fight-for-fifteen activists suffer from both political and substantive disadvantages when compared to proponents of the EITC. Politically, fighting for a higher minimum wage has become an important and visible rallying for Democrats since Obama's presidency, but that also has made it a partisan issue that activates powerful blocking coalitions. This is true even though minimum wage regulations do not explicitly show up on government budgets, except where they apply to government employees or contractors. Substantively, higher minimum wages can cost jobs and are financed from some combination of lost wages, higher prices, and lower business profits. The EITC, by contrast, has unambiguous positive effects on employment and is paid for out of general revenues.

Seeking a Political Future for the EITC

Working to expand and improve the EITC is both better policy and better legislative politics than increasing the minimum wage, although the two efforts need not be in competition. The EITC has long enjoyed bipartisan support and, unlike the minimum wage, has not become partisan. An expanded EITC would improve the well-being of low- and middle-income wage earners, making work pay better for those whose wages have long been stagnant. The costs of the EITC are widely shared and paid for largely through progressive income taxes, though in the near term the credit may also be financed through increased federal debt.

The moral argument for providing economic security through higher wages is clear, and it's an argument that proponents of higher minimums and the EITC can make. But while businesses will frequently oppose minimum wage increases, enhancing the EITC can garner support from businesses, especially small businesses. With effective leadership from EITC advocates, business interests, which benefit from the higher after-tax wages supported by the EITC, might be coaxed into supporting reform. Their resources can help move this issue onto legislative agendas. Expanding the benefits of the EITC into the middle class and increasing the credit for workers without children are both viable proximate goals. Reducing or eliminating marriage penalties—or even providing some bonuses for low- and moderate-income parents to marry—might attract social conservatives into a supporting coalition.[47] As with other tax expenditures, once entrenched, these achievements can be expanded. What has been missing is effective leadership.

True, it has been possible in some states to increase minimum wages. But the EITC enjoys greater bipartisan support in state legislatures. Most states have supplemented and enhanced the EITC but have not increased their minimum wages. Instead Republican-controlled state legislatures have been blocking local governments from increasing minimum wages. In principle, there is no reason that an expanded EITC cannot be combined with an increased minimum wage.[48] But combining the two might undermine support for an expanded EITC.

Policy analysts continue debating the merits of a universal basic income, and some regard it as superior to the EITC and minimum wage. As we have said, a UBI enjoys champions from both the left and the right. But the UBI is a political nonstarter. Its inclusiveness is its Achilles heel: the prospect of transferring annual income to idlers and the enormously wealthy defeats a politically viable moral argument. That alone ensures that it will endure only in the world of punditry and academic debate, notwithstanding the resources that its Silicon Valley advocates might be prepared to deploy on its behalf. One need look only to its failures in Europe to realize that UBI is a distraction. Expanding and strengthening the EITC is both better politics and better policy.

CHAPTER SIX

From Unemployment
to Reemployment

Americans are often more vulnerable to job and wage losses than their counterparts in most other advanced industrial countries.[1] That's because the US has more flexible labor markets and fewer legal protections for employees, as well as less robust social insurance protections. Among the reasons for this are the limited and declining influence of trade unions since the 1950s and the relative weakness of the Democratic Party when compared with many of Europe's social democratic parties. The divergence between US and foreign workers might be diminishing, as unions have recently been declining and center-left parties have been fragmenting and weakening across much of the industrial world.[2] But other factors, notably federalism and the corrosive effects of racial antipathies on class solidarity, suggest that the US workforce might continue as one of the most vulnerable to employment insecurity for some time to come.

Tempting Diversions

Politicians often blame job loss and wage stagnation on competition from low-wage foreign workers. Expanded international trade in goods and services in recent decades has made focus on international trade as the culprit even more politically appealing. For a long time, complaints about the costs to American workers from international trade came from Democrats and their union supporters, who called for tougher labor law and environmental protections in trade treaties as ways to raise the costs of foreign-produced goods and services. Traditionally, Republicans advocated removing barriers to trade. Until 2017, presidents of both parties resisted calls for protectionist measures. Both Bill Clinton and Barack Obama counted agreements expanding cross-border trade among their signature accomplishments: Clinton in signing the North American Free Trade Agreement (NAFTA) inherited from the George H. W. Bush administration—with the addition of modest side agreements on labor and the environment—and Obama in negotiating the Trans-Pacific Partnership (TPP). Both needed Republican support in Congress to enact these agreements.

This pattern of bipartisan support for trade agreements changed dramatically with Donald Trump's election in 2016. Once in office, Trump set about proving that "trade wars are good and easy to win."[3] His opening salvo was an executive order on the third day of his presidency withdrawing the United States from the TPP, which he had attacked relentlessly on the campaign trail. In 2016 President Obama had signed TPP with eleven Pacific nations representing 800 million people and 40 percent of the world's GDP. TPP would have eliminated 18,000 tariffs on agricultural products and checked China's burgeoning economic power in the region. While Trump insisted that his move was a "great thing for the American worker," skeptics emphasized that the main effect of the US withdrawal was to help China consolidate its power over East Asian regional trade.[4] Some economists estimated that, by 2030, Trump's withdrawal would decrease US economic growth by $131 billion and increase China's by $250 billion.[5]

Undeterred, Trump followed his action on TPP with a similar attack on NAFTA, which he blamed for US trade deficits with Mexico and Canada. He also imposed new tariffs on the Europeans and other trading partners.[6] On October 1, 2018, Trump claimed a great victory for American workers after making a handful of changes to NAFTA and relabeling it the United States-Mexico-Canada Agreement. Unacknowledged was the fact that most of the updated provisions in this agreement were taken from the TPP he had trashed two years earlier.[7]

It is uncontroversial among the great majority of economists that freer trade has enriched the American economy. Updating a comprehensive 2005 study, Gary Hufbauer and Lucy Lu estimate that, from 1950 to 2016, trade liberalization, combined with cheaper transportation and communications, increased total US GDP by $2.1 trillion. Per capita GDP rose by more than $7,000 and per household GDP by $18,131, with most of the gains accruing to lower-income households. They estimate potential GDP gains from further trade liberalization, especially in services, of another $1,670 per capita by 2025.[8] This is hardly news. Economists have known for centuries that protecting national markets with tariffs and subsidies undermines the logic of comparative advantage and breeds retaliatory trade wars from which all sides eventually lose. Trump's attachment to protectionism is about politics not economics.

Trump is not the first president to seek political advantages from protectionism, despite its economic costs. Herbert Hoover's Smoot-Hawley tariffs of 1930 are typically portrayed as the most damaging example, but there are others. In the 1950s, when US oil cost about one dollar a barrel and Saudi oil sold for about five cents, President Dwight Eisenhower imposed import quotas to keep foreign oil out of the country. This kept oil prices high enough to keep US oil companies happy but not so high as to make consumers fret. Its main effect was to use up US oil when it was cheap rather than Middle East and Venezuelan oil when they were much cheaper. The United States paid the price for that misguided policy for half a century.[9]

When Trump announced a 25 percent tariff on steel imports in March 2018, he was reprising a long list of presidential efforts to limit imports to protect the US steel industry. Lyndon Johnson, Richard Nixon, and Ronald Reagan all imposed steel import quotas. Jimmy Carter put a price floor on steel imports, using a mechanism similar to a tariff except that the US Treasury did not get the additional revenue the policy generated. In 2002 George W. Bush placed tariffs of 8 to 30 percent on steel products, but he removed them the next year in response to adverse economic consequences and international retaliations. Barack Obama imposed tariffs on certain types of steel in an effort to limit Chinese imports.[10] Just recounting this history demonstrates its ineffectiveness. It also reminds us of the political power of the Youngstown-steel-industry resurrection myth. In 2018 the US had fewer steelworkers than manicurists.[11]

Along with steel tariffs, Trump announced a 10 percent tariff on aluminum. He based his legal authority on a trade law that allows the president to impose tariffs to protect national security.[12] Steel and aluminum are inputs for many products, including construction and heavy equipment, airplanes, and cars. Trump initially exempted imports from allies, including the European Union, Japan, Mexico, and Canada, the largest source of imports to the US. But in June 2018 he ended the exemptions, prompting widespread retaliation as those trading partners raised tariffs on US agricultural and other imports. A year after that, Trump removed the tariffs on metal imports from Canada and Mexico. The spuriousness of his national security justification was obvious—captured nicely by Catherine Rampell in a *Washington Post* column entitled "So you're telling me my Subaru is a national security threat?"[13]

Trump subsequently expanded his unilateral imposition of tariffs to $34 billion of Chinese imports, enlarged by an additional $200 billion in May 2019, while threatening to impose tariffs on up to $300 billion more. He and his political advisors viewed bashing China as an effective political tactic, allowing him to look tougher than any Democrat. The erstwhile Trump strategist Steve Bannon said proudly, "The politics now drive the economics."[14] China responded in kind, focusing initially on US agricultural exports such as soybeans, corn, pork, and poultry. No one knew how Trump's trade war might end.

Trump's initial tariffs were focused on intermediate supply inputs rather than consumer products, hitting US multinational supply chains.[15] Stories soon emerged of companies and localities fretting about, working around, and in some cases suffering from the tariffs.[16] Stripmatic Products, an Ohio manufacturer of sausage stuffers, had to raise its prices, lost a major bid, and threatened to close.[17] Plug Power, a Latham, New York, fuel cell assembler, warned the US trade representative that more than 600 employees "could potentially lose their livelihood, not to mention jobs associated with our customers, supply chain partners and others that support the distribution and sale of our products."[18] Harley-Davidson, the iconic American motorcycle manufacturer once lauded by Trump as a special favorite, said it was moving some manufacturing to Thailand and Europe.[19] The Mid Continent Nail Corporation in Poplar Bluff, Missouri, the nation's largest nail manufacturer, laid off 50 of its 600 workers and threatened to move to Mexico unless it got an exception from the steel tariffs.[20]

Prices for washers and dryers in the US rose by 12 percent by the end of 2018.[21] The US had collected about $82 million in additional revenues from the tariffs by February 2019. The best estimate of the short-run effects of Trump's trade war on the US economy is that it cost American consumers and producers nearly $69 billion (0.37 percent of GDP) in 2018 because of higher prices. Along with the additional revenues, these higher prices largely translated into higher profits for domestic producers, so that the net effects that year were small: an aggregate loss of $7.8 billion.

Economists estimate that Trump's tariffs will cost anywhere from three to ten times as many jobs as they save. Wages did at first increase a bit for workers in sectors protected by the tariffs, but the price effects were substantially larger, so that families' disposable income decreased by 0.7 percent on average.[22] In May 2019 trade experts at the Peterson Institute for International Economics estimated that Trump's steel tariffs had cost American consumers and businesses about $900,000 for every job they saved or created—thirteen times the typical steelworker's salary.[23] This is to say nothing of the many local disruptions resulting from the trade war. China's 25 percent retaliatory tariff on lobsters was a big hit to the Little Bay Lobster Company of Newington, New Hampshire. Little Bay once took 50,000 pounds of weekly orders from China, but those buyers switched to a less expensive Canadian supplier. Pistachios that had been shipped from California to China faced a 45 percent tariff and were replaced by nuts from Iran.

In an effort to stimulate political backlash to Trump's actions, America's trading partners have focused retaliatory tariffs on areas where support for him and his allies is strong. Agricultural interests were targeted and Midwestern producers suffered. Mike Nang, Iowa's Republican secretary of agriculture, told a crowd gathered at a state fair that the trade war should end. "When retaliation comes targeted at agriculture, we are bearing the brunt," he said. "We cannot continue to bear the full brunt." In South Dakota, the costs to farmers and ranchers were estimated at hundreds of millions of dollars in the first few weeks of retaliatory tariffs. Canada's retaliatory tariffs on paper products threatened the viability of exports from Wisconsin that had amounted to $2 billion during the previous decade.[24] Leaders from Mobile, Alabama, to New London, Connecticut, sounded alarm over the potential for Trump's tariffs to damage their local economies. Trump responded with a $12 billion "pacifier for farmers," as Illinois soy bean farmer Dave Kestel dismissed it. This was little more than a stopgap attempt to blunt the fallout in the run-up to the 2018 midterms.[25] But Trump stuck with it. As the 2020 Presidential primary season began and China upped the ante, Trump added another $16 billion in support for farmers harmed by tariffs.[26] How much this would help him with angry rural voters was debatable, not only because, as Kestel notes, farmers want markets for their products not pacifiers, but also because the great bulk of this money was expected to go to farms with annual revenues of several million dollars.[27]

It was, in any case, not enough. In August 2019 China cancelled all purchases of US farm exports in response to Trump's decision to slap a 10 percent tariff on $300 billion of Chinese imports. Zippy Duval, president of the American Farm Bureau, called it a "body blow to thousands of farmers and ranchers who are already struggling to get by." By then Chinese agricultural imports from the US had dropped from $19.5 billion in 2017 to $9.2 billion in 2018 and, even before the new escalation, were on track to fall by an additional 20 percent in 2019. This compounded the massive stress for an industry in which crop yields had been diminished by successive years of record flooding and extreme heat waves. The combined effect: US farm income fell 45 percent from $123.4 billion in 2013 to $63 billion in 2018. "Trump is ruining our markets," declared North Dakota farmer Bob Kuylen, noting that the only thing keeping him farming was his massive sunk cost. "It's killing us," said wheat and soybean farmer Mark Watne, who is president of the North Dakota Farmers Union. Like Kestel, he doesn't believe that taxpayers should subsidize farmers "just because of what I see as a mistake of a trade war." But he does think that the Trump administration would have little choice other than to pay off farmers. "Either you let a bunch of farmers go broke or you do another payout."[28]

The best estimates of the political effects of Trump's trade war show that while the US tariffs were targeted to help workers in politically competitive counties, retaliatory tariffs were targeted at US exports from heavily Republican counties, especially those in agriculture.[29] Rural Americans were particularly hard hit.[30] Trump's apparent calculation was that workers who kept their jobs or even saw a slight increase in their wages would appreciate his efforts, while the consumers who paid higher prices would overlook them or at least not blame him. He also seemed to think that his confrontation with China would make him look strong. The *Washington Post* reported that he told his advisors and allies that the trade war with China is "highly popular with his political base and will help him win reelection in 2020 regardless of any immediate economic pain."[31]

If there were any doubts that Trump's tariffs were about politics, not economics, he put them to rest in May 2019 when he announced that he would impose a 5 percent tariff on imports from Mexico—potentially rising to 25 percent—unless that country "substantially stops" immigrants from crossing the border with the US. This action was opposed not only by all of his economic advisors but also by his aggressive trade negotiator with China. After a week of noisy brinksmanship with the Mexican government, he called off the tariffs, announcing an agreement requiring Mexico to do more to stem the flow of Central American migrants.[32] Trump was transparently reminding the insecure Americans for whom he had done little or nothing in his first term that their troubles were all due to imports from low-wage foreigners and immigrants threatening to take American jobs. His message, like that of nativist populists around the world: it's not your fault; it's those foreigners.

Despite protectionism's costs, its political allure seemed unlikely to dissipate any time soon. In targeting convenient villains, Trump's trade war fed a potent ideological narrative: America's trade agreements are unfair to hardworking Americans and benefit low-wage foreign workers. Incompetent US bureaucrats—aided and abetted by the cosmopolitan, uncaring, and inattentive elites whom Bannon christened the "globalists"—were out-negotiated, perhaps even bamboozled, by clever foreign leaders focused on improving the lives of their citizens. These foreigners—especially the Chinese—secured trade agreements that provided good, if relatively low-paying, jobs to their workers and cost middle-class Americans their jobs and beggared their children's futures. The still-hollowed-out steel factories of Youngstown offered testimony to the failed policies that the hero of *The Art of the Deal* was determined to remedy.

A Republican Congress would not—and could not—stop him. Invoking national security is sufficient to impose tariffs, even when manifestly bogus. Trump cynically conceded as much when Canadian Prime Minister Justin Trudeau questioned how his country posed a national security threat to the US. Trump's facetious retort: "Didn't you guys burn down the White House?"[33] This discretion enables presidents to evade the veto players who typically insulate the status quo, making it hard for Congress to rein in a president determined to impose tariffs. Curbing presidential authority would require new legislation, which would have to pass both houses of Congress with veto-proof two-thirds majorities. To be sure, some members of Congress urge their colleagues to reinvigorate the legislative branch's constitutional prerogatives concerning trade, ceded for decades to the executive branch. But their exhortations, like the ritual hand-wringing when presidents violate the War Powers Act by engaging in military action not authorized by Congress, will likely prove fruitless.[34]

Nor were business interests—despite their hostility to tariffs—able to muster effective coalitions to block tariffs.[35] Even if they could solve the conflicts among differently affected businesses and take a united stand, they would inevitably confront formidable opposition. Attacking trade agreements, especially agreements with China or Mexico, garners support from unlikely coalitions of ethnic nationalists, workers who want to acquire or maintain jobs in protected industries, and liberals who vilify trade agreements as inattentive to environmental concerns and complicit in brutal labor conditions abroad. These political realities made it easy for Trump to ignore with impunity denunciations from economists, business groups, and the Republican political establishment.

Political resistance to protectionism is further confounded by the intensity and distribution of voter attitudes. The benefits of free trade are spread widely across the population in lower prices, while the costs are often concentrated—either geographically or in groups whose members lack the skills or sway to avoid downward mobility. Generations of commentators following Mancur Olson have observed that governments can overspend on well-organized interests because the benefits are concentrated, while the costs—higher taxes or public debt—are dispersed among millions of voters (including unborn voters in the case of debt) who lack the incentives and means to organize themselves into an effective opposition. This logic implies that those who experience concentrated costs from free trade will be easier to mobilize than the millions of beneficiaries. And, as we have noted, people react more intensely to losses than to gains. It is therefore unsurprising that the losers from globalization are more easily mobilized than are the winners.[36]

Trump's tariff gambit was also helped by his highly visible proximate goals. Rather than announce a general protectionist strategy, he cleverly identified specific foreign tariffs on US goods that he declared objectionable and wanted lowered or eliminated. Canadian tariffs on dairy products and European tariffs on US automobiles were prominent targets. In July 2018 German Chancellor Angela Merkel said that she would be willing to consider reducing the latter, and later that month Trump and European Commission President Jean-Claude Juncker initialed an agreement to "work towards" zero tariffs on non-auto industrial goods and reduce barriers to trade in services and other areas.[37] As with the revised NAFTA, such actions allowed Trump to claim victory: he was quick to declare the Juncker agreement a "very big day for free and fair trade"—even though all that had been agreed to was a temporary halt in the trade war Trump had himself started.

Whether all of this maneuvering would amount to anything other than the inevitable costs of a trade war was another matter. In 2018 it didn't even reduce the US trade deficit, which two years after Trump began his trade war reached $891.2 billion, the largest such deficit in American history. Even the bilateral deficit with China set a record at $419 billion.[38] Not that these numbers mean anything to average Americans or even to the economy at large.[39] More importantly, there was no reason to expect that Trump's trade policies would alleviate the economic insecurities of more than tiny numbers of US workers, despite the significant costs. His farm bailouts and subsidies did not even stem the rising tide of family-farm bankruptcies, which increased from 467 filings between mid-2017 and mid-2018 to 514 the next year, most of them concentrated in the Midwest.[40]

Trump has often trumpeted Pyrrhic trade victories, as when the White House and its allies used a carrot-and-stick approach to prevent the heating and air-conditioning firm Carrier from closing an Indiana plant and moving 1,100 jobs to Mexico. While the administration threatened hefty tariffs if the company went forward with offshoring, the State of Indiana gave Carrier $7 million in tax incentives in exchange for making a $16 million investment in the plant. But much of that investment went to automation.[41] As Greg Hayes, CEO of Carrier's corporate parent United Technologies, conceded, "We will make that plant competitive just because we'll make the capital investments there. But what that ultimately means is there will be fewer jobs." About 800 jobs were saved, but Carrier still cut 300 to 600 along with another 700 at another facility nearby. The costs to Indiana taxpayers far exceeded the wages paid to Carrier employees whose jobs were saved in the short run, but that was irrelevant to Trump's politics.[42] His victory claims fed off his nationalist narrative and concomitant disdain for the multilateral institutions nurtured by the United States since the end of World War II. His relentless attacks on the European Union, the G-7, the World Trade Organization, and NATO buttressed an "America First" ideology that harkens back to nativist isolationists of the 1930s such as Charles Lindbergh. It is hostile to all multilateral agreements and institutions.[43]

Despite this ideology's potency for mobilizing disaffected Americans, there is no reason to believe that Trump's trade wars will produce better results for the US or the world in the 2020s and 2030s than protectionism did in the 1920s and 1930s. Open markets are best for the overall economy, but their benefits do not flow to everyone. Those who cannot adapt often face painful dislocation. These prospects become all the more terrifying in an era when capital's increased mobility has left unions—where they exist at all—with greatly diminished capacity to defend workers, and when technological innovation requires constant retooling that is beyond the capacities of many people. As the Carrier story underscores, it is technology rather than trade that is likely going to be the chief culprit in job loss going forward, even though this will not stop politicians from attacking trade. Heading off protectionism depends on finding better ways to address the insecurity of those workers who bear the brunt of change.

Shortcomings of Unemployment Insurance

The best protections from economic insecurity that the US government provides are for the elderly. Social Security has been the country's most successful anti-poverty program; Medicare provides significant health insurance; and Medicaid offers health insurance for the poor and children and long-term care coverage for many elderly who are too poor to afford it.

The weakest link in US social insurance is protection from job loss during the working years.[44] A major political challenge of our time is to find ways to help laid-off workers avoid downward mobility and dislocation. This is especially important now, when globalization and technological changes are producing widespread—and well-grounded—fears of downward mobility. Economists often treat job losses resulting from company reorganizations, takeovers, mergers, plant closures, the substitution of technology for labor, downsizing, and even offshoring as the inevitable by-products of capitalism's creative destruction. But this invites politicians to attack immigrants and push self-defeating protectionism as we have seen. The better choice is to build support for policies that deal directly with the sources of employment insecurity.

In virtually all developed countries, unemployment insurance is provided by the national government. In the US the unemployment insurance system was created as part of the Social Security Act of 1935, but it was marred from the outset by doubts about whether the Supreme Court would uphold as constitutional a federal social insurance program. This resulted in a unique state-based system with coverage and eligibility determined by the states and unemployment insurance funded by a dedicated tax on employers. Unemployment insurance still depends on an unfortunate mix of federal, state, and local responsibilities designed more than eight decades ago in the shadow of now-archaic constitutional concerns. The federal role is essentially limited to providing some guidelines and oversight, supplying financial backing in hard times, and funding the states' administrative costs. This structure creates additional obstacles to the provision of protections: whatever their party, state legislators worry that improving protections will produce a perverse race to the top, making their states magnets for vulnerable or unemployed workers.

As a result the US system remains a complex patchwork of more than fifty programs that fail to provide basic economic security for jobless workers or adequate countercyclical stability to the national economy during downturns. The states typically provide up to twenty-six weeks of benefits, although eight states have reduced this period to less than sixteen weeks.[45] Benefit-coverage levels and duration vary considerably depending on where a worker happens to live.

Unemployment insurance is also becoming less useful as the structure of work changes. The system was designed to help traditional full-time workers who lose their jobs and presumes a relatively short interval before they return to full-time work. But the number of workers who are independent contractors or are hired on a contractual or temporary basis is growing, and these workers often cannot take advantage of unemployment insurance. Lawrence Katz and Alan Krueger have estimated that these kinds of workers accounted for 94 percent of all job growth between 2005 and 2015.[46] The *New York Times* reports that in 2019 Google's temporary workers and independent contractors, whose pay ranges from $16 to $125 an hour, number 120,000, working side-by-side with the company's 102,000 full-time employees—a ratio only slightly higher than is typical for technology firms.[47] Criteria for unemployment insurance eligibility vary from state to state, but most still exclude part-time or contractual workers despite their growing role in the workforce. At best, unemployment insurance provides limited support for workers who lose part-time jobs or who take them during or after periods of unemployment.

The percentage of jobless workers who receive unemployment benefits has been shrinking, underscoring how ineffective our inherited system is, given today's employment insecurity. In 2016 only 27 percent of unemployed workers received benefits, down from 36 percent in 2007.[48] Low-wage workers are the least likely to be covered. On average, unemployment benefits replace about 45 percent of prior earnings, but replacement rates vary widely, from 55 percent in Rhode Island and Hawaii to 37.5 percent in Louisiana and 33.3 percent in Alaska. The benefits are generally not sufficient to prevent lower-income unemployed workers and their families from falling into poverty.[49]

Employers pay state and federal taxes for unemployment insurance, but the costs of the tax ultimately come out of workers' paychecks. The federal tax is 0.6 percent of the first $7,000 of earnings. State unemployment insurance taxes vary widely, from 0.1 percent to 15.1 percent depending on a variety of factors, including each business's history of firing workers. The minimum taxable wage base is the same as for the federal tax, a level that has not increased since 1983. The five highest state taxable wage bases ranged from about $35,000 to nearly $50,000 in 2019. Because the wages subject to unemployment insurance taxes are capped, their burden is particularly regressive, falling disproportionately on low-wage workers.[50] Financing is complex, inconsistent, and unfair.

America's ethos of bootstrapping and individual responsibility makes moral arguments supporting unemployment insurance shaky, except at times like the Depression or Great Recession when job loss is manifestly due to factors beyond workers' control. This is one reason why politicians have linked support for expanded unemployment protections to trade agreements. Workers who lose their jobs to foreign competition can scarcely be blamed, particularly when the competition from abroad has been made easier by trade deals pursued by their government. This is why it has been tempting to build coalitions supporting trade deals by promising expanded assistance for workers who are adversely affected by trade. Tactically appealing as this might seem, it rests on dubious logic that ends up being self-defeating.

The Perverse Politics of Trade Adjustment Assistance

The idea that the government should help workers who lose jobs due to foreign competition was first advanced in the US in 1950 by economist Clair Wilcox. Eleven years earlier, Nicholas Kaldor had famously maintained that the British had benefitted in 1846 from repealing the Corn Laws—tariffs that had been designed to keep grain prices high to favor domestic producers—because the winners could have compensated the losers and still been better off.[51] Exhibiting a tin ear for politics, Kaldor never urged that any compensation actually be paid.[52] As Paul Samuelson has noted, such arguments call to mind Marie Antoinette's proclaiming "Let them eat cake!" without transferring any sugar or flour to her subjects.[53] The more worldly Wilcox did not propose paying compensation either, but he did argue that the federal government should help displaced workers find new employment.[54] But nothing came of his recommendation until the Kennedy administration.[55] "When considerations of national policy make it desirable to avoid higher tariffs," JFK declared, "those injured by that competition should not be required to bear the full brunt of the impact. Rather, the burden of economic adjustment should be borne in part by the Federal Government."[56]

Congress adopted Trade Adjustment Assistance (TAA) as part of the Trade Expansion Act of 1962 to ease transitions for workers who would be displaced by the tariff reductions envisaged in the legislation. TAA provided for income maintenance at 65 percent of the worker's wages for up to a year, relocation funds, and—most important—free training for anyone who needed it. New York Democrat Eugene Keogh, the bill's floor manager in the House, declared that intensive training "will be aimed at getting these workers trained in skills which will enable them, in as short a time as possible, to take their rightful place in the economy." TAA was not meant "to tide a worker over a lull in his employment but to assist him in attaining new skills and talents to be applied in a new job."[57] Keogh was echoing President Kennedy, who had insisted that TAA must be neither a subsidy nor government paternalism. Instead, it should "afford the time for American initiative, American adaptability, and American resiliency to assert themselves."[58]

Initially, Kennedy's initiative looked promising. The bill picked up backing from businesses by also promising loans and technical support to firms that suffered due to tariff reductions. Organized labor was onboard. AFL-CIO president George Meany made it clear that adjustment assistance was vital to union acquiescence in the tariff-reduction provisions. Meany endorsed TAA strongly, declaring that it "would strengthen both our domestic economy and our world competitive position by helping companies and workers to increase their efficiency, either in their present field or a new one."[59] Kennedy trumpeted the bill as a deftly crafted, "constructive, businesslike program of loans and allowances tailored to help firms and workers get back into the competitive stream." He endorsed the aspiration that "instead of the dole of tariff protection, we are substituting an investment in better production."[60]

But TAA was stillborn. Lyndon Johnson, who took over as president when Kennedy was assassinated the following year, focused on other priorities. From 1962 to 1969, the US Tariff Commission—charged with administering the program—failed to approve a single TAA request. Eligibility requirements were loosened somewhat thereafter, but the commission still stymied workers' applications by demanding that they produce data that was available only from former employers or from the commission itself. Only about 35,000 workers received adjustment allowances in the next several years, and few of them received any training. Union leaders came to regard the government's program as a ruse. By 1973 Meany had written TAA off as inadequate to address the challenges accompanying tariff reductions and the AFL-CIO was lambasting it as "burial insurance." This was a fateful failure, as Steve Charnovitz observes, to take advantage of the window of opportunity when organized labor had backed free trade.[61]

Labor's abandoning support for TAA in the early 1970s was especially unfortunate because by then major business interests had moved from being skeptics—as they were in the 1960—to robust advocates. Business lobbyists were working to block strongly protectionist measures such as the Burke-Hartke bill, which threatened to regulate US companies' employment practices abroad, while calling for better worker training to compensate for the losses from free trade. In 1973 former Nixon administration official Fred Bergsten led a Chamber of Commerce task force that recommended major government investments in manpower training. Noting that freer trade dislocates some workers and industries for the benefit of the economy as a whole, Bergsten argued to the House Ways and Means Committee that those who are hurt "should be compensated adequately for their losses, and the opportunity should be seized to enable them to increase their contribution to the national welfare." Pepsi CEO Donald Kendall—chair of the Emergency Committee on American Trade, which was leading the opposition to the Burke-Hartke bill—told the committee that it was "inexcusable that instead of a national program of industrial adaptation that would allow the worker to retain pension and other rights, our economy offers only inadequate training or the dole."[62] But with the AFL-CIO now opposing TAA as unfairly narrow in helping only workers displaced due to international trade, this business support came too late.

By contrast, in countries like Denmark, whose legal employment protections are as weak as those in the United States, workers who lose their jobs automatically get substantial financial support and retraining. Unemployment insurance covering up to 60 percent of lost wages is paid for up to four years, provided that the worker enrolls in job-search and retraining programs crafted by the government in close collaboration with unions and companies. Danish unemployment rates have consistently been lower than those in the United States, suggesting that fears of moral hazard are overblown.[63] Other countries, including Canada, Japan, and Sweden, have shifted some of the burdens of employment support to former employers by making them provide or pay for outplacement or training services.[64]

Congress tried to revive TAA as part of the Trade Act of 1974. That bill relaxed eligibility criteria, shifted TAA administration to the Department of Labor, increased the assistance to 70 percent of previous wages up to a ceiling of the average national manufacturing wage, set up a trust fund financed by tariffs to enhance payments for training, and created out-of-town job-search support. Nevertheless, perhaps because they knew that the Nixon administration had lost interest in the program, the AFL-CIO correctly predicted that TAA would remain ineffective. The Office of Management and Budget refused to implement the TAA trust fund, and the Labor Department and relevant state agencies lacked sufficient staff to manage the program. The result: it took some fourteen months to respond to the average claimant, too long to do much good. The Labor Department did allocate some training funds from other sources, but they were small drops in huge buckets. For instance, Ohio requested $2.7 million in 1976 and received $400,000. Even when the Ford administration introduced a fast-track procedure for cases of serious unemployment in a number of industries, the Labor Department failed to expedite TAA benefits.

The Carter administration did no better. President Carter rejected a proposed overhaul of TAA as too expensive, with the perverse result that, although the program grew, it failed to become more effective. By the end of 1980, about a million workers had received some $2.4 billion in readjustment funds since the program's inception, two-thirds of that amount having been spent in the final year due to massive layoffs in the auto industry. By then, the Labor Department had cut its allocation for adjustment assistance by half, so that only 19 percent of those who received allowances got career counseling, 3 percent secured

training, and less than 1 percent obtained job-search or relocation aid.

This combination of increased costs and limited effectiveness
made the program an easy target in 1981 for the incoming Reagan
Administration. In his first address to Congress, Reagan adopted—
perhaps unconsciously—what by then had long been the AFL-
CIO's stance: he declared it unfair that people who lost jobs because
of foreign competition were eligible for help unavailable to those
who became unemployed due to domestic competition. Benefits
were reduced, recipients were required to accept any job that paid
more than their state's unemployment benefit, and the Labor
Department was allowed to require recipients to choose between
retraining and relocation after eight weeks.

By 1986 TAA had become, according to Charnovitz, "a cruel
caricature of what adjustment was intended to be." Lack of leadership after President Kennedy's death, chronic underfunding, and
ineffective administration combined to ensure that the bulk of the
$2,954 the program spent per worker since 1975 had been allo-
cated to income support, with only 2.5 percent spent on adjustment help—including training. Training was in any case not generally available, let alone required as a condition for support as
the law mandated. Early enthusiasm by organized labor had been
squandered, with the AFL-CIO instead demanding domestic-
content requirements for manufactured goods. Business interests
had split; some supported TAA, but firms in import-sensitive industries hoped TAA would fail, bolstering their case for protectionism. Nor did economists speak with one voice. The great majority favored free trade, but many also resisted government
intervention in labor markets and were therefore hostile to TAA's
adjustment provisions. And federal and state bureaucrats often
found the law too complex to administer and enforcement too expensive to invest in, given the resources at their disposal.[65]

In short, the story of adjustment insurance in the US has been a tragedy of errors. The better course for organized labor, after TAA's sputtering debut in the Johnson administration, would have been to continue pushing it as a proximate goal despite its flaws, lobby to fix its administrative problems, and endeavor to extend it to wider circumstances of job loss. The political prospects for such an effort would have been better had business gotten on board before organized labor bailed. Despite this history of missed opportunities, there are signs that comprehensive expansion of adjustment insurance is an idea whose time has come.

Efforts at Revival and Expansion

When Bill Clinton signed NAFTA three decades after TAA's inception, the program was expanded to cover not only unemployment due to imports but also losses from jobs shifted to Mexico and Canada. By the early 2000s TAA had been further expanded to encompass shifts in production to any country with which the US has a trade agreement and to cover workers in factories producing inputs for goods facing competition from imports.[66] By then TAA provided quite generous support, but only to a small number of workers: 37,000 in 2002.[67] At that point the Democratic-controlled Senate and Republican-majority House enacted a significant enlargement of TAA as a condition for renewing President Bush's fast-track authority to negotiate trade agreements. In provisions projected to cost $10 billion over the next decade, income benefits were expanded from fifty-two to seventy-eight weeks, a tax credit for health insurance was added, job-search and relocation benefits were increased, and coverage was added for farmers, ranchers, older workers, and secondary workers upstream and downstream from industries affected by job losses to Mexico and Canada.[68] Congressional Democrats extracted additional enhancements in 2015, creating a new public workforce-development system.[69] This program relies on local control and local businesses in an effort to enhance training opportunities and improve credentials for employees.[70] But through the end of the Obama administration, Congress failed to appropriate the necessary funds, repeating the pattern of chronic underfunding that has persisted for decades.[71] In 2017 the incoming Trump administration shifted to its protectionist agenda, abandoning the tariff reductions that had helped build political support for expanding and extending TAA.

The upshot is that US adjustment assistance remains meager. Every other advanced economy spends at least twice as much as the US; Germany and France spend five times as much.[72] Denmark spends more than 2 percent of GDP to help unemployed workers reenter the workforce—twenty times as much as the US. Even with its recent enhancements, TAA has had little impact. Between 2000 and 2007, imports from low-wage countries rose from 15 to 28 percent of total US imports, yet the system failed to keep up. As David Autor and his colleagues observed of this time period, "Labor market adjustment to trade shocks is stunningly slow, with local labor-force participation rates remaining depressed and local unemployment rates remaining elevated for a full decade or more after the shock commences."[73] Given the inadequacies of TAA, workers instead increasingly apply for and get Social Security disability payments, portending their permanent exit from the labor force.[74]

This is hardly surprising. Both TAA and unemployment insurance are inadequate in the face of the insecurities inherent in today's labor markets.[75] When workers find new jobs, they typically are paid considerably less than previously. Republican and Democratic Congresses have consistently refused to appropriate enough funds to support firms, communities, or displaced workers to help them adapt to a new reality marked by the diminishing half-life—if not permanent obsolescence—of many kinds of human capital. As businessman Alex Sheford—who was forced to lay off workers when his firm Century Furniture downsized because of the influx of Chinese imports—lamented, TAA is "a Band-Aid for an economy that has a sliced artery."[76] Nothing less than a major transformation of adjustment assistance and unemployment insurance will suffice.

Universal Adjustment Assistance

Ensuring long-term income security for workers must become the central focus of adjustment assistance. This means providing transitional resources to help those who can adapt to the demands of changing labor markets and a safety net that delivers basic necessities for those who cannot. Even in an economy with full employment, there will be discouraged workers—those who want work but have stopped trying to find a new job—and others so frustrated that they no longer even want jobs. Discouraged workers grew by 15 percent over the eight years after the Great Recession, and the number who no longer wanted jobs grew even more—so that the labor-force participation rate (the ratio between the labor force and the working-age population) fell from 66 percent to 63 percent between 2008 and 2016 despite steadily falling unemployment after 2010.[77]

Much conventional wisdom holds that that our double ambition—to guarantee long-term income support as well as transitional resources—is potentially at war with itself. Providing people with income might undermine their incentives to do what they must to survive in the labor market. This is what Bill Clinton claimed when introducing his welfare-reform legislation in 1996: "The current welfare system undermines the basic values of work, responsibility and family, trapping generation after generation in dependency and hurting the very people it was designed to help." He argued that placing time limits—including lifetime limits—on public support would "make welfare what it was meant to be: a second chance, not a way of life."[78] How do we avoid the moral hazard Clinton identified? How do we ensure that transitional support serves as a springboard and not a hammock? The short answer is that incentives can be structured to diminish that risk, even if it cannot be eliminated entirely.

In principle TAA benefits are now generous and robust. Eligible displaced workers who are engaged in training for a new job are supposed to be able to get cash benefits for up to two years by combining unemployment and TAA benefits. Moderate-income workers aged fifty or older who are less likely to be reemployed at their prior wage level may, in principle, be eligible for wage insurance to make up at least some of the difference between their new lower wage and their previous higher salary. Health insurance for displaced workers is partially subsidized through a refundable tax credit. And TAA, in the law at least, contains special provisions intended to help firms and communities weather disruptions from liberalized international trade.

In practice we have seen that, like unemployment insurance, resources for adjustment depend on a woefully inadequate patchwork of state and federal programs.[79] Among TAA's administrative headaches is the perplexing necessity of establishing which jobs meet the criterion of having been lost because of trade rather than for other reasons. This slows down awards and contributes to perceptions that the benefits are arbitrary and unfair, making an easy political target for blocking coalitions. If it ever made sense to prefer assistance for people harmed by trade over other sources of involuntary job loss, that time has passed. Going forward, whatever the source of unemployment, transitional assistance, often including retraining, will be needed. As Edward Alden observes, "While many other countries have overhauled, refined, and expanded their labor market adjustment schemes," the US has not changed its support significantly since the adoption of unemployment insurance in 1935. Then unemployment was episodic and cyclical, not due to permanent changes in labor markets that require workers to develop new skills. As Alden notes, this failure was "one of the bigger mistakes of US government economic policy, one that has resulted in an enormous waste of human capital and in eroding popular support for international trade and US engagement with the world."[80]

Historically, retraining efforts have often been underwhelming. One 1998 World Bank study of retraining programs in OECD countries found that they did no better than job-search assistance in increasing either the likelihood of reemployment or postintervention earnings, whether for workers who have been laid off en masse or for the long-term unemployed.[81] More recent research has been more encouraging about the effects on subsequent earnings of retraining versus other kinds of intervention even for older workers, though the opportunity costs of retraining older workers are higher than for those with longer work lives ahead of them.[82] It is also true that dire predictions—as old as the hills—of growing levels of permanent unemployment due to technological innovation have often been exaggerated. But what does seem clear is that skills decay more rapidly today than ever before, and this is unlikely to change. One 2017 Deloitte study found that many skills are obsolete within five years.[83] The challenge is less that robots will make humans redundant and more that changing technologies perpetually require people to develop new skills. One recent Aspen Institute / Accenture study found that, in the artificial-intelligence era, physical, operational, and simple analytical skills are becoming less important than higher-level creativity, more complex reasoning skills, and socioemotional skills.[84] Whatever mix of retraining and other kinds of transitional help is needed going forward, this is clearly going to require substantial help from governments.

In the US the best way forward is to combine TAA and unemployment insurance into one national program, which we call Universal Adjustment Assistance. UAA would provide adequate unemployment coverage and benefits to any worker—including independent contractors and part-time or seasonal workers—who loses a job without fault and who is actively seeking employment. The highly regressive current financing structure of unemployment insurance should be reformed as it is folded into UAA. This means increasing expenditures for TAA, unemployment insurance, and job training already on the books and moving primary responsibility for unemployment coverage and benefits to the federal government. Assistance should also be provided to workers and their families relocating to take new jobs. An urgent task is to build support in both political parties and among labor and especially business interests for the federal government to fund this program.

An enduring American myth—which often serves to impede legislation—is that Americans are able to pull themselves up by their bootstraps. One way to do that when confronted with unemployment is for people to move whenever and wherever opportunity knocks, an attitude memorialized in the nineteenth-century admonition to "go West, young man, go West." Measuring people's movements for jobs is difficult, but migration within the

US apparently peaked around 1980, and has declined substantially since then. An aging population, the prevalence of two-earner families, and cyclical downturns in labor or housing markets only partially explain the decline.[85] The geographer Thomas J. Cooke estimates that one-fifth of the decrease in Americans' willingness to move is attributable to what he describes as rootedness, which makes moving increasingly rare.[86] Relying on individuals to move on their own to where jobs are more plentiful or pay better now offers the prospect of only limited success.

This is worrisome given the potential benefits from moving. In 2019 Federal Reserve economists found 22 million openings for good jobs—defined as jobs paying more than the national median wage—across wide varieties of occupational categories for workers without college degrees, taking various areas' cost of living into account.[87] Many of these jobs were in the Midwest and only a few in the large coastal cities where the cost of living is substantially higher. Raj Chetty and his colleagues have also found that moving with young children to better neighborhoods offers opportunities to increase children's prospects of attending college and earning more income. It therefore stands to reason that supporting the mobility of workers and their families will improve their economic opportunities and produce large payoffs.[88]

This is why modern adjustment assistance needs to help workers and their families relocate. Such assistance could be built into UAA. Alternatively, EITCs could be increased temporarily when workers move for a new job. Or workers could be given additional refundable tax credits to help defray the costs of such a move. (The 2017 tax legislation moved in the opposite direction by repealing a previously available tax deduction for moving expenses incurred when taking a new job.) This approach avoids the well-known difficulties associated with empowering public officials to "pick winners" by supplying place-based incentives to firms in hopes of creating employment, a subject that we take up in chapter 8. It also ensures that the funds spent actually go to workers, rather than disappear in consulting fees, padded executive compensation packages, and stock buy-backs. Underwriting the geographic mobility of Americans carries the added advantage of diversifying political constituencies, militating against the partisan tribalism that is aggravated by blue-state / red-state sorting and the concentration of red-state liberals in blue cities. This, in turn, would increase the incentives for both major parties to back policies like an expanded EITC and UAA instead of self-defeating protectionism.[89]

These policies are good proximate goals around which to build new political coalitions, but they are just a beginning. New strategies—including strategies that have been deployed elsewhere, such as in Rhode Island, Germany, and Denmark—are also needed to help workers remain attached to the workforce and to help displaced workers find new jobs. Work-sharing, where two workers temporarily fill one part-time job, is one possibility. Another is increased support for self-employment assistance for jobless workers with the skills and motivation to find entrepreneurial alternatives to unemployment. Reemployment bonuses can be offered to unemployed workers who find work within specified periods, or who participate in targeted employment counseling and training programs. There are also good reasons to invest in reemployment initiatives focused on the needs of older workers who have been out of work for more than six months—a subset of employees who often end up applying for Social Security Disability Insurance or early retirement benefits. Creating tax incentives for people to build nest eggs to help see them through difficult transitions or for further education or training can also be part of an answer for some. But this is at best a partial solution, and it will take a long time to become effective unless Congress authorizes employees to use their retirement-account funds while these accounts build up.[90]

Creative efforts to change the moral commitments surrounding job loss are essential for political success. President Clinton's mantra that welfare should be "a second chance, not a way of life" fed off and reinforced the patronizing presumption that unemployment is usually the worker's fault: displaced workers should be given one and only one chance to shape up and atone for their failures.[91] The fault narrative belies too many stubborn facts in today's world. It feeds destructive self-denigration and stokes resentment that makes it harder to build coalitions in support of constructive policies like those we propose. Blame is all too easily pressed into the service of blocking coalitions. The message that downward mobility and job loss are due to personal failings intensifies the antagonism toward "cutting in" that Arlie Hochschild encountered in Louisiana, along with hostility toward public assistance more generally. The effort to change moral commitments and build supportive coalitions can be helped by the reality that the need for UAA is not just a poor person's problem. Lifetime employment is disappearing for much of the middle class, as the durability of many skills continues falling and the returns to continuous retooling grow. Some will be able to bear the costs themselves, but most will not.

The gains from trade and technology are more than adequate to fund compensation and training for those who suffer downward wage pressures or job losses. Until now, businesses have captured the lion's share of these gains without bearing significant costs. They have enjoyed enormous returns from technological and financial innovations. They have taken advantage of lower labor costs through global supply chains and increased profits, and often they have escaped taxes using the increased mobility of their capital and intellectual property. Countries around the world have lowered their business taxes as nations have competed for investments and mobile assets. So far at least, businesses have garnered these gains without major threats to their autonomy or hegemony. Some companies have responded in important and effective ways to local challenges, but in state and federal legislatures, they have sought and largely gotten their way for decades. Today's politics demonstrate that this approach is shortsighted.

Like the EITC, public spending on the continuous enhancement of workers' human capital may in effect become a subsidy for employers. This is true of education generally because better educated workers are more productive than less educated ones; factoring in the costs of alternatives makes this undeniable. Unemployed and comparatively less productive workers will need to be supported one way or another, and those with greater capacity to pay are going to end up bearing many of the costs. Far better to spend dollars enhancing workers' opportunities and productivity than to pay for opioid addiction. If workers are not helped in ways that make them attractive to the private sector, pressures to increase costly public-sector employment will also grow. The potential costs of adding millions of workers to federal and state payrolls are hard to estimate, but, depending on the numbers of employees and their wage levels, they could add hundreds of billions of dollars to public budgets and disrupt private labor markets.

To have a chance of succeeding, efforts to revamp and modernize TAA and unemployment insurance will need strong support from business, not least because of organized labor's diminished political sway. Securing this support will not be easy. Opposing coalitions are sure to coalesce around small-government conservatives, advocates for state over federal control (taking advantage of the status quo bias in favor of state rather than federal unemployment insurance), anti-tax Republicans, and business managers and owners who have been reaping the benefits of trade liberalization and technological innovation for decades without bearing their costs. These groups have resources and leaders willing and able to step forward to resist change. The effort to build business support for a modern UAA program of the sort we have outlined might, however, be advanced through argument. Activists should point out that failing to implement UAA will lead to increased pressure for regulations limiting business flexibility to fire workers and to greater support for employee labor protections—not to mention protectionist policies. But winning this argument will not be easy.

To make the politics even more challenging, there is no obvious coalition to step into the breach. Unlike Social Security, with its armada of elderly supporters and their effective lobbying from the AARP, and unlike Medicare and Medicaid, which benefit from the determined defense of doctors, hospitals, and pharmaceutical companies, greater unemployment and adjustment assistance do not yet enjoy the support of a powerful political constituency. No one wants to believe that they are going to need unemployment coverage or reemployment assistance. But as experience of the difficult and changing demands of modern labor markets becomes more widespread, this indifference will likely diminish. It will then become more rewarding for politicians to replace moral commitments based on failure and fault with ones that emphasize investing in a more productive national workforce.

Far-sighted political leadership will be essential for success. The emergence of this kind of leadership is impossible to predict, but we argue in the final chapter that there are opportunities—indeed, imperatives—for business leaders to make a constructive difference. Instead of caviling at the traumatizing political ramifications of snowballing economic insecurity that have been playing out since 2016, business leaders would do better to focus on cures and deploy their energy and resources to organize, fund, and lead coalitions supporting EITC expansions and UAA.

In this chapter and the previous one, we have showed how to make jobs pay better and how to ease transitions between jobs. One compelling and urgent way to deploy a better-paid workforce is the subject we take up next.

CHAPTER SEVEN

Waiting for Infrastructure

Following Donald Trump's election in 2016, a number of Democratic aspirants to the presidency began calling for the government to serve as the employer of last resort for healthy Americans unable to secure a job in the private sector.[1] These calls were echoed and detailed by left-leaning think tanks.[2] Typically, the candidates' plans offer a $15 hourly minimum wage, health insurance, and paid family and sick leave for employees—better pay and benefits than in many private sector jobs.[3]

The idea that the government should ensure that everyone able and willing to work can get a job—a government job if necessary—is hardly new. In his January 1944 State of the Union Address, the first item in Franklin Roosevelt's Economic Bill of Rights was the "right to a useful and remunerative job."[4] The Universal Declaration of Human Rights promulgated by the United Nations in 1948 includes among the "inalienable rights of all members of the human family," "the right to work, to free choice of employment, to just and favorable conditions of work and to protection against unemployment."[5] But not even the New Deal's Works Progress Administration and Civilian Conservation Corps guaranteed every healthy American a job.

Just what role the federal government should play in assuring employment has long been a subject of intense debate. Fears of limited private-sector opportunities—especially for workers without college degrees—are well-founded, and polls show that a large number of Americans support the idea of a government jobs guarantee. But Americans remain skeptical of major expansion of the federal government's civilian workforce.[6]

Yet annual federal spending is a large multiple of what it was in 1960, amounting to about $4 trillion in 2019. Seven new cabinet agencies have been added since then, including the Departments of Education, Energy, and Homeland Security, along with a host of subcabinet agencies, such as the Environmental Protection Agency and the Federal Emergency Management Agency. Federal statutes have also multiplied, now dealing with new subjects such as school quality, environmental protection, and greatly expanded lists of federal crimes. Federal regulations have increased by about 100,000 pages since 1960. But the size of the federal civilian workforce has remained essentially the same: 2.1 million employees under Donald Trump, about 300,000 more than when John F. Kennedy was elected in 1960 and 100,000 fewer than when Ronald Reagan was reelected in 1984.[7] The largest decline in the civilian workforce occurred under Bill Clinton. The largest nonmilitary government employer is the Department of Veterans Affairs with about 375,000 workers.

How did the federal government expand its spending, regulation, and criminal law so much without employing more workers? By devolving more responsibilities to state and local governments, whose workforces have more than tripled since 1960 to nearly 20 million, and by greatly expanding the number of employees who work for nonprofit and for-profit organizations fulfilling contracts for the federal government. Estimates of the number of federal contract employees vary from year to year and are not totally reliable, but the best estimates are that the number grew from about 5 million workers in 1990 to about 7.5 million in 2017. John J. DiIulio, Jr., has estimated that, in 2017, there were about 12 million workers who were not federal government employees yet earned their living from federal dollars, about six times as many as in 1960.[8]

The upshot is that many Americans and their legislators want the goods and services provided by federal dollars, and they support some government regulation, such as of environmental polluters, but they do not want federal "bureaucrats" to administer the programs that Congress enacts. The IRS has hired private contractors to collect its debts, and the Defense Department contracts out many of its responsibilities to private organizations.[9] Criminals and undocumented immigrants are routinely held in private prisons, which house a growing share of America's inmate population.[10] State and local governments also now contract with private entities to provide many services, and local government itself is increasingly being privatized in the South and the West.[11] Proposals that the government employ anyone who cannot find a job might be useful to some political campaigns, but mustering a political coalition to guarantee a government job to anyone who fails to secure private-sector employment is fanciful.

A more realistic goal is greater government finance of private-sector work. An especially promising arena for combining government and private finance and expertise to create employment is to rebuild and modernize US infrastructure: transportation facilities, including roads, bridges, tunnels, and airports; communications, including internet access; electrical facilities, such as electric power production and grids; and schools, from preschool to community colleges.

Infrastructure improvements create jobs, and not just jobs directly involved in those improvements. Estimates vary from 11,000 to 40,000 jobs per billion dollars of infrastructure investment, depending on where and how the improvements are done. No one doubts that the impact is substantial.[12] And there are additional benefits. Improving and expanding public transportation allows people who could not otherwise do so to get to jobs, improving neighborhoods as well.[13] In recent decades communities with high levels of broadband access have enjoyed faster growth in employment, number of businesses, and number of IT intensive businesses.[14] Employed workers foster additional job creation when they spend their incomes, even if this can be hard to measure.[15] Improving infrastructure also enhances private-sector productivity, contributing to better wages and more robust economic growth.[16] And sometimes infrastructure improvements are essential to avoid costly disasters.

The Works Progress Administration instituted by Franklin Roosevelt in 1935 built or improved 651,000 miles of roads, 953 airports, 124,000 bridges and viaducts, 1,178,000 culverts, 8,000 parks, 18,000 playgrounds and athletic fields, and 20,000 swimming pools. It constructed 40,000 buildings (including 8,000 schools) and repaired 85,000 more.[17] One reason that America's infrastructure desperately needs repair and upgrading is that—with the important exception of the construction of the Interstate Highway System that began in 1956—no comparable effort has been undertaken since.[18]

This inattention has resulted in extensive degradation. In 2017 the American Society of Civil Engineers gave US infrastructure a grade of D+ (down from a C in 1988) and said raising that grade would require $2 trillion of "wise" investments over the next decade. The needs are pervasive; the society rated airports, dams, roads, bridges, levees, ports, inland waterways, mass transit, public parks, schools, drinking water, electricity, hazardous waste, and waterworks, and among these only bridges, ports, and rail earned a grade above a D. Bridges and ports earned a C+. The only B grade was for rail, thanks in no small part to freight railroad companies that spent more than $27 billion on improvements in 2015 alone. The society estimated that the US has 56,000 structurally deficient bridges, 15,000 high-hazard dams, and a $536 billion shortfall in highway maintenance.[19]

Leaders across the political spectrum agree that the nation's infrastructure needs major investment, and that, if done right, improvements would contribute substantially to US economic growth and Americans' well-being. In 2014 President Obama described US infrastructure as "embarrassing," and the Treasury and Transportation Departments produced detailed studies of how to enlist the private sector in improving it.[20] A year later Bernie Sanders urged federal spending of $1 trillion "to rebuild our crumbling infrastructure and create up to 13 million good paying jobs."[21] In January 2017, California Democratic Senator Kamala Harris tweeted, "Here's the truth: infrastructure spending isn't a transportation issue for most Americans—it's a human rights issue."[22] In his presidential campaign, Donald Trump vowed to "build the greatest infrastructure on the planet Earth—the roads and railways and airports of tomorrow." The nation's "crumbling roads and bridges" and "the dilapidated airports," he said, "can all be fixed, but ... only by me."[23]

In February 2017, less than a month after taking office, President Trump sent Congress a fifty-three-page "Legislative Outline for Rebuilding Infrastructure in America."[24] This "framework," as it was dubbed, described US infrastructure as "in an unacceptable state of disrepair" and called for "at least $1.5 trillion in new investment" over the subsequent decade. Even two-thirds of this could have created 11 million jobs over that time span.[25] But the Trump administration proposed only $200 billion in federal funding. Where the remaining $1.3 trillion would come from was a mystery.[26] In June the White House "unpacked" its infrastructure commitment at an "Infrastructure Summit" in the ornate Indian Treaty Room of the Old Executive Office Building next to the White House. Speaking to a group of governors, mayors, county commissioners, agricultural commissioners, and tribal leaders, Vice President Mike Pence declared that rebuilding America is a "bipartisan enterprise." Describing the nation's infrastructure as "in a truly sorry state," Pence told the group that President Trump "is committed to making historic investments in our national infrastructure so that America has the best roads, the best bridges, the best highways, the best waterways, and the best airports we have ever had in the history of this country." The audience applauded; Pence said this had been "a banner week for infrastructure" and promised his audience that President Trump would meet the largest "infrastructure challenges" that America has "ever faced in the modern era."[27] But even though Republicans controlled the White House and both chambers of Congress, nothing happened.

The Democrats' return to control of the House in January 2019 held out the possibility of a different—bipartisan—dynamic on infrastructure. After all, both the Obama and Trump administrations had called for major infrastructure projects, and both their Transportation and Treasury Departments had described innovative ways of enlisting public-private partnerships in that effort.[28] Maybe the 116th Congress would turn out to offer an opportunity for one of the "big wins" across the aisle that candidate Trump had predicted in 2016 but had failed to deliver. But by May 2019, that seemed unlikely. A seemingly encouraging meeting between Trump and Democratic House and Senate leaders created the illusion of an agreement to explore a $2 trillion infrastructure initiative, but that balloon was almost immediately popped by Trump's chief of staff and Senate Republicans who said that it would never happen. Trump subsequently called it off, insisting that Democrats choose between infrastructure and investigations of potential wrongdoing by himself, his staff, and his campaign. By then the Trump White House's seven "Infrastructure Weeks" had become a running Washington joke.[29]

Waiting for major infrastructure improvements in the United States has become a lot like waiting for Godot. Plenty of talk, little action, and Godot never arrives. Republicans and Democrats have long debated the need for massive infrastructure improvements but with conspicuously little effect. Why is improving the nation's infrastructure so difficult?

Importantly, while infrastructure upgrades are needed in every state, the vast majority of improvements would mainly have local or regional impact. Potential benefits and costs vary greatly among localities and states, which complicates putting together the coalitions necessary to produce and allocate federal funds. Even without the polarization and partisanship that characterize today's politics, it is difficult to convince legislators from New York or New Jersey to support infrastructure improvements in Indiana, and vice versa. Moreover, the biggest bang for the buck, in terms of improvements in citizens' welfare, typically occurs with infrastructure projects in urban, suburban, and exurban locations, which makes it difficult to attract support from representatives of rural communities—a problem made worse by rural resentment of urban "elites."[30] The elimination in 2011 of congressional earmarks—which had allowed key legislators to obtain funds for their (sometimes-wasteful) pet projects in exchange for votes for other public works—removed the frequently useful grease in the wheels of effective coalition building when it came to important infrastructure projects.

This means that at the federal level—and often within the states—combining rural and urban projects is often essential to creating viable coalitions that can secure legislation to push infrastructure projects forward. This might be a challenge, but there are enough needs across the country that such combinations, or even set-asides for rural improvements, are possible. There are also vital infrastructure projects, like refurbishing deep-water harbors, that serve both rural and urban interests.

There have been some notable successes at the state and local levels, but federal support is often needed. State and local governments can take the lead in setting priorities, overseeing work, and obtaining financing, but the federal government often must supply financing and institutional support to facilitate projects—especially in their formative stages. At a minimum, the federal government is often needed to reduce regulatory barriers.[31]

Moving forward in improving infrastructure often also requires a push from businesses interests. This obviously includes firms in the construction industry and their suppliers, but also firms with stakes in infrastructure improvements. That means trucking and transportation supply companies along with manufacturers, agricultural firms, and wholesalers, all of which rely on efficient transportation to get their goods to market. The surge in extracting natural resources from shale in places such as North Dakota has created new businesses in rural areas with large stakes in efficient and cost-effective transportation. Infrastructure coalitions might also include businesses and workers reliant on US ports, companies in the water and electricity industries, and financial institutions, which will collect large fees from creating and marketing the financial instruments required to raise the necessary funds. Attracting a broad business coalition is easier the larger, more comprehensive, and more ambitious the infrastructure program. In short, size matters.

The imperative to enlist rural-urban coalitions and business interests in support of major infrastructure improvements enhances the importance of effective leadership. At the federal level, this inevitably requires strong presidential leadership. Presidents are crucial both in developing the substance of infrastructure plans and securing the essential congressional support, at least from members of their own party.[32] Although both Presidents Obama and Trump urged large infrastructure improvements, neither provided the requisite leadership.

The Obama administration failed to obtain major new infrastructure legislation, other than $47 billion of infrastructure spending enacted in the American Recovery and Reinvestment Act, the stimulus legislation enacted in February 2009 in response to the financial crisis. Only three Senate Republicans, Susan Collins and Olympia Snowe of Maine and Pennsylvania's Arlen Spector (who later switched to the Democratic Party) voted for the legislation, which passed the Senate by a 61–37 vote. The House bill passed by 244–188, with 11 Democrats and 177 Republicans opposed. Even with Democratic majorities in the House and Senate, the legislation provided more than $5 of tax cuts for every dollar of infrastructure spending—$275 billion to $47 billion. During the remainder of 2009 and in 2010, while Democrats held control of both the House and Senate, President Obama never made infrastructure a legislative priority, focusing his muscle instead on health insurance, financial regulation, and climate change legislation.

After the 2010 midterms, Republicans controlled the House, and in the 2014 elections they recaptured the Senate.[33] The opportunity to secure infrastructure legislation with Democratic majorities in both chambers had ended by 2011. Republican Speakers of the House John Boehner and Paul Ryan both followed the so-called Hastert rule, named for their predecessor Dennis Hastert, which requires support by a majority of Republican House members to bring legislation to a vote in the chamber. This gave veto power to a group of Tea Party House Republicans known as the Freedom Caucus, who opposed any substantial federal infrastructure spending. In the Senate, Majority Leader

McConnell, fulfilling his promise to thwart Obama's agenda at every turn, never brought infrastructure legislation to the floor for a vote. Key players in the Obama administration—who had fashioned a clever proposal combining a large increase in infrastructure spending with business tax reform, a Republican priority—insisted that there would have been majority support in both the House and Senate had floor votes ever been permitted. But we will see that the Obama "compromise" was insufficiently bold.

Although Trump sent his infrastructure proposals to Congress soon after taking office, he quickly turned instead to partisan Republican priorities: to repeal and replace the Obama health insurance legislation and enact costly tax cuts. The first of these attempts failed, but the latter succeeded. By reducing federal revenues, tax cuts make financing infrastructure improvements even harder. Trump's first term might have been very different— and far more successful—had he begun by deploying his political capital and energy behind the bold bipartisan infrastructure improvements that he called for in his 2016 campaign.

It is impossible to predict when voters will elect a president who adopts infrastructure as a genuine priority, and no one knows whether the congressional stars will align when that happens. But it is worth considering what kinds of projects are feasible and would be propitious from the perspective of battling economic security, if and when effective leadership materializes. What can we learn from past efforts about how major infrastructure projects can be funded, sited, and successfully completed?

Challenges of Financing Infrastructure with Taxes

Along with bridging the urban-rural divide, the most difficult challenge for major infrastructure improvements is obtaining necessary financing—a challenge made more difficult because of anti-government and anti-tax attitudes that have been a centerpiece of Republican politics for more than four decades. This sometimes motivates efforts to abdicate federal responsibility entirely, as in July 2018 when Senators Ted Cruz (R-Texas), Mike Lee (R-Utah), and Marco Rubio (R-Florida) introduced the so-called Transportation Empowerment Act to repeal the federal gas tax and give states and localities more control over infrastructure spending. Even while urging that Washington get out of the business of infrastructure decision-making and funding, Cruz acknowledged that growing and strengthening American infrastructure "is necessary to our economic future."[34]

In 1956, to facilitate construction of the highway system, Congress transformed the federal role in highway finances. Before that, federal appropriations for highways had been relatively small and came out of general revenues through the normal appropriations process. The legislation that year increased a number of taxes on drivers, most notably the federal gas tax (then three cents a gallon), and established a highway trust fund to finance completion of the interstate system over the next sixteen years. The federal share of the costs was 90 to 95 percent, and federal control ensured that roads would connect across state lines.

But the federal government has not played such a dominant role in highway projects since then. In the 1970s such projects were only 70 percent federally funded, with 30 percent provided by the states.[35] Increasing the federal gas tax to a level that would adequately fund the needed improvements has proved daunting politically. The 1982 Surface Transportation Assistance Act, signed by President Reagan, increased the gas tax to nine cents a gallon, with one cent going into a new account to help finance improvements in mass transit. In 1990, as part of comprehensive budget legislation signed by President George H. W. Bush, the gas tax was raised by another nickel, half of which was diverted from the trust fund to reduce federal deficits. In 1993 President Clinton increased the gas tax by another 4.3 cents a gallon to 18.4 cents, with all of this increase going toward deficit reduction. In 1997, Congress redirected these funds into the Highway Trust Fund. In the more than twenty-five years since the 1993 increase, Congress has not raised the gas tax, despite inflation eroding its value by 40 percent.

The result: fuel-tax revenues are inadequate to fund the ongoing federal share of highway spending, much less pay for a substantial increase. In 2008 and 2009, for example, additional federal spending was deficit financed. Making up for Highway Trust Fund shortfalls has frequently required transfers from general revenues. Congress authorized $130 billion to be transferred between 2007 and 2021, $52 billion for 2016–2018 alone. By 2021 it will take a ten-cents-a-gallon increase just to fund the shortfall.[36] But raising national gas taxes to fund highway and mass transit projects has become extremely difficult even with support from some interested businesses, such as the trucking industry.[37]

State legislators have had more success. The first state gas tax was introduced in Oregon in 1919 at one cent per gallon, and federal and state gas taxes combined ranged in 2019 from a low of 33.06 cents a gallon in Alaska to a high of 79.06 cents in California. According to the American Petroleum Institute, the average combined gas tax in the US in 2019 was 52.64 cents a gallon.[38] State tolls also often are used to fund highways and bridges. But, like gas taxes, tolls are unpopular with the public.[39]

Like funding for highway construction and maintenance, financing to maintain and improve mass transit is challenging to obtain. One need only ride the busses in virtually any city or travel on the New York subways to see the shortfalls. Passenger fares do not suffice. About one half of all mass transit passengers use busses, but passenger miles on much faster commuter and light rail systems, which carry only about 10 percent of passengers, have recently been growing. Revenues from passenger fares vary greatly, but on average they fund about 37 percent of operating costs. State and local government assistance pays for roughly 54 percent of operations, with federal funds providing only a meager 8 percent. About two-thirds of the total operating expenses of public transit agencies pay for employees' wages and fringe benefits. In 2015 the roughly 425,000 mass transit employees in the US were paid an average of about $65,000 per year in cash wages, down from about $75,000 (in 2015 dollars) in the late 1980s.

Federal funds play a more significant role in financing capital expenditures for mass transit than for operating costs, providing about 43 percent of funds in 2015. On average, local governments contributed another 21 percent and the states provided about 15 percent. The politics at the state and national levels are challenging. Because most expenditures for mass transit occur in metropolitan areas, and most ridership occurs there, legislators who represent rural areas rarely support federal or state funding for mass transit operations and improvements. Instead, those lawmakers prefer directing any available infrastructure money to roads and highways.[40]

During Barack Obama's second term, members of his administration believed that they had discovered a large, relatively painless source of revenue for financing major infrastructure improvements: taxes on the foreign earnings of US-based multinationals. Before 2017 US parent companies had incentive to leave foreign earnings offshore rather than repatriate them, lest they be forced to pay residual US tax. By that year, these earnings exceeded $2.5 trillion. The administration was proposing a revenue-neutral tax reform that would reduce the US corporate tax rate from 35 to 28 percent and eliminate the tax on repatriations, but with a one-time "transition tax" on the foreign earnings. These revenues would be used to fund infrastructure improvements.[41]

But this proposal never came to a vote in the House or Senate. Instead, in December 2017, President Trump signed tax-cut legislation that Congress passed with only Republican votes. The law used the $340 billion in transition tax revenues to help fund a permanent reduction in business income taxes, including a 21 percent corporate tax rate.[42] Rather than the revenue-neutral tax reform that the Obama administration had wanted, the Republican tax bill was designed to lose at least $1.5 trillion in its first decade.[43] Not only was a politically promising and painless source of tax revenue to help finance infrastructure improvements lost, but the expansion of federal deficits and debt make it more difficult for the federal government to borrow to help finance infrastructure improvements. Throughout the twenty-first century, the US has been borrowing prodigious amounts to fund current consumption rather than the needed investments in a more productive future.

The Role for Debt Finance

Using debt to help finance infrastructure upgrades avoids the political obstacles of trying to finance long-term infrastructure improvements with tax increases. For more than a century, state and local governments have used long-term bonds to fund infrastructure—paying their lenders tax-free interest. The US municipal bond market is by far the most robust in the world, and it has long been used to leverage state and federal grants for infrastructure improvements.[44] But the practice of using municipal bonds to finance new projects has declined since early in this century, and current law unnecessarily limits use of these tax-free bonds when a project involves private-equity participation or ownership. Both the Obama and Trump administrations advocated removing this barrier to public-private infrastructure partnerships.[45]

During the financial crisis, Congress passed legislation (effective only for 2009–2010) allowing states and municipalities to issue Build America Bonds, taxable bonds with 35 percent of the interest costs directly subsidized by the federal government rather than through an exemption from income taxes. This greatly increased the market for state and local bonds by making them competitive with corporate bonds for tax-exempt investors such as pension funds, sovereign wealth funds, and university endowments. Despite its success and potential for helping to fund infrastructure improvements, the taxable-bond option was not renewed after the Republican midterm victory in 2010.

Rahm Emanuel, Obama's first chief of staff, was famous for his admonition never to let a serious crisis to go to waste, but that is exactly what the administration did in this instance.[46] It would have been more far-sighted to take advantage of the window of opportunity created by the financial crisis to put this policy in place for the longer run. Making these two legislative changes—expanding opportunities for tax-free state and local bonds in public-private infrastructure projects and expanding the market for these bonds by restoring a federally subsidized taxable-bond alternative—remains a realistic goal. Achieving it would substantially enhance opportunities for using low-cost public debt in public-private infrastructure partnerships. Both proposals could attract a broad bipartisan coalition of legislators and support from a wide range of business interests, as well as from governors and mayors. What is needed is effective leadership to get the ball rolling when the opportunity next arises.

Managing Risks

All infrastructure projects carry risks, which can vary greatly. All projects have design, construction, demand, and maintenance risks. Sometimes these risks are borne by public entities, and sometimes they are shifted to private parties. Often private-sector experts are better able to evaluate, manage, and mitigate such risks. New projects, often referred to as greenfield projects, tend to have the greatest risks of inadequate demand. Design and construction risks are low for some projects, such as highways, and greater for others, such as underwater tunnels, which may face serious technological challenges. The ability to shift such risks from the public to private entities and to obtain private funding are potential advantages of public-private infrastructure partnerships.

The gold standard of such risk shifts to private partners is realized when private entities have the responsibility to design, build, finance, operate, and maintain a project. A public entity must then retain oversight to ensure that the public-private entity fulfills its obligations in a timely manner with appropriate quality control. This public-private partnership structure often offers both risk-reducing and political advantages over traditional infrastructure procurement. In traditional cases the responsible government entity owns the property but issues separate contracts for the design, building, maintenance, and operation of the infrastructure asset. Various private businesses win these contracts, typically through a competitive bidding process.

Enlisting private firms to agree to pay down the debt or supply equity for an infrastructure enterprise requires committing at least some level of revenues from the project to compensate them for the financing they supply and the risks they bear. These revenues can come from various sources, but many infrastructure projects generate revenues directly from users. Public and private water and electricity suppliers charge customers based on usage. States also have long histories of charging tolls for use of roads and bridges. Pennsylvania, New Jersey, and Maine have operated toll roads since shortly after World War II. Each of these states financed these roads with bonds paying interest rates from 1.5 to 2.6 percent, depending on whether the bonds were secured by the state's full faith and credit or only by the tolls. All three collected significant surpluses in operating revenues almost immediately. By 1954 fifteen other states had nearly 1,400 miles of toll roads under construction, with plans for an additional 3,400 miles. Technological advances now allow tolls to be collected without toll collectors or slowing traffic. In principle this means that tolls can be much more widely deployed and can vary between residents and nonresidents.

Airports offer the best prospects for user-based funding of operating expenses and improvements in transportation infrastructure. Many airports, especially busy ones, have the potential to generate sufficient revenues to service and retire debt incurred in construction and also cover operating expenses. Potential revenues include landing fees and terminal leases to airlines, leases to rental car agencies, parking fees, departure and other passenger taxes and fees. Now that many of the best shopping malls and food courts are located in airports, commercial leases can also produce substantial income. In some cases airlines will finance upgrading and expanding the terminals that they occupy.[47] The potential for such revenue is greatest in cities that serve lots of passengers, such as large cities and cities used strategically as hubs in the common airline hub-and-spoke systems. In some instances, privatization of airports might be possible and even desirable. For example, the British Airport Authority, which controls seven major airports including London's Heathrow, Gatwick, and Stansted, was privatized in 1987 through a $2.5 billion offering of shares to the public.

Full privatization, however, can result in the transfer of valuable public assets to private investors. This comes with risks, which are greatest with respect to existing assets, especially those that do not require major upgrading. The poster child for such bad deals is the 2008 privatization of Chicago's parking meters, which, along with the also-privatized Chicago skyway, had served as an important source of ongoing city revenues. To avoid raising the city's property taxes, Mayor Richard M. Daley sold the parking meters in 2008 to a group of US and international investors who formed an entity called Chicago Parking Meters LLC (CPM). When the meters were sold, they were producing less than $24 million annually for the city's coffers. After numerous parking fee increases by CPM, the meters took in more than $134 million in 2017. The private investors were then expected to recover their entire $1.16 billion investment by 2021, when sixty-one years will remain on their lease. To add insult to injury, the lease requires the city to make "true-up" payments to CPM for any parking spaces that become unavailable for any reason. In 2017 those payments totaled $21.7 million.

This example underscores yet another kind of political risk: that instead of producing efficiency gains, privatization agendas might be hijacked by people who line their pockets at the public's expense. Political economists have long known that powerful industry groups are better placed than voters and consumers to influence lawmaking and regulation. Their coalitions are better organized and more enduring, they have larger war chests for lobbying, and the benefits they derive are concentrated while the costs imposed on others are borne by millions of widely dispersed consumers.[48] And while politicians attend to consumers as well as to producers—they need votes as well as money—voter attention is often fleeting, whereas industry lobbyists play a long game.[49] These considerations suggest that bad privatization deals like the Chicago parking meter scheme might be hard to prevent.

A significant barrier to expanding public-private infrastructure partnerships is the absence of state legislation authorizing such projects, or in some states inadequately comprehensive authorizing legislation.[50] Fewer than twenty states have sufficiently broad enabling legislation. In a few states, voters must approve individual projects before they go forward. Assuring adequate public oversight and institutional capacity to effectively administer and protect the public's interest in such partnerships is a challenge for such legislation, but the goal of removing state inhibitions on such projects should attract broad coalitions of support as long as adequate safeguards are included. That can be a tall order, as suggested by the partial privatization of Fannie Mae discussed in chapter 3. Morgenson and Rosner supply chapter and verse of the highly effective stratagems employed by James Johnson and his associates to weaken congressional oversight of their Government Sponsored Entity, yet no one was ever held to account for the subsequent debacle or for the fact that Johnson was able to retire with a multimillion-dollar severance package before the house of cards collapsed.[51]

Some Success Stories—and Some Notable Failures

LaGuardia Airport. In a 2012 survey by *Travel and Leisure* magazine, travelers ranked LaGuardia Airport, one of the busiest in the world, as the worst airport in the United States—worst at security and check-in, worst at baggage handling, the worst Wi-Fi, and the worst design and cleanliness.[52] In February 2014 Vice

President Joe Biden famously—and correctly, if politically incorrectly—described LaGuardia as the kind of airport travelers would find in a third-world country. Opened in 1939, with its main terminal dating from 1964, LaGuardia serves nearly 30 million passengers annually. In June 2016 New York governor Andrew Cuomo announced an $8 billion upgrade scheduled to be completed by 2022.

The Port Authority of New York and New Jersey entered into an agreement with a special-purpose partnership, LaGuardia Gateway Partners (LGP), to design, build, finance, operate, and maintain a new Terminal B, the central terminal building which serves most of the airport's passengers.[53] LGP was the winner from among four bidders.[54] The main risk that the Port Authority wanted to shift to private parties was potential cost overruns during construction.[55] LGP was awarded a lease for the terminal through 2050 under which it pays the Port Authority rent of $15 million annually; the Port Authority is obligated to pay LGP up to a total of $1 billion in passenger-facilities charges over the lease term.[56] The $4 billion cost of the terminal was financed by $2.5 billion in revenue bonds to be repaid by LGP through a combination of passenger-facility charges, airline fees, and retail and other concession revenue. LGP private shareholders contributed about $200 million in equity, and the Port Authority contributed the remainder.[57] In July 2018 a vice president of the construction company said that the work on Terminal B was being done by 2,400 professional and trade workers from 28 unions.[58] The Port Authority estimated that this project would produce $1.3 billion in wages and $5.2 billion in additional economic activity in the region.[59]

In addition to this arrangement for Terminal B, the Port Authority entered into a new lease until 2050 with Delta Airlines, which agreed to participate in an additional $4 billion project to upgrade the terminals it occupies (Terminals C and D). The Port Authority contributed $600 million, including $185 million for a new electrical substation and $215 million for new road and supporting infrastructure.[60] Delta agreed to contribute $300 million in equity investments and to finance the remaining $3.4 billion through revenue bonds.[61] The terms of the lease between the Port Authority and Delta were not made public.[62] In 2016 the Port Authority estimated that the Delta-funded replacement of Terminals C and D would generate 8,000 direct and 10,000 indirect jobs, $1.3 billion in wages, and $5.2 billion in economic activity.[63] Upgrading LaGuardia is a major—long overdue—improvement, but only time will tell whether the returns to the private investors are excessive.

Light rail serving the Denver airport. In 2004 voters approved a $4.7 billion plan for a "FasTracks" light rail system through the Denver metropolitan area to be funded by a 0.4 percent increase in the city's sales tax to pay off the project's borrowing costs over a twenty-year period. Political leadership was provided by John Hickenlooper, then Denver's mayor. Hickenlooper convinced the mayors in the eight counties surrounding Denver to join a supporting coalition along with local business leaders, who believed that the rail system would unclog the roads, and environmental groups concerned with abating the increasing smog from traffic congestion. This coalition secured passage of the referendum by a 58 percent majority.[64]

But, even with the sales tax increase, the twenty-three-mile rail line to the Denver airport needed a $2.2 billion public-private partnership, the first for a US transit project.[65] A private entity, Denver Transit Partners (DTP), contributed about $460 million to the project, about one-fourth of the project's total cost. DTP entered into an agreement with the Regional Transportation District (RTD) to design, build, finance, operate, and maintain the project for thirty-four years. Under this agreement, the public authority RTD remains the owner of all the assets and has the right to set and retain fares and to keep all the revenues from the project, but it must make fixed payments to DTP, the private partner, based on performance metrics.[66]

Despite the participation of the private entity, the majority of funds for this project came from federal grants and loans. The loans are secured, and will be paid, by a 1 percent sales tax increase in metropolitan Denver. This project was estimated to have produced 7,000 jobs and added $1.3 billion to Denver's economy by September 2015.[67] As of March 2016, over 10,000 people had been employed at different points, earning $246 million in wages, with another $555 million spent on equipment, services, and supplies and $624 million on subcontractors.[68]

By the spring of 2016, the rail spur from the Denver airport to downtown was complete, along with seventy-five additional miles at a total cost of $7.6 billion. The rail system, which spans an area the size of Delaware, transformed neighborhoods, including a new $2 billion downtown development in the vicinity of Union Station, an area described as "a bustling urban hive of restaurants, shops, and residential towers that only six years ago was a gravelly no man's land."[69]

The Port of Miami. The Port of Miami operates as a Miami-Dade County government enterprise, and it is expected to pay all of its operating and capital costs. Given its reliance on bonds, the port is one of the most indebted government entities in the country. Its revenues are derived from docking ships, user fees, and rents. In order to diversify its funding sources and increase rents from commercial real estate, the port has entered into public-private partnerships with several private cruise lines to develop new cruise terminals. Passenger cruise lines generate more revenue per use than cargo activities, and they increase potential retail and advertising revenue.[70] Royal Caribbean's Terminal A, which can dock cruise ships carrying 5,500 passengers, opened in November 2018.[71] Disney made an agreement under which a new terminal would accommodate 360,000 passengers annually by 2023.[72] The Swiss company MSC Cruises made an agreement to accommodate its 7,000-passenger ships.[73] And a partnership with Virgin Voyages provides for a new $150 million terminal funded by Virgin and the port's capital fund. The port will impose a surcharge on Virgin's passengers in order to recoup much of its investment.[74]

In some of these cases, the port has allowed private enterprise fully to fund terminal construction (with bond support) in exchange for annual rental payments based on guarantees of passenger traffic and user fees for passengers who embark and disembark there. The new terminals have improved both the quality of the facilities and the port's financial footing.

In 2016, prior to the completion of any of these projects, a private study estimated that cruise activity in the port generated 14,616 direct jobs, 8,690 indirect jobs (employment at firms supporting the port's activity), and 6,187 induced jobs (jobs resulting from the spending of those directly and indirectly employed). In 2016 the port served 5.1 million passengers. By 2018 the port served nearly 5.6 million passengers, growth that exceeded the estimate in the port's 2035 master plan.[75]

Replacing the Tappan Zee Bridge. Not all successful infrastructure projects involve public-private partnerships. In some cases, creative public financing will suffice. The new Mario M. Cuomo bridge—a nearly $4 billion replacement for the Tappan Zee Bridge between Westchester and Rockland Counties in New York—was fully paid for out of public funds.[76] The construction was done by a consortium of private designers, builders, and engineers under a fixed-price contract after analyses indicated that building a new bridge would cost less than repairing the old

Tappan Zee. New York State contributed about $1.1 billion of the bridge's costs from its Thruway Stabilization Fund, which had been funded with $1.3 billion of settlements with financial institutions and $700 million of normal state appropriations. About $2.9 billion was debt-financed, with about $1.3 billion of that in revenue bonds to be repaid from tolls on the New York Thruway and bridges. The remaining $1.6 billion was financed by loans to the state from the federal Department of Transportation's Transportation Infrastructure Finance and Innovation Act loan program, which provides cheaper and more flexible debt for the state than issuing additional revenue bonds. The federal loan permits the state to defer any repayment until five years after the project is completed, allowing New York to defer toll increases at least until 2021. The tolls on the new bridge, from the more than 140,000 cars that cross it daily, are expected to increase to nearly $8 for commuters with a New York E-Z Pass and to more than $11 for other cars, pretty much in line with tolls on other New York City bridges and passenger-car tunnels. Drivers on other parts of the New York State Thruway may also face toll increases of about 24 percent.[77]

Los Angeles transit. In a Herculean effort to reduce substantially the number of Angelenos clogging the city's expansive freeway system, the city and county of Los Angeles together embarked on an extensive expansion and modernization of mass transit so that Los Angeles now has the third-most comprehensive system in the United States.[78] A large majority of Los Angeles voters, nearly 70 percent, voted to increase the local sales tax, first by half a cent and then beginning in 2039 by another half a cent. When fully phased in, the sales tax increase is expected to bring in an additional $560 million annually for decades. This revenue will pay interest and principal on the debt issued to add a new light rail line to Los Angeles International Airport, a new subway line, and extensions of existing subway lines. Los Angeles Mayor Eric Garcetti, who led a broad business coalition in support of the sales tax referendum, described its enactment as the key to the city's future.[79]

One notable project was the Metro Expo Line, which opened in 2016 and runs 15.2 miles from downtown LA to Santa Monica and the Pacific Ocean. It was the first time since 1953 that Los Angeles had rail service from downtown to the beach. This line, which is expected to carry 64,000 passengers daily by 2030, took decades to build, and the economic activity it has spurred has not been welcomed by all.[80] Plans for apartments, single-family homes, and commercial development near Expo Line station stops have evoked complaints from local homeowners and tenants who worry about gentrification and displacement and from Santa Monica residents who blame an increase in crime on Expo Line riders.[81] This experience demonstrates that some might view even successful infrastructure projects as mixed blessings. But the downsides of success are typically mild compared with the costs of failure.

The Gateway tunnel. Perhaps the most notorious failure of a major infrastructure improvement has been the inability, so far, to construct a new tunnel under the Hudson River between New York and New Jersey. The tunnel is intended to replace a 107-year-old, ten-mile, two-track railroad tunnel between Newark, New Jersey, and Pennsylvania Station in New York City. Elsewhere in the Northeast Corridor, railroads have three or four tracks, but the aging tunnel is a high-risk choke point for 200,000 daily commuters and most of Amtrak's 6.7 million annual passengers. If the existing tunnel—which was severely damaged by Superstorm Sandy—were to become inoperative, it could cost the US economy as much as $100 million per day.[82]

During the Obama administration, the federal government committed $3 billion to the Gateway project—more money than for any other transit project in the US—and the Port Authority of New York and New Jersey committed a similar amount. But on October 5, 2010, New Jersey Governor Chris Christie announced that he was abandoning the project because of cost overruns. New Jersey Democratic Senator Frank Lautenberg described Christie's stopping the tunnel project as "one of the biggest public policy blunders in New Jersey history." Christie wanted to divert state highway tolls that had been committed to Gateway to other projects and did not want to raise the state's gas tax to pay its share of the costs.[83] This decision increased the newly elected governor's profile in the Republican Party as an antispending warrior, and Christie no doubt thought it would enhance his potential as a Republican presidential candidate in the 2016 election. Obama's transportation secretary, Ray LaHood, insisted that the cost overruns were within the original cost estimates for the Gateway project, and he demanded that New Jersey return to the federal government $271 million that had been advanced before Christie killed the project.[84]

Seven years later, in a September 7, 2017, meeting with Republican and Democratic lawmakers from New York and New Jersey, President Trump seemed ready to resurrect the Gateway tunnel project. Noting that the new tunnel was vital to the economy and comparing it to air conditioning projects in the basement of his hotels, Trump said, "Nobody's gonna see it, but you still gotta do it." After the meeting ended, however, Trump told Democratic Senate Minority Leader Chuck Schumer of New York that he would get the tunnel only if Trump got funding for his wall along the Mexican border, a trade that Schumer refused to make. After that, Trump threatened to veto a $1.2 trillion transportation bill if it included even one dollar of funding for Gateway, and his secretary of transportation voided the Obama administration's commitment to fund half of the project's costs through a combination of federal grants and loans. Marcia Hall, president of Building America's Future, a bipartisan coalition of elected officials committed to major infrastructure improvements, said, "No question, this is the most desperately needed infrastructure effort in the country. It's crazy that it isn't happening."[85]

California's high-speed rail. If Gateway epitomizes essential infrastructure project that has been stymied by contrary political leadership, the $100 billion high-speed-rail project between Los Angeles and San Francisco is one that should never have been started and surely will not be completed. In 2008 Californians voted for a nearly $10 billion bond issuance as a down payment on the project, which was then estimated to cost $40 billion. In May 2018 only 31 percent of Californians told pollsters that they wanted the project to continue. Nevertheless, in July construction work was underway at twenty-one sites across five counties in central California, and proponents were insisting that the 500-mile railway will be completed by 2033.[86] In the two years from 2016 to 2018, with relatively low inflation, costs on the 119-mile segment from Madera to Bakersfield in the Central Valley increased by almost 36 percent from $7.8 billion to $10.6 billion.[87] Of the projected $100 billion cost—which would certainly rise if the project reached completion—the rail authority has only $30 billion, not enough to extend the line from Bakersfield to San Francisco. California's Democratic Governor Jerry Brown had insisted on pressing forward, but his successor, Gavin Newsom, was more circumspect. Proponents believed that completing the Madera-Bakersfield stretch would cause businesses and individual Californians to rally behind completing the project, but in early 2019, with conservatives gathering signatures to defund the effort by ballot initiative the following year, Newsom mothballed the project.[88] With no visible signs of progress in either Los Angeles or San Francisco, the prospects for reviving it are dim.

Morals of the Story

There are compelling moral arguments to support major investments in infrastructure improvements across the nation. Not only would construction provide jobs, but well-selected projects also promise long-term employment benefits, improvements in neighborhoods, and reduced congestion, which would decrease pollution and increase public well-being. Yet, despite bipartisan congressional support and expressions of enthusiasm from Democratic and Republican presidents, opportunities to move forward have proved elusive.

This is partly because infrastructure projects are location-specific, and putting together a package of projects to satisfy coalitions of urban and rural constituencies is challenging. More importantly, it is often difficult to raise taxes to pay off the debt used to finance infrastructure projects. Even when appropriate urban-rural packages exist, veto players in Congress have extraordinary ability to prevent votes on projects that would enjoy majority support. This is largely due to the fear of primary challenges to Republicans from their right. This, along with weak party controls, gives extraordinary power to extreme factions, most visibly the Freedom Caucus.[89] This has made effective presidential leadership all the more important, yet both Presidents Obama and Trump have been tepid and ineffective on this front. Neither was willing to make infrastructure a major priority or to match expressions of enthusiasm with genuine commitments of federal dollars. Effective leadership has therefore had to come from states and cities.

When financing requires private investments and public-private partnerships, overcoming the potential risks of bad deals is essential, but in practice often hard. Whenever a bad deal, such as the Chicago parking meter sale, occurs, opportunities arise for demagogic opposition. This is exemplified by Bernie Sanders's insistence that "Trump's public-private partnership model is good for Wall Street but bad for America."[90] Sanders exaggerates his claims and overlooks the Obama administration's support for public-private infrastructure projects.[91] Sanders also ignores the kinds of success stories we have described here and punts on the dearth of alternatives for funding infrastructure projects and getting them built.[92] Nevertheless, his complaints portend challenges to such partnerships from the Democratic left, even when private debt repayment and equity investments are essential for infrastructure improvements to come to fruition.[93]

Opportunities for effective infrastructure-improvement coalitions are plentiful, and the needs are unquestionably great. Proximate goals abound: there are opportunities for valuable infrastructure improvements throughout the country and at every level of government. State and local bonds offer the potential for inexpensive long-term financing, and, as Denver and Los Angeles voters have demonstrated, the public can be convinced to support sales tax increases when voters believe that potential projects offer substantial public benefits. Some states are now also looking at taxes on sales of newly legalized marijuana as a potential source of infrastructure funding.[94]

Ignoring America's decaying and increasingly outmoded infrastructure creates the potential for major disasters. It also foregoes the potential for worthwhile short- and long-term job creation. Once a start has been made, projects can usually achieve traction, particularly—as with ports, airports, and toll roads and bridges— if they can generate revenue streams into the future. Perhaps the greatest obstacles concern the need to pay immediate costs for long-term benefits and the rarity of committed political leadership.

At the national level, crises create opportunities, but infrastructure is a chronic problem, rarely a crisis. Franklin Roosevelt's creation of the Works Progress Administration in 1935 was exceptional because unemployment had reached crisis levels in the early 1930s (23.6 percent in 1932, 24.9 percent in 1933, 21.7 percent in 1934, and 20.1 percent in 1935), and it never fell below 14 percent until the US entered World War II. By contrast, during the Great Recession unemployment peaked at 9.9 percent in 2009 and fell steadily thereafter to 4.7 percent by the end of Obama's presidency.[95] In the Obama era, elites no longer feared communist ideology creeping into the American workforce, as many had during the Depression, reducing the pressure for concerted stabilizing action. So it is hardly surprising that Obama did not make employment creation through infrastructure a major priority.

The underlying challenge is that politicians like projects when the benefits for their constituents show up quickly and the costs are borne by others or deferred into the future. Investments in infrastructure frequently do not come to fruition until after current politicians have left office. Joel Simmons has shown that when political parties are weak, as they are in the US, politicians are less likely to invest in infrastructure, because they have few incentives to concern themselves with their party's long-run standing or reputation.[96] Thus providing health insurance to millions of uninsured voters before the 2010 midterms was bound to have more appeal for Obama and the Democrats on Capitol Hill. For Trump and congressional Republicans, giving away a one-time windfall from corporate tax reform to their core constituencies was likewise more attractive than infrastructure investment.

The cost side of the infrastructure equation can be somewhat mitigated through user charges, debt financing, and public-private partnerships, as we have seen, although issuing more debt might face powerful blocking coalitions, especially when there are state or city legal barriers or borrowing costs are especially high. Adequate monitoring of public-private partnerships can be difficult. But these formidable challenges should not be overstated. During the Obama administration, the federal government provided funding for a number of important projects, including the Denver rail line, the Tappan Zee Bridge replacement, and the failed efforts in New Jersey and California. There is considerable support for infrastructure spending in both parties. The fact that it is seldom a legislative priority often makes it an uphill battle that demands determined leadership, persistence, and ingenuity.

In short, it is not preordained that waiting for infrastructure must be like waiting for Godot, even though the political challenges are often formidable. Solutions will frequently have to be local and regional, and they will sometimes require substantial private-sector participation. States and cities can deploy resources and incentives to attract private investment to infrastructure and other employment-creating projects, though we will see in the next chapter that this too is sometimes easier said than done. Success will be more likely if efforts are conditioned by a sober appreciation of the hurdles that their proponents must overcome.

CHAPTER EIGHT

What More Is to Be Done?

It is essential that society helps people who are left behind or who are in danger of it. Otherwise these people might reject the social contract and succumb to the poisonous snake oil peddled by political charlatans. This central imperative of democratic capitalism has led us to focus on employment markets, the main underlying cause of growing economic insecurity, rather than policies like support for home ownership, which are at best orthogonal to the problem and have historically been pursued in ways that made it worse. We have also rejected approaches like providing a universal basic income. If feasible at all politically, it would have to be set at such a low level—and likely at the cost of abolishing so much of the existing social safety net—that it would likely increase the insecurity of millions of Americans.

Instead we have focused on policies such as an expanded earned income tax credit, universal adjustment assistance, and infrastructure programs that can succeed and for which the necessary political coalitions can plausibly be mustered and sustained. These policies should be key parts of a program geared toward the realities of a twenty-first century economy in which globalized capitalism's creative destruction requires ever more nimble labor markets. That program must embody a collective responsibility to enable people adapt to, live with, and thrive in a world of perpetual change. Without a viable program of this sort, the US will fall behind countries with more dynamic, self-renewing labor markets, and it will continue having to cope with ugly, self-defeating politics at home. Rather than an aberration, the 2016 elections will turn out to have been a harbinger of things to come.

Vital as these policies are, they are scarcely an exhaustive catalog of what is needed to address the gnawing insecurity that plagues tens of millions of Americans. Even if better paying jobs become available and peoples' ability to transition among them is greatly improved, they still need access to child care and affordable health insurance to take advantage of these enhanced possibilities. And retraining programs can only achieve so much if basic skills are not developed in the first place, a major problem in many of America's dilapidated and underperforming public schools.

We take up these issues in this chapter, interrogating them from the standpoint of our distinctive focus on good policy in light of viable politics. We also discuss policies that are designed to reinvigorate local and regional economies. Place-based policies confront well-known hazards and often fail, but there are also success stories from which we can learn. Even these are no panacea and surely no substitute for effective national policy. But especially when national politics are as polarized and sclerotic as in the United States today, it is important to consider subnational efforts as well.

Bottom-Up Medicare expansion

For the population under age sixty-five, employment-based coverage and Medicaid are the two main sources of health insurance.[1] Medicaid and the Children's Health Insurance Program are most important sources for the poor and near poor: in 2019 58 percent of the 37 million people under 65 with income below 150 percent of the federal poverty level were enrolled in one of these two programs.[2] Employer-based coverage also varies greatly by income. About 90 percent of the 93 million people under age sixty-five with incomes of 400 percent or more of the federal poverty level had employer-based coverage, compared to 63 percent with incomes between 150 and 400 percent. The Congressional Budget Office expects these patterns to continue in the absence of major legislation.

Obamacare was meant both to increase coverage dramatically and to begin controlling costs. But we have seen that the compromises needed to enact it, followed by relentless Republican efforts to undermine it, have limited its effectiveness. Despite these setbacks, coverage has increased substantially, mostly because many states have expanded their Medicaid coverage in response to incentives created by the law. In some states, however, many of these gains are threatened by new work requirements. Ongoing success is hardly guaranteed; Obamacare's future remains uncertain despite its increasing popularity with the public.

Federal subsidies for health insurance are large. In 2019 the subsidies, including tax breaks for employer-related coverage for people under age sixty-five, totaled about $257 billion; they are expected to amount to $4.2 trillion over the decade from 2020 to 2029.[3] Federal subsidies for Medicaid and the Children's Health Insurance Program combined are of roughly the same magnitude, while Medicare spends about one-fourth as much on 8 million Americans under age sixty-five.[4] Altogether, these expenditures totaled $733 billion in 2019 and are projected to be nearly $10 trillion in 2020–2029. Medicare expenditures for the elderly are estimated to cost an additional $10.5 trillion over that decade.[5]

Total health expenditures in the US in 2019 were estimated at $3.8 trillion, with a little more than 10 percent of that paid out of pocket by individuals.[6] The US spends massive amounts more on health care costs than other countries do—about 17 percent of GDP, compared to between 9 and 11 percent in Australia, Canada, France, Germany, Italy, Spain, and the United Kingdom. What do we get for all of our trillions? More preventable deaths than these other countries; more uninsured people: 30 million, nearly 9 percent of the population; and more underinsured people: one quarter of the population, 86 million who forego medical care because their deductibles, copayments, or prescription drugs are unaffordable. More and more workers are finding an ever-increasing share of their compensation going into the costs of health insurance and health care.[7] As the Kaiser Family Foundation reported, the typical health insurance premium for a family of four increased at double the inflation rate in 2015, having shot up by 55 percent in the previous decade.[8]

Obamacare retained employer-based coverage as the linchpin of health insurance for working-age Americans.[9] But although employer-based coverage is expected to remain relatively stable over the next decade, fighting economic insecurity over the longer term requires a sustainable move in the direction of health insurance that can become independent of employer-based plans. The basic reason is obvious: as lifetime employment becomes increasingly rare and labor becomes more mobile both geographically and across occupations, growing numbers of people will lose their insurance periodically, and they won't know when next they will have a job or what health coverage—if any—it will include. Over the four years following the 2008 recession, the number of people unemployed for a year or longer increased six-fold, from 704,000 in 2007 to 4.3 million in 2011. By 2017—almost a decade after the collapse—that number was still 1.1 million, 50 percent above its 2007 level.[10] The anxiety that results from this kind of employment insecurity grows as people age and their health risks increase.[11]

The expectation that people will buy private health insurance founders against the well-known problems of adverse selection and moral hazard. Healthy people must buy insurance in order to make insurance pools viable for providers, but they might not buy it because they underestimate the likelihood of serious illness and know that emergency room care is in any case available. Insurance companies, for their part, have strong incentives to avoid covering the people who most need insurance or to set prohibitively high prices for them. Given the large political and economic obstacles to containing health care costs, these problems will only get worse. Some combination of regulation and subsidies is therefore inevitable. The question is, what combination?

Many policy analysts of varying ideological stripes have concluded that a single-payer national system like Canada's would guarantee virtually universal coverage and would be the most cost-effective health insurance system overall. In the 2020 presidential campaign, several Democratic candidates proposed a version of a Medicare-for-all plans for the United States. Many of their congressional colleagues have advanced similar proposals. In his 2016 campaign, Bernie Sanders estimated this would cost $1.38 trillion a year.[12] The left-leaning Urban Institute and the right-leaning Mercatus Center, however, both put the expected costs at closer to $3 trillion a year.[13] Estimates such as these all assume that families with better insurance coverage will use more health care and that current administrative costs would be significantly reduced. But estimating costs is tricky because lots of the plans lack many relevant details.[14] Will there be premiums and copayments, and what will they cost? What medical services will be covered? What methods will be used to determine how much physicians, hospitals, and pharmaceutical companies will be paid? What private options, if any, will remain available for employer-based and other private insurance?

Even if total health expenditures do not increase much—the Rand Corporation estimates an increase of less than 2 percent a year—the way these costs are paid would undergo tremendous changes.[15] In the current US system, many health care costs are invisible to voters. Economists agree that employers' payments for their employees' health insurance reduce cash wages and ultimately come out of the employees' pockets, but employees never see that. The payroll and income tax subsidies for employer coverage cost the federal government more than $180 billion annually, but by reducing both government spending and taxes, these subsidies appear to make the government smaller, not larger. Moving the bulk of these costs to public budgets will generate vigorous opposition from anti-tax legislators who will fight against adding hundreds of billions of dollars to the federal budget regardless of the overall savings for Americans.

The Canadian plan for the US—even relabeled as Medicare for all—is a political fantasy. For one thing, the political demand is lacking. The proportion of Americans covered by employer-based health insurance fell from 60 percent to about half over the decade ending in 2018, but that still amounts to nearly 160 million people. Two-thirds of them are satisfied with their health care, although that number edges downward as employer-based coverage becomes skimpier and costlier for businesses and workers. Most of the elderly, who might otherwise be a powerful lobby through the AARP, are already covered through Medicare and Medicaid, which garner even higher satisfaction rates.[16] They have no incentive to mobilize in favor of universal care. If anything they might fear that such a move would leave them with diluted or more expensive coverage. Add to this the staunch opposition of the private health insurance industry, which would be wiped out, and hostility from the National Federation of Independent Businesses, other conservative small business groups, and much of the medical and hospital establishment.

Any doubt about the political impossibility in the US of enacting a mandatory single-payer plan like Canada's should recede when looking to the experience in New York, where bills to establish a state-wide single-payer system have been introduced in the legislature every year since 1992. The combination of weak supportive coalitions and powerful hostile ones has doomed this legislation even when Democrats have controlled both legislative chambers and the governorship.[17]

True, businesses that pay for their employees' insurance would benefit from shifting these costs to taxpayers. Aside from the savings, they could pay more in cash wages that employees would see as income—unlike the employer contributions to insurance plans, which employees generally don't view as pay. That is a considerable advantage. But this has been true for decades without motivating any significant business support for a single-payer system. It is hard to see why that would change. Business is too divided, and for many the path of less resistance is to imitate companies like Walmart by relying more on part-time or temporary workers and independent contractors who may be denied coverage altogether. Who will stop them, given the collapse of organized labor in the private sector and the status-quo bias in the American political system?

Rather than try to move boldly to universal public coverage, a better course is to devise a strategy for expanding Medicare coverage on a voluntary basis. Jacob Hacker—who inspired the public option for Obamacare, which, as we discuss in chapter 4, was scrapped to get the necessary vote of Connecticut Senator Joe Lieberman—has described a proposal he calls Medicare Part E.[18] That is "E" for everyone. This plan would require employers either to provide coverage for their employees or to pay for Medicare Part E—a play-or-pay requirement. It would also provide automatic enrollment, enhance Medicare benefits, and better coordinate Medicare and Medicaid to ensure coverage of the poor and children. The Center for American Progress has advanced a similar proposal, and legislation along these lines has been sponsored by Democrats in both the House and Senate.[19]

Expanding Medicare on a voluntary basis and improving its benefits offers the greatest promise for increasing health care coverage and controlling costs. But this does not mean that even this somewhat more modest change can be enacted. What if we went smaller, by for instance, lowering the Medicare eligibility age to 55 or even 50? The trouble is that changes at this scale won't generate the kind of traction that will ultimately produce universal coverage and lower costs. As Hacker has put it, this sort of change might "stall out."[20]

We need to think, then, of other possible options for reform. A better place to start is by extending Medicare to the youngest working-age people, who are also the cheapest to insure. This mitigates both the political sticker shock and the per capita costs of Medicare by expanding its risk pool to mostly healthy people. People below the age of thirty could be eligible immediately, after which they would be able to keep their coverage for as long as they want or switch to an employer plan if they prefer. Newborns would be enrolled automatically unless their parents opt out. Over a generation, Medicare would slowly become available to all, but on a voluntary, subsidized basis. As with Hacker's proposal, when employees elect into Medicare, their employers would have to make additional contributions to Medicare. Insured individuals would also contribute some payments for premiums. Cash wages received in lieu of employer-based coverage would be subject to federal income and payroll taxes.

During the gradual transition, cost savings would accrue. A large source of savings would be administrative costs. In the case of employer plans, these costs are significantly higher than Medicare's, which amount only to about 2 percent of its total costs. And the impact of gradual expansion on the federal budget would, at least initially, be modest. Most people who buy into the system will not want to lose their coverage because it will likely be cheaper and better coverage than they could otherwise get. Private health insurers will also have to become more efficient and cost effective to compete.

This Medicare option would, over time, operate much as the public option was intended to under Obamacare: as a competitor to private insurers to keep them honest, and as a source of cost control. Creating a Medicare option does not preclude adding a public option to Obamacare later, should the political stars align. But the potential per capita cost savings for Medicare from adding young people might well offer greater political opportunities to expand coverage. Current Medicare coverage would continue to be automatically available at age sixty-five.

An important advantage of this plan is that the status-quo bias would start working in favor of Medicare coverage for all rather than against it. As the number of people who are covered increases, the political constituency for keeping the program will grow too. The history of public support for Obamacare is salutary in this regard. The botched initial rollout of the program, combined with relentless Republican attacks, depressed public support. But this reversed once there was a serious prospect of eliminating coverage altogether. Even a united Republican Congress with the avid support of President Trump failed in its efforts to repeal Obamacare in 2017.[21] A Medicare expansion will likely enjoy a similar improvement in political climate. It may be that once all Americans become eligible, the public would even support a requirement that people not covered by private insurance elect into the expanded Medicare option.

Obamacare, precarious though it is, has become the most successful expansion of coverage since the creation of Medicare and Medicaid in 1965. Even so, the project of ensuring that all Americans have access to affordable health insurance—an ongoing concern of Democrats and Republicans since the New Deal—is unfinished. A remedy remains vital to alleviating a major source of economic insecurity in the United States. The effort to control rising costs is similarly incomplete. Bottom-up voluntary expansion of Medicare offers a realistic proximate goal—more realistic, certainly, than trying all at once to institute Medicare for all. After a century of failure to provide universal coverage, we can tolerate a transitional generation on the way to truly universal health care.

Child Care and Universal Pre-K

Much economic insecurity is aggravated by family circumstances. In particular, millions of parents with young children need more affordable child care and preschool in order to be able to work outside the home.

In December 1971, not long after women's liberation groups had found their footing and six months after Richard Nixon announced that he would make an unprecedented visit to Communist China, the president vetoed the comprehensive Child Development Act. This legislation would have funded child care facilities open to all children aged three to five in any locality with a population of 5,000 or more. It had passed the Senate on a bipartisan 63-17 vote, thanks largely to the leadership of Minnesota Senator Walter Mondale. It passed the House by a narrower 210-186 margin. Local governments and nonprofit groups would have been responsible for creating and running the child care facilities. Poor children could have attended for free, and families with above-poverty incomes would have been subject to a sliding scale of fees based on their incomes.

Nixon's veto was ironic. A year earlier the White House had declared child care a national priority and held a highly publicized conference on children's well-being. Nixon himself had said, "What happens to the child from a nutritional standpoint, from an educational standpoint, from an environmental standpoint, in the years between one and five may affect that child for the balance of his life regardless of what may happen after that time."[22] That year nearly one-third of married women with children under age six were employed, compared to fewer than 14 percent two decades earlier.[23] (In 2018 the figure was close to two-thirds.[24])

Nixon's veto was a response to opponents' claims that national child care would be a form of communism, leading to the "Sovietization" of American children; to governors who objected that the program empowered local rather than state governments; to social conservatives who contended that national child care created an additional threat to family control over children's upbringing; and to the legislation's costs. In his veto message, Nixon described public provision of child care as "family-weakening" and said that it "would commit the vast moral authority of the National Government to the side of communal approaches to child rearing over the family-centered approach." It would be, he insisted, "a long leap into the dark for the United States government and the American people," a very "radical" undertaking.[25] The US has never again come this close to a universally available child care program.

Universal child care was not actually so radical, nor a long leap into the dark for the US. The federal government had provided heavily subsidized, universal child care successfully a generation earlier, during World War II. Recognizing that Rosie could not do her riveting without someone to care for her children while her husband was off to war, Congress in 1940 enacted the Lanham Act to enable mothers with children from infancy through age twelve to contribute to wartime production. More than $1 billion (in 2012 dollars) was distributed to more than 635 communities in every state (except New Mexico) for the construction and maintenance of child care facilities, teacher pay and training, and for children's meals. The child care centers provided educational material and outdoor play, hot lunches, and regular naps for preschool children. The program operated from 1943 to 1946. During its short life, universal child care made it easier for mothers to work and generated sizable increases in their employment, which continued years after the legislation expired. It also had a positive impact on the children it served, improving their long-term health, educational attainment, and prospects for employment. The benefits were greatest for the most economically disadvantaged families.[26]

After the 1971 failure of child care legislation, efforts to create broadly available child care frequently foundered. In 1987, for example, the Alliance for Better Childcare, a coalition of more than seventy nonprofit and child-advocacy organizations, pushed legislation for federal child care support targeted at low-income families that ultimately failed. The legislation irked some members of Congress because it would have provided funds to the states, rather than directly to families through tax credits or vouchers, and it did not provide funding to religious organizations. But in 1990 George H. W. Bush signed legislation that created Child Care Development Block Grants to the states. This law provided choice for parents, along with some expansion of the EITC and additional tax credits for families with infant children. The Personal Responsibility and Work Opportunity Reconciliation Act of 1996—welfare legislation signed by President Clinton—transformed these block grants into the Child Care and Development Fund, a single block grant program that still provides federal funds to the states for child care.[27] In 2018 Congress increased funding for this program by $2.4 billion, the largest increase since its inception.[28]

In addition to these block grants, the federal government spends about $4 billion a year on income tax credits for a portion of child care expenses. These credits are capped at $1,050 for one child, $2,100 for two. This is about one-fifth of the annual cost of child care in Alabama and Mississippi, less than 10 percent in California, Illinois, Massachusetts, and New York.[29] The tax credits enable a very small minority of families with one child to pay 10 percent or less of their incomes on child care.

Because child care costs so much and is often of poor quality, and because increasing government subsidies to families will increase child care prices, Gamesh Sitarman and Anne Alstott have proposed a new system designed to moderate costs and set higher standards. They recommend building local child care facilities open to the public and funded by the federal or state governments. Fees would be capped at a certain percentage of family income, with specified staff-to-child ratios, space requirements, and educational program, if any. Such an investment would not be out of the norm; it would put the US in the same league as its global counterparts. As Sitarman and Alstott stress, US spending on child care is relatively low, ranking thirty-fifth out of thirty-six developed countries as a percentage of GDP, behind Bulgaria, Mexico, and Slovenia.[30] France has long had a public child care system somewhat similar to the one they propose, providing state-run centers available to all children age three months and up. Fees for these "creches" are set according to a sliding scale based on income.[31] Standards for health and safety are set by the government.[32]

Lists of facilities can be found at town halls, and anyone can apply for a slot for their child. Demand exceeds supply, however, so parents are told to apply when pregnant or when they apply for adoptions.[33]

The US also has a public child care system, although relatively few people know about it. The Department of Defense funds and runs a child development program for children from six weeks old to age five. As in France, military personnel pay for their children's placement on an income-dependent sliding scale, but the fees are hardly inexpensive: in 2017–2018, they ranged from a low of $222 per month per child to $944. More than 100,000 children under age three were served by these centers. Again, demand outstrips supply. The Defense Department also subsidizes some nonmilitary child care programs that comply with the department's regulations and pays some costs of home-based child care serving up to six children at a time. The latter cost about half as much as places in the child development centers.[34]

There also have been encouraging state and local developments for children aged three and four. Pre-kindergarten education has recently become widely available in the United States. Forty-four states now offer programs that vary widely in their potential to produce substantial long-term employment, health, and quality-of-life benefits for the children enrolled. These pre-K programs include a mix of public schools, Head Start, and private alternatives. Cities like Boston, New York, and Washington, DC—controlled by Democrats, with mayors who made pre-K an important campaign issue—have instituted public preschool programs. The Boston program is rated as one of the country's best in quality but falls short on funding and serves only about half of the city's four-year-old children.[35] New York's program, initiated in 2014, served 70,000 four-year-olds in 2018. Mayor Bill de Blasio announced that the program would be expanded to three-year-olds by 2021.

As in Boston, funding is a challenge. The mayor proposed funding his pre-K initiative with an increase in city income taxes for residents earning $500,000 a year or more, but Governor Andrew Cuomo objected and instead transferred to the city $300 million of state funds for the pre-K program.[36] As in Boston, finding enough spaces to serve the city's young children is an obstacle.

Washington, DC, may have the most successful of the city pre-K programs. It provides two years of free, full-day preschool in public schools, charter schools, and private community-based nonprofit facilities. In 2017 the program served 90 percent of the city's four-year-olds and 70 percent of the city's three-year-olds, and it improves the children's academic and social skills and their readiness for school. In the decade of availability of preschool in DC, the labor force participation of mothers of children under age five increased by 12 percent, with 10 percentage points of this increase attributed to the expansion of pre-K opportunities. DC, however, is also an outlier on costs, spending roughly $17,000 per pupil annually, which comes from a combination of federal and city sources.[37]

Even the Washington, DC, program is modest by international standards. France, for example, began in the 1830s instituting *écoles maternelles* that combine schooling and child care for children of low-income families. Today these schools enroll 95 percent of all French children aged three to five.[38] In September 2015 France required all children to begin school at age three.[39] Given the long-standing *écoles maternelle*, this was hardly a revolutionary change.

State pre-K programs in the US span the nation, including many Republican states. The earliest state pre-K program began with a 1980 pilot in Oklahoma, which now serves 75 percent of the state's four-year-olds. It is a highly ranked program, provided almost entirely in public schools at a cost of about $7,700 per child annually. About $3,500 of that comes from state coffers, with the remainder from the federal Head Start program.[40] Florida's free preschool program, which began in 2005, enrolls the highest percentage of four-year-olds of any state offering. In contrast to Oklahoma students, Florida's are taught in private facilities at a cost of less than $2,500 per pupil each year. This has resulted in large class sizes, shorter hours, and relatively low quality.[41] Alabama's program was ranked highest in quality in 2017 by the National Institute for Early Education Research, but it served only a quarter of the state's four-year-olds. Enrollment has been rising annually, largely because of increased federal funding.[42]

All of this activity shows that universally available pre-K combines good policy with good politics. Most importantly, providing preschool to three- and four-year-olds faces no potential blocking coalition. Importantly, teachers unions should not object. Preschool does not threaten the livelihood of teachers, who often resist large-scale political reforms of education. In fact, universal pre-K might offer prospects for expanding teachers' employment and their unions over time. For conservatives, who often advocate trimming welfare rolls through work requirements for single mothers of young children, universal pre-K is a positive development. High child care costs are a barrier to work; universal pre-K removes that barrier. At the same time, pre-K improves opportunities for disadvantaged children and promises to increase the earnings and the productivity of their parents. Universal pre-K is also supported by a wide range of constituents—both Democrats and Republicans—for whom reducing child care costs is a priority. Builders and construction workers benefit from opportunities to build or rehabilitate facilities. And many nonprofits and child advocacy organizations are effective proponents. Building and holding together a supportive coalition should not be difficult.

Expanding child care and preschool opportunities contributes significantly in allowing mothers to work. The labor force participation rate for single mothers has grown by four percentage points since 2015, with most of that increase coming from single mothers without college degrees.[43] A growing economy with expanding job opportunities has been important to this development, so the increasingly widespread availability of public preschool offers only a partial explanation for this growth, but it has undoubtedly helped. Directing more federal funds to ensure universal availability of preschools and affordable child care for younger children could help even more, as would expanding paid family leave.[44] In June 2019 Connecticut became the seventh state to establish a paid family leave program, over the objections of the state's business community. It was financed by a 0.5 percent payroll tax on private-sector employees.[45]

Insisting on family-centered care for preschool children is archaic in a world in which able-bodied adults are expected, in dominant moral outlooks, to work—particularly if they get income support from the government. Ironically, given the role that threats of communistic childcare played in Nixon's 1971 veto, China now offers a model for the kind of family-based child care that conservatives had hoped for a generation ago. In China, grandparents frequently migrate from their hometowns to cities and move in with their children in order to take care of their grandchildren. Forty-three percent of China's 15 million elderly migrants in 2018 moved in order to take care of their grandchildren. This migration accounted for more than half of the elderly who moved to the larger, more economically developed cities, such as Beijing, Shanghai, Guangzhou, and Shenzhen.[46] This contributes to China's high female labor force participation rate, higher than in the US or UK. But this is one thing that China cannot export to the US.[47] What happens in China, in this case, stays in China: the days when extended family would supply an appreciable portion of US child care ended long ago.

K-12 Education

Of all the proposals that have been advanced for improving low- and middle-income security in the US, none is as ubiquitous as calls for improving the quality of public education. And with good reason. After all, how can we retrain workers for the technological age when they are not well educated in the first place? Major reform of America's K-12 educational system is clearly needed. In 2015 US fifteen-year-olds ranked fortieth in the annual Program for International Student Assessment survey, a notable decline over previous years and significantly below the average for participating nations. Americans are treading water in reading and science literacy, ranked twenty-fourth and twenty-fifth respectively.[48] As Robert Putnam reports in *Our Kids: The American Dream in Crisis*, things are especially dire for children near the bottom of the income distribution, whose educational opportunities are now worse than they have been for decades in both absolute and relative terms. Between 1970 and 2010, the share of children in the top income quartile receiving a college degree has risen from 40 percent to 80 percent, while the share in the next quartile has grown from about 15 percent to 30 percent, and the share in the bottom two quartiles has remained virtually flat at around 10 percent. Surely this is the place to start?

In principle, yes, but the limitations of Putnam's recommendations signal the depressing scope of this challenge. He calls for more investment in existing schools, extending school hours and extracurricular and enrichment activities, and more experimentation with charter schools, vocational training, and community colleges—arguably plausible goals. But he says nothing about the political coalitions that might support such measures, and fails to establish that, even if adopted, they would have a significant impact on the problem. Putnam himself notes that family background is a better predictor of the likelihood of college graduation than student test scores; that growing class segregation is a significant cause of differences in children's educational experiences; that residential segregation "is deeply rooted in growing income inequality, and that the financial equity that middle-class American have embodied in their homes makes efforts to reduce class segregation fiercely resisted." Changes in zoning ordinances and the home interest mortgage deduction, which make the problem worse, also "are objects of great political contention."[49]

That's putting it mildly. A large obstacle to meaningful change is our funding of K-12 education mainly out of local property taxes, which, as Putnam notes, reinforces the status-quo of resource-starved schools in poor neighborhoods—not to mention endemic economic and racial segregation. Former Federal Reserve Chair Janet Yellen has emphasized the role that funding plays for "families below the top" and blamed the virtually unique system of funding public schools out of local property taxes as a major reason for the United States' educational shortcomings.[50] Those with the resources to opt out do so, either by sending their children to private schools or by moving to neighborhoods that are beyond the reach of poor families. Decades of efforts to increase funding for public schools have run into brutal opposition from anti-tax groups, the most dramatic of which was California's Proposition 13 initiative, which generally limits property taxes to 1 percent of assessed value. The multiple exit options from the public system drain the people and organizations that would otherwise be forces for its improvement. As Albert Hirschman pointed out half a century ago, people with easy exit options have few incentives to spend time and effort trying to improve declining organizations.[51]

Policies pushed by forces on the political right also predictably run into powerful blocking coalitions. The most frequent are proposals for the introduction of choice through voucher systems in public schools and calls to create charter schools within them.[52] Both are hotly contested: voucher systems on the grounds that, by reducing exit costs for those who can leave, they subject those who cannot to remain in bad schools that might well decline further, and charters for the same reason and also because of their mixed record on quality.[53] Regardless of who is right, conservative proposals run into buzz saws of opposition from public school administrators, teachers unions, and the politicians allied with them. Typical is the six-day strike of 30,000 Los Angeles teachers in January 2019. The strike was motivated in part by class sizes, wages, and other working conditions, but teachers also sought to stop the spread of charter schools, which, they contend, drain resources from the rest of the system. Bernie Sanders and Democratic Senators Kamala Harris, Cory Booker, Sherrod Brown, and Kirsten Gillibrand all immediately came out in support of the strike.

Booker came to this position the hard way. In 2008, then mayor of Newark and a rising star in Democratic politics, Booker declared at the Democratic National Convention, "Ten years ago when I talked about school choice . . . I was literally brought into a broom closet by a union and told I would never win office if I kept talking about charters."[54] He persisted nonetheless, netting for his school-choice agenda a $100 million gift from Facebook founder Mark Zuckerberg matched by another $100 million raised from foundations and other individual donors. The goal was to turn around Newark's public schools, which had become so bad by 2010 that more than 60 percent of students in third through eighth grade were below grade level in reading and math, nearly half of students dropped out, and the school system had been taken over by the state government. This school-turnaround venture became a political train wreck, as told in four-part harmony by Dale Russakoff in *The Prize*.[55] There was plenty of blame to go around, emanating from what one Newark educational leader, Dominique Lee, dubbed the "school failure industry": overpaid and ignorant consultants; heavy-handed, top-down reformers who lack essential local knowledge; Booker's well-heeled donors and political cronies; and ideologues appointed by Governor Christie. But implacable opposition from the teachers unions was also a major factor. Booker has sided with the unions ever since.

Backlash against the school-reform movement is not restricted to Newark, where in 2014 anti-charter candidate Ras Baraka became mayor after defeating Shavar Jeffries, who would go on to become president of the pro-charter Democrats for Education Reform. Baraka was reelected with over 77 percent of the vote in 2018.[56] In 2013 de Blasio's victory in New York with 73 percent of the vote came on the back of a strident anti-charter campaign, ushering in an era of feuding with charter proponents and the wider school-reform movement.[57] He was reelected with 66.5 percent of the vote five years later.[58] In Chicago, mayor and reform advocate Rahm Emanuel won a close bid for reelection in a runoff in 2015, and soon found that "backlash against charter schools has been so fierce that few new schools have been authorized."[59] During her campaign for the Democratic presidential nomination in 2016, Hillary Clinton reversed her longstanding support for charter schools. According to press reports, she sounded "less like a decades-long supporter of charter schools . . . and more like a teachers union president."[60]

The 2019 strike in Los Angeles followed a year of teacher walkouts cross the country, including six in conservative and swing states. America's schools lost some 1.5 million worker days to these stoppages, almost double the combined days lost to strikes in all other industries and the largest number in twelve years.[61] This militancy did not dissipate, partly because Betsy DeVos, multibillionaire heir to the Amway fortune and Donald Trump's secretary of education, has been a relentless advocate of charters and voucher programs and a lightning rod for teacher activism. A month after the Los Angeles strike, lawmakers in West Virginia abandoned a bill to expand charters and private school vouchers in response to a statewide teachers' walkout.[62] Democrats have been loath to challenge the teachers, even if they might have done so in the past. As Dana Goldstein noted in the *New York Times*, it has become "practically impossible for a national Democrat to profess anything short of full-throated support for picketing educators."[63]

That erstwhile Democratic defenders of charter schools either reversed themselves or fell silent on school reform did not mean they were entirely wrong. School reform has been successful in some circumstances. KIPP (Knowledge is Power Program) schools, to take one example, have notched notable records in a number of cities, and many children have done well at charter schools in Newark, Washington, DC, and other cities. Even though charters do not outperform traditional public schools on average, the best of them deliver impressive results, and research shows that public schools that adopt their practices can make large academic gains.[64] Impartial evaluation is difficult, partly because charters often enroll children of better-resourced and motivated parents, and charter schools sometimes obtain more resources than other schools in their districts.

And there is always the challenge of the effect on the remaining public schools. Echoing Hirschman's observation about exit, former Newark schools Superintendent Cami Anderson described Booker's backing of charters as "the lifeboat theory of educational reform." In effect, she said, Booker was creating two educational systems. His plan was to grow the charters to 40 percent of enrollments in five years, leaving the other 60 percent of students to sink or swim on the big ship. "I did not come here to shuffle the deck chairs on the *Titanic*," she said.[65] Even Anderson's more modest effort at reform—creating a citywide lottery that ostensibly gave parents greater choice—ran into trenchant opposition from teachers unions and community groups. She quit in 2015. As an outsider and the first non-African American superintendent in decades, perhaps she was destined to fail. By 2016 she had, in any case, joined the critics of the reform movement she had once championed, arguing that it was abandoning those most in need of help. "Why has the school reform community been largely silent," she asked at a Teach for America summit, "about the school-to-prison pipeline?"[66]

Even if the powerful coalitions blocking school reform could be overcome, the Supreme Court has created hurdles to educational equity that are all but insuperable for many public schools. In 1973 the Court rejected a claim by the San Antonio Independent School District for redress for students who were being underserved due to their neighborhood district's low property tax base. In the course of dismissing the claim that spending should be equalized across school districts, the Court declared that there is no fundamental right to education in the US Constitution. Moreover, poor students are not a "suspect class" that stands in need of protection under the Fourteenth Amendment.[67] The following year the justices further hobbled any possibility of addressing the soft apartheid fostered by the neighborhood-based public school system. Unless there is a deliberate policy of segregation, the Court held, school systems are not at fault; they cannot be held responsible for *de facto* segregation. In any event segregation cannot be addressed by remedies that cross district lines, even in highly segregated cities like Detroit.[68] Litigation under state constitutions that do provide an explicit right to education has sometimes fared better, helping to equalize funding. But US public schools remain highly segregated and starkly unequal financially.

National legislative solutions have fared little better than litigation. The most ambitious of these in recent decades was No Child Left Behind (NCLB) in 2001, a signature effort of the George W. Bush administration that continued a tradition of failure dating from the 1940s. For instance, in 1965 Congress passed the Elementary and Secondary Education Act (ESEA) as part of the Great Society's War on Poverty. ESEA was meant to expand educational access and to narrow achievement gaps through remedial spending, professional development of teachers, and programs fostering better parental involvement. It was a legislative breakthrough after previous attempts by Presidents Truman and Kennedy that had been stymied. It was tough to get reforms past coalitions of conservatives who resisted expanding the federal role in primary and secondary education, Catholics who were more interested in parochial schools that would not benefit from expanding the federal role, and urban liberals in Congress—such as Adam Clayton Powell, Jr., of Harlem—who opposed federal aid bills that would have supported segregated schools. ESEA became possible because the Democrats' huge victory in 1964 sidelined conservatives, because LBJ bought off the Catholic lobby by cleverly devising a bill that provided federally assisted programs directly to the children rather than to the parochial schools, and because people like Powell were turned around by the Civil Rights Act, which had prohibited federal funding for segregated schools.[69]

Initially ESEA was judged by many to be a success. The bill called for $1 billion ($8 billion in 2018 dollars) in federal spending in the coming year, which rose to $4.2 billion in 1968 ($31 billion in 2018 dollars)—more than ten times the $375 million that had been spent a decade earlier. This increased the federal share of total educational spending from less than 3 percent to 10 percent.[70] But the legislation soon came under intensifying attacks, partly due to the resurgent Republican tide and partly because it was poorly implemented, with local administrators doing end runs around the guidelines to cover routine expenses and overhead. As James Patterson reports, "By the early 1970s it was an open secret that a great deal of federal educational money aimed at the poor was missing its target."[71]

Alongside these political and administrative concerns, the efficacy of remedial spending on education was increasingly coming into question. Northeastern and Midwestern cities, reeling from the effects of vanishing industrial jobs, were further devastated by botched programs of urban renewal. In Newark, as Russakoff recounts, the result was the destruction of longstanding neighborhoods. Residents were relegated to large housing projects like Newark's Central Ward. By the late 1960s, more than 18,000 mostly low-income minority residents were jammed into this mile-and-a-half radius, living in high-rise silos that lacked ground-floor restrooms and had minimal grass or open space. Parents had a hard time knowing where their children were, making supervision virtually impossible. Russakoff reports an unidentified Newark official's testimony to the US Commission on Civil Rights, describing the Central Ward as "one of the most volatile ghettos anywhere on the eastern seaboard."[72] And, as Douglas Rae has noted, similar patterns were playing out in other industrial cities.[73]

For schoolchildren growing up in and going home to such circumstances every day, the question was whether money spent on compensatory education could make a real difference. The 1966 Coleman Report, commissioned by the National Center for Education Statistics and led by the sociologist James Coleman, had answered this question with a decisive, if reluctant, no. The Coleman Report documented a reality similar to that which Putnam would describe five decades later. The report concluded that family circumstances, the quality and ethos of neighborhoods (including how segregated they are), and peer attitudes mattered more than spending per pupil, increases in which often seemed not to improve education attainment in a measurable way.

Spending is not irrelevant, but it will have only limited impact unless these basic issues are addressed.[74] Studies have found that when compensatory programs appear to work, the gains are often not maintained over the summer. This was the case in one study showing that third-graders who began a remedial program a full year behind grade level in reading ended it with only a five-month deficit. Then summer came, and the students entered the next year as far behind as they would have been without the remedial help.[75] Perhaps unsurprisingly, although spending per pupil increased from 1964 onward, average SAT scores fell steadily.[76] By the early 1970s, growing numbers of school reformers were in agreement that without addressing the economic and social disadvantages of poor inner-city students, their life chances were unlikely to dramatically improve.[77]

Twenty-first century efforts have also largely crashed and burned on the hard rock of this enduring reality. No Child Left Behind was an ambitious reauthorization of ESEA, enacted by large bipartisan majorities. NCLB expanded the federal government's role by providing substantial resources conditioned on annual testing, benchmarks for progress, and increased teacher accountability. The standardized tests that were deployed as metrics were soon attacked by some as too narrow, promoting anti-educational "teaching to the test." Others thought the standards were too punitive because schools that made significant absolute improvements—but had not achieved the requisite proficiency levels—were nonetheless penalized. Both criticisms were accurate, as were complaints that many school districts gamed the system by lowering standards in order to meet them. The Atlanta public schools engaged in outright cheating.[78] This was hardly surprising. As conservative commentator Charles Murray noted, by requiring every child to test at grade level by 2014, the law in effect required all children to be above the previous average within just a few years.[79] As criticism mounted from all ideological directions, Congress reduced funding, shifting the burden to heavily strapped state budgets and forcing state legislators to make other cuts to meet the law's requirements.[80]

In December 2015 Congress passed the Every Student Succeeds Act, and President Obama signed it. The law's title defied Murray's contention that not all students can attain proficiency, but the legislation actually pursued no such goal. Instead it turned over most of what was left of NCLB to the states, shrinking the federal role in education for the first time since the 1980s. Conservatives welcomed it as a victory.[81] This did not actually change things much, because NCLB had not been reauthorized since 2007 due to lack of bipartisan agreement. In any case the Obama administration had for years been granting schools waivers as long as they were making some absolute improvements. The 2015 law retained residual oversight of school-district goals by the Department of Education, but in 2017 GOP lawmakers and the incoming Trump administration eliminated even those accountability regulations.[82]

It is hard not to conclude from this depressing history that the focus on schools—like the mortgage assistance discussed in chapter 3—might be too far downstream from the root problems to have much impact, at least in the near term. A major difference between education and housing is that, whereas housing financing can be changed significantly, in education the blocking coalitions are so powerful that significant reform is not likely to be enacted. If enacted, it is not likely to be implemented successfully. This might be why many political leaders are focused on preschools or community colleges. There will be exceptions, as in the relatively clean slate created in New Orleans after hurricane Katrina destroyed many of the existing schools in 2005.[83] But, while no one should gainsay attempts to improve K–12 education throughout the land, for the most part it may be wiser to conclude, as Mark Zuckerberg did in the wake of his failed effort in Newark, that are no quick fixes for K–12 education and that resources might be better directed at tackling poverty and economic insecurity.

Zuckerberg and his wife Priscilla Chan have also concluded that top-down educational reform is bound to fail in the US. The Newark experience convinced them that they had failed to engage sufficiently with the people they were trying to help. "We can't empower people if we don't understand the needs and desires of their communities," they wrote. Russakoff agrees, noting that the decision by reformers like Christie, Booker, and Anderson to bypass local communities was "not only politically calamitous, but also produced an agenda that didn't equip the district's schools with resources to address the profound emotional needs children were bringing into classrooms every day—needs that parents and teachers could have highlighted, had they been consulted."[84] Compelling as this epitaph might be, it suggests that progress—when it comes—is likely to arrive school district by school district, if not school by school, or even child by child. It is hard to avoid this conclusion in view of the funding structure of American K–12 education, the interests vested in maintaining the existing system, the stance of the federal courts, and public backlash against the reform efforts of both the Bush and Obama administrations. Russakoff also suggests that, as with place-based policies more generally, there is little prospect that an efficacious national strategy could be adopted or successfully implemented.

Place-Based Policies

Providing increased take-home pay, better transitional assistance, infrastructure jobs, universal health insurance, and universal pre-K make for an essential quintet of policies geared to fighting insecurity. But will they be enough? Perhaps more geographically focused policies are needed, especially in collapsed and collapsing communities that have been devastated by industrial decline, opioid abuse, and disintegrating families. The suggestion that place-based policies might be essential is buttressed by the extensive work of Raj Chetty and colleagues in his Equality of Opportunity Project, now called Opportunity Insights. This research demonstrates the importance of neighborhoods to children's prospects and outcomes.[85] There is no longer any doubt that place—where people grow up and live—is vital to their well-being. But as *New York Times* columnist Eduardo Porter has observed, devising effective, politically realistic policies to address place-based differences is challenging—especially for the federal government.[86]

Economists have long been skeptical of place-based policies. David Neumark and Helen Simpson summed up the conventional wisdom in 2015: "A major shortcoming of the research on place-based policies is that even the most positive evidence on their effectiveness does not establish that they create self-sustaining economic gains."[87] As with special economic zones in the developing world, place-based policies are widely criticized for giving national governments tasks for which they are often ill-equipped: picking winners and determining what communities need and how to deliver it. Place-based policies are also susceptible to capture, rent-seeking, and other forms of corruption.[88] Even when corruption is absent, political considerations and influence often dominate economic needs. It is fair to worry that place-based policies misallocate resources and lead to remedies that are not worth what they cost.

Yet some economists have begun questioning the conventional skepticism. Edward Glaeser, who affirmed the standard view in 2008, has since changed his mind. Writing with Benjamin Austin and Lawrence Summers, he now argues that the exceptional joblessness of working-aged men—especially in what he calls the "eastern Heartland"—coupled with a decline in labor mobility calls for more investment in place-based policies by the federal government.[89] Glaeser and his coauthors want to see some infrastructure projects selected because they will create employment, and they want an expanded EITC, especially for single workers. They also call for consideration of place-based economic distress in decisions about siting military bases and other government facilities.

In 2017 Congress illustrated the difficulties of fashioning effective place-based policies. As part of that year's tax legislation, the federal government sought to stimulate economic activity in distressed communities by incentivizing investments in designated "opportunity zones." Previous federal efforts to provide tax incentives to benefit specific distressed areas had proved largely ineffective. For example, in 1993, during the Clinton administration, tax legislation advantaged "empowerment zones." These were selected areas where 20 percent of the residents had incomes below federal poverty thresholds and the unemployment rate was at least 6.3 percent, plus some specific rural areas in Kentucky, Mississippi, and Texas. Along with $100 million in block grants directed to these zones, businesses in them received a 20 percent wage credit (with a ceiling of $3,000) for each worker who lived in the zone and additional incentives for locating plant and equipment there. Empirical analysis, however, has generally found little or no evidence that this program lifted people out of poverty. Instead, it often resulted in gentrification of the better-off areas of the zones by higher-income households moving into the area, which served mainly to increase housing prices.[90]

Despite the limited or unverifiable success of previous efforts, at the urging of Senator Tim Scott of South Carolina, the Republican Congress in 2017 enacted new tax benefits for investors in designated opportunity zones. The tax breaks were estimated to cost $1.6 billion over ten years, increasing thereafter.[91] The claim that tax benefits for investors in opportunity zones will produce widespread gains is a classic instance of trickle-down economic thinking.[92] Details are complex, but generally the rules provide tax deferrals, tax reductions, and tax exemptions on capital gains for investors in real estate funds or equipment or in shares of businesses that operate significantly in designated opportunity zones.[93] Following enactment, about 8,700 areas were designated as opportunity zones by governors of all 50 states and some mayors. On average, these zones have lower-income households than the national average, but the inclusion of some is hard to fathom: among the zones are locations where investors would be happy to buy in without the tax breaks. Examples include Long Island City, gentrifying parts of Oakland, and an area in Las Vegas where a new NFL football stadium is being built.[94] Much of the early investment in opportunity zones was in real estate, with New York City, Los Angeles, and Phoenix being the hottest markets.[95] The tax breaks for investors in these zones become more valuable as investment returns increase. There is no requirement that the investments actually be motivated by the incentives: investments in an opportunity zone planned before the zone was designated can still earn the tax break. There also is no requirement that jobs be made available to residents of the zones. Promoters say that $6 trillion of potential capital gains may be able to escape taxes through opportunity zones; Treasury Secretary Steven Mnuchin put the number at $10 billion. Either way, the $1.6 billion of lost revenue is surely an underestimate. Economist Martin Sullivan insists that the "lion's share of tax benefits [will go] to areas that don't need investment incentives while leaving many truly needy locations unaffected."[96]

Evaluation of the program's impacts on jobs, growth, and poverty rates within the designated areas will be a long time in coming. Prior experience, however, is hardly encouraging. The choice of targeted areas is often based more on political than economic advantages and on the political connections of investors. Once a place is designated, the combination of loss aversion and status quo bias makes it difficult to remove from the list. More promising policies include removing barriers to mobility such as occupational licensing requirements, especially for jobs that do not require higher degrees, and providing more affordable housing for workers who do move.[97]

There are some encouraging examples of place-based policies from states and cities. Utah in 2012 embarked on an ambitious program to combat intergenerational poverty, with a special focus on childhood poverty.[98] Since then, Utah's upward-mobility record has been strong for the US, roughly as strong as Denmark's and Norway's, whose records are among the best in the world.[99] Utah's child poverty rate in 2017 was 10.7 percent, compared to the national level of 15.4 percent.[100] Another example: in July 2017 Newark launched a jobs initiative called Newark 2020 to combat poverty. The proximate goal was to employ 2,020 unemployed Newark residents in full-time work paying a living wage by

2020.[101] This endeavor engaged local for-profit and nonprofit institutions in efforts to hire Newark residents, who had previously held a relatively small percentage of the jobs generated by the resurgence in the economic vitality of downtown. Newark's efforts also sought to spur an increase in the businesses' purchases of local goods and services. Involving local universities and hospitals as anchor institutions in such efforts has been successful elsewhere, including West Philadelphia (where a shift in spending by local enterprises is estimated to have generated 160 new jobs and $5 million in additional local wages), Baltimore (through Hopkins Local), and Cleveland (through the Evergreen Cooperative Institute).[102]

Another potentially effective intervention by state and local governments would be to expand the vocational educational capacity of community colleges. Improved community colleges, which are organized and generally funded by states and localities, can enhance the earning capacities of their students, including workers transitioning among careers. Unlike many place-based policies, investing in community colleges does not empower government officials to pick winners to whom dollars will be allocated, diminishing the risks of political cronyism.

Some cities have responded well to shocks from international trade. Unlike Youngstown, where the search for alternatives failed to arouse much local political energy and decline has not abated, some comparably challenged cities have changed with the times. Allentown, Pennsylvania, about which Billy Joel sang, "They're closing all the factories down," is a case in point. Like Youngstown, Allentown also lost its manufacturing industries, but its population actually grew from 104,000 in 1980 to more than 121,000 in 2017.[103] In 2016 Allentown was the fastest growing city in Pennsylvania and one of six cities named a "national success story" by the Urban Land Institute.[104] Allentown's success is largely attributable to its shift toward service jobs, especially in health, transportation, and warehousing. In a comprehensive study of Allentown, Sean Safford also credits entrepreneurial innovations based on local capital combined with leadership from local politicians and CEOs as well as the city's ties to universities.[105]

Then there is Hickory, North Carolina, an industrial city hit hard by Chinese furniture imports. Hickory's furniture industry was identified by the *Wall Street Journal* as emblematic of the "China shock" that spurred the rise of Donald Trump. At its peak in 1990, Hickory was the center of 60 percent of the nation's furniture production. But twenty-five years later, the town was on life support.[106] Between 2000 and 2015, Chinese furniture imports to the US nearly quintupled from $4.4 to $20.4 billion. By 2007 Chinese imports had cost Hickory 16 percent of its manufacturing jobs. Disability rolls filled, mostly with older, unemployed workers. Nearly one-fifth of Hickory's population between ages twenty-five and thirty-four moved away.[107]

But Hickory's furniture producers responded. They adjusted by moving into custom production for niche markets, a strategy that by 2016 had begun paying off. "We have gone from the worst of times to the best of times in a short cycle," declared John Brug, chairman and Chief Executive of Vanguard Furniture."[108] Vanguard and other local furniture firms report that custom business models are proving viable, providing at least a partial solution to the jobs problem, although companies are employing fewer workers than they had earlier.[109]

Hickory has adapted in other ways, too. Old textile mills now house offices and restaurants. The defunct, but historic, Lyerly Full Fashioned Mill is now the headquarters of the global supply-chain management firm Transportation Insight.[110] CommScope and Corning Optical Communications now manufacture fiber optic products in Hickory for export. Apple, Alphabet (Google), and Facebook have all opened data storage and processing facilities there. Unlike many cities stung by globalization and technology, Hickory is growing. Its population of 20,000 in 1980 doubled to more than 40,000 in 2015. Hickory's unemployment rate, which was 9.4 percent in 2010, was below 5 percent by 2016.

Dan St. Louis, director of Hickory's Manufacturing Solutions Center, which helps small startups, says, "We have been telling kids for 20 years, don't get into manufacturing, it will all be gone, it will all be in China." He adds, "Today, however, businesses that have invested in robotic machines or in development of high-tech fabrics for medical, sports, or other industries cannot find qualified workers."[111]

Allentown and Hickory notwithstanding, people often must move away from smaller cities to improve their opportunities. Recognizing that high housing costs can be barriers to attracting workers, a number of cities have tried to create more affordable housing. New York City has set a goal of building or preserving 200,000 affordable apartments over a ten-year period through zoning and other changes. Between 2014 and 2018, the city helped finance nearly 122,000 affordable residences, albeit with mixed reviews.[112] In December 2018 Minneapolis revised its zoning rules to permit the development of three-family homes in the city's single-family residential neighborhoods as part of an effort to obtain more affordable housing. The name of the project, Minneapolis 2040, signals that the program will take decades to evaluate.[113] In 2019 state legislatures in Oregon and California both considered rules that would end single-family zoning in order to increase opportunities for building multifamily dwellings. But both efforts faced vigorous opposition from many homeowners and their coalitions.[114] San Francisco—which has become notorious for median housing prices five times the national average—has made minimal progress in creating affordable homes. Zoning laws intended to preserve the city's character often bar building more affordable housing.[115]

Sometimes local businesses can be induced to help. Microsoft is a case in point. In January 2019 the company responded to the decline in government spending on affordable housing and to the city of Seattle's threats to impose new taxes on its largest business. That month Microsoft announced a $500 million commitment to help create more affordable housing. The company says that $225 million will go toward preserving and building middle-income housing in six cities near its Redmond, Washington, headquarters, and $250 million will be used for low-income housing in the region.[116] The remaining $25 million will go to local nonprofits working to combat homelessness.[117] Not to be outdone, in June Google announced a $1 billion initiative to support more affordable housing in the San Francisco area.[118] According to the National Low Income Housing Coalition, the federal government spent about one-third as much on housing programs in 2018 as it did in the 1970s. When companies like Microsoft and Google are willing to deploy capital to address low- and middle-income housing needs in areas like Seattle and San Francisco, where ordinary workers are often priced out of the market, this creates opportunities for state and local governments to issue tax-exempt debt to leverage those resources through public-private partnerships. As Matthew Gordon Lasner, a professor of urban studies and planning, told the *New York Times*, Americans are often more comfortable with private-sector solutions, but when it comes to housing, "they're not enough to cope with the challenge," making government action essential.[119] Ironically, on the day that Microsoft announced its pledge, the Department of Housing and Urban Development was closed due to a government shutdown.

State and local policies can succeed and often do, but sometimes they fail. When states and localities offer tax incentives to business to attract jobs to particular areas, they often fare no better than the federal government. A salutary illustration: the New Jersey Economic Development Authority has had little success with its tax incentives, which are supposed to encourage companies to create and retain jobs and revitalize communities. In January 2019 the state comptroller released a performance audit of these programs, which had granted $3.4 billion in tax incentives to 401 projects that were expected to create more than 50,000 new jobs, retain an additional 33,727 jobs, and generate $9.3 billion in capital investments. The comptroller found numerous failures of oversight, monitoring, and compliance reporting. The audit also found overstated job data that had resulted in millions of dollars in overpayments. The number of actual jobs created or retained was uncertain, making it impossible to assess costs versus benefits.[120]

The report recommended twenty-one oversight improvements, some of which might help. but that raises a larger question: When do local incentives to attract private capital succeed? The empirical research on this question reveals that tax incentives are most successful when aimed at small, young firms rather than large, mature ones. The evidence suggests that the jobs created by major firms would have materialized even without tax incentives. The recent research also finds that incentives to attract new capital fare best when they are part of a development strategy that includes policies that support existing local firms and startups.[121]

In short, the politics of place-based policies at the federal level will often produce patronage as well as politically driven efforts like the tax breaks for investments in opportunity zones. Although state and local efforts do not always succeed, they can be more effective at targeting incentives in light of local knowledge, so that the benefits actually reach the intended low- and middle-income residents. Spillover effects for local communities will also more likely be positive, though there is always the concern that rent increases and related gentrification might harm the most vulnerable local populations.[122] State and local governments are better positioned than is the federal government to innovate with place-based policies, but we should not underestimate the barriers to doing so.

Right Policies, Good Politics

A substantially enlarged EITC, major investments in infrastructure, universal adjustment assistance, transforming unemployment insurance into reemployment insurance, a path to stable health insurance for all, more affordable child care, and universal pre-K constitute an ambitious agenda in a today's polarized America. There are, to be sure, many other problems that increase economic insecurity, such as overly punitive and discriminatory criminal law and enforcement, drug addiction without affordable treatment options, domestic violence, and other causes of family dysfunction. Tackling those challenges would take another book.

The policies proposed here are not pie-in-the-sky. We have emphasized fighting economic insecurity by improving opportunities to obtain jobs, making them pay better, and reducing the costs of job transitions and periods of unemployment. The politics will not be easy, but we have identified proximate goals geared to advancing this agenda, latent coalitions that can be built to support them, and realistic approaches to generating the necessary resources. We have also identified moral arguments that creative leaders can deploy to mobilize and expand support. As the constituencies who benefit from these policies grow, those people can be counted on to resist backsliding, taking advantage of the inertia and veto points in the system to protect, entrench, and build on the gains. We have advanced the kind of agenda that John Rawls once dubbed "realistically utopian." It is designed to "extend what are ordinarily thought of as the limits of practical possibility."[123] Unlike Rawls, however, we have also sketched how to achieve proximate goals that can become waystations on a road to a better future. The biggest political challenge is raising the taxes needed to finance these changes.

CHAPTER NINE

Paying for Change—or Not

Creative bond financing, user fees, and public-private partnerships can help fund infrastructure projects, but expanding the EITC, creating universal adjustment assistance, broadening medical insurance coverage, and other measures proposed here will require additional revenue. Where will it come from? Borrowing has been the path of least resistance in Washington since the turn of this century. But with a national debt exceeding $17 trillion in 2020 and annual deficits set to reach $1 trillion in 2020 and to average $1.2 trillion or more for the next decade, that path is not sustainable.[1] The unavoidable conclusion is that funds must be raised through additional taxation. But political leaders in both parties behave as though this is an untouchable third rail in American politics, even though higher taxes would fund spending that they deem essential. How did that happen?

Legacy of the Anti-Tax Movement

The story of how the US became incapable of matching tax revenues to its spending levels would take another book. The short take is that since the late 1970s, anti-tax politics and policies have been the glue that holds the Republican coalition together. When Ronald Reagan was governor of California in 1978, he saw first-hand the political force of the anti-tax movement that added

Proposition 13 to the state's constitution. Upon entering the Oval Office three years later, he was determined to work from that playbook by enacting a major federal tax cut.[2] He succeeded, providing large tax reductions for both individuals and businesses, perhaps most famously reducing the top tax rate from 70 percent first to 50 percent in 1981, then to 28 percent in 1986.

Even more importantly, the 1981 legislation indexed the tax brackets and other important income tax parameters to inflation. This transformed national tax politics. No longer could Washington politicians rely on inflation to move people into higher brackets, and, in turn, increase revenues to finance larger spending or tax cuts. Deprived of these invisible revenue increases, it appeared that Congress would have to raise taxes to fund increased spending. Republicans insisted that, as revenue became inadequate, Congress would have to cut spending. But as Bruce Bartlett has detailed, this "starve the beast" strategy failed dramatically.[3] The federal government simply borrowed more to fund additional spending. In his 2019 book *Fiscal Therapy*, William Gale aptly describes the Republicans' refusal to raise taxes as a watershed in US fiscal history. "Never before," he says, "had intentional policy decisions, not driven by war or depressions, caused a sustained rise in the debt-to-GDP ratio."[4] Keeping the federal deficit and debt under control has been a major challenge ever since.

By 1990 President George H. W. Bush had come to believe that the nation's out-of-control deficits required substantial reduction. But Democratic Senate Majority Leader George Mitchell made it clear that he would only consider significant spending cuts and tighter budget rules if the White House agreed to tax increases. Bush relented. In doing so, he violated his famous "read my lips: no new taxes!" pledge. But he did it because he was convinced that it was the right thing for the country. He also believed—erroneously as it turned out—that his exceptionally strong popularity following the successful US expulsion of Iraq from Kuwait in 1991 might insulate him from the political fallout. Bush failed to win reelection in no small part because he was betrayed by Newt Gingrich, who correctly intuited that by breaking with the president he could fuel his ambition to become the first Republican Speaker of the House in a generation.[5] President Bush gave his Treasury secretary, Nicholas Brady, a signed copy of the 1990 Budget Act with an inscription: "Someday people will understand that we did the right thing."[6] Three decades later, it is hard to find a Republican who does.

In January 1995 Gingrich did indeed become Speaker. Bill Clinton had raised taxes in 1993, again to address deficits—this time with only Democratic votes. The following year the Republicans captured the House of Representatives for the first time since 1954. Since then, the political courage to raise the revenue needed to fund the government's spending has become vanishingly scarce.

By the time of the 2012 election, 238 of the 242 House Republicans, 41 of the 47 Senate Republicans, and many Republican state legislators and governors across America had signed Grover Norquist's "Taxpayer Protection Pledge." They promised not to raise taxes under any circumstances. In 2019, when Donald Trump discussed with House and Senate Democrats a $2 trillion infrastructure initiative to be partially funded by a federal gas tax increase, Norquist was incensed. He warned Trump that if he raised the tax, which hadn't changed since 1993, he would be putting his "fingerprints on the murder weapon" that would kill Republicans' chances in the next election.[7]

When George W. Bush moved into the White House in January 2001, federal revenues were robust because of the deficit-reduction legislation of the previous decade, coupled with the burst of economic growth and the stock market rise of the late

1990s. Federal revenues were at a postwar high of 20.4 percent of GDP, and spending was extraordinarily low at 17.6 percent. The ratio of federal debt to GDP had fallen from nearly 50 percent in the early 1990s to 34 percent in 2000. Government and private economists were predicting surpluses for the next decade and the consequent eradication of the federal debt. Federal Reserve Chairman Alan Greenspan told Congress in March 2001 that all of the federal debt would soon be paid off, and, unless taxes were cut, the federal government would have to start buying corporate stock, an idea that he abhorred.

Then—proving that the apple sometimes falls far from the tree—the second President Bush enacted large tax cuts in 2001 and 2003. Federal revenues fell to 15.6 percent by 2004.[8] In 2003 Bush also proposed, and Congress enacted, an expensive Medicare prescription drug benefit. It was the first time the federal government had instituted a new entitlement without establishing a revenue source to pay for it. In addition, the so-called War on Terror proved expensive, costing nearly $6 trillion between 2001 and 2018.[9] By 2008, the year that Greenspan and other economists had predicted the debt would be paid off, the federal debt was 39 percent of GDP and rising fast because of the recession. In 2012, when the Obama administration agreed to make virtually all of the Bush tax cuts permanent, the ratio of federal debt to GDP had nearly doubled to 70 percent..

Long after it became laughable to claim that starving the beast would keep spending down, Republicans still do all they can to cut taxes and block any and all tax increases.[10] In 2017 Trump and the Republican majorities in Congress enacted another huge tax cut, even though the growing economy did not need stimulus and US public debt relative to the size of the economy was at its highest level since World War II.[11] Unlike the World War II debt, 95 percent of which was owed to Americans, nearly half of today's federal debt is owed to foreigners, not all of whom are interested in boosting the US. At some point, especially when interest rates rise, it will become clear that the US will face strong—perhaps irresistible—pressure to inflate the dollar to pay its debts. Even with the advantages of the world's reserve currency, which make it attractive for foreigners to buy US federal debt, the government can't continue perpetually taking in revenues of 17 percent of GDP while spending in excess of 20 percent of GDP.

Democrats did not adopt the Republicans' adamantine resistance to any and all tax increases. But once Republicans captured the House in the 1994 midterm elections, Democrats became skittish about raising taxes, except on the "rich." The 2008 presidential primary contest between Barack Obama and Hillary Clinton, in which both candidates pledged not to increase any taxes on "people making less than $250,000 a year," solidified Democrats' reluctance. George Stephanopoulos, the ABC debate moderator, recognized the importance of the moment and asked if this was an "absolute, read-my-lips pledge." Both Obama and Clinton answered that it was.[12] In fact, both promised "middle-class" tax cuts. In January 2013 President Obama fulfilled his pledge by extending and making permanent all of the Bush tax cuts of 2001 and 2003 except for those affecting individuals with incomes over $250,000 or wealth exceeding $5 million ($10 million for a married couple).[13] By then raising taxes only on the rich had become orthodoxy in the Democratic Party.

Taxing the Super-Rich?

By 2019 the Democrats' targets had narrowed further, focusing on the very highest levels of income and wealth. In January New York freshman Democratic Representative Alexandria Ocasio-

Cortez proposed to increase the top income tax rate to 70 percent on income that exceeds $10 million a year, an idea that seemed to strike a chord with a majority of Americans.[14] The *Washington Post* estimated that this might raise as much as $720 billion over ten years, but Ocasio-Cortez was not clear whether she meant her proposal to apply only to income ordinarily taxed at the top rate or also to income, such as capital gains, currently taxed at much lower rates.[15] The conservative Tax Foundation estimated that, if the tax hike excluded capital gains, her proposal would raise nearly $300 billion between 2019 and 2029. But if capital gains were included, the measure would lose revenue in the first two years and raise only about $50 billion total over the same period because it would induce a dramatic decline in sales of assets currently eligible for a lower capital gains rate.[16]

The last time the US income tax rates topped out at 70 percent was before Reagan's tax cuts in 1981, and then that rate was easy to avoid.[17] Since 1990 top income tax rates have fluctuated between 31 and 40 percent. In 2019 the top rate was 37 percent. As with French Socialist President François Hollande's ill-fated 2012 effort to assess a 75 percent supertax on incomes above €1 million, Ocasio-Cortez's proposal is unlikely to become law—however much it excites her political base.[18]

Even if, as seems unlikely, a Democratic administration and Congress imposed a 70 percent tax rate on incomes above $10 million, the rate change would not be stable. Effective repeal coalitions, like effective blocking coalitions, are predictable. Combined state and federal income taxes in many states would exceed 80 percent, giving even some liberal Democrats pause. Many Americans who believe that top income tax rates are too low nonetheless believe that the government should not take more than half of a person's earnings. Even the top rate of 40 percent that prevailed under President Clinton and again under President

Obama did not last long. All Republicans will certainly fight such a high rate. Owners of small and medium-size businesses, their financial backers, and their effective lobbies would lead the opposition. Their successes since 2001 in dramatically reducing the federal estate tax—the most progressive US tax and the only federal tax on wealth—demonstrate their political sway.

A few days after Ocasio-Cortez proposed her 70 percent top income tax rate, Massachusetts Democratic Senator Elizabeth Warren advanced an annual 2 percent wealth tax on Americans with net worth above $50 million, 3 percent on net wealth above $1 billion. The tax was designed in part by Emmanuel Saez and Gabriel Zucman, frequent collaborators of Thomas Piketty. Saez and Zucman estimated that the tax would apply to only about 75,000 families, the wealthiest 0.1 percent, and that it would raise revenues equal to 1 percent of GDP annually ($219 billion in 2019). But they assumed that the tax would be comprehensive, without any exceptions, such as for farms or illiquid assets including art and other collectibles. They also assumed that revenues from the tax would grow at 5.5 percent a year. And they assumed that rich people would not substantially evade the tax by changing their residence or citizenship, borrowing to reduce their net worth, making charitable gifts during their lifetimes rather than charitable bequests, transferring assets to future generations through trusts, or via any other method.[19] Finally, Saez and Zucman assumed that wealth would always be taxed at its true value without any discounts for illiquidity or minority shareholding, an assumption belied by experience with local property taxes, the federal estate tax, and wealth taxes elsewhere.[20]

The promise of wealth taxes is oversold. At the turn of the century, ten developed countries had wealth taxes, but in 2019 only three did: Switzerland, Norway, and Spain.[21] Before their repeal, European wealth taxes—with various thresholds, rates, and tax bases—raised about 0.2 percent of GDP. That's about one-fifth the level estimated by Saez and Zucman.[22] Lawrence Summers observed in a *Washington Post* op-ed that he had "often been struck by how much his judgments regarding tax revenue based on published economic statistics have differed from those of professional revenue estimators." He and fellow economist Natasha Sarin estimated that Warren's wealth tax might raise as little as one-eighth of what Saez and Zucman predicted and that a "maximally optimistic" estimate would be 40 percent as much.[23]

Countries with wealth taxes have faced high administrative and compliance costs, as well as difficult controversies over valuations. A 2010 study of OECD countries' wealth taxes also found strong support for the claim that such taxes hamper economic growth.[24] Compliance problems, especially posed by very rich individuals concealing their wealth abroad or changing their residence, no doubt contributed to Piketty's decision to propose a global wealth tax, knowing full well that there is no global government to enact or enforce it.

Wealth is considerably more unequally distributed than income, with the top 10 percent holding about 70 percent of all household wealth and the top 1 percent owning more than the bottom 90 percent.[25] So it is hardly surprising that many liberal Democrats want to raise taxes on wealthy Americans. But from 2001 through 2017, Congress weakened the federal estate tax. In 2000, the tax rate of 55 percent applied to assets above $675,000; by 2018 the rate had dropped to 40 percent and the exemption had been raised to $11.18 million.

We previously have written a book detailing the triumphs of advocates for repeal of the estate tax, explaining how they produced effective and surprising coalitions and moral arguments that merged capitalist economics and the Protestant ethic to emphasize values of thrift and hard work.[26] Democrats found themselves powerless to stop them, even though the tax was paid only by the wealthiest 2 percent of Americans and most of it by the top 1 percent or higher. An annual wealth tax would confront similar arguments, not to mention challenges from Republican state attorneys general, who would argue that it is an unconstitutional, unapportioned "direct" tax.[27] Comparable constitutional challenges to Obamacare were widely dismissed as frivolous, but ultimately proved debilitating to that legislation's goals by reducing the expansions of coverage through Medicaid that Congress had enacted. It is difficult to have confidence that today's even more conservative Supreme Court would uphold an annual federal wealth tax.

Other Approaches

It would be more realistic to tax the receipts of large gifts or bequests as income. Taxing transfers of wealth to recipients at top income tax rates clearly would pass constitutional muster and would deprive its opponents of their most persuasive moral arguments. These recipients of large gifts and bequests neither created the wealth nor saved it. They are not "job creators" but instead beneficiaries of windfalls resulting from luck: they were born into rich families. As Theodore Roosevelt emphasized when he first proposed a tax on inheritances more than a century ago, large inheritances undermine important American commitments to equality of opportunity and against an economic aristocracy.

There are additional ways to increase both income tax revenues and progressivity. The Congressional Budget Office estimates that raising the tax rates on ordinary income in the top two brackets (35 percent and 37 percent) by one percentage point each would raise revenue by $123 billion over ten years. Lifting all brackets by one percentage point would raise $905 billion. Raising the tax rates on dividends and capital gains from their current high of 20 percent to 22 percent would generate about $70 billion more. In fact, the dividend rate could be increased by much more without adverse economic effects. Until 2003, dividends had been taxed at the same rates as ordinary income, but since then they have been taxed at the much lower capital gains rates. The 2017 tax cut legislation reduced the corporate rate from 35 to 15 percent, but it failed to raise the dividend rate and to tax stock buybacks like dividends. Changing the tax treatment of gains on assets transferred at death to match the treatment of gifts would pick up another $105 billion.[28] If gains on assets transferred at death were taxed, instead of forgiven as they now are, the revenue gain would be about six times that amount.

There are also many tax breaks for businesses and their owners that could be eliminated. Real estate businesses and investments are especially favored by rules that allow owners routinely to escape paying income taxes. These include deductions for depreciation even when an asset is increasing in value and the funds to purchase it are borrowed. In addition, it is easy to avoid income tax on gains of sales of real estate as long as the funds are reinvested in other real estate.[29] Hedge fund and private equity managers are permitted to pay tax on their compensation at lower capital gains rates rather than standard income tax rates. This also enables them to avoid paying payroll taxes that fund Medicare. Small business owners, too, can use corporations and partnerships to avoid their share of Medicare and self-employment taxes, costing the Social Security and Medicare Trust funds more than $350 billion per decade.[30] There are also special tax breaks for natural resource exploration and development, credit unions, insurance companies, and large agriculture firms.[31]

Eliminating tax breaks for specific industries would be unlikely to incite opposition from a broad-based business coalition. At a minimum the current write-offs of equipment purchases, which provide tax advantages for robots over workers, could be repealed. Curtailing the various tax benefits could produce many hundreds of billions in additional revenue going forward, and all of the potential changes listed here would increase tax progressivity.

Additional billions could be garnered simply by funding the IRS in a manner that would allow that agency to better collect the taxes that are due. Since 2010 information that reveals potential individual and corporate tax avoidance and evasion has become readily available to the IRS, including much information from abroad. But fewer than 1 in every 161 people was audited in 2017, only 4.4 percent of those with more than $1 million in income.[32] It is the wealthy on whom the IRS should be focusing most of its auditing efforts, since they have the largest amount to hide from the taxman, and the greatest ability to hide it. The IRS is also completely outmanned by private lawyers and accountants when it comes to detecting and investigating tax avoidance by high-income business owners with complex corporate and partnership structures. Every dollar added to the IRS enforcement budget would yield a substantial multiple in additional revenues.

If raising tax income rates is being considered, the emphasis should generally be on individual rather than businesses taxes: higher individual taxes carry fewer disadvantages for the economy's international competitiveness. Broad business tax increases are also harder to enact than cutting back on targeted tax breaks. Moreover, it is important to enlist business participation in coalitions backing the job creation and increased wages essential to enhance economic security.

We have emphasized in this book the impact of globalization and technological change on middle- and low-income families, but those forces have also exerted important influences on income tax systems around the world. Tax reductions for corporations and high-income individuals have occurred throughout the developed world, even where anti-tax attitudes, supply-side economics, and Republican policies favoring the top are absent. Technology and globalization are largely responsible.[33] The movement of capital across borders means that high taxes on business income in one nation tend to shift business activity to countries with lower taxes, often along with attendant jobs. Individual investors, in contrast, are more likely to stay in their country of residence, and any decline in domestic investments by US residents is likely to be offset by increased investments in the US by foreigners.

The Political Power of Concentrated Wealth

In a *New York Times* op-ed published a few days after Alexandria Ocasio-Cortez announced her proposal for a top income tax rate of 70 percent, Saez and Zucman argued that the purpose of such a rate is not to raise revenue but instead to combat extreme concentrations of wealth that distort democratic politics. Just as the point of taxing carbon might be to reduce carbon emissions rather than raise revenue, they argue, the point of high tax rates on "sky-high incomes" is to stop the "oligarchic drift that, if left unaddressed, will continue undermining the social compact and risk killing democracy."[34]

Saez and Zucman make an important point. Faced with economic threats of wage stagnation and job loss from technological innovation and globalization, lower- and middle-income workers have become demoralized and made more insecure because of their lack of political clout. They understand all too well that politicians are responsive to donors and wealthy constituents.[35]

Many commentators attribute this disparity to the destructive system of campaign finance that became entrenched in the United States after a series of constitutional decisions by the Supreme Court beginning in the 1970s that declared money in politics to be the same as speech and therefore protected under the First Amendment.[36] In effect this eliminates any real prospect of shielding our politics from the influence of wealthy donors, except by constitutional amendment or by major changes in the composition of the Court—both of which are at least decades away. That might be why Saez and Zucman are looking to high income tax rates or an annual wealth tax as substitutes. Others are looking to change the rules of corporate governance and antitrust law.[37] Still others are calling for resurrection of the political power of private-sector unions to represent the political, as well as economic, interests of workers.[38] But, whatever their merits might be, income tax hikes, a wealth tax, corporate governance reform, and antitrust law are not up to this task. And restoring the political and economic power of private-sector unions to their 1950s levels is a pipe dream.

Changing the Tax Conversation

The fundamental problem is twofold. First, Republicans refuse to raise any taxes, insisting that all Americans are overtaxed. Second, Democrats now embrace as a nonnegotiable political tenet that all but the very richest Americans are overtaxed. The parties have adopted these dogmas to serve their political ambitions. For the Democrats, it is also a consequence of focusing on inequality—income and wealth at the very top rather than the economic insecurities of the rest. Democrats also obsess about the progressivity of income tax rates while paying less attention to how much

Americans are actually taxed and how the revenue is spent. Taking state taxes into account, the US in 2017 had lower taxes as a share of its economy than any of the thirty-six OECD countries except Chile, Ireland, Mexico, and Turkey. US federal and state taxes combined were about 27 percent of GDP, compared to the OECD average of about 34 percent. And in 2017 the US enacted another large tax cut. It is hardly surprising that other developed countries spend much more on addressing economic insecurity and on infrastructure than the US does.[39]

Moreover, in other countries that provide considerably more economic security to their low- and middle-income residents and more progressive spending policies than the United States, taxes are often less progressive. This is the case even when their top income tax rates are higher.[40] In the Nordic countries, for example, top income tax rates of up to 60 percent kick in at about $60,000 to $70,000 of income.[41] A national tax on domestic consumption of goods and services—a value-added tax (VAT) or, as it is sometimes called, a goods-and-services tax—helps finance public spending. The details are often complex, but a VAT is essentially a sales tax with collections before the retail level. The tax is now often imposed at rates from 20 to 25 percent. The US is the only OECD country without such a tax, which can be found in nearly 170 countries worldwide. Sales taxes and VATs can be regressive, but there are many techniques for protecting low- and moderate-income workers from the effects.[42]

In 1955 the liberal lion John Kenneth Galbraith explained in *The Affluent Society* why liberals should support a VAT, an explanation that is hard to improve on more than sixty years later. Galbraith regarded promises to concentrate taxes on people with extraordinarily high incomes or wealth as a classic liberal mistake. The "rational liberal," Galbraith said, "will not hesitate to accept [tax] increases that are neutral as regards the distribution of income." Otherwise, Galbraith explained, the needs for "pressing public services" and the "poverty of people, which can only be corrected at increased public costs, must wait while we debate the ancient and unresolvable question of whether the rich are too rich." A liberal who insists that any tax increase be carried more than proportionately by the higher income brackets in effect becomes "a co-conspirator with the conservative in reducing taxes." "Meanwhile," he added, "the individuals with whom he sympathizes and whom he seeks to favor . . . would be among the first beneficiaries of the better education, health, housing, and other services," which would result from adopting a sales tax. Arguing for a national sales tax to fund a list of community improvements, Galbraith noted that his kind of tax "has been recommended for years by the most impeccable of conservatives." Indeed, even the National Association of Manufacturers supported a sales tax—a "blessing from those who speak with the prestige of producers." He concluded, "As a political point, this is not negligible."[43]

In 2019 liberal economist Leonard Burman proposed an 11 percent VAT to fund a universal wage subsidy of 100 percent of up to $10,000 of earnings and to increase refundable tax credits for children. Burman's wage subsidy and child credit proposals are closely related to the expansions of the EITC we recommend in chapter 5, but his subsidy would be available to all individuals without any ceiling on eligible wages. Burman analogized his proposal for using a dedicated flat-rate consumption tax to fund increased wages to Franklin Roosevelt's decision to fund Social Security with a flat-rate payroll tax. Using modern economic tools, Burman demonstrates that although his VAT is regressive, his overall proposal is quite progressive. The wage subsidies and child credits that low- and-middle income workers would receive are much greater than the new taxes they would pay. Burman estimates that under his proposal the bottom 80 percent would see an increase in their after-tax incomes, while the top 20 percent would face an additional burden of almost 5 percent of their after-tax income and the top 1 percent just over 7 percent more. Burman estimates that his 11 percent VAT would raise more than $11 trillion in its first decade. The Congressional Budget Office apparently agrees.[44]

CBO has also estimated the revenue potential of other options that have been proposed by some legislators. Among these are a $25-per-metric-ton carbon tax, which would translate into about a 25-cents-per-gallon increase in the gasoline tax, some electricity price increases, and about $1.1 trillion in revenue over ten years. Another possibility is an annual fee of 0.15 percent of the liabilities of banks operating in the US with assets of $250 million or more. This would raise about $90 billion over the same period. Finally a tax of 0.1 percent of the value of traded securities, including payments for derivatives, would raise $776.7 billion by 2028.[45] CBO also describes potential increases in the federal share of unemployment taxes, along the lines we suggest in chapter 6.

These three possibilities might enjoy some political advantages over a broad-based VAT. A carbon tax is widely seen as an essential element of any program to battle climate change by reducing fossil fuel consumption and would likely enjoy support from a coalition of environmental groups and businesses, including businesses with stakes in clean energy.[46] If a carbon tax were accompanied by the reduction of some environmental regulations, it might garner support from representatives of oil and gas companies and utilities. This would be a delicate project, though. Any regulatory rollbacks must be carefully designed so as not to threaten support from environmental organizations.

Likewise, a tax on financial institutions based on their liabilities would not likely induce opposition from other industries. It might win public support as payback for the risk-taking that led to the financial crisis. Again, blocking coalitions might be weakened or avoided if some burdensome regulations were simultaneously reduced. The tax on financial trading has the advantage of targeting the same industry, and especially short-term or high-volume traders. Its economic impact at a very low rate would be slight, given the large drops in trading transactions costs that have occurred in recent decades. The concern that will generate opposition from Wall Street is that trading will simply move offshore to avoid the tax, vitiating both its benefits and its potential revenue. But that risk might be manageable at a 0.1 percent rate, and European countries have also been considering such a tax.

The revenues from such sources should be earmarked for financing the kinds of economic security protections proposed here. Not only would that address progressivity concerns, but earmarked taxes also are more popular with the public. After all, referendums to fund infrastructure improvements using sales taxes have frequently been successful. History also suggests that earmarked taxes are often more difficult to cut or repeal.

Given almost unanimous Republican resistance to any tax increases, there is no doubt that it will be challenging to enact any of these new taxes. The tax law adopted in 2017 already has additional future tax cuts built in. The 2017 budget resolution required tax cuts not to exceed $1.5 trillion over ten years in order to be enacted through "reconciliation," a procedure that allowed the tax legislation to pass the Senate with only fifty-one votes. As with the George W. Bush tax cuts in 2001, Congress in 2017 enacted sunsets of tax cuts that dramatically understate their likely real revenue costs. Expirations of the tax cuts scheduled between 2020 and the end of 2025 would cost almost another $1.5 trillion to maintain for another decade, and nearly one-third of those tax increases would be paid by families below the top quintile of income. Federal deficits of more than $1 trillion are anticipated for every year after 2019. Unsurprisingly, the fastest growth in future spending will be interest on the federal debt, rising from 1.6 percent of GDP in 2018 to 6.7 percent in 2050 and accounting for 69 percent of all projected spending increases as a share of GDP.[47] Much of that interest will go to foreigners, so there is little reason to believe that it will be ploughed back into the US economy. Republican deficit hawks like retired Senator Bob Corker of Tennessee, who had vowed that he would not vote for any tax legislation if it "added one penny to the deficit," became hummingbirds when the tax cut legislation came up for a vote. Corker later confessed that if the law ends up costing what CBO predicts, "it could well be one of the worst votes I've made."[48] It was. The 2017 tax reductions, along with the subsequent tax cuts built into that law, amplify the daunting challenges of raising adequate revenue. Redirecting the tax conversation away from a myopic focus on the progressivity of income tax rates to funding a fiscal system that will be progressive in its effects is vital.

Costs of Failing to Act

But it will not be enough. In 1976 Herb Stein—who had chaired the Council of Economic Advisors for Presidents Nixon and Ford—announced what has become known as Stein's Law: "If something cannot go on forever, it will stop." But stopping the ongoing tax cuts and raising revenues to fund the expenditures necessary to alleviate economic insecurity will take unusual political courage and leadership. In the absence of a crisis, political courage is rare—often vanishingly rare. If Democrats achieve control of the White House and Congress, it might become possible to raise taxes to fund a more robust EITC, universal adjustment assistance, more affordable child care, infrastructure improvements, and better health coverage. Short of full Democratic control, change is unlikely until our chronic fiscal problems turn into another full-blown crisis. But then it might be too late.

Businesses lobbyists will resist corporate income tax rate increases, but business has every reason to support a VAT or a carbon tax to fund important enhancements to economic security. If there is no threat of a broad-based increase in business taxes, there is no reason for businesses and their advocacy organizations to form blocking coalitions. Indeed, business leaders should see that it is in their interest to go further. They should build and sustain coalitions with organizations that advocate for poor and middle-income families to advance the kinds of proposals we have advocated here. The moral imperative for addressing economic insecurity is clear.

Finally, several commentators have noted that in areas such as information technology, pharmaceuticals, defense, aviation, space exploration, and green-energy innovation, the government often makes high-risk upfront investments from which private companies derive substantial profits—in effect having taxpayers pay for the greatest risks and privatizing the rewards. One conspicuous example is computer technology. As economist Mariana Mazzucato has documented, every component of the iPhone and the internet technology on which it depends was developed in government-funded labs or otherwise underwritten by the government. Steve Jobs's fame as an innovative entrepreneur notwithstanding, his genius actually was seeing new ways to integrate these technologies into user-friendly applications and products.[49] Mazzucato proposes that the government take a small equity share in companies that commercialize technologies that it funds. Others have echoed her arguments, proposing that governments take royalties from companies that profit from public investments. For a long time, the US has done just this with natural resources developed on federal lands. Singapore and other countries have also earned returns on their investments in resources and technologies exploited by private firms, without paying any measurable efficiency costs.[50] Royalties and equity shares offer the possibility of revenue: returns on taxpayers' investments, while bypassing the difficulties associated with taxing multinationals that have been able to shift profits around to avoid paying.

When he was a political advisor to Bill Clinton, James Carville famously remarked that he would like to be reincarnated as the bond market because the bond market can intimidate anyone. The underlying idea, which had currency in the 1990s and was integral to the economic dogma of the Clinton administration, was that pressure from the markets would curb reckless economic behavior by politicians. But the bond markets seem to have taken this century's deterioration of the US government's financial position with hardly a ruffle. Perhaps someday they will move with a vengeance to confirm Stein's law, and an economic crisis will prompt action. But that kind of reckoning might be remote. In the meantime, debt financing will remain on the table. This is clearly the case for funding infrastructure as we saw in chapter 7. As long as interest rates remain relatively low, additional debt finance might remain viable for a time.[51] But without a new source of revenue, this is just kicking the can down the road. The status quo is untenable.

CHAPTER TEN

The Wages of Insecurity

Capital in the Twenty-First Century has been the most widely discussed work of political economy in a generation. Thomas Piketty chronicles and purports to explain the growth in inequality over the past four decades across the industrialized world, and his message is as memorable as it is concise: the rich get richer than everyone else because the returns to capital exceed the rate of economic growth and therefore the returns to labor. Over time, the advantages of wealth cumulate. His argument has provoked blizzards of commentary about whether and to what extent those in the top 1 percent, or an even smaller subgroup, actually are accumulating more income and wealth than everyone else, and, if so, whether Piketty is right about why this is happening. The debates turn on abstruse challenges to measuring pre- and post-tax income in various countries, whose tax systems have evolved over time.[1] The results depend on what forms of compensation count as income; which measures of inflation one uses; how inheritances are divided; and what counts as causing or contributing to economic growth over time. These debates will not be resolved any time soon. They are not our subject.

What matters here is that Piketty and the debate he has spawned divert the spotlight from the concerns of most people on the wrong side of globalization and the technological revolution: job insecurity, the prospect of downward mobility for themselves and their children, and perceptions of local injustice that matter much more to tens of millions of alienated voters than what is or is not happening with the top 1 percent. Piketty's proposals to redress the growth of inequality are also distractions. In his book he recommends a global wealth tax; more recently, he has promoted a transnational European assembly armed with taxing and redistributive powers. Both ideas are so utterly deaf to anything that is feasible politically that it is hard to take them seriously.[2] This is not to gainsay the sense of urgency that motivates his advocacy. But debating his analysis and his proposals shifts attention away from finding viable ways to address the inequalities and insecurities fueling the populist politics that Piketty rightly fears.

Inequalities that Matter Most

In a video that went viral in April 2013, Dutch ethologist Frans de Waal vividly demonstrates capuchin monkeys' resentment of unequal treatment. The monkeys are part of an experiment. To get a reward, they must carry a rock from one portal to another, taking it from and then handing it back to the lab technician. In the key demonstration, a pliant capuchin is initially content to perform the task in return for a chunk of cucumber. But once he sees the capuchin in the next cage being rewarded for the same task with a more desirable grape, he becomes enraged. He hurls the cucumber at the researcher and refuses to perform the task in return for the compensation that previously had satisfied him. "That's the Wall Street Protester!" De Waal comments at the end of the demonstration, bringing down the house as the aggrieved capuchin pounds furiously on the side of his cage.[3] A similar response to inequality has been found in many other social animals.

The capuchin monkey's fury is suggestive, but de Waal—like many who are outraged by Piketty's findings about the top

1 percent—draws the wrong conclusion from his demonstration. To be sure, the capuchin's impulse and behavior are all too recognizably human; one has only to think of the child who is happy with a cracker but becomes resentful when his sibling gets a cookie. But that's the point: like the angry capuchin, the child is upset by being treated differently than someone he regards as his peer. After all, the monkey is not troubled by the fact that the lab technician has bowls of both cucumbers and grapes in plain view. What bothers him is that a capuchin just like him is getting better rewarded for the same task. The real question about the Wall Street protesters, with their singular focus on investment bankers, is whether they are typical of most people. The evidence suggests that generally they are not.

People do care what others have, but this has more to do with local comparisons than beliefs about the fairness of the overall distribution of income and wealth. A college professor might be irked to learn that she is paid $500,000 less than the attorney who lives next door, but she will be seriously upset if she finds she's paid $10,000 less than the professor of comparable rank in the next office. Up and down the occupational scale, people make comparisons to others similarly situated. When women object to earning less than men, they focus on gender-based salary gaps in similar jobs: "equal pay for equal work!" Understanding the inequalities that people regard as unfair requires knowing what their reference group is. It is all about "choosing the right pond," as one scholar of status markets famously put it.[4] Karl Marx believed that this reference group would expand, that workers would eventually start comparing their share of the wealth they produce to the share that capitalists get.[5] But Marx's expectation that this would radicalize workers seems to have gone the way of his other predictions: people continue making more local comparisons.

Nowhere is this more true than with the white working-class voters Arlie Hochschild studied in Louisiana. They were profoundly aggrieved, but their central complaints had nothing to do with global inequality or resentment of the wealthy. Rather, their complaints were rooted in the humiliation they experienced from losing their jobs and needing public support—support doled out by officials these voters resented for their job security and perhaps also because of their race. The grievances that did have a distributive edge stemmed from the belief that their misfortunes were due to "cutting in" on the part of unspecified others. This captured their understanding of affirmative action. Of course, this policy was itself redressing previous unfair advantages of a different sort— "when affirmative action was white," as Ira Katznelson puts it—but their anger was no less potent politically for that fact.[6] However inaccurately, they were convinced that others were getting ahead in ways that were pushing them back in line. They were unconcerned with what people at the top of the income distribution were getting. If the wealthiest 1 percent bothered them at all, they did not talk about it with Hochschild enough for her to report it.

Falling and the Fear of It

Perceived cutting in is doubly aggravating. As well as feeding the belief that someone less deserving than you is being rewarded at your expense, the notion of cutting in assumes that you are being deprived of something that is—or otherwise would have been— yours. We now know that loss aversion is a more powerful motivator of human action than is the prospect of gain. People react more strongly to losing a dollar than they do to foregoing the possibility of getting one.[7] There are many theories about why this is so. Perhaps the most convincing is that for millennia humans lived so close to the edge of survival that even a small loss might well have been catastrophic. Whatever the explanation, the finding is robust, and it is no longer limited—if ever it was—to people at or near starvation. This is closely related to what behavioral economists describe as the endowment effect: the widespread finding that people will pay more to keep something that they own than to gain that same thing if they don't already own it, and that they will often decline to trade something they have been given for something else of the same or even greater value.[8] The bottom line is that we don't like losing things that we have or believe we are rightfully going to have. Even comparatively wealthy people will balk at the prospect of losing $40,000 a year in Social Security benefits if the program were to be abolished. They can therefore be counted on as part of a blocking coalition against efforts to abolish or undermine it.

Understanding endowment effects and loss aversion also makes it easier to know which voters are available for mobilization by populist politicians. Since the 2016 election, widespread assertions that Trump voters were overwhelmingly working class have been debunked. About a third of his supporters in the Republican primaries earned less than $50,000 a year, the national median, but a third made between $50,000 and $100,000 and another third more than $100,000. "If being working class means being in the bottom half of the income distribution," Nicholas Carnes and Noam Lupu note, then most of Trump's supporters in the primaries were not working class. In the general election, too, only about 35 percent of his supporters made less than the median income. Moreover, while 70 percent of Trump primary voters lacked college degrees, the same was true of voters for all Republican primary candidates. Sixty-nine percent of his supporters in the general election lacked college degrees, but 60 percent of the total still earned more than the median income.[9] Their relative lack of education did not necessarily mark them as working class, even if it did not immunize them from the snobbery and derision of elites.

What matters is not so much where voters lie in the overall income distribution as whether they are experiencing or worrying about losses. The most telling political effect of globalization and technological change is that so many Americans are in this position. In one 2019 poll conducted for the World Economic Forum, almost two-thirds of US respondents said it was no longer commonly the case that hard work proved to be a path from poverty to prosperity. And only 10 percent regarded successful bootstrapping as extremely common. The expectation that hard work would lead to advancement was higher in many developing countries.[10] Some of this loss of faith in the possibility of advancement stems from decades of wage stagnation or even falling real incomes, often resulting in the need to add a second earner or a second job to make a family's ends meet. Lost confidence is also traceable to flat or downward mobility, as people are forced to trade jobs that are highly esteemed by their peers for those that are less so—often from skilled or semi-skilled occupations to lower-skilled service work. People who once designed and built things and had achieved seniority and status in their companies over many years do not like admitting to their neighbors that they are now telemarketing, flipping burgers, or working menial shifts at the local hospital. Job insecurity is made worse by the change from lifetime employment, once frequently protected by union contracts, to the contemporary world in which there is high employee turnover and increased reliance on "self-employed" contractors even by large industrial corporations.

The shift from a world of lifetime employees to temporary or contract workers need not intimidate people on the winning side of the technological revolution. Young graduates from top universities with good informational and other technical skills might pull a three-year stint at McKinsey or bounce through a few startups before settling on another lucrative job or enterprise. Or perhaps in their late twenties they will return to school for an MBA and network their way more deeply into the webs of opportunity that structure modern economies. For these people, the prospect of changing jobs multiple time over a working life may seem less a threat than an empowering source of freedom. Their principal asset is the human capital that they have the wherewithal to market and replenish to create their own security, while they accumulate retirement savings and other financial assets. For them, "independent contractor" is a badge of their success and independence. They achieve favorable economic prospects along with a measure of freedom that has seldom been available to anyone in human history.

But for those on the losing side of the tech revolution, "independent contractor" is a euphemism for perpetual vulnerability. They might be hired for relatively brief periods on term contracts to meet the ever-changing needs of companies or even become seasonal workers. Lacking the leverage to negotiate health insurance, retirement, or other benefits, they are price takers in relatively low-skilled labor markets in which they can easily be replaced and from which unions have all but disappeared. Even if reasonably well compensated when they work, this new "precariat" of permanently insecure workers is unlikely to age well.[11] They lack the wherewithal to self-insure against an unexpected illness or to build a nest egg for secure retirement. They have to run as long as they can on treadmills that they did not design and cannot control. Eventually they will fall off for good, discarded by the relentless logic of creative destruction. Increasingly, they know this is coming and fear it.

Blindsided as many were by these developments, they had been forecast—and not just by the likes of Patrick Buchanan, who has been beating his anti-elitist and nativist drums on cable television to little effect since his failed bids for the presidency in the last century.[12] In 1998 liberal philosopher Richard Rorty warned that sooner or later blue-collar workers would realize "that their government is not even trying to prevent wages from sinking or to prevent jobs from being exported" and that "suburban white-collar workers—themselves desperately afraid of being downsized—are not going to let themselves be taxed to provide social benefits for anyone else." At that point, Rorty predicted, "something will crack. The nonsuburban electorate will decide that the system has failed and start looking for a strongman to vote for—someone willing to assure them that, once he is elected, the smug bureaucrats, tricky lawyers, overpaid bond salesmen, and postmodernist professors will no longer be calling the shots."[13]

What Businesses Should Fear

We saw in chapter 4 that the New Deal's success was partly due to the forbearance of powerful business elites, who did not often join blocking coalitions against the legislation's major social protection provisions. Many business interests supported New Deal policies, at least tacitly, and some did so actively. This was partly motivated by the need to combat the economic ravages of the depression.[14] But the economic considerations were leavened by the fear that millions of vulnerable or unemployed workers might conclude, as Marx and Engels had hoped they would almost a century earlier, that they had nothing to lose but their chains.[15] The totalitarian realities of Stalinism and the Soviet Union's sclerotic inefficiency were not yet common knowledge, and communist-influenced trade unions—particularly in the CIO— were competing for the hearts and minds of American workers. Business elites had good political reasons to support basic social protections for workers who might otherwise become radicalized.

These incentives looked very different after the Soviet empire's collapse between 1989 and 1991 and the subsequent demise of orthodox communist economic models in countries, like China and Vietnam, that remained nominally Marxist. The 1990s and 2000s, until disaster struck, were a period of unprecedented confidence in capitalist democracy, which seemed not only to be secure but also spreading to much of the developing world. By the turn of the century, the number of democracies in the world exceeded nondemocracies for the first time in human history. And if some countries resisted democratization, capitalism was surely on the march, pulling hundreds of millions out of poverty in Asia and Latin America, with Africa seemingly next. Inequality was growing within the developed Western countries, but it was declining worldwide.[16] There seemed little cause to challenge the policy trifecta of freer trade, deregulation, and privatization that came to be known at home as neoliberalism or, when preached to the developing world or insisted upon as a condition for aid and foreign investment, the Washington consensus.

It was not all plain sailing, to be sure. Latin America spent much of the 1990s recovering from the debt crises of the 1980s, which erupted again in 1995, with Mexico needing a $50 billion IMF bailout of its peso and Argentina collapsing into a full-scale depression at the end of the decade. Financial crises in Thailand, Indonesia, and South Korea took the gloss off the Asian Tiger narrative in 1997. Russia defaulted the following year; the dot-com bubble burst two years after that; and then Argentina defaulted on $132 billion of debt—a seventh of the money borrowed by the entire developing world. But these events, while serious, were managed and contained. Few saw systemic threats on the horizon. The terrorist attacks of September 11, 2001 shook the confidence of some in the West about what Francis Fukuyama, among others, had heralded as a benign end of history.[17] But whatever challenge the rise of militant Islam might pose to Western democratic institutions, it was notably devoid of an alternative to capitalism.

Where Islamist governments had come to power in countries like Iran and Afghanistan, they just ran their economies badly. Capitalism reigned supreme, and along with it came a widespread consensus that Western technocrats knew how to manage it successfully—smoothing the peaks and troughs of the business cycle into a "great moderation," as Federal Reserve governor and future chairman Ben Bernanke declared in 2004.[18]

Harvard President Lawrence Summers exemplified the brimming mainstream confidence in this consensus the following year at the annual Jackson Hole meeting of top central bankers and economists. As President Clinton's Treasury secretary, Summers had pushed hard for passage of the Gramm-Leach-Bliley bill that in 1999 repealed key provisions of the Glass-Steagall Act of 1933, which had separated the activities of commercial and investment banks. Summers heralded Gramm-Leach-Bliley as "historic legislation that will better enable American companies to compete in the new economy.[19] He did not even try to conceal his irritation when Chicago economist Raghuram Rajan sounded alarm at unprecedented levels of intermediation by financial institutions, which facilitates transactions but also potentially increases appetite for risk.[20] Dismissing Rajan as a Luddite, Summers upbraided him for having the temerity to provoke ignorant lawmakers who might create troublesome new regulations.[21]

Perhaps the most dramatic indicator of the breadth of this confident consensus was the degree to which parties of the traditional left embraced it. Tony Blair's New Labour shed Clause IV of its constitution that had called for widespread nationalization, granted operational independence to the Bank of England, and continued Margaret Thatcher's commitments to deregulation and privatization. Bill Clinton's New Democrats made comparable triangulating moves, embracing fiscal discipline and reducing welfare benefits in 1996. Germany's Social Democrats behaved similarly under Gerhard Schröder, adopting the business-friendly Hartz IV Reforms in 2003.[22] Rather than argue the merits of social democracy and mixed economies, these leaders concluded that their only viable path to winning and retaining power was to show that they could manage capitalism at least as well as—and, they argued, better than—center-right parties. To differentiate themselves electorally, they turned instead to cultural issues: abortion, gender equality, gay rights, and multicultural identity politics. There were quibbles over the levels and progressivity of marginal tax rates, but questioning the merits of managed capitalism was off the table almost everywhere.

Overwhelming confidence in the government's ability to manage a neoliberal order that faced no competitive threat was bound to engender complacency. The path of least resistance, reinforced by the increasing geographic stratification of urban life that Douglas Rae has dubbed "segmented democracy," was to move to the suburbs, sometimes behind gates, where those left behind were out of sight—and also out of mind.[23] Potentially troublesome populations were dealt with by an increasingly punitive criminal justice system. America's imprisoned population more than quadrupled from about half a million in 1980 to more than 2.2 million in 2015, largely due to the war on drugs, mandatory minimum sentencing, and habitual-offender laws that mandated life sentences upon a third felony conviction.[24] These "three-strikes" laws, adopted in more than half of the states, were added to the federal system by the Clinton administration in 1994—another way in which Democrats felt it more important to mimic Republicans than to differentiate themselves.[25]

The complacent consensus was not shattered even by the crisis of 2008. Franklin Roosevelt had refused to endorse Herbert Hoover's emergency economic measures during the four-month interregnum between his election in November of 1932 and his inauguration the following March, but candidate Barack Obama endorsed the Bush administration's decision and agreed with Democrats in Congress to infuse up to $700 billion into the banking system in September 2008.[26] Once in office, the new president accepted the arguments of Summers, then director of the National Economic Council, and Treasury Secretary Timothy Geithner, who said the Obama administration should continue working with Wall Street insiders to resolve the crisis. Working together turned out to include allowing AIG to pay $165 million in bonuses to its executives, even though the company needed a $182 billion bailout for what Federal Reserve Chairman Ben Bernanke had denounced as its reckless use of credit default swaps to boost profits.[27] Summers and Geithner insisted that the alternative would be a systemic failure that would usher in another Great Depression. Those advocating a more aggressive response that would have held banking elites culpable were ignored, so much so that even the bankers were surprised by how little was demanded of them.[28]

But the complacent technocrats in both parties were flouting the simmering voter rage that would erupt with a vengeance eight years later. There had been ominous signs from the start. Early versions of the bank bailout bill provoked furious voter backlash in many constituencies. Even once modifications guaranteeing additional oversight and transparency had been added, bipartisan agreements between House leadership and members came unstuck, and the bill was initially voted down. Democrat Lloyd Doggett objected that the oversight rules would hand sweeping new powers to an administration that was responsible for allowing the crisis to develop. Republican Jeb Hensarling denounced the modified bailout bill as "the slippery slope to socialism" that would leave taxpayers responsible for "the mother of all debt."[29] Main street and rural Republicans refused to vote for the final bill, leaving President Bush humiliatingly dependent on Democrats in both Houses to pass it.[30]

Rick Santelli's rant on the Chicago Mercantile Exchange that allegedly inspired the Tea Party had focused on the moral hazard of helping out underwater home owners with taxpayer dollars, but moral hazard was also at hand in bailing out financial institutions without holding their executives to account. Even for Americans who don't care about overall inequality, shelling out billions of dollars to protect the salaries and bonuses of manifestly culpable executives is another matter. In 2015 and 2016, first Bernie Sanders and then Donald Trump mobilized this rage at financial elites by attacking Hillary Clinton for her close association with Goldman Sachs—epitomized by private speeches delivered at the company's request (she refused to release the transcripts), for which she had reputedly been paid hundreds of thousands of dollars. In January 2016 Goldman paid $5 billion to resolve claims that it had engaged in deceptive marketing and sold faulty mortgage securities to its clients in the run-up to the crisis. Secretary Clinton might as well have penned Trump's "Crooked Hillary!" narrative herself.

By 2016 it was clear that the financial crisis had left the technocratic consensus in political tatters. Three weeks before the Brexit referendum in late June, Tory Justice Minister and Brexiteer Michael Gove declared that "people in this country have had enough of experts."[31] Gove's comment quickly went viral, underscoring the political mileage that could be garnered from attacking establishment elites as incompetent or even corrupt. Candidate Trump worked from the same playbook, seldom missing opportunities to attack America's leaders for being self-dealing fools. As conservative commentator Tucker Carlson crowed in the wake of Trump's unexpected victory, "Trump's election wasn't about Trump. It was a throbbing middle finger in the face of America's ruling class. It was a gesture of contempt, a howl of rage, the end result of decades of selfish and unwise decisions made by selfish and unwise leaders. Happy countries don't elect Donald Trump," Carlson continued, "desperate ones do."[32]

It is this rage and desperation that business elites should fear. The complacency that prevailed from the Great Moderation into the financial crisis blinded too many to the reality that desperate people do desperate things. The US and UK votes in 2016 provided the wakeup call that the people left behind by globalization and the technological revolution are every bit as threatening to well-functioning democratic capitalism as their predecessors were in the early 1930s, despite the current absence of a communist or any other alternative regime vying for their allegiance. Falling or stagnant incomes, insecurity about jobs and social status, and resentment of self-dealing elites make for a potent brew in which populist politics easily thrive. In its right-wing forms, populism combines trade protectionism with anti-immigrant xenophobia, both of which undermine healthy economies by subsidizing inefficiency and distorting labor markets. Left-wing populism also breeds demands for damaging protectionism, usually along with pressure for tax regimes that hamper competitiveness. High corporate taxes make for one of the easiest political sells to voters who believe they have been shafted by multinational corporations.

The longer it takes economic elites to learn that insecurity breeds populism—and the longer it takes them to internalize the implications of this lesson—the more costly the results will be. There will surely be growing pressure for mandated minimum or living wages, stronger protections for workers in vanishing jobs, limits to immigration that might be beneficial in many sectors, and perhaps even modern variants of machine-breaking as jobs keep disappearing to technology. Businesses will likely find themselves paying more for health insurance and facing more demands for paid family leave, child care facilities, and payments for transition relief when they fire employees or outsource production.

For reasons we have advanced throughout this book, relying on employer-based protections is second- or even third-best policy and fosters economic risks that could and should be avoided. But employer-based protections offer the substantial political advantage of requiring neither additional taxes nor spending, and so all too easily become the path of least resistance for beleaguered or opportunistic politicians.

Yet considerably more than the US economy and US politics are on the line, even if many among America's business and professional elites do not yet realize it. Adam Tooze has recently documented the hitherto unappreciated extent to which the Federal Reserve bailed out not only the US economy during the financial crisis but also the rest of the world. The Fed poured trillions of dollars into European and Asian economies to prevent a catastrophic global collapse.[33] It is hard to imagine the Fed having the political leeway to take comparable action to head off another crisis of that magnitude until the anxieties that are fueling populist rage at home are addressed.

Similarly, vital aspects of international relations are now at risk from populism. Like fish who cannot see the water they are swimming in, we take the goods and services of the international system for granted, but now we are poised to lose them. Robert Kagan has forcefully reminded us that for decades the US underwrote a fragile global order through NATO and other alliances, ensuring that economic competition among the major capitalist powers did not metastasize into war, as happened so often in the past.[34] As Kagan, Tooze, and other students of international relations have long understood, the world's dominant powers historically have found it worthwhile to bear the costs of providing global public goods that otherwise will not be sustained.[35] America's retreat from this role, which began with Obama and accelerated under

Trump, will also not reverse until the domestic forces that fuel our new brand of America Firstism are addressed.

Populists on the left and the right agree that domestic politics are rigged against middle-class Americans who have little or no sway over what policies are enacted. Among Hillary Clinton's problems in 2016 was that many voters, as well as Sanders, believed that the nominating contest was rigged in her favor. As it turns out, they were right.[36] The political science literature also confirms that policymaking is rigged against ordinary Americans. Martin Gilens and Benjamin Page have shown that support for a legislative proposal among average Americans has no effect on its potential for being adopted.[37] Research by Larry Bartels reaches similar conclusions.[38] Yet these scholars have found that economic elites and organized business interests have a substantial impact on US public policy, as have we.[39] The accurate perception that the system is rigged eats away at the legitimacy of a political order that business elites have too long taken for granted.

Yet until now American business leaders and organizations have showed few signs of advancing or supporting the kinds of policies we have argued for in this book. The diminished scope and power of unions and the demise of any serious communist or even socialist challenge have made any threats that might be thought to emanate from such quarters seem hollow. Right-wing populism, such as that fostered by the Tea Party after 2009, has not been hostile to business interests outside the financial sector, supplying business leaders with few reasons to worry. But alarming winds of change are blowing. In Europe populist parties and groups like the Five Star Movement and the League in Italy and the French Yellow Vests are furiously hostile to technocratic management of the status quo. They also are hard to locate on a left-right continuum, so the political causes for which they might be mobilized are difficult to predict. But these challenges are unlikely to be sanguine from the standpoint of business.

The economic insecurity that fueled much of the rage behind Donald Trump's election has shaken the complacency of some business leaders. One 2017 McKinsey survey of some 300 executives from companies with more than $100 million in annual revenues found that 62 percent believe they will have to replace or retrain more than a quarter of their workforce before 2023. Seventy percent of executives at companies with more than $500 million in annual revenues see technological disruption affecting more than a quarter of their workers by then. Yet these numbers have yet to be translated into meaningful action. The same report notes that public spending on labor-force training and support has fallen steadily for years in most OECD countries and in the US. And even though 66 percent of the executives surveyed regard improving workers' technical skills as a top-ten priority, and 30 percent include it in their top five, American businesses have yet to substantially increase their commitments to employee training budgets. Nor have they attempted to muster support for effective policies to combat the scourge of economic insecurity.[40]

This is not to say that business is universally tone deaf to the policies that would actually work. People like JP Morgan Chase CEO Jamie Dimon and Berkshire Hathaway's Warren Buffett have endorsed major expansions of the EITC and reemployment training.[41] But these are rather isolated voices. Like the Republican political establishment, the bulk of America's corporate elites have gone along with Trump's agenda. They tut-tut at his trade wars and xenophobia while lapping up the tax cuts that—as with the squandering of the corporate tax reform dividend that might have been spent on infrastructure—have made it harder to advance the kinds of policies called for here. For the most part, concerned business leaders such as George Soros and the Koch brothers have limited themselves to contributing to their preferred candidates' campaigns. As Jane Mayer reminds us in *Dark Money*, many billions in resources are being invested in causes that push in the wrong direction.[42] This is to say nothing of the conceit that the answer to America's challenges might be staring at business elites from the bathroom mirror, as Howard Schultz, Mark Cuban, Tom Steyer, and other moguls thought in the run-up to 2020 presidential election.[43]

To be sure, some wealthy business leaders have engaged in productive philanthropic efforts. Mark Zuckerberg's venture with the Newark schools might have been ill-conceived, but others have done better. Jeff Bezos, Amazon CEO and the world's richest person, has pledged $2 billion to fund preschool for low-income families and fight homelessness. That comes on top of close to $100 million he spent on these causes by 2019.[44] Michael Dell of Dell Technologies has committed over $1.2 billion to health care and education, subsidizing public schools, supplementary tutoring programs for poor children, and college tuition.[45] Bridgewater founder Ray Dalio has committed $100 million to Connecticut's schools, and Robert F. Smith of Vista Equity Partners promised to pay off the student loans of Morehouse College's class of 2019.[46] Others could surely be named.

But no matter how well-meaning or generous, philanthropy cannot address the pervasive economic risks and insecurities we have discussed here. Michael Bloomberg noted as much when announcing his $1.8 billion pledge to make admission to Johns Hopkins, his alma mater, need-blind. It was the largest donation to a college ever, but Bloomberg made clear that personal philanthropy is impotent to fight a $1.8 trillion student debt problem. That, he argued, will take major government commitments.[47]

Some executives ignore the reality that philanthropy is no substitute for effective public policy. In November 2018 San Francisco passed Proposition C, increasing the tax on annual gross receipts above \$50 million by half a percent. The measure, expected to generate between \$250 million and \$300 million a year, would double the amount that the city spends to fight homelessness. It was strongly supported by Salesforce CEO Marc Benioff, who ploughed \$7 million into the Prop C campaign in the month before the vote. But Twitter and Square CEO Jack Dorsey fought hard to kill it, as did executives of companies like Lyft and Stripe.[48] This is ironic in view of the fact that many Silicon Valley tech companies have recognized the city's chronic homelessness problem as warranting major philanthropic commitments on their part.[49]

Holding public policy hostage to the whims of feuding billionaires is folly. A better approach for corporate leaders would be to convene business groups to build support for the kinds of legislative initiatives outlined in this book. Indeed, given our emphasis on the critical role that coalitions—rather than median voters—play in the legislative arena, mustering business support is essential. The 2019 announcement by the Business Roundtable that nearly 200 large US multinationals have abandoned their exclusive focus on shareholders is encouraging. These companies have pledged to support their employees and communities, in addition to their customers, suppliers, and shareholders, As Steven Pearlstein—a Pulitzer Prize–winning journalist who has criticized the corporate obsession with maximizing stockholder profits as the source of what has gone wrong with American capitalism—observed, this revision of corporate governing principles is a long overdue correction to American business norms.[50]

But the hard work remains to be done. It will take resources and leadership. And it depends on building and sustaining effective coalitions. Politicians must be lobbied and empowered to enact and entrench well-formulated proximate goals, goals that can jump-start our politics onto a path toward a better future. Large and growing numbers of Americans need help in responding to well-founded worries of being discarded, and they need resources to cope with a future that has already arrived. The political events of 2016 and thereafter sound unmistakable warnings to business leaders that they take exceptional risks for themselves and their companies if they continue behaving as if this is not their problem.

Here we have focused centrally on improving opportunities during the working years as vital to address the debilitating fear and despair of economic insecurity. Reducing insecurity requires creating more jobs through infrastructure improvements that everyone agrees are essential. It demands increasing take-home pay by building on and expanding earned income tax credits that have enjoyed bipartisan support for this purpose for nearly a half century. And it calls for expanded and modernized adjustment assistance, which should help all workers who lose their jobs—not just those who lose jobs because of trade. We have also urged improving child care and pre-K opportunities to better enable parents to work and ensuring that everyone has access to affordable health care. In all these areas we have shown that although the necessary reforms will be challenging to implement, there are potentially viable paths to political success.

Many conservatives will insist that we are crying wolf. Rising forces on the left will contend, to the contrary, that nothing less than the destruction of existing economic and political arrangements, and perhaps of capitalism itself, will suffice. To them, the changes we call for here will seem the least we can do. They might be: the wolf is at the door.

GLOSSARY

Aid to Families with Dependent Children (AFDC): Federal assistance program that provided financial support to families with children and little or no income. In effect from 1935 to 1996.

American Association of Retired Persons (AARP): Interest group whose mission is to "empower people to choose how they live as they age." An influential lobbying organization that focuses mainly on issues affecting the elderly.

American Federation of Labor and Congress of Industrial Organizations (AFL-CIO): The largest federation of trade unions in the United States. Engages in substantial political spending, lobbying, and activism.

Business for Innovative Climate and Energy Policy (BICEP): A coalition pressing the US government to pass broad, bipartisan energy and climate legislation.

Center for Budget and Policy Priorities (CBPP): Progressive think tank that analyzes the impact of federal and state government spending with emphasis on low- and moderate-income families.

Children's Health Insurance Program (CHIP): Insurance program that provides health coverage at a low cost to families that earn too much money to qualify for Medicaid but cannot afford to buy private insurance.

Committee for Economic Development (CED): Nonprofit, nonpartisan, business-led public policy organization designed to sustain and promote free enterprise, improve education and health care, improve corporate governance, and reform campaign finance.

Congressional Budget Office (CBO): Nonpartisan federal agency that provides budget and economic information to Congress.

Earned Income Tax Credit (EITC): Refundable tax credit for low-to moderate-income workers. The amount of the credit depends on the filer's income and the number of children they count as dependents.

Elementary and Secondary Education Act (ESEA): Enacted during Lyndon Johnson's administration, a law that provides federal funding to primary and secondary schools.

Equal Rights Amendment (ERA): Proposed constitutional amendment intended to guarantee equal legal rights regardless of sex. It had passed both houses of Congress by March 1972 but failed to win ratification by three quarters of the states before the 1979 deadline. Efforts to extend the deadline failed, and the ERA never became law.

Family Assistance Plan (FAP): Proposed by President Nixon but never implemented, FAP would have provided low-income, working families with a guaranteed annual income.

Government-Sponsored Enterprise (GSE): Type of financial services corporation created by Congress, designed to increase credit flow to targeted sectors of the economy, improve efficiency in those segments of the market, and reduce risk to investors.

Home Affordable Modification Program (HAMP): US government program introduced in 2009 as part of the Making Home Affordable program (MHA). Designed to help struggling homeowners avoid foreclosure by reducing the interest costs of their mortgages.

Homeownership and Opportunity for People Everywhere (HOPE): Pilot program to sell public housing to tenants. Proposed by Housing and Urban Development Secretary Jack Kemp in 1989, HOPE was later abandoned as too expensive.

National Federation of Independent Business (NFIB): Nonprofit entity whose goal is to advance the interests of small business owners. The largest small business association in the United States.

National Labor Relations Board (NLRB): Independent governmental agency charged with enforcing labor law in cases of collective bargaining and unjust labor practices.

National Welfare Rights Organization (NWRO): An advocacy organization active from 1966 to 1975 that fought for welfare rights, particularly for women and children. Its goals were to ensure adequate income, dignity, and justice and to inspire democratic participation.

Negative Income Tax (NIT): Tax-and-transfer scheme in which people earning income above a threshold level are taxed and people earning below that level received transfers. Proposed in Congress but never adopted.

No Child Left Behind Act (NCLB): Adopted by Congress in 2001 as part of its reauthorization of the Elementary and Secondary Education Act, NCLB was a standards-based education reform, which required states to develop assessments in basic skills. It was replaced by the Every Student Succeeds Act of 2015.

North American Free Trade Agreement (NAFTA): Trade agreement signed by Canada, Mexico, and the United States that came into force on January 1, 1994, creating a trilateral trade bloc in North America. In 2017 and 2018 the Trump administration renegotiated aspects of the agreement and renamed it the United States-Mexico-Canada Agreement (USMCA).

Patient Protection and Affordable Care Act (ACA): Comprehensive health care reform enacted in 2010 with the goal of expanding the Medicaid program, supporting innovative medical care delivery methods, and making affordable health insurance accessible to more people. Commonly known as Obamacare.

Supplemental Nutrition Assistance Program (SNAP): Formerly known as the Food Stamp program, SNAP provides low-income people living in the United States with food-purchasing assistance.

Supplemental Security Income (SSI): Federal program that pays benefits to disabled adults and children with limited income and resources. Benefits are also payable to those aged sixty-five and older without disabilities who meet the financial requirements.

Temporary Assistance for Needy Families (TANF): Federal program that provides grants to states and territories for the purpose of providing families with temporary financial assistance and support services such as child care, job preparation, and work assistance. Replaced Aid to Families with Dependent Children as part of the 1996 welfare reform.

Trade Adjustment Assistance (TAA): US government program adopted as part of the Trade Expansion Act of 1962 with the goal of mitigating the costs of imports on certain areas of the economy. TAA provides individuals and businesses harmed by foreign competition with transitional assistance.

Trans-Pacific Partnership (TPP): Trade agreement between Australia, Brunei, Canada, Chile, Japan, Malaysia, Mexico, New Zealand, Peru, Singapore, and Vietnam. The United States took part in the negotiations, and President Obama signed the agreement in February 2016. But Congress did not ratify it, and President Trump withdrew the US in 2017.

Transportation Infrastructure Finance and Innovation Act (TIFA): Federal program adopted by Congress in 1998 and run by the Department of Transportation, TIFA provides credit assistance for qualified regional and national ground transportation projects.

Unemployment Insurance (UI): Established as part of the Social Security Act of 1935, UI provides short-term income to qualifying workers who lose their jobs.

United States Climate Action Partnership (USCAP): A cooperative group of businesses and environmental organizations that lobbied the US government to mandate significant reductions in greenhouse gas emissions.

United States Department of Housing and Urban Development (HUD): Cabinet department in the executive branch that focuses on developing and executing housing policies and development projects in cities.

Universal Basic Income (UBI): Proposal to provide all citizens or residents of a country with a guaranteed payment that is unrelated to employment.

Value-Added Tax (VAT): Tax on sales of goods and services determined according to the amount by which the value of an article has been increased at each stage of production or distribution. Also known as a goods-and-services tax.

Working Tax Credit (WTC): UK refundable tax credit since 2003, paid to working members of low-income families.

Works Progress Administration (WPA): New Deal agency that employed millions of individuals, mostly unskilled men, to complete public works projects such as the construction of public buildings and roads.

NOTES

Introduction

1. Michael Batty, Jesse Bricker, Joseph Briggs, Elizabeth Holmquist, Susan McIntosh, Kevin Moore, Eric Nielsen, Sarah Reber, Molly Shatto, Kamila Sommer, Tom Sweeney, and Alice Henriques Volz, "Introducing the Distributional Financial Accounts of the United States," Finance and Economics Discussion Series 2019-017, Federal Reserve Board, 2019, https://www.federalreserve.gov/econres /feds/files/2019017pap.pdf

2. Bernie Sanders, "A threat to American democracy," speech from the United States Senate floor, March 27, 2014, https://www.youtube.com/watch?v =fQOCfweYLrE.

3. Robert Frank, "The top 1% of Americans now control 38% of the wealth," CNBC, September 27, 2017, https://www.cnbc.com/2017/09/27/the-top-1 -percent-of-americans-now-control-38-percent-of-the-wealth.html; Emmanuel Saez, "Striking it richer: The evolution of top incomes in the United States (updated with 2012 preliminary estimates)," University of California Berkeley Working Paper, September 3, 2013. https://eml.berkeley.edu//~saez/saez -UStopincomes-2012.pdf.

4. MJ Lee, Dan Merica, and Jeff Zeleny, "Bernie Sanders Endorses Hillary Clinton," CNN Politics, July 12, 2016, https://www.cnn.com/2016/07/11/politics /hillary-clinton-bernie-sanders/index.html.

5. "We're the party that wants to see an America in which people can still get rich." Ronald Reagan, remarks at a Republican congressional dinner, Washington, DC, *Public Papers of the Presidents of the United States,* Ronald Reagan: 1982, Book 1 (Washington, DC: U.S. Government Printing Office, 1982), 558.

6. Arlie Russell Hochschild, *Strangers in Their Own Land: Anger and Mourning on the American Right* (New York: New Press, 2016).

7. Daniel Kahneman and Amos Tversky, "Prospect Theory: An Analysis of Decision under Risk," *Econometrica* 47, no. 2 (1979): 263–291.

8. Katherine J. Cramer, *The Politics of Resentment: Rural Consciousness in Wisconsin and the Rise of Scott Walker* (Chicago: University of Chicago Press, 2016).

9. Adam Tooze, *Crashed: How a Decade of Financial Crises Changed the World* (New York: Viking, 2018), chapters 19–25.

10. In the May 2019 elections to the European Parliament, Britain's new Brexit party, led by Nigel Farage, easily beat Labour and the governing Conservatives, who came in fifth place. Mainstream parties lost ground across the continent, with Marine Le Pen's National Rally beating Emanuelle Macron's governing En Marche! in France and in Matteo Salvini's Lega Nord taking 33 percent of the vote in Italy.

Sarah Wolff, "Forget the Brexit party surge in the UK, the rest of Europe has delivered a more important message," *The Independent*, May 27, 2019, https://www .independent.co.uk/voices/european-elections-brexit-party-far-right-green-lib -dems-socialist-democrats-a8931951.html.

11. Tess Townsend, "Steve Case: 47 States Have to Fight for 25 Percent of Venture Capital Dollars," Recode, June 1, 2017, https://www.recode.net/2017/6/1 /15725826/steve-case-revolution-rise-rest-left-behind-venture-capital-dollars. In 2018 New York, Massachusetts, and California were the first, sixth, and seventh most unequal states. Estelle Sommeiller and Mark Price, "The New Gilded Age: Income Inequality in the U.S. by State, Metropolitan Area, and County," Economic Policy Institute, July 19, 2018, https://www.epi.org/files/pdf/147963.pdf.

12. James M. Curry and Frances E. Lee, "Non-Party Government: Bipartisan Lawmaking and Party Power in Congress," *Perspectives on Politics* 17, no. 1 (2019): 47–65; James M. Curry and Frances E. Lee, "What Is Regular Order Worth? Partisan Lawmaking and Congressional Processes," unpublished manuscript, September 5, 2018.

13. Frances McCall Rosenbluth and Ian Shapiro, *Responsible Parties: Saving Democracy from Itself* (New Haven: Yale University Press, 2018), ch. 5.

14. Richard Pildes, "Romanticizing Democracy, Political Fragmentation, and the Decline of American Government," *Yale Law Journal* 124 (2014): 828–844.

15. "Truth about Catnip," WebMD, https://pets.webmd.com/cats/catnip-effects -on-cats.

16. Lael Brainard, "Is the Middle Class within Reach for Middle-Income Families?" speech at the 2019 Federal Reserve System Community Development Research Conference, Washington, DC, May 10, 2019, https://www.federalreserve .gov/newsevents/speech/brainard20190510a.htm.

17. Neil Bhutta and Lisa Dettling, "Money in the Bank? Assessing Families' Liquid Savings Using the Survey of Consumer Finances," FEDS Notes, Board of Governors of the Federal Reserve System, November 19, 2018, https://www .federalreserve.gov/econres/notes/feds-notes/assessing-families-liquid-savings-using -the-survey-of-consumer-finances-20181119.htm.

18. Desmond S. King and Rogers M. Smith, *Still a House Divided: Race and Politics in Obama's America* (Princeton: Princeton University Press, 2013); Christopher H. Achen and Larry M. Bartels, *Democracy for Realists: Why Elections Do Not Produce Responsive Government* (Princeton: Princeton University Press, 2017); John Sides, Michael Tesler, and Lynn Vavreck, *Identity Crisis: The 2016 Presidential Campaign and the Battle for the Meaning of America* (Princeton: Princeton University Press, 2018).

1. Then and Now

1. *The Adventures of Ozzie and Harriet* premiered on television in October 1952 after eight years on radio and remained popular for fourteen seasons, through 435 episodes.

2. In 1965, for example, Harvard's tuition was $1,760, and median white family income was nearly four times greater: $6,900. In 2019 Harvard's tuition was $47,730. The total cost with room and board was $69,607, while median household income was $63,368. "Yale, Princeton increase tuition," *Harvard Crimson*,

November 18, 1965, https://www.thecrimson.com/article/1965/11/18/yale
-princeton-increase-tuition-pyale-and; Frank Olito, "How the cost of Harvard has
changed throughout the years," *Business Insider,* June 10, 2019, https://www
.businessinsider.com/how-the-cost-of-harvard-has-changed-throughout-the
-years2019-6.

3. Alexis de Tocqueville, *Democracy in America,* vol. 2 (1840; New York: Perennial
Classics, 2000), 513.

4. Robert Putnam convincingly relates how, since the 1970s, American have
socialized less with their neighbors, participated less with organizations that meet
regularly, and even spent less time with their families. *Bowling Alone: The Collapse
and Revival of American Community* (New York: Simon and Schuster, 2000),
31–147.

5. GDP grew from $228 billion in 1945 to nearly $1.3 trillion by 1972.

6. Milton Friedman actually said, "In one sense, we are all Keynesians now; in
another, nobody is any longer a Keynesian." "The Economy: We Are All Keynesians
Now," *Time,* December 31, 1965.

7. "The Living Room Candidate: Presidential Campaign Commercials 1952–
2016," Museum of the Moving Image, 2019, http://www.livingroomcandidate.org
/commercials/1952.

8. These efforts were hardly an economic panacea. Black household income rose
from 46 percent of white household income in 1965 to just over 61 percent in
2015.

9. See Reva B. Siegel, "Constitutional Culture, Social Movement Conflict and
Constitutional Change: The Case of the De Facto ERA," *California Law Review* 94,
no. 5 (2006): 1323–1419; Michael J. Graetz and Linda Greenhouse, *The Burger
Court and the Rise of the Judicial Right* (New York: Simon and Schuster, 2016),
255–268.

10. Quoted in Betty K. Koed, "The Politics of Reform: Policymakers and the
Immigration Act of 1965" (Ph.D. diss., University of California, Santa Barbara,
1999), 171–172.

11. Hugh Davis Graham, *Collision Course: The Strange Convergence of Affirmative
Action and Immigration Policy in America* (Oxford: Oxford University Press, 2002),
Table 5.1, 95.

12. For an extended analysis, see, generally, Graham, *Collision Course.*

13. Kevin Phillips, *The Emerging Republican Majority* (New York: Arlington
House, 1969).

14. Quoted in James Boyd, "Nixon's Southern Strategy—It's All in the Charts,"
New York Times, May 17, 1970.

15. Thomas Byrne Edsall and Mary D. Edsall, *Chain Reaction: The Impact of Race,
Rights, and Taxes on American Politics* (New York: W. W. Norton, 1991). See also
Robert Kuttner, *Revolt of the Haves: Tax Rebellions and Hard Times* (New York:
Simon and Schuster, 1980).

16. Michael J. Graetz and Ian Shapiro, *Death by a Thousand Cuts: The Fight over
Taxing Inherited Wealth* (Princeton: Princeton University Press, 2005), 287.

17. See, generally, Michael J. Graetz, *The End of Energy: The Unmaking of
America's Security, and Independence* (Cambridge, MA: MIT Press, 2011); Meg
Jacobs, *Panic at the Pump: The Energy Crisis and the Transformation of American
Politics in the 1970s* (New York: Hill and Wang, 2016).

18. Henry David Thoreau, *The Heart of Thoreau's Journals*, ed. Odell Shepard (Boston: Houghton Mifflin, 1927; New York: Dover Publications, 1961), 56. Thoreau's full journal entry for September 1, 1851, reads, "Is not disease the rule of existence? There is not a lily pad floating in the river but has been riddled by insects. Almost every shrub and tree has its gall, oftentimes esteemed its chief ornament and hardly to be distinguished from the fruit. If misery loves company, misery has company enough. Now, at midsummer, find me a perfect leaf or fruit."

19. Haynes Johnson, "The Heartbreak of Ohio's Steel Valley," *Washington Post*, October 26, 1980.

20. Bruce Springsteen. "Youngstown," track 4 on *The Ghost of Tom Joad*, Columbia Records, 1995, compact disc.

21. These numbers are from David Skolnick, "Presidential Visits to Valley in Odd-Numbered Years Rare," *Vindicator*, July 24, 2017.

22. Remarks of President Barack Obama on the economy, V&M Star Plant, Youngstown, Ohio, May 15, 2010.

23. "French Company Christens New Pipe Facility; 350 Jobs in Youngstown," Marcellus Drilling News, June 13, 2013.

24. Jenna Johnson, "Steel Valley's Youngstown Is Much More Complicated than Trump Portrays," *Washington Post*, July 25, 2017.

25. United States Census, Quickfacts, Youngstown City, Ohio, https://www.census.gov/quickfacts/youngstowncityohio 01-29-2019.

26. Quoted in Johnson, "Heartbreak."

27. Mike Patton, "U.S. Role in Global Economy Declines Nearly 50%," *Forbes*, February 29, 2016. To determine the current GDP of the US and other countries, see the World Bank's World Development Indicators: https://databank.worldbank.org/reports.aspx?source=world-development-indicators.

28. "World Trade Statistical Review 2018," World Trade Organization, Table A4, 122, https://doi.org/10.30875/0ab3aa40-en.

29. "2017 ITPF International Scorecard," *International Tax Policy Forum*, August 22, 2017, https://www.itpf.org/scorecard_2017.

30. Gareth A. Jones, "The Geographies of *Capital in the Twenty-First Century*: Inequality, Political Economy, and Space," in *After Piketty*, ed. H. Boushey, J. B. DeLong, and M. Steinbaum (Cambridge, MA: Harvard University Press, 2017), 283.

31. Thomas B. Edsall, "Can the Democratic Party Find New Voters?" *New York Times*, June 15, 2017.

32. Susan Chira, "Men Don't Want to Be Nurses. Their Wives Agree," *New York Times*, June 24, 2017.

33. Daron Acemoglu and Pascual Restrepo, "Robots and Jobs: Evidence from US Labor Markets," NBER Working Paper No. 23285, National Bureau of Economic Research, Cambridge, MA, March 17, 2017. But see Lawrence Mishel and Heidi Shierholz, "Robots, or Automation, Are Not the Problem: Too Little Worker Power Is," Economic Snapshot, Economic Policy Institute, Washington, DC, February 21, 2017, https://www.epi.org/publication/robots-or-automation-are-not-the-problem-too-little-worker-power-is.

34. Laura Tyson and Michael Spence, "Exploring the Effects of Technology on Income and Wealth Inequality," in Boushey, DeLong, and Steinbaum, eds., *After Piketty*, 202–205.

35. See, for example, Joseph Francois, Laura M. Baughman, and Daniel Anthony, "'Trade Discussion' or 'Trade War'? The Estimated Impacts of Tariffs on Steel and Aluminum," Policy Brief, Trade Partnership, June 5, 2018, https://tradepartnership .com/wp-content/uploads/2018/06/232RetaliationPolicyBriefJune5.pdf. The Tax Foundation tracks the number of jobs being lost from Trump's tariffs. See Erica York, Kyle Pomerleau, and Robert Bellafiore, "Tracking the Economic Impact of U.S. Tariffs and Retaliatory Actions," Tax Foundation, continually updated since May 31, 2019, https://taxfoundation.org/tracker-economic-impact-tariffs.

36. David H. Autor, David Dorn, and Gordon H. Hanson, "The China Syndrome: Local Labor Market Effects of Import Competition in the United States," *American Economic Review* 103, no. 6 (2013): 2121–2168.

37. James Manyika, "Technology, Jobs, and the Future of Work," McKinsey Global Institute, May 2017, https://www.mckinsey.com/featured-insights /employment-and-growth/technology-jobs-and-the-future-of-work.

38. Tim Brown, "Farmers to Trump: 'We Don't Want Handouts . . . We Want a Quick Return on Free Trade,'" Sons of Liberty Media, July 25, 2018, https:// sonsoflibertymedia.com/farmers-to-trump-we-dont-want-handouts-we-want-a -quick-return-to-free-trade.

39. David M. Kennedy, *Freedom from Fear: The American People in Depression and War 1929–45* (Oxford: Oxford University Press, 1999), 165, 218–248.

40. On American exceptionalism, see Louis Hartz, *The Liberal Tradition in America: An Interpretation of American Political Thought since the Revolution* (New York: Harcourt Brace Jovanovich, 1955).

41. Kennedy, *Freedom from Fear,* 244–245, 270.

42. Unemployment fell to below 15 percent in 1937 but shot back up to almost 20 percent in the 1938 recession and did not fall significantly until the war economy ramped up after 1940. American Social History Project, Graduate Center, City University of New York, https://herb.ashp.cuny.edu/items/show/1510.

43. Kennedy, *Freedom from Fear,* 238–242; Huey Long, "Share Our Wealth: Every Man a King," speech, February 23, 1934, Huey Long Website, https://www .hueylong.com/programs/share-our-wealth-speech.php.

44. On one occasion Roosevelt referred to the need to "steal Long's thunder." Raymond Moley, *After Seven Years* (New York: Harper and London, 1939), 305.

45. Kennedy, *Freedom from Fear,* 245–246.

46. Katherine J. Cramer, *The Politics of Resentment: Rural Consciousness in Wisconsin and the Rise of Scott Walker* (Chicago: University of Chicago Press, 2016); Arlie Russell Hochschild, *Strangers in Their Own Land: Anger and Mourning on the American Right* (New York: New Press, 2016).

47. "Number of Jobs, Labor Market Experience, and Earnings Growth among Americans at 50: Results from a Longitudinal Survey," Bureau of Labor Statistics, News Release, August 24, 2017, https://www.bls.gov/news.release/pdf/nlsoy.pdf.

48. The best compilation and description of this research that we have found is Jennie E. Brand, "The Far-Reaching Impact of Job Loss and Unemployment," *Annual Review of Sociology* 41 (2015): 359–375. The discussion that follows is largely based on this work.

49. Brand, "Far-Reaching Impact," 363, citing Kenneth A. Couch and Dana W. Placzek, "Earning Losses of Displaced Workers Revisited," *American Economic Review* 100, no. 1 (2010): 572–589; and Jennie E. Brand and Till Von Wachter,

"The Economic and Social Consequences of Job Loss and Unemployment," Population Reference Bureau (PRB), November 20, 2013, http://www.prb.org /Multimedia/Video/2013/job-loss-webinar.aspx.

50. Kathleen Thelen, "The American Precariat: U.S. Capitalism in Comparative Perspective," *Perspectives on Politics* 17, no. 1 (2019): 5–27, Figures 3 and 12, https://doi.org/10.1017/S1537592718003419.

51. David H. Autor and Mark G. Duggan, "The Growth in the Social Security Disability Rolls: A Fiscal Crisis Unfolding," *Journal of Economic Perspectives* 20, no. 3 (2006): 71–96, 71–72.

52. Erika Edwards, "U.S. Death Rates from Suicides, Alcohol and Drug Overdoses Reach an All-Time High," NBC Health News, June 12, 2019, https://www.nbcnews.com/health/health-news/u-s-death-rates-suicides-alcohol -drug-overdoses-reach-all-n1016216.

53. Lester C. Thurow, *The Zero-Sum Society* (New York: Basic Books, 1980).

54. Reagan was referring to the economic crisis at the time. Inaugural Address of Ronald Reagan, January 20, 1981, https://www.reaganfoundation.org/media /128614/inauguration.pdf.

55. Marshall Steinbaum, "Inequality and the Rise of Social Democracy: An Ideological History," in Boushey, DeLong, and Steinbaum, eds., *After Piketty*, 440. It is now clear that Thomas Piketty and others overestimate the share of gains at the top in the postwar period. Gerald Auten and David Splinter, "Income Inequality in the United States: Using Tax Data to Measure Long-Term Trends," unpublished manuscript, August 23, 2018.

56. Lael Brainard, "Is the Middle Class within Reach for Middle-Income Families?" speech at the Federal Reserve System Community Development Research Conference, Washington, DC, May 10, 2019, https://www.federalreserve .gov/newsevents/speech/brainard20190510a.htm.

57. AnnaMaria Andriotis, Ken Brown, and Shane Shifflett, "Families Go Deep in Debt to Stay in the Middle Class," *Wall Street Journal*, August 1, 2019; Heather Long, "'This doesn't look like the best economy ever': 40% of Americans say they still struggle to pay bills," *Washington Post*, July 4, 2019.

58. National Low Income Housing Coalition, "Out of Reach 2017: The High Cost of Housing," June 9, 2017, http://nlihc.org/sites/default/files/oor/OOR17 _MembersLaunch_Webinar_060917.pdf.

59. See, generally, Sandra E. Black and Paul J. Devereux, "Recent Developments in Intergenerational Mobility," in *Handbook of Labor Economics*, vol. 4, part B (2011): 1487–1541. There is debate over whether the family environment, school quality, or even genetics has as much causal impact on intergenerational mobility as parental income, and perhaps even more causal impact. See, for example, Eric R. Nielsen, "Human Capital and Wealth Before and After *Capital in the Twenty-First Century*," in Boushey, DeLong, and Steinbaum, eds., *After Piketty*, 163. But there is no doubt that the incomes of parents and their children are highly correlated.

60. Jed Kolko, "Trump Was Stronger Where the Economy Is Weaker," FiveThirtyEight, November 10, 2016, https://fivethirtyeight.com/features/trump -was-stronger-where-the-economy-is-weaker; and Ben Casselman, "Stop Saying That Trump's Win Had Nothing to Do with Economics," FiveThirtyEight, January 9, 2017, https://fivethirtyeight.com/features/stop-saying-trumps-win-had -nothing-to-do-with-economics.

61. See Graham, *Collision Course.*

62. Stephen Rose, "White Working-Class Men in a Changing American Workforce," Third Way, June 19, 2017, https://www.thirdway.org/report/white -working-class-men-in-a-changing-american-workforce.

63. David Runciman, "Stiffed," review of Janet Byrne, ed., *The Occupy Handbook* (Boston: Back Bay, 2012), *London Review of Books* 34, no. 20, October 25, 2012, 7–9.

64. Brandon DeBot, "Harsh Tradeoff at Core of GOP Health Bill: Keep Medicaid Expansion or Cut Taxes for the Wealthy?" Center for Budget and Policy Priorities, June 22, 2017, https://www.cbpp.org/sites/default/files/atoms/files/6-21 -17health2.pdf.

65. See Michael J. Graetz and Linda Greenhouse, *The Burger Court and the Rise of the Judicial Right* (New York: Simon and Schuster, 2016), 258–268.

2. Building Blocks of Distributive Politics

1. Antoine de Saint-Exupéry, *The Little Prince* (1944; Eugene: Harvest, 1971), 10–11.

2. Vilfredo Pareto, *Manual of Political Economy* (1906; New York: Augustus Kelly, 1971).

3. "In 1871 at a conference of the First International in London, resolution IX which had the support of Marx and Engels read: 'Against the power of the propertied classes the proletariat can only act as a class by turning itself into a political party.'" Robin Cox, "The Parliamentary Road to Socialism," Socialist Party of Great Britain, https://www.worldsocialism.org/spgb/socialist-standard/1970s /1978/no-889-september-1978/parliamentary-road-socialism.

4. The median voter model was proposed by Harold Hotelling, "Stability in Competition," *Economic Journal* 39, no. 153 (1929): 41–57 and Anthony Downs, *An Economic Theory of Democracy* (New York: Harper, 1957). Its application to the distribution of income and wealth was proposed by Allan H. Meltzer and Scott F. Richard, "A Rational Theory of the Size of Government," *Journal of Political Economy* 89, no. 5 (1981): 914–927.

5. The attribution might be apocryphal. The statement was reported by Mitch Ohnstad of the *New York Herald* at the time of Sutton's arrest in February 1952, but Sutton later claimed no memory of having said it. Willie Sutton and Edward Linn, *Where the Money Was: Memoirs of a Bank Robber* (New York: Broadway, 2004).

6. Michael J. Graetz and Ian Shapiro, *Death by a Thousand Cuts: The Fight over Inherited Wealth* (Princeton: Princeton University Press, 2005); Susan Dynarski, "Hope for Whom? Financial Aid for the Middle Class and Its Impact on College Attendance," NBER Working Paper No. 7756, National Bureau of Economic Research, Cambridge, MA, June 2000.

7. Thomas Frank, *What's the Matter with Kansas? How Conservatives Won the Heart of America* (New York: Holt, 2005); and Christopher H. Achen and Larry M. Bartels, *Democracy for Realists: Why Elections Do Not Produce Responsive Governments* (Princeton: Princeton University Press, 2016).

8. For a survey off the various factors scholars have identified that limit redistribution in democracies, see Ian Shapiro, *The State of Democratic Theory* (Princeton: Princeton University Press, 2003), ch. 5.

9. Chaim D. Kaufmann and Robert A. Pape, "Explaining Costly International Moral Action: Britain's Sixty-Year Campaign against the Atlantic Slave Trade," *International Organization* 53, no. 4 (1999): 631–668; and Seymour Drescher, *Econocide: British Slavery in an Era of Abolition,* 2nd ed. (Chapel Hill: University of North Carolina Press, 2010), 113–186.

10. "That Gini Might Give You a Headache," Rolling Alpha, September 25, 2013, http://www.rollingalpha.com/2013/09/25/that-gini-might-give-you-a -headache; Cara Anna, "Post-Apartheid South Africa Is World's Most Unequal Country," Associated Press, May 7, 2019, https://www.apnews.com/a1cd5ebc5ed 24a7088d970d30bb04ba1; "South African Youth Unemployment Rate," Trading Economics, 2019, https://tradingeconomics.com/south-africa/youth -unemployment-rate.

11. Michael Moore, "The Purpose of Occupy Wall Street Is to Occupy Wall Street," *The Nation,* April 2, 2012, 12.

12. David Runciman, "Stiffed," review of Janet Byrne, ed., *The Occupy Handbook* (Boston: Back Bay, 2012), *London Review of Books* 34, no. 20, October 25, 2012, 7–9.

13. Susan Dunn, *Jefferson's Second Revolution: The Election Crisis of 1800 and the Triumph of Republicanism* (New York: Houghton Mifflin, 2004), 264–265.

14. For a survey of the literature on minimum winning coalitions see Dennis C. Mueller, *Public Choice III* (Cambridge: Cambridge University Press, 2003), 281–284, 290–291.

15. Mancur Olson, *The Logic of Collective Action: Public Goods and the Theory of Groups* (Cambridge, MA: Harvard University Press, 1965), 51, 60–64, 72–76, 133–134, 139–141.

16. See Donald Green and Ian Shapiro, *Pathologies of Rational Choice Theory: A Critique of Applications in Political Science* (New Haven: Yale University Press, 1994), 72–97.

17. Graetz and Shapiro, *Death by a Thousand Cuts,* 34–49.

18. Mayling Birney, Ian Shapiro, and Michael J. Graetz, "The Political Uses of Public Opinion: Lessons from the Estate Tax Repeal," in *Divide and Deal: The Politics of Distribution in Democracies,* ed. Ian Shapiro, Peter Swenson, and Daniela Donno (New York: NYU Press, 2008), 298–340.

19. Daniel Henninger, "Barack Obama Gets the Last Laugh," *Wall Street Journal,* July 21–23, 2017, A13.

20. Graetz and Shapiro, *Death by a Thousand Cuts,* 263–265.

21. David Goldfield, *America Aflame: How the Civil War Created a Nation* (New York: Bloomsbury Press, 2011), 17–41; and David Brion Davis, *The Problem of Slavery in the Age of Revolution, 1770–1823* (Ithaca, NY: Cornell University Press, 1975), 523–556.

22. Steven Deyle, *Carry Me Back: The Domestic Slave Trade in American Life* (Oxford: Oxford University Press, 2005), 14–39.

23. Sven Beckert, *Empire of Cotton: A Global History* (London: Penguin, 2014), 242–273.

24. James McPherson, *Battle Cry of Freedom: The Civil War Era* (Oxford: Oxford University Press, 1988), 369–391.

25. Olivia Katrandjian, "Occupy Wall Street Protests Spread across the Country with No Unified Message," ABC News, October 8, 2011, http://abcnews.go.com /US/occupy-wall-street-protests-spread-country-clear-unified/story?id=14696466.

26. Julianne Pepitone, "Why Occupy Wall Street Isn't about a List of Demands," CNN Money, October 12, 2011, http://money.cnn.com/2011/10/12/technology /occupy_wall_street_demands/index.htm.

27. See the memorable portrayal by Tommy Lee Jones in the film *Lincoln,* directed by Steven Spielberg, Touchstone Pictures, 2012: https://www.youtube.com /watch?v=QTwKOCILJl0. For a less dramatic, if more historically accurate, account, see Doris Kearns Goodwin, *Team of Rivals: The Political Genius of Abraham Lincoln* (New York: Simon and Schuster, 2005), 684–696.

28. See Sidney Bland, "New Life in an Old Movement: Alice Paul and the Great Suffrage Parade of 1913 in Washington, D.C.," *Records of the Columbia Historical Society* 71/72 (1971/1972), 657–678; Jen McDaneld, "White Suffragist Dis/Entitlement: The Revolution and the Rhetoric of Racism," *Legacy* 30, no. 2 (2013): 243–264; Garth E. Pauley, "W. E. B. Du Bois on Woman Suffrage: A Critical Analysis of His Crisis Writings," *Journal of Black Studies* 30, no. 3 (2000): 383–410; Suzanne M. Marilley, "Frances Willard and the Feminism of Fear," *Feminist Studies* 19, no. 1 (1993): 123–146.

29. See James Patterson, *The Eve of Destruction* (New York: Basic Books, 2012), 209–212.

30. On the changing law of marital rape in the US, see Deborah L. Rhode, *Justice and Gender* (Cambridge, MA: Harvard University Press, 1989), 249–251; Rene I. Augustine, "Marriage: The Safe Haven for Rapists," *Journal of Family Law* 29, no. 3 (1990–1991): 559–590; and Sandra Ryder and Sheryl Kuzmenka, "Legal Rape: The Marital Exception," *John Marshall Law Review* 24 (Winter 1991): 393–421.

31. See Reva B. Siegel, "Constitutional Culture, Social Movement Conflict and Constitutional Change: The Case of the De Facto ERA," *California Law Review* 94, no. 5 (2006): 1323–1419.

32. Ira Katznelson, *Fear Itself: The New Deal and the Origins of Our Time* (New York: Norton Liveright, 2013), 156–194. We skirt the debates over how much, if at all, FDR actually wanted to buck the Southern racist wing of his party and to what extent other considerations, such as administrative feasibility and imitation of the social insurance programs being created elsewhere, also contributed to the exclusion of agricultural and domestic workers from Social Security. See Larry DeWitt, "The Decision to Exclude Agricultural and Domestic Workers from the 1935 Social Security Act," *Social Security Bulletin* 70, no. 4 (2010): 1–15; and Richard Rodems and H. Luke Shaefer, "Left Out: Policy Diffusion and the Exclusion of Black Workers from Unemployment Insurance," *Social Science History* 40, no. 3 (2016): 385–404.

33. "Obama: I'm Not Responsible for Trump," *Politico,* November 15, 2016, http://www.politico.com/story/2016/11/obama-trump-not-my-fault-231411.

34. Martin Luther King, Sermon at Temple Israel of Hollywood, February 26, 1965, audio and transcript available at http://www.americanrhetoric.com/speeches /mlktempleisraelhollywood.htm.

35. Goldfield, *America Aflame*, 483–505.

36. Paul Pierson, *Dismantling the Welfare State? Reagan, Thatcher, and the Politics of Retrenchment* (Cambridge: Cambridge University Press, 1995). See also Paul Pierson, "When Effect Becomes Cause: Policy Feedback and Political Change," *World Politics* 45, no. 4 (1993): 595–628; and Daniel Béland, "Reconsidering Policy

Feedback: How Policies Affect Politics," *Administration and Society* 45, no. 2 (2010): 568–590.

37. Arthur M. Schlesinger, Jr., *The Coming of the New Deal* (Boston: Houghton Mifflin, 2003), 309.

38. "Bush's Final Approval Rating: 22 Percent," CBS News, January 16, 2009, http://www.cbsnews.com/news/bushs-final-approval-rating-22-percent.

39. Jane Mayer, *Dark Money: The Hidden History of Billionaires behind the Rise of the Radical Right* (New York: Doubleday, 2016), 165–300.

40. See Graetz and Shapiro, *Death by a Thousand Cuts*, 223.

41. In *Citizens United v. Federal Election Commission* 558 U.S. 310 (2010), the Supreme Court held that the First Amendment's guarantee of freedom of speech prohibits restrictions on independent political expenditures by nonprofit and for-profit corporations, labor unions, and other associations.

42. James MacGregor Burns, *The Crosswinds of Freedom*, vol. 3: *The American Experiment* (New York: Vintage, 1989), 410.

43. Daniel Massey, "Occupy Wall Street Takes a New Direction: Ad Hoc Leaders Push Movement toward a More Militant Stage," *Crain's New York Business*, November 13, 2011, http://www.crainsnewyork.com/article/20111113 /ECONOMY/311139975/occupy-wall-street-takes-a-new-direction.

44. Drake Bennett, "David Graeber, the Anti-Leader of Occupy Wall Street," *Bloomberg Business Week*, October 26, 2011, https://www.bloomberg.com/news /articles/2011-10-26/david-graeber-the-anti-leader-of-occupy-wall-street.

45. Richard Kluger, *Simple Justice: The History of Brown v. Board of Education and Black America's Struggle for Equality* (New York: Vintage, 2004).

46. Robert Caro, *The Years of Lyndon Johnson*, vol. 4: *The Passage of Power* (New York: Vintage, 2013), 201–227, 685–943.

3. Good Politics, Wrong Policy

1. The 1992 Clinton campaign's focus on globalization's challenge to the American middle class was immortalized in the film *Primary Colors* (directed by Mike Nichols, Universal Pictures, 1998), based on the anonymous novel of the same name subsequently revealed as the work of political columnist Joe Klein. John Travolta played the Clintonesque Jack Staunton, who tells New Hampshire voters that outsourced shipyard and other "muscle" jobs are never coming back, that weakened unions will not revive, and that the future depends on workers learning "to exercise the muscle between your ears." https://www.youtube.com/watch?v=sgXclrh–TpU.

2. William J. Clinton, "Remarks on the National Homeownership Strategy," The White House, Washington, DC, June 5, 1995, available at the American Presidency Project, https://www.presidency.ucsb.edu/node/220941; "The National Homeownership Strategy: Partners in the American Dream," U.S. Department of Housing and Urban Development, 1995, 1–2.

3. Marisa Chappell, "The Curious Case of Urban Homesteading," *Jacobin*, March 31, 2017, https://www.jacobinmag.com/2017/03/jack-kemp-hud-acorn -public-housing.

4. "[Waging War on Poverty] HOPE: Homeownership and Opportunity for People Everywhere," U.S. Department of Housing and Urban Development, 1991, ii.

5. Jason DeParle, "How Jack Kemp Lost the War on Poverty," *New York Times Magazine,* February 28, 1993.

6. "United States Home Ownership Tate," Trading Economics, https://tradingeconomics.com/united-states/home-ownership-rate.

7. Jo Becker, Sheryl Gay Stolberg, and Stephen Labaton, "Bush Drive for Home Ownership Fueled Housing Bubble," *New York Times,* December 21, 2008.

8. "The State of the Nation's Housing 2008," Joint Center for Housing Studies, Harvard University, 2008, 17–21.

9. Apostolos Fasianos and Stephen Kinsella, "What Drove Up US Household Debt?" Private Debt Project, Governor's Woods Foundatin, Philadelphia, n.d. [2015], Fig. 7, http://privatedebtproject.org/view-articles.php?What-Drove-Up-US-Household-Debt-18.

10. Debbie Gruenstein Bocian, Wei Li, and Keith S. Ernst, "Foreclosures by Race and Ethnicity: The Demographics of a Crisis," Center for Responsible Lending, Durham, NC, June 18, 2010, https://www.responsiblelending.org/mortgage-lending/research-analysis/foreclosures-by-race-and-ethnicity.pdf; Renae Merle, "Minorities Hit Harder by Foreclosure Crisis," *Washington Post,* June 18, 2010.

11. Nick Penzenstadler and Jeff Kelly Lowenstein, "Seniors Were Sold a Risk-Free Retirement with Reverse Mortgages. Now They Face Foreclosure," *USA Today,* June 13, 2019.

12. Sarah Burd-Sharps and Rebecca Rasch, "Impact of the US Housing Crisis on the Racial Wealth Gap across Generations," Social Science Research Council, June 2015, https://www.aclu.org/files/field_document/discrimlend_final.pdf.

13. Gretchen Morgenson and Joshua Rosner, *Reckless Endangerment: How Outsized Ambition, Greed, and Corruption Created the Worst Financial Crisis in Our Time* (New York: St Martins Press, 2011), 62–63, 68–71, 192–193, 246–248, 256–259.

14. The study was eventually published as Alicia H. Munnell, Geoffrey M. B. Tootell, Lynn E. Browne, and James McEneaney, "Mortgage Lending in Boston: Interpreting HMDA Data," *American Economic Review* 86, no. 1 (1996): 25–53, 51.

15. "Closing the Gap: A Guide to Equal Opportunity Lending," Federal Reserve Bank of Boston, 1993.

16. J. P. Morgan Chase settled for some $13 billion in restitution and fines, Bank of America $16.6 billion, Citigroup $7 billion, Morgan Stanley $3.2 billion, and Goldman Sachs $5 billion. Lucinda Shen, "Goldman Sachs Finally Admits It Defrauded Investors during the Financial Crisis," *Fortune* online, April 11, 2016, http://fortune.com/2016/04/11/goldman-sachs-doj-settlement.

17. Timothy Curry and Lynn Shibut, "The Cost of the Savings and Loan Crisis: Truth and Consequences," *FDIC Banking Review* 13, no. 2 (2000): 26–35, 26, 33.

18. More stringent regulation—most likely requiring substantially larger down payments, capital cushions, and stricter underwriting criteria—would have limited Fannie's ability to purchase and resell many loans. Once it became clear, however, that more regulation was inevitable, Johnson mounted an attack to ensure that the new regulations were minimal. By announcing Open Doors to Affordable Housing, a $10 billion initiative, and giving large grants to activist groups such as ACORN that supported increased homeownership for minorities, Johnson transformed erstwhile advocates of tighter regulation into allies. Fannie also managed to secure, through the Federal Housing Enterprises Financial Safety and Soundness Act, a

capital requirement of just 2.5 percent, rather than the 10 percent applicable to banks. And Johnson and his allies persuaded the HUD regulator to seek prior congressional approval for any new regulations, including those related to improved capital requirements. In effect, Johnson and his allies used both parties' commitments to the proximate goal of expanding low-income home ownership to neutralize efforts to limit Fannie's aggressive agenda. Morgenson and Rosner, *Reckless Endangerment,* 22–30.

19. Morgenson and Rosner, *Reckless Endangerment,* 70.

20. Potential whistleblowers were neutralized. In 1996 the Congressional Budget Office (CBO) produced a study documenting that in 1995 alone Fannie spent $2 billion on lobbying, executive compensation, and public relations. Johnson's well-funded allies on Capitol Hill responded by attacking the report and its authors to undermine their credibility. The CBO report was ignored. Taxpayers were paying for Fannie to lobby politicians on behalf of its own management and their perks. Small wonder that there was no effective opposition. Morgenson and Rosner, *Reckless Endangerment,* 82–90.

21. Wayne Duggan, "Financial Crisis Bailouts: What Did They Actually Cost Taxpayers?" *Yahoo Finance,* October 9, 2014, https://finance.yahoo.com/news /financial-crisis-bailouts-did-actually-184624029.html.

22. Morgenson and Rosner, *Reckless Endangerment,* 70.

23. Joshua Rosner, "Housing in the New Millennium: A Home without Equity Is Just a Mortgage with Debt," unpublished manuscript, June 29, 2001, rev. September 30, 2017, https://ssrn.com/abstract=1162456.

24. Karl E. Case and Robert J. Shiller, "Is There a Bubble in the Housing Market?" *Brookings Papers on Economic Activity* 2 (2003): 299–362.

25. Robert Shiller, *Irrational Exuberance,* 2nd ed. (Princeton: Princeton University Press, 2005).

26. Karl E. Case and Robert J. Shiller, "Full House," *Wall Street Journal,* August 30, 2006, A10; and Robert J. Shiller, "Bubble Trouble," Project Syndicate, September 17, 2007, https://www.project-syndicate.org/commentary/bubble-trouble.

27. John Geanakoplos, "Solving the Present Crisis and Managing the Leverage Cycle," Cowles Foundation Discussion Paper No. 1751, Yale University, January 2010, https://papers.ssrn.com/sol3/papers.cfm?abstract_id=1539488; John D. Geanakoplos and Susan P. Koniak, "Mortgage Justice Is Blind," *New York Times,* October 29, 2008; and John D. Geanakoplos and Susan P. Koniak, "Matters of Principal," *New York Times,* March 4, 2009.

28. John Geanakoplos, "Leverage, Default, and Forgiveness: Lessons from the American and European Crises," *Journal of Macroeconomics* 39 (2014): 313–333, 328–330.

29. John Geanakoplos, Testimony before the House Financial Services Committee, May 6, 2010, http://archives-financialservices.house.gov/Media/file /hearings/111/Printed%20Hearings/111–131.pdf.

30. Kenneth Harney, "A Lifeline for Underwater Homeowners," *The Real Deal: South Florida Real Estate News,* March 26, 2010, https://therealdeal.com/miami /2010/03/26/ken-harney-a-lifeline-for-underwater-homeowners.

31. Rick Santelli broadcast on CNBC Business News, February 19, 2009, https://www.youtube.com/watch?v=zp-Jw-5Kx8k&t=10s. On Santelli's subsequent

reflections, see Jamilah King, "Rick Santelli: Tea Party Rant 'Best Five Minutes of My Life,'" Colorlines, September 20, 2010, https://www.colorlines.com/content/rick-santelli-tea-party-rant-best-five-minutes-my-life.

32. Vanessa Williamson, Theda Skocpol, and John Coggin, "The Tea Party and the Remaking of American Conservatism," *Perspectives on Politics* 9, no. 1 (2011): 25–43.

33. A July 2009 study by the Boston Fed found that only 3 percent of seriously delinquent borrowers had their loans modified to enable lower monthly payments, and 5.5 percent had loans modified without altering their payments. Manuel Adelino, Kristopher S. Gerardi, and Paul S. Willen, "Why Don't Lenders Renegotiate More Home Mortgages? Redefaults, Self-Cures, and Securitization," Public Policy Discussion Paper No. 09-4, Federal Reserve Bank of Boston, July 2009, https://www.bostonfed.org/publications/public-policy-discussion-paper/2009/why-dont-lenders-renegotiate-more-home-mortgages-redefaults-selfcures-and-securitization.aspx.

34. Jenifer B. McKim, "Lenders Avoid Redoing Loans, Fed Concludes," *Boston Globe*, July 7, 2009.

35. "Remarks by Governor Ben S. Bernanke," meetings of the Eastern Economic Association, Washington, DC, February 20, 2004, https://www.federalreserve.gov/boarddocs/speeches/2004/20040220.

36. Shiller, *Irrational Exuberance,* 20–25.

37. Matt Phillips, "Most Germans Don't Buy Their Own Homes, They Rent. Here's Why," Quartz, January 23, 2014, https://qz.com/167887/germany-has-one-of-the-worlds-lowest-homeownership-rates.

38. The metaphor appears to have originated with Reinhard A. Hohaus, an actuary for the Metropolitan Life Insurance Company, in a 1949 speech at the Ohio Chamber of Commerce. He had different legs in mind, though: private insurance, group insurance, and Social Security. "Origins of the Three-Legged Stool Metaphor for Social Security," Research Note #1, Research Notes and Special Studies by the Historian's Office, Social Security Administration, https://www.ssa.gov/history/stool.html.

39. Francesca Eugeni, "Consumer Debt and Home Equity Borrowing," *Economic Perspectives* 17, no. 2 (1993): 2–13, 8.

40. See Michael J. Graetz, "The Truth about Tax Reform," *University of Florida Law Review* 40, no. 4 (1988): 617–639.

41. John V. Duca, "Making Sense of the U.S. Housing Slowdown," *Economic Letter,* Federal Reserve Bank of Dallas, vol. 1, no. 11, November 2006, 1–8; Vladimir Klyuev and Paul S. Mills, "Is Housing Wealth an 'ATM'? The Relationship between Household Wealth, Home Equity Withdrawal, and Savings Rates," *IMF Staff Papers* 54, no. 3 (2007): 539–561; and Guglielmo Maria Caporale, Mauro Costantini, and Antonio Paradiso, "Re-examining the Decline in the US Savings Rate: The Impact of Mortgage Equity Withdrawal," *Journal of International Financial Markets, Institutions and Money* 26 (2013): 215–225.

42. Becker, Stolberg, and Labaton, "Bush Drive for Home Ownership."

43. Alan S. Blinder, *After the Music Stopped: The Financial Crisis, the Response, and the Work Ahead* (Princeton: Princeton University Press, 2013).

4. The Essential Role of Business

1. In April 2019 the federal government reported that, during the first quarter of the year, the economy grew at an annual rate of 3.2 percent, payrolls had risen for 104 quarters in a row, and more than 20 million jobs were created since the end of the Great Recession in 2009. Average hourly earnings had risen by 3.2 percent in the previous twelve months. See Nelson D. Schwartz, "Job Growth Underscores Economy's Vigor; Unemployment at Half-Century Low," *New York Times*, May 3, 2019; Ben Casselman, "Why Wages Are Finally Rising, 10 Years after the Recession," *New York Times*, May 2, 2019.

2. For documentation of the large increase in the profit share of the US nonfinancial sector since the mid-1970s, see Simcha Barkai, "Declining Labor and Capital Shares," Working Paper, new series no. 2, Stigler Center for the Study of the Economy and the State, London Business School, November 2016, http://facultyresearch .london.edu/docs/BarkaiDecliningLaborCapital.pdf.

3. This was the line attributed to Charles Wilson in 1943, after President Eisenhower nominated him to be secretary of defense. In fact, when asked at his confirmation hearing whether he would be able to make a decision adverse to the interests of General Motors, Wilson said he would but added that he could not conceive of such a situation "because for years I thought what was good for the country was good for General Motors and vice versa." Justin Hyde, "GM's 'Engine Charlie' Wilson Learned to Live with a Misquote," *Detroit Free Press*, September 14, 2008, http://www.rasmusen.org/g406/chapters/Tex-and-diagram-files/photo-quote -sources/GM-s-Engine-Charlie-Wilson-learned-live-misquote.htm.

4. Daphne MacDonald, "20 of the Fastest-Growing Industries in the US Right Now," MSN Money, October 19, 2018, https://www.msn.com/en-us/money /markets/20-of-the-fastest-growing-industries-in-the-us-right-now/ss-AAyi71p.

5. Peter Swenson, "Varieties of Capitalist Interests: Power, Institutions, and the Regulatory Welfare State in the United States and Sweden," *Studies in American Political Development* 18, no. 1 (2004): 186–195.

6. Peter Swenson, *Capitalists against Markets: The Making of Labor Markets and Welfare States in the United States and Sweden* (Oxford: Oxford University Press, 2002), 192, 206–213, 220–223, 240. For the view that business support was somewhat more grudging, see Jacob S. Hacker and Paul Pierson, "Business Power and Social Policy: Employers and the Formation of the American Welfare State," *Politics and Society* 30, no. 2 (2002): 277–325.

7. David Kennedy, *Freedom from Fear: The American People in Depression and War, 1929–1945* (Oxford: Oxford University Press, 1999), 119–130.

8. James T. Patterson, *Grand Expectations: The United States, 1945–74* (Oxford: Oxford University Press, 1996), 53–55.

9. Harriman briefly joined the National Recovery Administration. He resigned in April 1934 over a disagreement with its director Hugh Johnson. Rudy Abramson, *Spanning the Century: The Life of W. Averell Harriman, 1891–1986* (New York: Morrow, 1992), 236–265.

10. Mark S. Mizruchi, *The Fracturing of the American Corporate Elite* (Cambridge, MA: Harvard University Press), 36–45; see also Rick Wartzman, *The End of Loyalty: The Rise and Fall of Good Jobs in America* (New York: Public Affairs, 2017), 11–19.

11. Committee for Economic Development, "Social Responsibilities of Business Corporations," June 1971, https://www.ced.org/pdf/Social_Responsibilities_of _Business_Corporations.pdf, 19–22, 27, 61.

12. "Real Gross Domestic Product: Historical Perspective," Bureau of Economic Analysis, U.S. Department of Commerce, https://apps.bea.gov/scb/account_articles /national/1199gdp/table6.htm.

13. Ronald Reagan, Inaugural Address, January 20, 1981, https://www.reagan foundation.org/media/128614/inauguration.pdf.

14. Michael J. Graetz, *The End of Energy: The Unmaking of America's Environment, Security, and Independence* (Cambridge, MA: MIT Press, 2011), 230.

15. David Vogel, *Fluctuating Fortunes: The Political Power of Business in America* (New York: Basic Books, 1989), 198–199.

16. Jerome L. Himmelstein, *To the Right: The Transformation of American Conservatism* (Berkeley: University of California Press, 1992), 140.

17. Barbara A. Bardes, Mack C. Shelley, and Steffen W. Schmidt, *American Government and Politics Today: The Essentials 2008* (Boston: Cengage Learning, 2009); Kelly LeRoux and Mary K. Feeney, *Nonprofit Organizations and Civil Society in the United States* (Abingdon-on-Thames, UK: Routledge, 2014); see also "FORTUNE Releases Annual Survey of Most Powerful Lobbying Organizations," Warner Media press release, November 15, 1999, http://origin-www.timewarner .com/newsroom/press-releases/1999/11/15/fortune-releases-annual-survey-of-most -powerful-lobbying.

18. Quoted in Graetz, *End of Energy*, 221.

19. See Leon H. Keyserling, "The Wagner Act: Its Origin and Current Significance," *George Washington Law Review* 29, no. 2 (1960): 199–233.

20. Quoted in Leon H. Keyserling, "In the Beginning: Why the Wagner Act?" in *The Wagner Act: After Ten Years*, ed. Louis Silverberg (Washington, DC: Bureau of National Affairs, 1945), 13.

21. William T. Dickens and Jonathan S. Leonard, "Accounting for the Decline in Union Membership, 1950–1980," *Industrial and Labor Relations Review* 38, no. 3 (1985), 323.

22. "Union Membership Rate 10.7 Percent in 2016," TED: The Economics Daily, Bureau of Labor Statistics, Department of Labor, February 9, 2017, https://www.bls.gov/opub/ted/2017/union-membership-rate-10-point-7 -percent-in-2016.htm.

23. James A. Gross, "Conflicting Statutory Purposes: Another Look at Fifty Years of NLRB Law Making," *Industrial and Labor Relations Review* 39, no. 1 (1985): 7–18, 7, 12.

24. A. H. Raskin, "Elysium Lost: The Wagner Act at Fifty," *Stanford Law Review* 38, no. 4 (1986): 945–955, 945, 949.

25. For an excellent account of union decline, focusing on the 1970s, see Jefferson Cowie, *Stayin' Alive: The 1970s and the Last Days of the Working Class* (New York: New Press, 2010).

26. Joseph A. McCartin, *Collision Course: Ronald Reagan, the Air Traffic Controllers, and the Strike That Changed America* (New York: Oxford University Press, 2011), 10.

27. Quoted in Jefferson Cowie, "How Ronald Reagan Broke the Air Controllers Union—And Why That Still Matters," *Dissent*, March 25, 2012.

28. William B. Gould IV, "Some Reflections on Fifty Years of the National Labor Relations Act: The Need for Labor Law and Labor Board Reform," Stanford *Law Review* 38, no. 4 (1986): 937–944. For discussion see Michael J. Graetz and Linda Greenhouse, *The Burger Court and the Rise of the Judicial Right* (New York: Simon and Schuster, 2016), 237–296.

29. *Howard Johnson Co. v. Detroit Local Joint Executive Board*, 417 U.S. 249 (1974); *NLRB v. Bildisco and Bildisco*, 465 U.S. 513 (1984).

30. See Kyle Peterson and John Crawley, "American Airlines Seeks to Void Labor Contracts," *Reuters*, March 27, 2012, https://www.reuters.com/article/us-amr-labor/american-airlines-seeks-to-void-labor-contracts-idUSBRE82R00H20120328.

31. *Linden Lumber Division, Summer & Co. v. NLRB*, 419 U.S. 301 (1974).

32. Employee Free Choice Act of 2009, H.R. 1409, 111th Cong. (2009), 560.

33. *Janus v. American Federation of State, County, and Municipal Employees*, 585 U.S., 138 S.Ct. 2448 (2018).

34. 138 S. Ct. at 2499 (dissenting opinion of Justice Ginsburg).

35. *Epic Systems Corp. v. Lewis*, 584 U.S., and 138 S.Ct. 1612 (2017). This exception for performance-based compensation was repealed in 2017.

36. 138 S. Ct at 2502 (dissenting opinion of Justice Kagan).

37. See Kim Hill and Emilio Brahmst, "The Auto Industry Moving South: An Examination of Trends," Center for Automotive Research, Ann Arbor, MI, December 15, 2003.

38. For a brief tour of this intellectual history, see Mizruchi, *Fracturing of the American Corporate Elite*, 204–208; Wartzman, End of Loyalty, 257–288.

39. Milton Friedman, "A Friedman Doctrine," New York Times Magazine, September 13, 1970.

40. Rakesh Khurana, *From Higher Aims to Hired Hands: The Social Transformation of American Business Schools and the Unfulfilled Promise of Management as a Profession* (Princeton: Princeton University Press, 2010), 291–361.

41. Recounted in conversation with Ian Malcolm and confirmed to the authors, via Malcolm, on June 27, 2019.

42. See Wartzman, *End of Loyalty*, 270–275.

43. Internal Revenue Code §162(m). This exception for performance-based compensation was repealed in 2017.

44. This is not to say that all companies are obsessed with keeping wages low. The classic comparison is between competitors Walmart and Costco. The average wage in 2006 at Costco was $17 an hour, while a full-time worker at Walmart made $10.11. At Sam's Club, a Walmart affiliate, the average wage also was about $10 an hour. Eighty-two percent of Costco's workers have employer-based health insurance, compared to fewer than half at Walmart. Walmart paid about 8 percent of their employees' health insurance premiums, while Costco paid about one-third of employees' premiums. Unsurprisingly, employee turnover is much lower at Costco than at Walmart. See Wayne F. Cascio, "The High Cost of Low Wages," *Harvard Business Review*, December 2006.

45. Wartzman, End of Loyalty, 275.

46. Mizruchi, *Fracturing of the American Corporate Elite*, 218. See also Wartzman, *End of Loyalty*, 232–236, 240–247.

47. Nathaniel Parish Flannery, "Executive Compensation: The True Cost of the 10 Largest CEO Severance Packages of the Past Decade," Forbes, January 19, 2012.

48. Wartzman, *End of Loyalty*, 269.

49. Mizruchi, *Fracturing of the American Corporate Elite*, 209–212, 215–216.

50. Wartzman, *End of Loyalty*, 268. Many insist that shareholder wealth maximization is required by Delaware corporate law, but the "business judgment rule" gives corporate managers wide discretion. Stephen M. Bainbridge, "Corporate Purpose in a Populist Era," Law and Economics Research Paper No. 18-09, UCLA School of Law, March 2019, and sources cited therein.

51. Mizruchi, *Fracturing of the American Corporate Elite*, 265.

52. Quoted in Michael J. Graetz, *The End of Energy: The Unmaking of America's Environment, Security, and Independence* (Cambridge: MIT Press, 2011), 236.

53. For more, see Graetz, *End of Energy*, chapter 13.

54. Graetz, *End of Energy*, 237, 241.

55. Ryan Lizza, "As the World Burns," New Yorker, October 3, 2010.

56. See Jacob S. Hacker, *The Great Risk Shift* (Oxford: Oxford University Press, 2006), 137–163.

57. For further discussion see Frances McCall Rosenbluth and Ian Shapiro, *Responsible Parties: Saving Democracy from Itself* (New Haven: Yale University Press, 2018), 95–127.

58. Wartzman, *End of Loyalty*, 325.

59. Sylvester J. Schieber and Steven A. Nyce, "Health Care USA: A Cancer on the American Dream," Council for Affordable Health Coverage and Willis Towers Watson, August 31, 2018, 31–36, https://www.willistowerswatson.com/en-US/insights/2018/08/health-care-usa-a-cancer-on-the-american-dream.

60. Mizruchi, *Fracturing of the American Corporate Elite*, 256.

61. Rosenbluth and Shapiro, *Responsible Parties*, 96.

62. Timothy Noah, "Obama's Biggest Health Reform Blunder," Slate, August 6, 2009, http://www.slate.com/articles/news_and_politics/prescriptions/2009/08/obamas_biggest_health_reform_blunder.html.

63. During the remainder of the Obama administration, Republicans repeatedly promised to repeal Obamacare. But they failed even after they gained control of the House, Senate, and White House in 2017. The tax bill they passed in December of that year attempted to eviscerate the law by repealing the requirement that everyone have health insurance coverage, a mandate that had been thought necessary to make insurance pools work well. Together with a series of regulatory changes adopted by the Trump administration and a lawsuit it supported, this threatened to unravel Obamacare's gains in health coverage.

64. Jan Fichtner, Eelke M. Heemskerk and Javier Garcia-Bernardo, "Hidden Power of the Big Three? Passive Index Funds, Re-Concentration of Corporate Ownership, and New Financial Risk," *Business and Politics* 19, no. 2 (2017): 298–326, 311.

65. Larry Fink, "A Sense of Purpose," January 16, 2018, https://seekingalpha.com/article/4137819-larry-finks-2018-letter-ceos-sense-purpose (emphasis added).

66. Larry Fink, "Purpose and Profit," [n.d.] 2019 https://www.blackrock.com/corporate/investor-relations/larry-fink-ceo-letter.

67. Quoted in Andrew Edgecliffe-Johnson, "Beyond the Bottom Line: Should Business Put Purpose before Profit?" *Financial Times*, January 4, 2019.

68. Colin Mayer, *Prosperity: Better Business Makes the Greater Good* (Oxford: Oxford University Press, 2019), 9, 15, 35.

69. Joseph L. Bower and Lynn S. Paine, "The Error at the Heart of Corporate Leadership," *Harvard Business Review*, 95, no. 3 (2017): 50–60. Senator Elizabeth Warren (D-MA) in 2019 proposed a mandatory federal charter that would require businesses with more than $1 billion of revenues to consider explicitly the interests of their communities, customers, and employees as well as of their investors. Elizabeth Warren, "Accountable Capitalism Act," August 15, 2018.

70. Jamie Dimon, "Letter to Shareholders," April 4, 2019, https://www.jpmorganchase.com/corporate/investor-relations/document/ceo-letter-to-shareholders-2019.pdf.

71. Caroline Kelly, "Freshman Democrat Presses JPMorgan CEO Jamie Dimon over Pay Disparity," CNN Politics, April 11, 2019, https://www.cnn.com/2019/04/10/politics/katie-porter-jamie-dimon-bank-employees/index.html.

72. Ray Dalio, "Why and How Capitalism Needs to Be Reformed," *Bridgewater Daily Observations*, April 5, 2019; and Ray Dalio, "My Diagnosis of Why Capitalism Is Now Not Working Well for the Majority of People," *Bridgewater Daily Observations*, April 6, 2019.

73. Quoted in Andrew Edgecliff-Johnson, "Why American CEOs Are Worried about Capitalism," *Financial Times,* April 23, 2019.

74. Business Roundtable, "Business Roundtable Redefines the Purpose of a Corporation to Promote 'An Economy That Serves All Americans,'" August 19, 2019, https://www.businessroundtable.org/business-roundtable-redefines-the-purpose-of-a-corporation-to-promote-an-economy-that-serves-all-americans.

75. Richard Henderson and Patrick Temple-West, "Group of US Corporate Leaders Ditches Shareholder-First Mantra," *Financial Times*, August 19, 2019.

76. Edgecliff-Johnson, "Why American CEOs Are Worried."

5. Making Work Pay

1. Randolph had founded and led the Brotherhood of Sleeping Car Porters, the first African American union. See William P. Jones, *The March on Washington: Jobs, Freedom, and the Forgotten History of Civil Rights* (New York: Norton, 2014), 121–200.

2. "A National Call for Moral Revival," Poor People's Campaign, https://www.poorpeoplescampaign.org.

3. Renata Sago, "Low-Wage Workers Are Reviving Dr. King's 1968 Poor People's Campaign," *Marketplace,* Minnesota Public Radio, May 8, 2018, https://www.marketplace.org/2018/05/04/wealth-poverty/grassroots-campaign.

4. Steven Greenhouse, "Low-Wage Workers Are Finding Poverty Harder to Escape," *New York Times,* March 16, 2014.

5. Peter Cappelli, "Career Jobs Are Dead," *California Management Review* 42, no. 1 (1999): 146–167.

6. Martin Luther King, *Where Do We Go from Here: Chaos or Community?* (New York: Harper and Row, 1967; Boston: Beacon Press, 2010), 171. See also Jordan Weissmann, "Martin Luther King's Economic Dream: A Guaranteed Income for All Americans," *Atlantic,* August 28, 2013.

7. Daniel Patrick Moynihan, *The Politics of a Guaranteed Income: The Nixon Administration and the Family Assistance Plan* (New York: Random House, 1973), 327–337, 532–533.

8. Donald Clark Hodges, *Class Politics in the Information Age* (Champaign: University of Illinois Press, 2000), 108; "Weighted Average Poverty Thresholds for Families of Specified Size," Historical Poverty Tables: People and Families—1959 to 2017, U.S. Census Bureau, U.S. Department of Commerce, https://www.census.gov/data/tables/time-series/demo/income-poverty/historical-poverty-people.html.

9. See Guida West, *The National Welfare Rights Organization: The Social Protest of Poor Women* (New York: Praeger, 1981).

10. Christopher Howard, *The Hidden Welfare State: Tax Expenditures and Social Policy in the United States* (Princeton: Princeton University Press, 1997).

11. For an overview of UBI debate, see Sarah Glazer, "Universal Basic Income," *CQ Researcher* 27, no. 31 (September 2017): 725–748.

12. Michelle Chen, "Could a Universal Basic Income Work in the US?" *The Nation*, August 15, 2017. See also Fred Block and Frances Fox Piven, "A Basic Income Would Upend America's Work Ethic—And, That's a Good Thing," *The Nation*, August 23, 2017.

13. Chris Weller, "8 High-Profile Entrepreneurs Who Have Endorsed Universal Basic Income," *Business Insider*, November 9, 2016, https://www.businessinsider.com/entrepreneurs-endorsing-universal-basic-income-2016-11; "$10 Million Project to Study Basic Incomes Launched," *Philanthropy News Digest*, December 16, 2016, https://philanthropynewsdigest.org/news/10-million-project-to-study-basic-income-programs-launched.

14. Andy Stern and Lee Kravitz, *Raising the Floor: How a Universal Basic Income Can Renew Our Economy* (Washington, DC: Public Affairs, 2016).

15. Charles Murray, *In Our Hands: A Plan to Replace the Welfare State* (Washington, DC: AEI Press, 2016), 11.

16. Quoted in Anne Nova, "More Americans Now Support a Universal Basic Income," CNBC, February 26, 2018, https://www.cnbc.com/2018/02/26/roughly-half-of-americans-now-support-universal-basic-income.html.

17. See Philippe Van Parijs, "Why Surfers Should Be Fed: The Liberal Case for an Unconditional Basic Income," *Philosophy and Public Affairs* 20, no. 2 (1991): 101–131. See also John Zogby, "Public Opinion toward Universal Basic Income," Utica College Center of Public Affairs Election Research, December 5, 2018, https://www.ucpublicaffairs.com/home/2017/12/5/public-opinion-toward-univerisal-basic-income-by-john-zogby. Unlike the UBI, Milton Friedman's negative income tax would not provide cash benefits to the rich.

18. "Switzerland's Voters Reject Basic Income Plan," BBC News, June 5, 2016, http://www.bbc.com/news/world-europe-36454060.

19. See John Henley, "Finland to End Basic Income Trial after Two Years," *Guardian*, April 23, 2018.

20. The Personal Responsibility and Work Opportunity Act of 1996 replaced Aid for Families with Dependent Children with the conditional and time-limited Temporary Aid for Needy Families. See "The Personal Responsibility and Work Opportunity Reconciliation Act of 1996," Office of the Assistant Secretary for Planning and Evaluation, U.S. Department of Health and Human Services, https://aspe.hhs.gov/report/personal-responsibility-and-work-opportunity-reconciliation-act-1996.

21. Ashley Kirzinger, Bianca DiJulio, Liz Hamel, Bryan Wu, and Mollyann Brodie, "Kaiser Health Tracking Poll—June 2017: ACA, Replacement Plan, and Medicaid," Kaiser Family Foundation, June 23, 2017, https://www.kff.org/health -reform/poll-finding/kaiser-health-tracking-poll-june-2017-aca-replacement-plan -and-medicaid.

22. John H. Cushman, Jr., "Russell B. Long, 84, Senator Who Influenced Tax Laws," *New York Times,* May 11, 2003.

23. V. Joseph Hotz and John Karl Scholz, "The Earned Income Tax Credit," in *Means-Tested Transfer Programs,* ed. Robert A. Moffitt (Chicago: University of Chicago Press, 2003).

24. Congressional Record, September 30, 1972, at 33010–33011. See, generally, Margot L. Crandall-Hollick, "The Earned Income Tax Credit (EITC): A Brief History," Congressional Research Service, March 20, 2018.

25. David Wessel, "Expanded Earned-Income Tax Credit Emerges as the Anti-Poverty Program of Choice for Many," *Wall Street Journal,* July 13, 1989, quoted in Crandall-Hollick, "Earned Income Tax Credit." See also Anne L. Alstott, "Why the EITC Doesn't Make Work Pay," *Law and Contemporary Problems* 73 (2010): 285–313.

26. "Working Income Tax Benefit—Overview," Government of Canada, April 10, 2019, https://www.canada.ca/en/revenue-agency/services/child-family -benefits/canada-workers-benefit.html.

27. For an example of how relief for low-income workers and their families might be separated into worker and child credits, see Michael J. Graetz, "The Tax Reform Road Not Taken—Yet," *National Tax Journal* 67, no. 2 (2014): 419–440, 419, 431–432.

28. Elaine Maag, Kevin Werner, and Laura Wheaton, "Expanding the EITC for Workers without Resident Children," Urban Institute, May 2019, https://www .urban.org/sites/default/files/publication/100130/expanding_the_eitc_for_workers _without_resident_children_3.pdf.

29. See Jonathan Grossman, "Fair Labor Standards Act of 1938: Maximum Struggle for a Minimum Wage," U.S. Department of Labor, https://www.dol.gov /general/aboutdol/history/flsa1938.

30. *Schecter Corp. v. United States,* 295 U.S. 495 (1935).

31. *Morehead v. Tipaldo,* 298 U.S. 587 (1936).

32. *West Coast Hotel Co. v. Parrish,* 300 U.S. 379 (1937).

33. Franklin D. Roosevelt, "Annual Message to Congress," January 3, 1938, 1–14, *Public Papers and Addresses,* [vol. 7]: *1938* (New York: Random House, 1941), 6.

34. Franklin D. Roosevelt, "The President Recommends Legislation Establishing Minimum Wages and Maximum Hours," May 24, 1937, 209–218, *Public Papers and Addresses,* [vol. 6]: *1937* (New York: Random House, 1941).

35. Frances Perkins, *People at Work* (New York: John Day Company, 1934), 138.

36. Quoted in Teresa Tritch, "FDR Makes the Case for the Minimum Wage," *New York Times,* March 7, 2014.

37. Franklin D. Roosevelt, "The Goal of the National Industrial Recovery Act," June 16, 1933, *Public Papers and Addresses,* [vol. 2]: *1933* (New York: Random House, 1938), 246.

38. Jordain Carney, "Sanders, Democrats Introduce $15 Minimum Wage Bill," *The Hill,* May 25, 2017, https://thehill.com/blogs/floor-action/senate/335227 -sanders-democrats-introduce-15-minimum-wage-bill.

39. Congressional Budget Office, "The Effects of a Minimum Wage Increase on Employment and Family Income," July 2019, https:www.cbo.gov/system/files/2019 -07/CBO-55410-MinimumWage2019.pdf, 6.

40. The House vote was 315–116. All the no votes were cast by Republicans. Eighty-two Republicans supported the increase. In the Senate forty-three Republicans blocked the minimum wage increase until a tax cut for small businesses was included. The Senate ultimately voted 94–3 for the bill, which also included veterans-care provisions and relief for victims of Hurricane Katrina.

41. "Executive Order 13658, Establishing a Minimum Wage for Federal Contractors: Annual Update," May 14, 2015, U.S. Department of Labor, Wage and Hour Division, https://www.dol.gov/whd/flsa/eo13658/index.htm.

42. National Conference of State Legislatures, "State Minimum Wages: 2019 Minimum Wage by State," January 7, 2019, http://www.ncsl.org/research/labor-and -employment/state-minimum-wage-chart.aspx.

43. Executive Office of the President, "Raising the Minimum Wage: A Progress Update," October 2016, https://obamawhitehouse.archives.gov/sites/default/files /minimum_wage/6_october_2016_min_wage_report-final.pdf.

44. See Chelsea Bowling, "State Preemption of Local Minimum Wage Laws," unpublished manuscript, Yale Law School, January 2017.

45. Lance Williams, "Tennessee Leads Nation for Minimum Wage Workers," *The Tennessean,* March 25, 2014, https://www.tennessean.com/story/money/2014/03 /25/tennessee-leads-nation-minimum-wage-workers/6865841.

46. "Americans Support Greater Federal Efforts to Reduce Poverty," Program for Public Consultation, University of Maryland School of Public Policy, June 1, 2017, https://www.publicconsultation.org/federal-budget/americans-support-greater -federal-efforts-to-reduce-poverty.

47. This might be easier done by disaggregating the amount of the credit based on wages from the amount based on the number of children. See James R. Nunns, Elaine Maag, and Hang Nguyen, "An Option to Reform the Income Tax Treatment of Families and Work," Urban Institute, December 5, 2016, https://www.urban.org/research/publication/option-reform-income-tax -treatment-families-and-work.

48. See Isabel V. Sawhill and Quentin Karpilow, "Raising the Minimum Wage and Redesigning the EITC," Brookings, January 30, 2014, https://www.brookings .edu/research/raising-the-minimum-wage-and-redesigning-the-eitc.

6. From Unemployment to Reemployment

1. See Michael J. Graetz and Jerry L. Mashaw, *True Security: Rethinking American Social Insurance* (New Haven: Yale University Press, 1999); Jacob S. Hacker, *The Great Risk Shift* (Oxford: Oxford University Press, 2006); Kathleen Thelen, "The American Precariat: U.S. Capitalism in Comparative Perspective," *Perspectives on Politics* 17, no. 1 (2019): 5–27, Figs. 7, 8, and 9.

2. Many of the challenges we describe in the US are emerging in European democracies as well. See Christian Salas, Frances Rosenbluth, and Ian Shapiro, "Political Parties and the New Politics of Insecurity," in *The New Politics of Insecurity,* ed. Frances Rosenbluth and Kathleen Thelen (forthcoming).

3. Kevin Liffey, "Trump Tweets: Trade Wars Are Good, and Easy to Win," *Reuters*, March 2, 2018, https://www.reuters.com/article/us-usa-trade-trump/trump-tweets-trade-wars-are-good-and-easy-to-win-idUSKCN1GE1E9.

4. Peter Pham, "Why Did Donald Trump Kill This Big Free Trade Deal?" *Forbes*, December 27, 2017; Adam Taylor, "A Timeline of Trump's Complicated Relationship with the TPP," *Washington Post*, April 13, 2018.

5. Robin Harding, "Trump's Withdrawal from TPP Creates High Stakes Turmoil," *Financial Times*, May 4, 2017.

6. Donald Trump, Presidential Memorandum Regarding Withdrawal of the United States from the Trans-Pacific Negotiations and Agreement, January 23, 2017.

7. Mark Landler and Alan Rappeport, "Trump Hails Revised NAFTA Trade Deal and Sets Up a Showdown with China," *New York Times*, October 1, 2018.

8. Gary Hufbauer and Zhigaho (Lucy) Lu, "The Payoff to America from Global Integration: A Fresh Look with a Focus on Costs to Workers," Policy Brief 17–16, Peterson Institute for International Economics, Washington, DC, May 2017.

9. For further discussion, see Michael J. Graetz, *The End of Energy: The Unmaking of America's Environment, Security, and Independence* (Cambridge, MA: MIT Press, 2011).

10. This history is recounted in Bob Bryan, "Trump's Trade Policy Has Been Tried Before—and It Was Terrible for the US Economy," Business Insider, March 2, 2018, https://www.businessinsider.com/what-is-a-tariff-trump-on-steel-aluminum-economic-impact-2018-3.

11. Lawrence H. Summers, "Trump's Trade Policy Violates Almost Every Strategic Rule," *Washington Post*, June 4, 2018.

12. Section 232 of the Trade Expansion Act of 1962, 232, 19 U.S.C. (1962). See also "Section 232 of the Trade Expansion Act of 1962," In Focus, Congressional Research Service, July 16, 2019, https://fas.org/sgp/crs/misc/IF10667.pdf.

13. Catherine Rampell, "So You're Telling Me My Subaru Is a National Security Threat?" *Washington Post*, May 24, 2018.

14. Mark Landler and Ana Swanson, "Trump Sees a China Trade Deal through a New Prism: The 2020 Election," *New York Times*, May 10, 2019.

15. Mary E. Lovely and Yang Liang, "Trump Tariffs Primarily Hit Multinational Supply Chains, Harm US Technology Competitiveness," Policy Brief 19–12, Peterson Institute for International Economics, May 2018.

16. Thomas Franck, "Tariffs Are Being Mentioned on 40 Percent of Earnings Calls," CNBC, July 25, 2018, https://www.cnbc.com/2018/07/25/here-are-the-companies-talking-about-trumps-tariffs.html; Laura Sparks and Jason Dean, "What Companies in Your State Are Avoiding Trump's Steel Tariffs?" WiscNews, June 24, 2019. https://www.wiscnews.com/news/national/what-companies-in-your-state-are-avoiding-trump-s-steel/article_5ccec3e7-9848-5b6a-a37b-990617666fe7.html.

17. David J. Lynch, "This Ohio Factory Thought It Could Bring U.S. Jobs Back from China. Then Trump Got Involved," *Washington Post*, June 6, 2018.

18. Quoted in Jim Tankersley, "This Factory Was Ready to Expand. Then Came the Trump Trade Wars," *New York Times*, June 1, 2018.

19. Rick Barrett, "Trump Responds as Harley-Davidson Announces Plans to Move More Motorcycle Products Overseas," *Milwaukee Journal Sentinel,* June 27,

2018, https://www.jsonline.com/story/money/2018/06/25/response-tariff-harley -davidson-moving-more-production-overseas/729995002.

20. Chris Isidore, "Largest US Nail Manufacturer 'On the Brink of Extinction' Because of the Steel Tariffs," CNN Money, June 26, 2018, https://money.cnn.com /2018/06/26/news/companies/steel-tariffs-job-losses/index.html.

21. Aaron Flaaen, Ali Hortaçsu, and Felix Tintelnot, "The Production Reloca- tion and Price Effects of US Trade Policy: The Case of Washing Machines," Working Paper No. 2019-61, Becker Friedman Institute, University of Chicago, April 2019.

22. Pablo D. Fajgelbaum, Pinelopi K. Goldberg, Patrick J. Kennedy, and Amit K. Khandelwal, "The Return to Protectionism," NBER Working Paper No. 25638, National Bureau of Economic Research, Cambridge, MA, March 2019, 25, 27.

23. Heather Long, "Trump's Steel Tariffs Cost U.S. Consumers $900,000 for Every Job Created, Experts Say," *Washington Post*, May 7, 2019; Flaaen et al., "Production Relocation and Price Effects."

24. Tony Newmyer, "The Finance 202: Trump's Trade Offensive Is Producing Brutal Local Headlines," *Washington Post*, July 16, 2018.

25. "Soybean Farmer Calls Trump's $12 Billion Plan a 'Pacifier,'" CBS News, July 25, 2018, https://www.cbsnews.com/news/soybean-farmer-calls-trumps-12 -billion-bailout-a-pacifier.

26. Ana Swanson, "Trump Gives Farmers $16 Billion in Aid Amid Prolonged China Trade War," *New York Times*, May 23, 2019.

27. Michael Hiltzik, "Rich Farmers, Not Mom-and-Pop Farms, Will Collect Most of Trump's Tariff Bailout," *Los Angeles Times*, May 28, 2019.

28. Emma Newburger, "'Trump Is Ruining Our Markets': Struggling Farmers Are Losing a Huge Customer in the Trade War—China," CNBC, August 10, 2019, https://www.cnbc.com/2019/08/10/trump-is-ruining-our-markets-farmers-lose-a -huge-customer-to-trade-war----china.html.

29. Fajgelbaum et al., "Return to Protectionism," 29–30.

30. Paul Krugman, "Trump Is Terrible for Rural America," *New York Times*, May 9, 2019.

31. Jacqueline Alemany, "Power Up: Trump Wants a 2020 Fight over Tariffs That Will Test the Patience of His Base," *Washington Post*, May 15, 2019.

32. Michael D. Shear, Ana Swanson, and Azam Ahmed, "Trump Calls Off Plan to Impose Tariffs on Mexico," *New York Times*, June 7, 2019.

33. Daniel Victor, "No, Mr. Trump, Canada Did Not Burn the White House Down in 1812," *New York Times*, June 6, 2018.

34. In the summer of 2018, Senator Bob Corker (R–TN) introduced legislation to restrict the president's authority to impose tariffs on national security grounds. But the proposal didn't go anywhere. Haley Byrd, "Corker to Introduce Bill in Response to Trump's Steel, Aluminum Tariffs," *Weekly Standard*, June 5, 2018.

35. Even opposition by the Republican power brokers the Koch brothers didn't slow Trump. Tony Newmyer, "The Finance 202: Trump Draws Powerful Enemy in Trade Fight: The Koch Brothers," *Washington Post*, June 5, 2018.

36. Daniel Kahneman and Amos Tversky, "Prospect Theory: An Analysis of Decision Under Risk," *Econometrica* 47, no. 4 (1979); Jeffry A. Frieden, Debt, Development, and Democracy: Modern Political Economy and Latin America, 1965–85 (Princeton: Princeton University Press, 1992); James E. Alt, Jeffry Frieden,

Michael J. Gilligan, Dani Rodrik, and Ronald Rogowski, "The Political Economy of International Trade," *Comparative Political Studies* 29, no. 6 (1996): 689–717.

37. Brett Samuels, "Merkel Says She's Open to Reducing EU Tariffs on US Car Imports," The Hill, July 5, 2018, http://thehill.com/policy/international/395591 -merkel-says-shes-open-to-reducing-eu-tariffs-on-us-car-imports; Silvia Amaro, "US-EU Trade Agreement Lacks Specifics and Fails to Eliminate Issues with China," CNBC Europe News, July 26, 2018, https://www.cnbc.com/2018/07/26/us -eu-trade-agreement-lacks-detail-and-fails-to-end-issues-with-china.html.

38. David J. Lynch, "As Trade Deficit Explodes, Trump Finds He Can't Escape the Laws of Economics," *Washington Post*, March 6, 2019.

39. Patrick Gillespie, "Growing Up Poor Makes It Harder to Succeed: Janet Yellen," CNN Business, March 23, 2017, https://money.cnn.com/2017/03/23/news /economy/fed-yellen-income-inequality-poor-success-study.

40. Annie Gowen, "Left Behind: Farmers Fight to Save Their Land in Rural Minnesota as Trade War Intensifies," *Washington Post*, August 3, 2019.

41. Ylan Q. Mui, Matea Gold, and Max Ehrenfreund, "Trump Vows 'Conse-quences' for Firms Moving Offshore after $7M Deal with Carrier," *Chicago Tribune*, December 1, 2016.

42. Aaron Rupar, "Carrier Says It Will Spend Millions Automating Plant, Plans to Lay Off Workers Trump 'Saved,'" Think Progress, December 9, 2016, https:// thinkprogress.org/carrier-automation-trump-deal-more-layoffs-db2554f46297.

43. Louisa Thomas, "America First, for Charles Lindbergh and Donald Trump," New Yorker, July 24, 2016.

44. Graetz and Mashaw, True Security, 90.

45. Organisation for Economic Co-operation and Development (OECD), *Back to Work: United States: Improving the Re-employment Prospects of Displaced Workers* (Paris: OECD Publishing, 2016), 81.

46. Lawrence F. Katz and Alan B. Krueger, "The Rise and Nature of Alternative Work Arrangements in the United States, 1995–2015," NBER Working Paper No. 22667, National Bureau of Economic Research, Cambridge, MA, September 2016. See, generally, Conor McKay, Ethan Pollack, and Alastair Fitzpayne, "Modernizing Unemployment Insurance for the Changing Nature of Work," Future of Work Initiative, Aspen Institute, January 2018.

47. Daisuke Wakabayashi, "Google's Shadow Work Force: Temps Who Outnumber Full-Time Employees," *New York Times*, May 28, 2019.

48. National Employment Law Project Annual Report, 2016. In 2010 the Government Accountability Office (GAO) reported that, of the 15 million workers who lost jobs from 2007 to 2009, only about half received unemployment insurance. GAO found that low-wage workers were almost two-and-one-half times as likely as higher-wage workers to be out of work yet were about half as likely to receive unemployment benefits. "Unemployment Insurance: Economic Circumstances of Individuals Who Exhausted Benefits," GAO-12-408, February 17, 2012.

49. Most state unemployment insurance programs normally pay benefits to eligible workers for up to twenty-six weeks. An extended program may pay benefits for an additional thirteen to twenty weeks in states where unemployment is especially high. Since 2009 the extended benefits program has been 100 percent federally funded, and during severe recessions Congress has funded additional

temporary extensions. Extended benefits tend to encourage the long-term unemployed to keep looking for work instead of leaving the workforce altogether.

50. The low taxable earnings base for unemployment insurance stands in sharp contrast to that used for Social Security, which was $127,000 in 2017 and is indexed to keep pace with wage growth. Medicare hospital insurance funding is much more progressive, having no cap.

51. Nicholas Kaldor, "Welfare Propositions of Economics and Interpersonal Comparisons of Utility," *Economic Journal* 49 (September 1939): 549–552.

52. See I. M. D. Little, *A Critique of Welfare Economics* (Oxford: Oxford University Press, 1950), 84–116.

53. Paul A. Samuelson, "Where Ricardo and Mill Rebut and Confirm Arguments of Mainstream Economists Supporting Globalization," *Journal of Economic Perspectives* 18, no. 3 (2004): 135–146.

54. Clair Wilcox, "Relief for Victims of Tariff Cuts," American Economic Review 40, no. 5 (1950): 884–889.

55. Steve Charnovitz, "Worker Adjustment: The Missing Ingredient in Trade Policy," *California Management Review* 28, no. 2 (1986): 156–173.

56. John F. Kennedy, Special Message to the Congress on Foreign Trade Policy (January 25, 1962), Public Papers of the Presidents of the United States (Washington, DC: Government Printing Office, 1963), https://www.presidency.ucsb.edu /node/235741.

57. Representative Keogh, speaking on Trade Expansion Act of 1962 HR 11970, 87th Congress, Congressional Record, June 27, 1962, 11951, https://www.govinfo .gov/content/pkg/GPO-CRECB-1962-pt9/pdf/GPO-CRECB-1962-pt9-4.pdf.

58. Kennedy, Special Message to the Congress.

59. George Meany, Hearings before the Committee on Finance, U.S. Senate, July 24, 1962, p. 241; and Hearings Before the Committee on Ways and Means, U.S. House of Representatives, March 19, 1962, p. 1145. In fact labor leaders had been advocates of trade adjustment assistance since the Eisenhower administration. In 1953 United Steelworkers President David J. McDonald, a member of the Randall Commission on Foreign Economic Policy, proposed that decreasing tariffs should be accompanied by government funds for technical and financial assistance to encourage firms to seek out new lines of business. He also supported accelerated tax write-offs and preferential treatment in awarding government contracts. These would accompany unemployment assistance and job training for displaced workers. The Commission rejected his proposals. Edward Alden, *Failure to Adjust: How Americans Got Left Behind in the World Economy* (New York: Rowman and Littlefield, 2016), 116–117.

60. John F. Kennedy, Address Before the Conference on Trade Policy (May 17, 1962), Public Papers of the Presidents of the United States (Washington, DC: Government Printing Office, 1963), https://www.presidency.ucsb.edu/documents /address-before-the-conference-trade-policy.

61. Charnovitz, "Worker Adjustment," 159.

62. Quoted in Alden, *Failure to Adjust*, 113.

63. Alden, *Failure to Adjust*, 126.

64. OECD, *Back to Work*, 68–71.

65. Charnovitz, "Worker Adjustment," 159–168.

66. See, for example, Katherine Baicker and Marit M. Rehavi, "Policy Watch: Trade Adjustment Assistance," *Journal of Economic Perspectives* 18, no. 2 (2004): 239–255, esp. Table 7, p. 245; Hufbauer and Lu, "Payoff to America from Global Integration."

67. Baicker and Rehavi, "Trade Adjustment Assistance," 243–244.

68. "Provisions of the Trade Bill," PL 107–210 Signed by President George W. Bush on August 6, 2002, CQ Almanac, http://library.cqpress.com/cqalmanac /document.php?id=cqal02-236-10371-664236&type=toc&num=3.

69. $2.7 billion was added for worker retraining and education, and coverage was extended to service-sector workers. Jonathan Weisman, "House Approve Trade Bill's Expansion of Worker Aid," *New York Times*, June 25, 2015.

70. For a description see OECD, *Back to Work*, 119–122.

71. Mark A. McMinimy, "Trade Adjustment Assistance for Farmers," Congressional Research Service, August 1, 2016, https://fas.org/sgp/crs/misc/R40206.pdf.

72. Edward Alden, "How to Help Workers Laid Low by Trade—And Why We Haven't," PBS, November 16, 2018, https://www.pbs.org/newshour/economy /column-help-workers-laid-low-trade-havent.

73. David H. Autor, David Dorn, and Gordon H. Hanson, "The China Shock: Learning from Labor Market Adjustment to Large Changes in Trade," *Annual Review of Economics* 8 (2016): 205–240, 235.

74. Autor, Dorn, and Hanson, "China Shock," 230; David Autor and Mark G. Duggan, "The Rise in Disability Rolls and the Decline in Unemployment," *Quarterly Journal of Economics* 118, no. 1 (2003): 157–205.

75. See, for example, Baicker and Rahavi, "Trade Adjustment Assistance"; Kara M. Reynolds and John S. Palatucci, "Does Trade Adjustment Assistance Make a Difference?" *Contemporary Economic Policy* 30, no. 1 (2012): 43–59; Mark Muro and Joseph Parilla, "Maladjusted: It's Time to Reimagine Economic 'Adjustment' Programs," Brookings, January 10, 2017, https://www.brookings.edu/blog/the -avenue/2017/01/10/maladjusted-its-time-to-reimagine-economic-adjustment -programs.

76. Quoted in Bob Davis and John Hilsenrath, "How the China Shock, Deep and Swift, Spurred the Rise of Trump," *Wall Street Journal*, August 11, 2016.

77. Llewellyn Hinkes-Jones, "Long-Term Discouraged Workers Increase in Growing Economy," Bloomberg News, August 26, 2016.

78. Text of President Clinton's announcement on welfare legislation, *New York Times*, August 1, 1996.

79. See, for example, Baicker and Rahavi, "Trade Adjustment Assistance"; Reynolds and Palatucci, "Does Trade Adjustment Assistance Make a Difference?"; Graetz and Mashaw, *True Security*.

80. Alden, *Failure to Adjust*, 113.

81. Amit Dar and Indermit S. Gill, "Evaluating Retraining Programs in OECD Countries: Lessons Learned," *World Bank Research Observer* 13, no. 1 (1998): 79–101. This confirmed earlier conventional wisdom that had found scant evidence for the programs' effectiveness. See, for example, Organisation for Economic Co-operation and Development, *Employment Outlook* (Paris: OECD Publishing, 1993).

82. Carolyn J. Heinrich, Peter R. Mueser, and Kenneth R. Troske, "Workforce Investment Act Non-Experimental Net Impact Evaluation," IMPAQ Interna-

tional, December 2008, https://wdr.doleta.gov/research/FullText_Documents
/Workforce%20Investment%20Act%20Non-Experimental%20Net%20Impact%20
Evaluation%20-%20Final%20Report.pdf; Louis Jacobson, Robert J. Lalonde, and
Daniel Sullivan, "The Impact of Community College Retraining on Older
Displaced Workers: Should We Teach Old Dogs New Tricks?" *Industrial and Labor
Relations* 58, no. 3 (2005): 398–416.

83. Brett Walsh and Erica Volini, "Rewriting the Rules of the Digital Age,"
Deloitte, 2017, https://www2.deloitte.com/content/dam/Deloitte/global
/Documents/About-Deloitte/central-europe/ce-global-human-capital-trends.pdf.

84. "Missing Middle Skills for Human-AI Collaboration," Accenture and the
Aspen Institute, October 25, 2018, https://www.accenture.com/us-en/insights
/future-workforce/missing-middle-skills-human-ai-collaboration.

85. See, generally, Raven Molloy, Christopher L. Smith, and Abigail K. Wozniak,
"Internal Migration in the United States," NBER Working Paper No. 17307,
National Bureau of Economic Research, Cambridge, MA, August 2011. Renters are
more likely to move than homeowners; people under forty-five are more likely to
move than older persons; and mobility is greater as family income rises. Latinos and
African Americans are less mobile than whites. Thomas B. Foster, "Decomposing
American Mobility: Compositional and Rate Components of Interstate, Intrastate,
and Intracounty Migration and Mobility Decline," *Demographic Research* 37 (2017):
1515–1548.

86. Thomas J. Cooke, "It's Not Just the Economy: Declining Migration and the
Rise of Secular Rootedness," *Population, Space and Place* 17, no. 3 (2011): 193–203.

87. Kyle Fee, Keith Wardrip, and Lisa Nelson, "Opportunity Occupations
Revised: Exploring Employment for Sub-Baccalaureate Workers across Metro
Areas and over Time," Federal Reserve Bank of Cleveland, April 2019. For a
summary of their findings, see Eduardo Porter, "Where the Good Jobs Are," New
York Times, May 2, 2019.

88. Raj Chetty, Nathaniel Hendren, and Lawrence F. Katz, "The Effects of
Exposure to Better Neighborhoods on Children: New Evidence from the Moving
to Opportunity Experiment," *American Economic Review* 106, no. 4 (2016):
855–902.

89. See Frances McCall Rosenbluth and Ian Shapiro, *Responsible Parties:
Saving Democracy from Itself* (New Haven: Yale University Press, 2018), chs. 2, 3, 5,
and 12.

90. For proposals for personal accounts, see, for example, Lori G. Kletzer and
Howard Rosen, "Reforming Unemployment Insurance for the Twenty-First
Century Workforce," Brookings, September 1, 2006, https://www.brookings.edu
/research/reforming-unemployment-insurance-for-the-twenty-first-century
-workforce; Jonathan Gruber, "Security Accounts as Short-term Social Insurance
and Long-term Savings," Aspen Institute Future of Work Initiative, August 31,
2016, https://assets.aspeninstitute.org/content/uploads/2016/08/2security_accounts
_final.pdf.

91. Clinton was triangulating to his right, and sanctimoniously punitive welfare
reform was integral to that effort. On why triangulation is bad strategy even when it
is good tactics, see Michael J. Graetz and Ian Shapiro, *Death by a Thousand Cuts: The
Fight over Taxing Inherited Wealth* (Princeton: Princeton University Press, 2005),
263–265.

7. Waiting for Infrastructure

1. See Jim Tankersley, "Democrats' Next Big Thing: Government Guaranteed Jobs," *New York Times*, May 22, 2018; Matthew Yglesias, "Why Politicians Should Promise Every American a Job," Vox, April 27, 2018, https://www.vox.com/2018/4/27/17278052/case-for-jobs-guarantee-sanders-booker-gillibrand.

2. L. Randall Wray, Flavia Dantas, Scott Fullwiler, Pavlina R. Tcherneva, and Stephanie A. Kelton, "Public Service Employment: A Path to Full Employment," Levy Economics Institute, Bard College, April 2018, http://www.levyinstitute.org/pubs/rpr_4_18.pdf; Neera Tanden, Carmel Martin, Marc Jarsulic, Brendan Duke, Ben Olinsky, Melissa Boteach, John Halpin, Ruy Teixeira, and Rob Griffin, "Toward a Marshall Plan for America," Center for American Progress, Washington, DC, May 16, 2017, https://www.americanprogress.org/issues/economy/reports/2017/05/16/432499/toward-marshall-plan-america.

3. See The Federal Jobs Guarantee Development Act of 2018, introduced by Senator Cory Booker (D–NJ), April 25, 2018. S.2746, 115th Cong., 2nd Sess., https://www.congress.gov/115/bills/s2746/BILLS-115s2746is.pdf.

4. Franklin Delano Roosevelt, State of the Union message to Congress, January 11, 1944, http://www.fdrlibrary.marist.edu/archives/address_text.html.

5. UN General Assembly, "Universal Declaration of Human Rights," Article 23, no. 1, December 10, 1948, Paris.

6. According to Yglesias, "Why Politicians Should Promise," one poll by Civis Analytics found 52–49 percent support for a jobs guarantee; Sean McElwee, Colin McAuliffe, and Jon Green, "Why Democrats Should Embrace a Federal Jobs Guarantee," The Nation, March 20, 2018; a Rasmussen poll found 46 percent support. John Bowden, "46 Percent of Americans Support Government Jobs Guarantee: Poll," The Hill, May 2, 2018, https://thehill.com/blogs/blog-briefing-room/news/385840-46-percent-of-americans-support-government-jobs-guarantee-poll.

7. John J. DiIulio, Jr., "10 Questions and Answers about America's 'Big Government,'" Brookings, February 13, 2017, https://www.brookings.edu/blog/fixgov/2017/02/13/ten-questions-and-answers-about-americas-big-government; John J. DiIulio, Jr., *Bring Back the Bureaucrats* (West Conshohocken, PA: Templeton Press, 2014); Paul C. Light, "The True Size of Government: Tracking Washington's Blended Workforce, 1984–2015," Issue Paper, Volcker Alliance, October 2017, https://www.volckeralliance.org/sites/default/files/attachments/Issue%20Paper_True%20Size%20of%20Government.pdf.

8. DiIulio, "10 Questions and Answers."

9. Jon D. Michaels, *Constitutional Coup: Privatization's Threat to the American Republic* (Cambridge, MA: Harvard University Press, 2017), 3.

10. "Gaming the System: How the Political Strategies of Private Prison Companies Promote Ineffective Incarceration Policies," Justice Policy Institute, June 2011, 9–10, 30, http://www.justicepolicy.org/uploads/justicepolicy/documents/gaming_the_system.pdf; Kara Gotsch and Vinay Basti, "Capitalizing on Mass Incarceration: U.S. Growth in Private Prisons," The Sentencing Project, August 2, 2018, https://www.sentencingproject.org/publications/capitalizing-on-mass-incarceration-u-s-growth-in-private-prisons.

11. See Evan McKenzie, *Privatopia: Homeowner Associations and the Rise of Residential Private Government* (New Haven: Yale University Press, 1996); and

Evan McKenzie, *Beyond Privatopia: Rethinking Residential Private Government* (New York: Rowman and Littlefield, 2011).

12. One 1992 study estimated that $1 billion spent on infrastructure generates 40,000 jobs: Michael Montgomery and David Wyss, "The Impact of Infrastructure," DRI / McGraw-Hill U.S. Review (October 1992), reported in Edward V. Regan, "Infrastructure Investment for Tomorrow," Public Policy Brief no. 16, Levy Economics Institute, Bard College, November 1994, http://www.levyinstitute.org /publications/infrastructure-investment-for-tomorrow, 44. More recently Beth Bovino examined a $1.3 billion project, concluding that it would generate 36,600 jobs per $1 billion invested, 61 percent (29,000) of which would be construction jobs. Beth Ann Bovino, "U.S. Infrastructure Investment: A Chance to Reap More Than We Sow," Standard and Poor's Rating Services, McGraw Hill Financial, 2014, http://images.politico.com/global/2014/05/05/sp-usinfrastructure201405.pdf. Federal agencies have used different estimates. A 2007 Federal Highway Administration study suggests 27,800 job per $1 billion invested, while a study by the Council of Economic Advisors in connection with the proposed 2011 American Jobs Act figures 13,000 jobs per $1 billion invested. "Employment Impacts of Highway Infrastructure Investment," Federal Highway Administration, U.S. Department of Transportation, https://www.fhwa.dot.gov/policy/otps/pubs/impacts.

13. William Julius Wilson, *When Work Disappears: The World of the New Urban Poor* (New York: Vintage, 1996), ch. 8.

14. William Herndon Lehr, Carlos Osorio, Sharon E. Gillett, and Marvin A. Sirbu, "Measuring Broadband's Economic Impact," Working Paper Series, Engineering Systems Division, Massachusetts Institute of Technology, February 2006, https://dspace.mit.edu/handle/1721.1/102779; and Nina Czernich, Oliver Falck, Tobias Kretschmer, and Ludger Woessmann, "Broadband Infrastructure and Economic Growth," *Economic Journal* 121, no. 552 (2011): 505–532.

15. "Employment Impacts of Increased Highway Infrastructure Investment," New England Council, December 10, 2008, https://newenglandcouncil.com /assets/Employment-Generation-from-Federal-Aid-Highway-Projects-12-10 -08-.pdf.

16. The impact of infrastructure investment on economic growth varies by type of infrastructure investment and over time. Highways and other core infrastructure projects have had the most impact historically, though their effects have likely declined. Estimates of the overall results of a 1 percent increase in the value of transportation infrastructure vary from a long-run effect of about 0.12 percent GDP growth to about 0.56 percent. David Alan Aschauer, "Is Public Expenditure Productive?" *Journal of Monetary Economics* 23, no. 2 (1989): 177–200; Pedro R. D. Bom and Jenny E. Ligthart, "What Have We Learned from Three Decades of Research on the Productivity of Public Capital?" *Journal of Economic Surveys* 28, no. 5 (2014): 889–916.

17. Mickey Kaus, *The End of Equality* (New York: Basic Books, 1987), 259.

18. President Eisenhower's interstate highway construction, begun in the 1950s, is probably the closest analogue. The Comprehensive Employment and Training Act of the 1970s is widely considered to have failed, largely because states and localities simply substituted federally subsidized jobs for nonsubsidized ones.

19. "2017 Infrastructure Report Card," American Society of Civil Engineers, https://www.infrastructurereportcard.org.

NOTES TO PAGES 174-178

20. Justin Sink, "Obama: US Infrastructure 'Embarrassing,'" The Hill, December 3, 2014, https://thehill.com/homenews/administration/225875-obama-state-of-us-infrastructure-embarrassing; "Expanding the Market for Infrastructure Public-Private Partnerships: Alternative Risk and Profit Sharing Approaches to Align Sponsor and Investor Interests," Office of Economic Policy, U.S. Department of the Treasury, April 2015, https://www.treasury.gov/connect/blog/Documents/Treasury%20Infrastructure%20White%20Paper%20042215.pdf; "Expanding Our Nation's Infrastructure through Innovative Financing," Office of Economic Policy, U.S. Department of the Treasury, September 2014, https://www.treasury.gov/resource-center/economic-policy/Documents/3_Expanding%20our%20Nation's%20Infrastructure%20through%20Innovative%20Financing.pdf.

21. Glenn Kessler, "Bernie Sanders's Claims about His $1 Trillion Infrastructure Plan," *Washington Post,* November 16, 2015.

22. "Kamala Harris Calls Infrastructure Spending 'A Human Rights Issue'—and Twitter Wasn't Having It," CBS Los Angeles, January 25, 2017, https://losangeles.cbslocal.com/2017/01/25/kamala-harris-calls-infrastructure-spending-a-human-rights-issue-and-twitter-wasnt-having-it.

23. Melanie Zanona, "Trump: Nation's Infrastructure Can Be Fixed 'Only by Me,'" The Hill, June 22, 2016, https://thehill.com/policy/transportation/284532-trump-nations-infrastructure-can-be-fixed-only-by-me.

24. "Legislative Outline for Rebuilding Infrastructure in America," message to Congress, February 2017, posted at U.S. Department of Transportation, https://www.transportation.gov/briefing-room/legislative-outline-rebuilding-infrastructure-america.

25. Anthony P. Carnevale and Nicole Smith, "Trillion-Dollar Infrastructure Proposals Could Create Millions of Jobs," Center on Education and the Workplace, Georgetown University, 2017, https://cew.georgetown.edu/wp-content/uploads/trillion-dollar-infrastructure.pdf, 3.

26. "The President's Initiative for Rebuilding Infrastructure in America," U.S. Department of Transportation, February 2018, https://cms.dot.gov/sites/dot.gov/files/docs/briefing-room/305216/infrastructure-initiative-booklet.pdf.

27. "Remarks by Vice President Pence at Infrastructure Summit Working Luncheon," White House, June 8, 2017, https://www.whitehouse.gov/briefings-statements/remarks-vice-president-pence-infrastructure-summit-working-luncheon.

28. "Expanding the Market for Infrastructure"; "Expanding Our Nation's Infrastructure."

29. Chris Cillizza, "This Phrase Has Become a Running Joke on the Trump Administration," CNN, May 26, 2019, https://www.cnn.com/2019/05/23/politics/donald-trump-infrastructure-week/index.html.

30. Katherine J. Cramer, *The Politics of Resentment: Rural Consciousness in Wisconsin and the Rise of Scott Walker* (Chicago: University of Chicago Press, 2016).

31. Phillip K. Howard, "Two Years Not Ten Years: Redesigning Infrastructure Approvals," Common Good, September 2015, https://www.commongood.org/wp-content/uploads/2017/07/2YearsNot10Years.pdf.

32. Perhaps the best-known failure of presidential leadership with respect to infrastructure was Jimmy Carter's inability to halt nineteen (mostly dam) projects

NOTES TO PAGES 178–184

that he described as "pork barrel" spending. See Scott A. Frisch and Sean Q. Kelly, *Jimmy Carter and the Water Wars: Presidential Influence and the Politics of Pork* (Amherst, NY: Cambria Press, 2008).

33. In the 2010 midterm elections, Republicans picked up sixty-three House seats to regain their majority and six seats in the Senate, reducing the Democratic majority from fifty-eight to fifty-three (including two independents who caucus with the Democrats). In the 2012 elections, Barack Obama was reelected president, but the House retained a seventeen-seat Republican majority. In 2014 Republicans recaptured control of the Senate with fifty-four seats and gained an additional thirteen seats to expand their majority in the House.

34. "Sens. Cruz, Lee, Rubio Introduce Transportation Empowerment Act," Ted Cruz U.S. Senator for Texas, press release, July 11, 2018, https://www.cruz.senate .gov/?p=press_release&id=3942.

35. United States Federal Highway Administration, *America's Highways 1776–1976: A History of the Federal Aid Program* (Washington, DC: U.S. Government Printing Office, 1977), 226–228, https://archive.org/details /americashighways00unit.

36. "President's Initiative for Rebuilding Infrastructure," 11.

37. "A Framework for Infrastructure-Funding," American Transportation Research Institute, November 2017, https://atri-online.org/2017/11/08/a -framework-for-infrastructure-funding.

38. "Gasoline Tax," American Petroleum Institute, 2018, https://www.api.org/oil -and-natural-gas/consumer-information/motor-fuel-taxes/gasoline-tax, last accessed August 15, 2019.

39. Kevin Cirilli, "Poll: Put Brakes on Gas Tax," Politico, April 22, 2013, https://www.politico.com/story/2013/04/gas-tax-poll-090412; Ashley Halsey III and Scott Clement, "Most Americans Don't Want New Tolls to Pay for Road and Bridge Improvements, Poll Says," *Washington Post,* January 17, 2017.

40. "2017 Public Transportation Fact Book," American Public Transportation Association, March 2018.

41. See "The President's Framework for Business Tax Reform: An Update," White House and Department of the Treasury, April 2016, 24, https://www.treasury .gov/resource-center/tax-policy/Documents/The-Presidents-Framework-for -Business-Tax-Reform-An-Update-04-04-2016.pdf.

42. "Estimated Budget Effects of the Conference Agreement on H.R. 1, The 'Tax Cuts and Jobs Act,'" JCX-67-17, Joint Committee on Taxation, U.S. Congress, December 18, 2017, https://www.jct.gov/publications.html?func=startdown&id =5053.

43. Michael J. Graetz, "Foreword–The 2017 Tax Cuts: How Polarized Politics Produced Precarious Policy," *Yale Law Journal Forum* 128 (2018): 315–338.

44. Some state and local bonds are "revenue bonds" financed solely through revenues from infrastructure projects. Others are backed by the general revenues from the state's or municipality's taxes. For more detail, see "Expanding Our Nation's Infrastructure."

45. "Expanding Our Nation's Infrastructure," 8, 10; "President's Initiative for Rebuilding Infrastructure," 30–31.

46. Gerald F. Seib, "In Crisis, Opportunity for Obama," *Wall Street Journal,* November 21, 2008.

47. Doug Cameron and Patrick McGroarty, "Airlines Know You Hate the Airport, and Are Trying to Do Something about It," *Wall Street Journal,* April 11, 2018.

48. The classic statement is George J. Stigler, "The Theory of Economic Regulation," *Bell Journal of Economics and Management Science* 2, no. 1 (1971): 3–21.

49. Sam Peltzman, "Toward a More General Theory of Regulation," *Journal of Law and Economics* 19, no. 2 (1976): 211–240.

50. "Expanding Our Nation's Infrastructure," 15–16.

51. Gretchen Morgenson and Joshua Rosner, *Reckless Endangerment: How Outsized Ambition, Greed, and Corruption Led to Economic Armageddon* (New York: Times Books, 2011).

52. Patrick McGechan, "LaGuardia Airport to Be Overhauled by 2021, Cuomo and Biden Say," *New York Times,* July 27, 2015.

53. "Skanska Named Preferred Bidder for the Terminal Replacement Project at LaGuardia Airport in New York City," press release, Skanska, May 25, 2015, https://www.usa.skanska.com/who-we-are/media/press-releases/125344/Skanska -appointed-preferred-bidder-for-the-Terminal-Replacement-Project-at-LaGuardia -Airport-in-New-York-City; "About LaGuardia Gateway Partners," LaGuardia Gateway Partners, 2017, https://www.laguardiab.com/about-lgp.

54. Daniel Geiger, "One of Four LaGuardia Bidders Gets Grounded," *Crain's New York Business,* March 13, 2014, https://www.crainsnewyork.com/article/20140313 /REAL_ESTATE/140319928/one-of-four-laguardia-bidders-gets-grounded.

55. Hilary Russ, "$2.5 Bn Deal for LaGuardia P3 Tops U.S. Muni Sales Next Week," Reuters, May 13, 2016, https://www.reuters.com/article/usa-municipals -deals-idUSL2N18A10H.

56. "LaGuardia Airport Central Terminal Building Lease Agreement," LaGuardia Gateway Partners and the Port Authority of New York and New Jersey, June 1, 2016, https://partners.skanska.com/usa/projects/lga/contractdocs/Shared%20 Documents/Redacted%20Lease%20Agreement%20-%20V2.0.pdf, 72.

57. "About LaGuardia Gateway Partners."

58. Tom Stabile, "LaGuardia Shoehorns $8B Megaproject at Busy Site," *Engineering News Record New York,* July 10, 2018, https://www.enr.com/articles /44829-laguardia-shoehorns-8b-megaproject-at-busy-site.

59. "Port Authority Advances Major Modernization Projects at LaGuardia and Newark Liberty International Airports," *New Jersey Business Magazine,* March 25, 2016, https://njbmagazine.com/njb-news-now/21255-2.

60. Elizabeth Wolf, "Port Authority Approves Lease to Rebuild Delta Terminals at New York-LGA," Delta News Hub, January 5, 2017, https://news.delta.com/port -authority-approves-lease-rebuild-delta-terminals-new-york-lga.

61. Russ, "$2.5 Bn Deal"; Mack Burke, "Delta Lands $1.4B Construction Package for New $4B LaGuardia Terminal," *Commercial Observer,* May 11, 2018, https://commercialobserver.com/2018/05/delta-lands-1-8b-construction-package -for-new-4b-laguardia-terminal.

62. The rental rates are redacted in the lease agreement provided under the Freedom of Information Act. "18794-LPA," The Port Authority of New York and New Jersey, Public Records Fulfilled Requests, https://corpinfo.panynj.gov /documents/18794-LPA.

63. "Port Authority and Delta Air Lines Advance a $4 Billion Project for Second Phase of the Creation of a New LaGuardia Airport," *Metropolitan Airport News*, July 21, 2016, https://metroairportnews.com/port-authority-and-delta-air -lines-advance-a-4-billion-project-for-second-phase-of-the-creation-of-a-new -laguardia-airport.

64. Monte Whaley, "Denver Is Being Transformed by FasTracks, 10 Years after Key Vote," *Denver Post*, January 30, 2015, https://www.denverpost.com/2015/01/30 /denver-is-being-transformed-by-fastracks-10-years-after-key-vote.

65. William G. Reinhardt, "Denver Eagle P3 Financed, First U.S. Rail PPP," Public Works Financing, September 2010.

66. "Eagle Project," RTD FasTracks Initiative, U.S. Department of Transportation, https://www.transportation.gov/tifia/financed-projects/eagle-project. About $1.03 billion was acquired through a "new starts" Full Funding Grant Agreement from the Federal Transit Administration and $280 million through a credit agreement under the Department of Transportation's Transportation Infrastructure Finance and Innovation Act credit program. The project will receive an additional $62.1 million in other federal grants and roughly $450 million in private financing—$396.1 million in private activity bonds and $54.3 million in equity. The remainder of the funding comprises approximately $114.3 million in RTD sales tax revenue; $48.2 million in revenue-bond proceeds; $40.3 million in local, Colorado Department of Transportation, and other contributions; and $20.8 million from "other sources."

67. The sales tax increase was necessitated by early cost overruns of about $2.3 billion due to rising land and material costs, modifications of the plan, and lower ridership than had been anticipated on some on the new lines. Sales tax revenues were also below initial estimates. Greg Griffin, "Money Woes Could Derail FasTracks Completion," *Denver Post*, July 4, 2009, https://www.denverpost.com /2009/07/04/money-woes-could-derail-fastracks-completion.

68. "Eagle P3 Project Quarterly Report Newsletter: April–July 2016," FasTracks Regional Transportation District of Denver, April–July 2016, http://www.rtd -fastracks.com/ep3_156.

69. Colin Woodard, "The Train That Saved Denver," *Politico Magazine*, May 19, 2016, https://www.politico.com/magazine/story/2016/05/what-works-denver-rail -system-growth-213905.

70. "Port of Miami 2035 Master Plan," Miami-Dade County, 2011, Section 8: Phasing and Costs, https://www.miamidade.gov/portmiami/master-plan.asp.

71. Taylor Dolven, "Miami Can Now Host World's Largest Cruise Ships—And They're Visiting Soon," *Miami Herald*, November 2, 2018.

72. Anne Kalosh, "Two Ships for Disney and Possible New Cruise Terminal at PortMiami," *Seatrade Cruise News*, September 9, 2018, http://www.seatrade-cruise .com/news/news-headlines/two-ships-new-cruise-terminal-weighed-for-disney-at -portmiami.html.

73. Chabeli Herrera, "PortMiami's Third New Cruise Terminal Is Coming. It'll Fit MSC's 7,000-Passenger Ships," *Miami Herald*, July 11, 2018.

74. Taylor Dolven, "Adults-Only Virgin Isn't a 'Typical' Cruise Line. Neither Is Its New Miami Terminal," *Miami Herald*, November 28, 2018.

75. "The Local and Regional Economic Impacts of PortMiami," Martin Associates, March 28, 2017, http://www.miamidade.gov/portmiami/library/reports/2016

-economic-impact-full-story.pdf; "Port Guide 2018-2019," Miami-Dade County, https://www.miamidade.gov/portmiami/library/2019-port-guide.pdf; "Port of Miami 2035 Master Plan," Section 4: Cruise and Ferry.

76. Dan Clark, "Who's Paying for the $4 Billion Tappan Zee Bridge Replacement?" *Politifact New York*, August 21, 2017, https://www.politifact.com/new-york /article/2017/aug/21/whos-paying-4-billion-tappan-zee-bridge-replacemen.

77. "Bridging the Financial GAP: Funding the Governor Mario M. Cuomo Bridge," Citizens Budget Commission, New York, October 12, 2017, https://cbcny .org/research/bridging-financial-gap.

78. Vas Panagiotopoulos, "The Los Angeles Metro Is Great—So Why Aren't People Using It?" CityMetric, January 25, 2017, https://www.citymetric.com /transport/los-angeles-metro-great-so-why-aren-t-people-using-it-2742.

79. Alissa Walker, "Measure M: Angelenos Vote to Tax Themselves for Better Public Transit," Curbed Los Angeles, November 9, 2016, https://la.curbed.com /2016/11/9/13573924/measure-m-los-angeles-public-transit-results.

80. Joel Epstein, "How the Expo Line Got to Santa Monica," Huffington Post, April 12, 2017, https://www.huffpost.com/entry/how-the-expo-line-got-to_b _9665762; Bruce Ross, "Design-Build Facilitates Completion of L.A.'s Expo Line Phase 2," *Metro Magazine*, September 1, 2015, https://www.metro-magazine.com /rail/article/295131/design-build-facilitates-completion-of-l-a-s-expo-line-phase-2.

81. Laura J. Nelson, "L.A. Will Allow More Dense Development Near Five Expo Line Stations," *Los Angeles Times*, July 3, 2018; Laura J. Nelson, "Lawsuit Seeks to Overturn Plan That Would Allow Taller Buildings along the Metro Expo Line," *Los Angeles Times*, October 30, 2018; Terry Pristin, "In Westside Los Angeles, a Rail Line Stirs a Revival," *New York Times*, July 6, 2010; Tracy Jeanne Rosenthal, "Transit-Oriented Development? More Like Transit Rider Displacement," *Los Angeles Times*, February 20, 2018; and Thomas Harlander, "Some Santa Monica Residents Are Blaming a Spike in Crime on the Expo Line," *Los Angeles Magazine*, August 21, 2018, https://www.lamag.com/citythinkblog/santa-monica-crime-expo -line.

82. Testimony of John Pocari, Interim Executive Director, Gateway Development Corporation, before the New Jersey Senate Legislative Oversight and Assembly Judiciary Committees, September 25, 2017; Michael Grunwald, "The Tunnel That Could Break New York," *Politico Magazine*, July 6, 2018, https://www .politico.com/magazine/story/2018/07/06/gateway-tunnel-new-york-city -infrastructure-218839.

83. Patrick McGeehan, "Christie Halts Train Tunnel, Citing Its Costs," *New York Times*, October 7, 2010; Grunwald, "The Tunnel That Could Break New York."

84. Letter from Roy Lathod, Secretary of Transportation to Frank R. Lautenberg, New Jersey Senator, April 29, 2017.

85. Grunwald, "The Tunnel That Could Break New York"; see also Elise Young and Demetrios Pogkas, "How Trump's Hudson Tunnel Feud Threatens the National Economy," Bloomberg, March 5, 2018, https://www.bloomberg.com/graphics/2018 -hudson-river-amtrak-tunnel-american-economy.

86. Adam Nagourney, "A $100 Billion Train: The Future of California or a Boondoggle?" *New York Times*, July 30, 2018.

87. Jim Sheehan, "Is High-Speed Rail Dying? This Could be a Crucial Year for the Troubled Project," *Fresno Bee*, January 17, 2018, https://www.fresnobee.com /news/local/high-speed-rail/article195242539.html.

88. Jonathan J. Cooper, "Push to End Bullet Train in 2020 Could Signal GOP Strategy," Associated Press, September 25, 2018, https://www.apnews.com/66c50c5 882fe442ea4c241021fff2efc; Kathleen Ronayne, "California Governor Scales Back High-Speed Train," Associated Press, February 12, 2019, https://apnews.com/783b3 36c787a42fd9148986786ee73cf.

89. See Frances McCall Rosenbluth and Ian Shapiro, *Responsible Parties: Saving Democracy from Itself* (New Haven: Yale University Press, 2018), 95–127.

90. "Rebuilding Our Infrastructure: Why Trump's Public-Private Partnership Model is Good for Wall Street but Bad for America," Bernie Sanders press release, Medium, June 7, 2017, https://medium.com/senator-bernie-sanders/why-trumps -infrastructure-plan-is-good-for-wall-street-but-bad-for-america-7ff353db42af.

91. See Tim Worstall, "Trump v. Sanders on Infrastructure—Bernie Sure Can't Count, Can He?" *Forbes*, June 8, 2017.

92. "Expanding the Market for Infrastructure"; "Expanding Our Nation's Infrastructure."

93. Grunwald, "The Tunnel That Could Break New York."

94. See Craig Giammona and Jack Kaskey, "New Jersey Is Trying to Figure Out How to Tax Weed," Bloomberg, December 7, 2018, https://www.bloomberg.com /news/articles/2018-12-07/n-j-learns-pot-economics-to-ensure-it-can-get-its-300 -million.

95. Kimberly Amadeo, "Unemployment Rate by Year since 1929 Compared to Inflation and GDP," The Balance, May 21, 2019, https://www.thebalance.com /unemployment-rate-by-year-3305506.

96. Joel Simmons, *The Politics of Technological Progress: Parties, Time Horizons, and Long-Term Economic Development* (Cambridge: Cambridge University Press, 2016).

8. What More Is to Be Done?

1. All of the health insurance–coverage data here, including cost estimates, are from the Congressional Budget Office (CBO), "Federal Subsidies for Health Insurance Coverage for People under Age 65: 2019 to 2029," May 2019, https://www.cbo.gov/system/files/2019-05/55085-HealthCoverageSubsidies_0.pdf.

2. CBO, "Federal Subsidies for Health Insurance Coverage." CBO estimated the federal poverty level in 2019 as $12,490 for a single person, plus $4,420 for each additional person in the household.

3. CBO, "Federal Subsidies for Health Insurance Coverage," 17.

4. Medicare expenditures for noninstitutionalized people under age sixty-five are about one-eighth of total Medicare spending, net of tax and premium receipts. CBO, "Federal Subsidies for Health Insurance Coverage," 20. The federal share of Medicaid covers 60 percent of joint federal-state expenditures.

5. CBO, "Federal Subsidies for Health Insurance Coverage"; Congressional Budget Office, "Updated Budget Projections, 2019 to 2029," May 2019, https://www.cbo.gov/system/files/2019-05/55151-budget_update_0.pdf, Table 5.

6. Jody L. Liu and Christine Eibner, "National Health Spending Estimates Under Medicare for All," Rand Corporation, 2019, https://doi.org/10.7249 /RR3106.

7. Robert Pollin, "The Case for Medicare for All," *Wall Street Journal*, March 28, 2019; "Health Insurance Coverage and Health-Care Expenses," in "Report on the Economic Well-Being of U.S. Households in 2013," Board of Governors of the Federal Reserve System, August 15, 2014, https://www.federalreserve.gov/econresdata /2014-economic-well-being-of-us-households-in-2013-health-insurance-coverage .htm.

8. Quoted in Helaine Olen, "How Fox News Accidentally Revealed the Truth about Support for Medicare-for-All," *Washington Post*, April 17, 2019.

9. See Congressional Budget Office, "Federal Subsidies for Health Insurance Coverage for People under Age 65: 2018 to 2028," May 2018, https://www.cbo.gov /system/files/2018-06/53826-healthinsurancecoverage.pdf.

10. Evan Cunningham, "Great Recession, Great Recovery? Trends from the Current Population Survey," Monthly Labor Review, Bureau of Labor Statistics, U.S. Department of Labor, April 2018, https://www.bls.gov/opub/mlr/2018/article /great-recession-great-recovery.htm.

11. In 2019 people who paid Medicare taxes for fewer than thirty quarters had to pay a standard monthly premium of $437, or $5,244 per year. "Medicare Costs at a Glance" (2019 costs), U.S. Centers for Medicare & Medicaid Services, https://www.medicare.gov/your-medicare-costs/medicare-costs-at-a-glance.

12. "'Medicare for All' Could Cost $32.6 Trillion, George Mason Study Says," *Time*, July 30, 2018, https://time.com/5352950/medicare-trillions-bernie-sanders.

13. The Urban Institute estimate is $2.5 trillion a year, while the Mercatus Center estimates the cost to be $32 trillion over ten years. See John Holahan, Lisa Clemans-Cope, Matthew Buettgens, Melissa Favreault, Linda J. Blumberg, and Siyabonga Ndwandwe, "The Sanders Single-Payer Health Care Plan: The Effect on National Health Expenditures and Federal and Private Spending," Urban Institute, May 2016, https://www.urban.org/sites/default/files/publication/80486/200785-The -Sanders-Single-Payer-Health-Care-Plan.pdf; Charles Blahous, "The Costs of a National Single-Payer Healthcare System," Working Paper, Mercatus Center, George Mason University, 2018, https://www.mercatus.org/system/files/blahous -costs-medicare-mercatus-working-paper-v1_1.pdf.

14. For a good overview of these issues, see Congressional Budget Office, "Key Design Components and Considerations for Establishing a Single-Payer Health Care System," May 2019, https://www.cbo.gov/system/files/2019-05/55150 -singlepayer.pdf.

15. Liu and Eibner, "National Health Spending Estimates."

16. Zac Auter, "Americans' Satisfaction with Healthcare System Edges Down," Gallup, September 15, 2016, https://news.gallup.com/poll/195605/americans -satisfaction-healthcare-system-edges-down.aspx.

17. See Charles Urban-Mead, "The New York Health Act: Prospects for a Single Payer Plan," unpublished manuscript, Yale University, December 19, 2018.

18. Jacob S. Hacker, "The Road to Medicare for Everyone," American Prospect, January 3, 2015, https://prospect.org/article/road-medicare-everyone. See also Jacob S. Hacker, "Health Care for America," Briefing Paper No. 180, Economic Policy Institute, January 16, 2007, https://www.epi.org/publication/bp180.

19. See CAP Health Policy Team, "Medicare Extra for All: A Plan to Guarantee Universal Health Coverage in the United States," Center for American Progress, February 22, 2018, https://www.americanprogress.org/issues/healthcare/reports /2018/02/22/447095/medicare-extra-for-all.

20. Hacker, "Road to Medicare for Everyone," 22.

21. In November 2016, 43 percent of Americans held a favorable view of the Affordable Care Act. This number rose to 50 percent in July 2017, when the "Repeal and Replace" bill was voted down in the Senate. Support increased to 54 percent in early 2018, as the abolition of the individual mandate in the Tax Cuts and Jobs Act took effect, further threatening the law. "KFF Health Tracking Poll: The Public's Views on the ACA," Henry J. Kaiser Family Foundation, July 30, 2019, https://www .kff.org/interactive/kaiser-health-tracking-poll-the-publics-views-on-the-aca.

22. Jennifer Ludden, interviewed by Ari Shapiro, "How Politics Killed Universal Child Care in the 1970s," National Public Radio, October 13, 2016; Barbara A. Chandler, "The White House Conference on Children: A 1970 Happening," *Family Coordinator* 20, no. 3 (1971): 195–207.

23. Sally S. Cohen, *Championing Child Care* (New York: Columbia University Press, 2001).

24. According to the Bureau for Labor Statistics, 62.2 percent of women with children under age six were employed in 2018. "Employment Status of the Population by Sex, Marital Status, and Presence and Age of Own Children under 18, 2017–2018 Annual Averages," U.S. Bureau of Labor Statistics, April 18, 2019, https://www.bls.gov/news.release/famee.t05.htm.

25. Richard M. Nixon, "Veto of the Economic Opportunity Amendments of 1971," December 9, 1971, available at https://www.presidency.ucsd.edu/documents /veto-the-economic-opportunity-amendments-1971. See also William Roth, "The Politics of Daycare: The Comprehensive Child Development Act of 1971," Discussion Paper 369-76, Institute for Research on Poverty, University of Wisconsin-Madison, December 1976, https://www.irp.wisc.edu/publications/dps/pdfs/dp36976.pdf.

26. Chris M. Herbst, "Universal Childcare, Maternal Employment, and Children's Long-Run Outcomes: Evidence from the U.S. Lanham Act of 1940," *Journal of Labor Economics* 35, no. 2 (2017): 519–564.

27. Cohen, *Championing Child Care*, 96, 105, 129, 198–199.

28. Claire Cain Miller and Ernie Tedeschi, "Single Mothers Are Surging into the Work Force," *New York Times*, May 29, 2019.

29. Ganesh Sitaraman and Anne L. Alstott, *The Public Option: How to Expand Freedom, Increase Opportunity and Promote Equality* (Cambridge, MA: Harvard University Press, 2019), 153; Katha Pollitt, "Day Care for All," *New York Times*, February 9, 2019.

30. Sitaraman and Alstott, *Public Option*, 151–154.

31. Pamela Druckerman, "Catching Up with France on Day Care," *New York Times*, August 31, 2013.

32. "Starting Strong IV: Monitoring Quality in Early Childhood Education and Care Country Note: France," Organisation for Economic Co-operation and Development, 2016, http://www.oecd.org/education/school/ECECMN-France.pdf.

33. Sitaraman and Alstott, *Public Option*, 157.

34. "Military Child Development Program: Background and Issues," Congressional Research Service, August 10, 2018, https://www.everycrsreport.com/files

/20180810_R45288_a7cc07942954f4822d744758e5580b1d3b801c9c.pdf; "Military Child Care Programs," Military OneSource, U.S. Department of Defense, December 12, 2018, https://www.military onesource.mil/family-relationships/ parenting-and-children/childcare/military-child-care-programs.

35. "Pre-K in American Cities: Quality and Access Grow, but Cities are Missing Opportunities to Create Lasting Benefits for their Youngest Learners," National Institute for Early Education Research and City Health, 2019, http:// nieer.org/wp-content/uploads/2019/01/CH_Pre-K_H.1.23.19pdf.pdf.; Spencer Buell, "Whatever Happened to Universal Pre-K in Boston?" *Boston Magazine*, September 4, 2018, https://www.bostonmagazine.com/education/2018/08/30 /universal-pre-k-boston.

36. Eliza Shapiro, "Bright Spot for N.Y.'s Struggling Schools: Pre-K," New York Times, January 1, 2019; William Neuman, "De Blasio Finds Biggest Win in Pre-K, but Also Lasting Consequences," *New York Times*, October 31, 2017.

37. Rasheed Malik, "The Effects of Universal Preschool in Washington, D.C.," Center for American Progress, September 26, 2018, https://www.americanprogress .org/isues/early-childhood/reports/2018/09/26/458208/effects-universal-preschool -washington-d-c.

38. Claire Lundberg, "France Is 180 Years Ahead of American on Universal Pre-K," *Slate Magazine*, February 4, 2014, https://slate.com/business/2014/02 /universal-pre-k-france-is-about-180-years-ahead-of-america-on-preschool -education.html.

39. Alice Cuddy, "France to Make School Compulsory from the Age of Three," *Euronews World*, March 27, 2018, https://www.euronews.com/2018/03/27/france-to -make-school-compulsory-from-the-age-of-three.

40. "Early Childhood Fast Facts 2017," Oklahoma State Department of Education, 2017, https://sde.ok.gov/sites/ok.gov.sde/files/documents/files/Early%20 Childhood%20Fast%20Facts%202017.pdf; Suzy Khimm, "Is Oklahoma the Right Model for Universal Pre-K?" *Washington Post*, February 14, 2013.

41. Daphna Bassok, Luke C. Miller, Eva Galdo, and Amanda J. Johnson, "Florida's Voluntary Pre-Kindergarten Program: An Overview of the Largest State Pre-School Program in the Nation," EdPolicyWorks Report, Curry School of Education, University of Virginia, November 2014, http://curry.virginia.edu/uploads /resourceLibrary/EdPolicyWorks-Report-FL-VPK.pdf.

42. "2017 State of Preschool Report Highlights Progress in Alabama," Rutgers Graduate School of Education and National Institute for Early Education Research, April 18, 2018, http://nieer.org/wp-content/uploads/2018/04/YB2017 _Alabama_Release.pdf.

43. Miller and Tedeschi, "Single Mothers Are Surging."

44. Only eight countries do not guarantee paid family leave: Micronesia, Nauru, Palau, Papua New Guinea, the Marshall Islands, Suriname, Tonga, and the United States. Megan A. Sholar, "The History of Family Leave Policies in the United States," The American Historian website, Organization of American Historians, November 2016, https://tah.oah.org/november-2016/the-history-of-family-leave -policies-in-the-united-states.

45. Max Reiss, "Lamont Signs Paid Family & Medical Leave Act," NBC Connecticut, June 25, 2019, https://www.nbcconnecticut.com/news/local/Lamont -Signs-Paid-Family--Medical-Leave-Act-511801841.html.

46. "China Focus: Moving for Grandkids, Meet China's Millions of Elderly Migrants," Xinhua, May 14, 2018, http://www.xinhuanet.com/english/2018-05/14 /c_137178328.htm; Zhuang Pingui, "China's 'Elderly Vagabonds' Sacrifice Retirement to Care for Kids," *South China Morning Post*, November 4, 2017, https://www.scmp.com/news/china/society/article/2118219/chinas-elderly -vagabonds-sacrifice-retirement-care-grandchildren.

47. "Labor Force Participation Rate, Female (% of Female Population Ages 15)," World Bank, April 2019, https://data.worldbank.org/indicator/SL.TLF.CACT.FE.ZS.

48. Joe Heim, "On the World Stage, U.S. Students Fall Behind," *Washington Post*, December 6, 2016.

49. Robert Putnam, *Our Kids: The American Dream in Crisis* (New York: Simon and Schuster, 2016), 135–190, 251–258.

50. Janet Yellen, "Perspectives on Inequality and Opportunity from the Survey of Consumer Finances," speech at Federal Reserve Bank of Boston, October 17, 2014.

51. Albert O. Hirschman, *Exit, Voice, and Loyalty: Responses to Decline in Firms, Organizations, and States* (Cambridge, MA: Harvard University Press, 1970).

52. John E. Chubb and Terry M. Moe, *Politics, Markets, and America's Schools* (Washington, DC: Brookings, 1990); David Osborne, *Reinventing America's Schools: Creating a Twenty-First Century Education System* (New York: Bloomsbury, 2017).

53. Gary Miron, William Mathis, and Kevin Welner, "Review of Separating Fact & Fiction," National Education Policy Center, February 23, 2015, https://nepc .colorado.edu/thinktank/review-separating-fact-and-fiction.

54. Dana Goldstein, "Democrats Are United on Teacher Strikes, but They Are in a 'Gladiator Fight' over Education," *New York Times*, January 18, 2019.

55. Dale Russakoff, *The Prize: Who's in Charge of America's Schools?* (New York: Mariner Books, 2015).

56. Russakoff, *The Prize*, 210; Mark Bonamo and Heather Kays, "Baraka Wins Reelection in Newark Mayoral Race in a Landslide," *Essex County News*, May 9, 2018, https://www.tapinto.net/articles/baraka-wins-reelection-in-newark-mayoral-race-in-3.

57. Andrew Rotherham, "De Blasio vs. Everyone Else: New York's Mayor Takes on Charter Schools, and the National Educational Debate Hangs in the Balance," Slate, March 12, 2014, https://slate.com/news-and-politics/2014/03/bill-de-blasio -vs-charter-schools-a-feud-in-new-york-city-has-broad-national-implications .html; Eva Moskowitz, "The Mayor Continues His War on Charter Schools," *New York Daily News*, November 29, 2017, https://www.nydailynews.com/opinion/mayor -continues-war-charter-schools-article-1.3663503.

58. Matthew Bloch and Jasmine Lee, "Election Results: De Blasio Wins Second Term as New York City Mayor," New York Times, December 20, 2017.

59. Editorial, "Giving Illinois Children a Second Escape Route from Bad Schools," *Chicago Tribune*, September 5, 2017.

60. Rick Moran, "Hillary Clinton's Flip-Flop on Charter Schools," *American Thinker*, November 10, 2015, https://www.americanthinker.com/blog/2015/11 /hillary_clintons_flip_flop_on_charter_schools.html.

61. The combined number of days lost in all other industries was 832,000. Computed from Marisa Fernandez, "Teacher Walkouts Boosted Strikes to Highest Level since 2007," Axios, February 24, 2019, https://www.axios.com/bls-labor -strikes-education-teachers-079c2e8c-0633-4b09-bc09-ee8cc3ba27a2.html.

62. Moriah Balingit, "Hours after West Virginia Teachers Strike, Lawmakers Drop Measures Expanding Charter Schools and Private School Vouchers," *Washington Post*, February 19, 2019.

63. Goldstein, "Democrats Are United."

64. Sarah Cohodes, "Charter Schools and the Achievement Gap," *The Future of Children* (Winter 2018): 1–16.

65. Russakoff, *The Prize*, 118–119.

66. Valerie Strauss, "An Astonishing Admission from a Controversial School Reformer," *Washington Post*, February 7, 2016.

67. *San Antonio Independent School District v. Rodriguez*, 411 U.S. 1 (1973).

68. *Miliken v. Brady*, 418 U.S. 717 (1974).

69. James Patterson, *Grand Expectations: The United States* (Oxford: Oxford University Press, 1996), 569–570.

70. James Sundquist, *Politics and Policy: The Eisenhower, Kennedy, and Johnson Years* (Washington, DC: Brookings, 1968), 216–217.

71. Patterson, *Grand Expectations*, 571.

72. Russakoff, *The Prize*, 16. The unidentified Newark official is also quoted in Jean Anyon, *Ghetto Schooling: A Political Economy of Urban Educational Reform* (New York: Teachers College Press, 1997).

73. Douglas Rae, *City: Urbanism and Its End* (New Haven: Yale University Press, 2003), 312–360.

74. Patterson, *Grand Expectations*, 571–572.

75. Allen J. Matusow, *The Unraveling of America: A History of Liberalism in the 1960s* (New York: Harper and Row, 1984; Athens: University of Georgia Press, 2009), 225.

76. Patterson, *Grand Expectations*, 572.

77. Christopher Jencks, *Inequality: A Reassessment of the Effect of Family and Schooling in America* (New York: Harper, 1981).

78. Valerie Strauss, "How and Why Convicted Atlanta Teachers Cheated on Standardized Tests," *Washington Post*, April 1, 2015. An Atlanta Journal-Constitution timeline details this scandal from its discovery in 2008 to the criminal conviction of eleven defendants in April 2015, available at https://www.ajc.com /news/timeline-how-the-atlanta-school-cheating-scandal-unfolded /jn4vTk7GZUQoQRJTVR7UHK.

79. Charles Murray, "The Age of Educational Romanticism," *New Criterion*, May 2008, https://www.newcriterion.com/issues/2008/5/the-age-of-educational -romanticism.

80. "Bush Budget Proposal for FY 2007 Cuts Education Spending," *Urban Legislator*, February 2, 2006, https://web.archive.org/web/20101120172356 /http://www.cgcs.org/images/Legislative/Feb06.pdf; Gail L. Sunderman, James S. Kim, and Gary Orfield, *NCLB Meets School Realities: Lessons from the Field* (Thousand Oaks, CA: Corwin Press, 2005).

81. Lyndsey Layton, "Obama Signs New K–12 Education Law That Ends No Child Left Behind," *Washington Post*, December 10, 2015.

82. Andrew Ujifusa, "How Have Obama's K–12 Policies Fared under Trump," *Education Week*, June 19, 2018, https://www.edweek.org/ew/articles/2018/06/20 /how-have-obamas-k-12-policies-fared-under.html.

83. Osborne, *Reinventing America's Schools*, chs. 1–3.

84. Russakoff, *The Prize*, 223.

85. Raj Chetty, John N. Friedman, Nathaniel Hendren, Maggie R. Jones, and Sonya R. Porter, "The Opportunity Atlas: Mapping the Childhood Roots of Social Mobility," October 2018, https://opportunityinsights.org/wp-content/uploads/2018/10/atlas_paper.pdf.

86. Eduardo Porter, "The Hard Truths of Trying to 'Save' the Rural Economy," *New York Times*, December 14, 2018.

87. David Neumark and Helen Simpson, "Place-Based Policies," in *Handbook of Regional and Urban Economies*, ed. Gilles Duranton, J. Vernon Henderson, and William C. Strange, vol. 5 (Amsterdam: North-Holland, 2015), 1197–1287. A useful typology, lists of state programs, and review of some empirical studies of place-based tax incentives can be found in Michelle D. Layser, "A Typology of Place-Based Investment Tax Incentives," *Washington and Lee Journal of Civil Rights and Social Justice* 25, no. 2 (2019): 403–463.

88. Lotta Moberg, "The Political Economy of Special Economic Zones," *Journal of Institutional Economics* 11, no. 1 (2015): 167–190.

89. Benjamin Austin, Edward Glaeser, and Lawrence Summers, "Jobs for the Heartland: Place-Based Policies in 21st-Century America," Brookings Papers on Economic Activity (Spring 2018): 151–232. For Glaeser's earlier view see Edward L. Glaeser and Joshua D. Gottlieb, "The Economics of Place-Making Policies," Brookings Papers on Economic Activity (Spring 2008): 155–239. See also Neumark and Simpson, "Place-Based Policies."

90. See C. Lockwood Reynolds and Shawn M. Rohlin, "The Effects of Location-Based Tax Policies on the Distribution of Household Income: Evidence from the Federal Empowerment Zone Program," *Journal of Urban Economics* 88 (2015): 1–15. But there are studies that find positive labor effects from both federal and state enterprise-zone programs. See John C. Ham, Charles Swenson, Ayse Imrohoroglu, and Heonjae Song, "Government Programs Can Improve Local Labor Markets: Evidence from State Enterprise Zones, Federal Empowerment Zones and Federal Enterprise Community," *Journal of Public Economics* 95, no. 7 (2011): 779–797.

91. "Estimated Budget Effects of the Conference Agreement on H.R. 1, The 'Tax Cuts and Jobs Act,'" JCX-67-17, Joint Committee on Taxation, U.S. Congress, December 18, 2017, https://www.jct.gov/publications.html?func=startdown&id=5053.

92. Jesse Drucker and Eric Lipton, "How a Trump Tax Break to Help Poor Communities Became a Windfall for the Rich," *New York Times*, August 21, 2019.

93. Internal Revenue Code, Subchapter Z, §1400Z-1 and -2.

94. Samantha Jacoby, "Potential Flaws of Opportunity Zones Loom, as Do Risks of Large-Scale Tax Avoidance," Center on Budget and Policy Priorities, January 11, 2019, https://www.cbpp.org/research/federal-tax/potential-flaws-of-opportunity-zones-loom-as-do-risks-of-large-scale-tax.

95. Sophie Quinton, "'Opportunity Zones' Spur New State Tax Incentives," Pew Charitable Trusts, April 3, 2019, https://www.pewtrusts.org/en/research-and-analysis/blogs/stateline/2019/04/03/opportunity-zones-spur-new-state-tax-incentives.

96. Martin A. Sullivan, "Economic Analysis: New Zones Spin Complex Web for Real Estate Investors," Tax Notes, Tax Analysts, March 11, 2019.

97. See Raven Molloy, Christopher L. Smith, Ricardo Trezzi, and Abigail Wozniak, "Understanding Declining Fluidity in the U.S. Labor Market," Brookings Papers on Economic Activity (Spring 2016): 183–237.

98. The Intergenerational Poverty Mitigation Act, Utah Title 35A: Chapter 9 (2012).

99. David Leonhardt, "In Climbing Income Ladder, Location Matters," New York Times, July 22, 2013.

100. Utah Intergenerational Welfare Reform Commission, "Utah's Seventh Annual Report on Intergenerational Poverty, Welfare Dependency and the Use of Public Assistance, 2018," https://jobs.utah.gov/edo/intergenerational/igp18.pdf.

101. Elizabeth Weill-Greenberg, "Institute Joins City of Newark in Newark 2020 Launch," New Jersey Institute for Social Justice, June 26, 2017, https://www .njisj.org/institute_joins_city_of_newark_in_newark_2020_launch.

102. Descriptions and analyses of all these programs are contained in Emily Tu, "Local Thriving Initiatives: Newark 2020," unpublished manuscript, January 2019.

103. Sean Safford, Why the Garden Club Couldn't Save Youngstown: The Transformation of the Rust Belt (Cambridge, MA: Harvard University Press 2009), 135, 137, and 146.

104. Stacy Wescoe, "Downtown Allentown Called a National Success Story by Urban Land Institute," LVB.com, Lehigh Valley Business, April 28, 2016, https://www.lvb.com/downtown-allentown-called-a-national-success-story-by -urban-land-institute.

105. Safford, Why the Garden Club, 142–143.

106. Bob Davis and John Hilsenrath, "How the China Shock, Deep and Swift, Spurred the Rise of Trump," Wall Street Journal, August 11, 2016.

107. Howard Schneider, "Away from Spotlight, US Manufacturers Battle Back from 'China Shock,'" Reuters, August 4, 2016, https://www.reuters.com/article/us -usa-manufacturing-china-insight-idUSKCN10F0CT.; David H. Autor, David Dorn, and Gordon H. Hanson, "The China Shock: Learning from Labor Market Adjustment to Large Changes in Trade," NBER Working Paper No. 21906, National Bureau of Economic Research, Cambridge, MA, January 2016; Davis and Hilsenrath, "China Shock."

108. Quoted in Schneider, "Away from Spotlight."

109. Quoted in Davis and Hilsenrath, "China Shock."

110. Eric Cunningham, "No, Wall Street Journal, Chinese Imports Didn't Kill My North Carolina Hometown," The Federalist, August 16, 2016, https:// thefederalist.com/2016/08/16/no-wall-street-journal-chinese-imports-didnt-kill -my-hometown.

111. Quoted in Schneider, "Away from Spotlight."

112. NYC Housing, "De Blasio Administration Financed More Than 34,000 Affordable Homes in 2018—A New Record," January 16, 2019, https://www1.nyc .gov/office-of-the-mayor/news/035-19/de-blasio-administration-financed-more-34 -000-affordable-homes-2018--new-record; Ameena Walker, "Bill de Blasio's Affordable Housing Initiative Failing Low-Income New Yorkers Says Report," Curbed New York, September 12, 2017, https://ny.curbed.com/2017/9/16 /16319102/nyc-affordable-housing-crisis-bill-de-blasio-report.

113. Miguel Otárola, "Minneapolis City Council Approves 2040 Comprehensive Plan on 12–1 Vote," Star Tribune, December 7, 2018, http://www.startribune.com

/minneapolis-city-council-approves-2040-comprehensive-plan-on-12-1-vote
/502178121.

114. Emily Badger and Quoctrung Bui, "Cities Start to Question an American Ideal: A House with a Yard on Every Lot," *New York Times*, June 18, 2019.

115. Matt Weinberger, "This Is Why San Francisco's Insane Housing Market Has Hit the Crisis Point," Business Insider, July 8, 2017, https://www
.businessinsider.in/this-is-why-san-franciscos-insane-housing-market-has-hit-the
-crisis-point/articleshow/59505155.cms.

116. Karen Weise, "Microsoft Pledges $500 Million for Affordable Housing in Seattle Area," *New York Times*, January 11, 2019.

117. Emily Badger, "Microsoft's Leap into Housing Illuminates Government's Retreat," *New York Times*, January 18, 2019.

118. Roland Li and Melinda Russell, "Google Puts Up $1 Billion to Fight Housing Crisis in Its Bay Area Backyard," *San Francisco Chronicle*, June 18, 2019.

119. Badger, "Microsoft's Leap into Housing."

120. Michael Symons, "No Proof That $11b Corporate Tax Breaks Created Jobs, NJ Audit Finds," New Jersey 101.5. January 9, 2019, https://nj1015.com/no-proof
-that-11b-corporate-tax-breaks-created-jobs-nj-audit-finds.

121. Mary Donegan, T. William Lester, and Nichola Lowe, "Striking a Balance: A National Assessment of Economic Development Incentives," Working Paper 18-291, Upjohn Institute for Employment Research, Kalamazoo, MI, 2018, http://doi.org/10.17848/wp18-291.

122. This was one of the concerns encouraging local opposition to Amazon's plans for a headquarters in New York, which prompted the company to abandon the idea in February 2019. See Corey Kilgannon, "An 'Amazon Effect' on Queens Real Estate? Here's Why Brokers Say It's Real," *New York Times*, December 27, 2018.

123. John Rawls, *The Law of Peoples* (Cambridge, MA: Harvard University Press, 1999), 6.

9. Paying for Change—or Not

1. Congressional Budget Office, "An Update to the Budget and Economic Outlook: 2019 to 2029," August 2019, https://www.cbo.gov/system/files/2019-08/55551-CBO
-outlook-update_0.pdf. See also Bill Chappell, "U.S. National Debt Hits Record $22 Trillion," National Public Radio, February 13, 2019, https://www.npr.org/2019/02/13
/694199256/u-s-national-debt-hits-22-trillion-a-new-record-thats-predicted-to-fall;
Kimberly Amadeo, "Current US Federal Budget Deficit," The Balance, May 8, 2019, https://www.thebalance.com/current-u-s-federal-budget-deficit-3305783.

2. Thomas Byrne Edsall and Mary D. Edsall, *Chain Reaction: The Impact of Race, Rights, and Taxes on American Politics* (New York: W. W. Norton, 1992), 116–136.

3. Bruce Bartlett, "'Starve the Beast,' Origins and Development of a Budgetary Metaphor," *Independent Review* 12, no. 1 (2007): 5–26.

4. William Gale, *Fiscal Therapy: Curing America's Debt Addiction and Investing in the Future* (Oxford: Oxford University Press, 2019), 45.

5. The story of Gingrich's betrayal is told in Richard Darman, *Who's in Control? Polar Politics and the Sensible Center* (New York: Simon and Schuster, 1996).

6. Remarks by Nicholas F. Brady at a dinner honoring the thirtieth anniversary of the Brady Plan, April 10, 2019, Americas Club, New York, author in attendance.

7. Quoted in Toluse Olorunnipa and Mike DeBonis, "Trump Falls Short on Infrastructure after Promising to Build Roads, Bridges, and Consensus," *Washington Post,* May 20, 2019.

8. Gale, *Fiscal Therapy,* 43, 46.

9. "Summary of War Spending in Billions of Current Dollars," Costs of War, Watson Institute, Brown University, November 2018, https://watson.brown.edu /costsofwar/figures/2018/budgetary-costs-post-911-wars-through-fy2019-59-trillion.

10. Bruce Bartlett, "Tax Cuts and 'Starving the Beast,'" *Forbes,* May 7, 2010, https://www.forbes.com/2010/05/06/tax-cuts-republicans-starve-the-beast -columnists-bruce-bartlett.html; Christina D. Romer and David H. Romer, "Do Tax Cuts Starve the Beast? The Effects of Tax Changes on Government Spending," *Brookings Papers on Economic Activity* (Spring 2009): 139–214.

11. Michael J. Graetz, "Foreword—The 2017 Tax Cuts: How Polarized Politics Produced Precarious Policy," *Yale Law Journal Forum* 128 (2018): 315–338.

12. "Transcript: Democratic Debate in Philadelphia," *New York Times,* April 17, 2008.

13. The American Taxpayer Relief Act of 2012, P.L. 112–240, enacted January 2, 2013.

14. Janie Valencia, "Alexandria Ocasio-Cortez Wants to Raise Taxes on the Rich—And Americans Agree," FiveThirtyEight, January 18, 2019, https://fivethirty eight.com/features/Alexandria-ocasio-cortez-wants-to-raise-taxes-on-the-rich-and -americans-agree; Matthew Sheffield, "Poll: A Majority of Americans Support Raising the Top Tax Rate to 70 Percent," *The Hill,* January 18, 2019, https://thehill .com/hilltv/what-americas-thinking/425422-a-majority-of-americans-support -raising-the-top-tax-rate-to-70.

15. Jeff Stein, "Ocasio-Cortez Wants Higher Taxes on Very Rich Americans. Here's How Much Money That Could Raise," *Washington Post,* January 5, 2019.

16. Kyle Pomerleau and Huaqun Li, "How Much Revenue Would a 70% Top Tax Rate Raise? An Initial Analysis," Tax Foundation, Washington, DC, January 14, 2019, https://taxfoundation.org/70-percent-tax-initial-analysis.

17. See Laura Saunders, "How Wealthy Americans Like Jack Benny Avoided Paying a 70% Tax Rate," *Wall Street Journal,* January 18, 2019.

18. Anne Penketh, "France Forced to Drop 75 Percent Supertax after Meager Returns," *Guardian,* December 31, 2014.

19. Emmanuel Saez and Gabriel Zucman, letter to Elizabeth Warren, January 18, 2019, http://Gabriel-zucman.eu/files/saez-zucman-wealthtax-warren.pdf.

20. Gabriel Zucman, *The Hidden Wealth of Nations: The Scourge of Tax Havens* (Chicago: University of Chicago Press, 2015). See also Saunders, "How Wealthy Americans."

21. Andrew Chatzky, "Inequality and Tax Rates: A Global Comparison," Council on Foreign Relations, March 12, 2019, https://www.cfr.org/backgrounder /inequality-and-tax-rates-global-comparison.

22. "The Role and Design of Net Wealth Taxes in the OECD," OECD Tax Policy Studies no. 26, 2018, https://www.oecd.org/ctp/the-role-and-design-of-net -wealth-taxes-in-the-oecd-9789264290303-en.htm.

23. Lawrence H. Summers and Natasha Sarin, "A 'Wealth Tax' Presents a Revenue Estimation Puzzle," *Washington Post,* April 4, 2019.

24. "Role and Design of Net Wealth Taxes."

25. Michael Batty, Jesse Bricker, Joseph Briggs, Elizabeth Holmquist, Susan McIntosh, Kevin Moore, Eric Nielsen, Sarah Reber, Molly Shatto, Kamila Sommer, Tom Sweeney, and Alice Henriques Volz, "Introducing the Distributional Financial Accounts of the United States," Finance and Economics Discussion Series 2019-017, Federal Reserve Board, 2019, https://www.federalreserve.gov /econres/feds/files/2019017pap.pdf; Matthew Smith, Danny Yagan, Owen Zidar, and Eric Zwick, "Capitalists in the Twenty-First Century," NBER Working Paper No. 25442, National Bureau of Economic Research, Cambridge, MA, rev. June 2019, https://papers.ssrn.com/sol3/papers.cfm?abstract_id=3340159.

26. Michael J. Graetz and Ian Shapiro, *Death by a Thousand Cuts: The Fight over Taxing Inherited Wealth* (Princeton: Princeton University Press, 2005). See also Michael J. Graetz, "Death Tax Politics," *Boston College Law Review* 57, no. 3 (2016): 801–814.

27. The constitutional status of an annual wealth tax is uncertain. If a "direct" tax, its revenue would have to be apportioned to the states based on their population, which is not the plan. Senator Warren released two letters from constitutional law scholars indicating that the tax would be upheld without such apportionment. (Michael Hiltzik, "Elizabeth Warren's Wealth Tax Is Constitutional, Experts Say—and Necessary," *Los Angeles Times*, January 25, 2019.) Others disagreed. See James Freeman, "Elizabeth Warren's Unconstitutional Wealth Tax," *Wall Street Journal*, January 25, 2019. Similar articles appeared in publications as diverse as *Mother Jones* and *National Review*. We will not enter that debate here, other than to observe that if such a wealth tax were to be enacted, a constitutional challenge would surely be mounted. Based on language by Chief Justice Roberts in the Supreme Court's Obamacare decision implying that a tax on "real property" or on "personal property" might be a "direct" tax, such a challenge would not be frivolous. If such a tax is enacted, Congress should provide for a speedy resolution by the Supreme Court. See *National Federation of Independent Business v. Sebelius*, 567 U.S. 519, 571–572 (2017), upholding the individual mandate of the Patient Protection and Affordable Care Act as within Congress' power to tax. Emmanuel Saez and Gabriel Zucman, "Alexandria Ocasio-Cortez's Tax Hike Idea Is Not about Soaking the Rich," *New York Times*, January 22, 2019.

28. Congressional Budget Office (CBO), "Options for Reducing the Deficit: 2019–2028," December 2018, 204–205, 207, 219–220, https://www.cbo.gov /publication/54667.

29. David Barstow, Susanne Craig, and Russ Buettner, "Trump Engaged in Suspect Tax Schemes as He Reaped Riches from His Father," *New York Times*, October 2, 2018; Jesse Drucker and Emily Flitter, "Jared Kushner Paid No Federal Income Tax for Years, Documents Suggest," *New York Times*, October 13, 2018.

30. CBO, "Options for Reducing the Deficit."

31. CBO, "Options for Reducing the Deficit"; for many more examples, see Joint Committee on Taxation, "Estimates of Federal Tax Expenditures for Fiscal Years 2018–2022," JCX 81-18, October 4, 2018.

32. Andrew Ross Sorkin, "Tax the Rich? Here's How to Do It (Sensibly)," *New York Times*, February 25, 2019.

33. See Peter H. Egger, Sergey Nigai, and Nora M. Strecker, "The Taxing Deed of Globalization," *American Economic Review* 109, no. 2 (2019): 353–390.

34. Egger, Nigai, and Strecker, "Taxing Deed"; Saez and Zucman, "Alexandria Ocasio-Cortez's Tax Hike."

35. See Larry M. Bartels, *Unequal Democracy: The Political Economy of the New Gilded Age,* 2nd ed. (Princeton: Princeton University Press, 2017).

36. See Michael J. Graetz and Linda Greenhouse, *The Burger Court and the Rise of the Judicial Right* (New York: Simon and Schuster, 2016), 243–265.

37. See Tim Wu, *The Curse of Bigness: Antitrust in the New Gilded Age* (New York: Columbia Global Reports, 2018).

38. See Julius G. Getman, *Restoring the Power of Unions: It Takes a Movement* (New Haven: Yale University Press, 2010).

39. Gale, *Fiscal Therapy,* 29. Other developed countries also spend less on defense than does the US.

40. Chatzky, "Inequality and Tax Rates"; "American Taxes Are Unusually Progressive. Government Spending Is Not," *Economist,* November 23, 2017.

41. Kyle Pomerleau, "How Scandinavian Countries Pay for Their Government's Spending," Tax Foundation, June 10, 2015, https://taxfoundation.org/how -scandinavian-countries-pay-their-government-spending.

42. See Michael J. Graetz, *100 Million Unnecessary Returns* (New Haven: Yale University Press, 2010).

43. John Kenneth Galbraith, *The Affluent Society,* 40th anniv. ed. (Boston: Houghton Mifflin, 1998), 223–233.

44. Leonard E. Burman, "A Universal EITC: Sharing the Gains from Economic Growth, Encouraging Work and Supporting Families," Tax Policy Center, Urban Institute, and Brookings, May 20, 2019, 2, 18–23, https://www.taxpolicycenter.org /sites/default/files/publication/157206/a_universal_eitc_7.pdf. In December 2018 CBO estimated that a well-designed 5 percent federal value-added tax would raise nearly $3.1 trillion over the ten-year period 2019–2028. "Options for Reducing the Deficit," 289–291.

45. CBO, "Options for Reducing the Deficit," 292–298.

46. See Gilbert E. Metcalf, *Paying for Pollution: Why a Carbon Tax Is Good for America* (Oxford: Oxford University Press, 2019); Michael J. Graetz, *The End of Energy: The Unmaking of America's Environment, Security, and Independence* (Cambridge: MIT Press, 2011), 178–240.

47. Gale, *Fiscal Therapy,* 57.

48. Niv Elis, "Corker: Tax Cuts Could Be 'One of the Worst Votes I've Made,'" *The Hill,* April 11, 2018, https://thehill.com/policy/finance/382663-corker-tax-cuts -could-be-one-of-worst-votes-ive-made.

49. Mariana Mazzucato, *The Entrepreneurial State: Debunking Public vs. Private Sector Myths* (New York: Public Affairs, 2015), 93–120.

50. Aldo Musacchio and Sergio G. Lazzarini, *Reinventing State Capitalism: Leviathan in Business, Brazil and Beyond* (Cambridge, MA: Harvard University Press, 2014), 178–200; Joshua Kurlantzick, *State Capitalism: How the Return of Statism Is Transforming the World* (New York: Oxford University Press, 2016), 177.

51. Olivier Blanchard, "Public Debt and Low Interest Rates," *American Economic Review* 109, no. 4 (2019): 1197–1229.

10. The Wages of Insecurity

1. See, for example, Gerald Auten and David Splinter, "Top 1 Percent Income Shares: Comparing Estimates Using Tax Data," *AEA Papers and Proceedings,* 109 (2019): 307–311.

2. For details of the proposal by Piketty and colleagues, see "Manifesto for the Democratization of Europe," http://tdem.eu/en/manifesto. They seem entirely innocent of the intense voter hostility to elite pressure for greater European integration, which Tony Judt correctly predicted would accelerate once the EU hit a real crisis. See Judt, *Postwar: A History of Europe since 1945* (New York: Penguin, 2005), 723–732. In 2005, referendums in France and the Netherlands doomed the plan for a federal European constitution. A watered-down version was adopted as a series of intergovernmental agreements via the Lisbon Treaty of 2007, after a negative Irish referendum had revealed that the constitution otherwise would likely suffer the same fate. The fallout from the 2010 Eurozone and 2012 refugee crises continues, spawning growing ultranationalist parties across the continent. Then there was the 2016 Brexit vote. It should be obvious that European voters will not easily be sold on a new transnational assembly with taxing and redistributive powers.

3. Frans de Waal, "Moral Behavior in Animals," talk delivered at TEDxPeachtree, November 2011, https://www.ted.com/talks/frans_de_waal_do_animals_have_morals. Excerpt at https://www.youtube.com/watch?v=meiU6TxysCg.

4. Robert Frank, *Choosing the Right Pond: Human Behavior and the Quest for Status* (Oxford: Oxford University Press, 1985). This research dates back to Robert K. Merton, *Social Theory and Social Structure,* 2nd ed. (New York: Free Press, 1957); and Leon Festinger's "A Theory of Social Comparison Processes," *Human Relations* 7, no. 2 (1954): 117–140. For subsequent scholarship, see Joanne Wood, "Theory and Research Concerning Social Comparisons of Personal Attributes," *Psychological Bulletin* 106, no. 2 (1989): 231–248; Joachim Krueger, "The Projective Perception of the Social World: A Building Block of Social Comparison Processes," in *Handbook of Social Comparison: Theory and Research,* ed. Jerry Suls and Ladd Wheeler, 323–351 (Boston: Springer, 2000); Guillermina Jasso, "Some of Robert K. Merton's Contributions to Justice Theory," *Sociological Theory* 18, no. 2 (2000): 331–339; Armin Falk and Markus Knell, "Choosing the Joneses: Endogenous Goals and Reference Standards," *Scandinavian Journal of Economics* 106, no. 3 (2004): 417–435; and Jerry Suls and Ladd Wheeler, "Social Comparison Theory," in *Handbook of Theories of Social Psychology,* vol. 1, ed. Paul A. M. Van Lange et al., 460–482 (Thousand Oaks, CA: Sage, 2012).

5. Karl Marx and Friedrich Engels, *The Communist Manifesto* (1848; New Haven: Yale University Press, 2012), 84–92.

6. Ira Katznelson, *When Affirmative Action Was White: An Untold History of Racial Inequality in America* (New York: W. W. Norton, 2006).

7. Daniel Kahneman and Amos Tversky, "Prospect Theory: An Analysis of Decision under Risk," *Econometrica* 47, no. 2 (1979): 263–291.

8. Daniel Kahneman, Jack L. Knetsch, and Richard H. Thaler, "Experimental Tests of the Endowment Effect and the Coase Theorem," *Journal of Political Economy* 98, no. 6 (1990): 339–348.

9. Nicolas Carnes and Noam Lupu, "It's Time to Bust the Myth: Most Trump Voters Were Not Working Class," *Washington Post,* June 5, 2017. For the data

underlying this article, see Nicholas Carnes and Noam Lupu, "The White Working Class and the 2016 Election," unpublished manuscript, February 22, 2019, http://noamlupu.com/Carnes_Lupu_WWC.pdf.

10. SAP and Qualtrics, "Globalization 4.0: The Human Experience," World Economic Forum, January 18, 2019. http://www3.weforum.org/docs/WEF_globalization4_Jan18.pdf.

11. Guy Standing, "The Precariat: From Denizens to Citizens?" *Polity* 44, no. 4 (2012): 588–608.

12. Buchanan unsuccessfully sought the Republican presidential nomination in 1992 and 1996, stormed out of the party in 1999, and then sought—and won—the nomination of the Reform Party that had been founded by billionaire Ross Perot. Buchannan ran on a platform of withdrawing the US from the United Nations and expelling it from New York City; abolishing the IRS and the departments of Energy, Education, and Housing and Urban Development; ending affirmative action; and eliminating all taxes on inheritance and capital gains. In 2000 he won fewer than half a million votes, 0.42 percent of the total. "2000 Presidential and Popular Vote Summary," Federal Election Commission, December 2001, https://transition.fec.gov/pubrec/fe2000/prespop.htm.

13. Richard Rorty, *Achieving Our Country: Leftist Political Thought in America* (Cambridge, MA: Harvard University Press, 1998), 90.

14. For discussion of Rexford Tugwell and the other Columbia progressive "brain trusters" in the early New Deal, see David Kennedy, *Freedom from Fear: The American People in Depression and War, 1929–45* (Oxford: Oxford University Press, 1999), 119–124.

15. "Let the ruling classes tremble at a communistic revolution. The proletarians have nothing to lose but their chains. They have a world to win." Marx and Engels, *Communist Manifesto*, 102.

16. Branko Milanovic, *Global Inequality: A New Approach for the Age of Globalization* (Cambridge, MA: Harvard University Press, 2018).

17. Francis Fukuyama, *The End of History and the Last Man* (New York: Free Press, 1992).

18. Ben Bernanke, "The Great Moderation," remarks at the meetings of the Eastern Economic Association, Washington, DC, February 20, 2004, https://www.federalreserve.gov/boarddocs/speeches/2004/20040220.

19. Stephen Labaton, "Congress Passes Wide-Ranging Bill Easing Bank Laws," *New York Times*, November 5, 1999.

20. Financial intermediation is the process by which banks act as middlemen in transactions, borrowing money on their own accounts and lending it to others.

21. Adam Tooze, *Crashed: How a Decade of Financial Crises Changed the World* (New York: Viking, 2018), 67–68.

22. The Hartz IV reforms were the fourth in a series of business-friendly amendments to the German system of welfare and unemployment insurance. They were named for the chairman of the reform committee, former Volkswagen CEO Peter Hartz, and adopted by the Social Democratic–led government in 2003. The reforms reduced long-term unemployment insurance and required recipients to participate in supervised employment searches. See Nils Zimmermann, "German Issues in a Nutshell: Hartz IV," *Deutsche Welle*, June 5, 2017, https://www.dw.com/en/german-issues-in-a-nutshell-hartz-iv/a-39061709.

23. Douglas Rae, "Democratic Liberty and the Tyrannies of Place," in *Democracy's Edges*, eds. Ian Shapiro and Casiano Hacker-Cordón, 165–192 (Cambridge: Cambridge University Press, 1999).

24. Criminal Justice Fact Sheet, National Association for the Advancement of Colored People, https://www.naacp.org/criminal-justice-fact-sheet, last visited September 4, 2019.

25. Ahmed A. White, "The Juridical Structure of Habitual Offender Laws and the Jurisprudence of Authoritarian Social Control," *University of Toledo Law Review* 706 (2006): 705–745.

26. Richard Cowan, "Obama Gives Tentative Support to Financial Bailout," Reuters, September 28, 2008, https://www.reuters.com/article/us-financial-bailout-obama/obama-gives-tentative-support-to-financial-bailout-idUSTRE48R1UW20080928.

27. David Stout and Brian Knowlton, "Fed Chief Says Insurance Giant Acted Irresponsibly," *New York Times*, March 3, 2009. Adding insult to injury, these were not merit bonuses, paid for good performance. They were retention bonuses, paid to AIG executives to unwind credit default swaps whose markets had disappeared. In effect these executives were being rewarded for cleaning up the mess they had made. Kimberly Amadeo, "AIG Bailout, Cost, Timeline, Bonuses, Causes, Effects," The Balance, March 15, 2019, https://www.thebalance.com/aig-bailout-cost-timeline-bonuses-causes-effects-3305693.

28. This story is told in Ron Suskind, *Confidence Men: Wall Street, Washington, and the Education of a President* (New York: Harper, 2012) and Andrew Ross Sorkin, *Too Big to Fail: The Inside Story of How Wall Street and Washington Fought to Save the Financial System—and Themselves* (New York: Penguin, 2010). See also Tooze, *Crashed*, 166–201, 291–318.

29. Carl Hulse and David M. Herszenhorn, "House Rejects Bailout Plan; New Vote Is Planned," *New York Times*, September 29, 2008.

30. The final TARP bill passed the House with the support of 74 percent of Democrats but only 46 percent of Republicans. Tooze, *Crashed*, 195.

31. Henry Mance, "Britain Has Had Enough of Experts, Says Gove," *Financial Times*, June 3, 2016.

32. Tucker Carlson, *Ship of Fools: How a Selfish Ruling Class Is Bringing America to the Brink of Revolution* (New York: Free Press, 2018), 3.

33. Tooze, *Crashed*, 9–12, 202–203, 206–221.

34. Robert Kagan, *The Jungle Grows Back: America and Our Imperiled World* (New York: Knopf, 2018).

35. Scholars describe this tendency in the terms of "hegemonic stability theory," which dates back to Charles Kindleberger, *The World in Depression 1919–1939* (Berkeley: University of California Press, 1973). For useful accounts see Robert Gilpin, *The Political Economy of International Relations* (Princeton: Princeton University Press, 1987); Michael C. Webb and Stephen D. Krasner, "Hegemonic Stability Theory: An Empirical Assessment," *Review of International Studies* 15, no. 2 (1989): 183–198; and Barry Eichengreen, "Hegemonic Stability Theory and Economic Analysis: Reflections on Financial Instability and the Need for an International Lender of Last Resort," Center for International and Development Economics Research, University of California, Berkeley, 1996, https://escholarship.org/uc/item/7g49p8kj. On the historical evolution of

hegemonic powers, see Paul Kennedy, *The Rise and Fall of the Great Powers* (New York: Random House, 1987).

36. Will Drabold, "DNC Apologizes to Bernie Sanders and Supporters Over Leaked Emails," *Time*, July 25, 2016.

37. Martin Gilens and Benjamin I. Page, "Testing Theories of American Politics: Elites, Interest Groups, and Average Citizens," *Perspectives on Politics* 12, no. 3 (2014): 564–581.

38. Larry M. Bartels, *Unequal Democracy: The Political Economy of the New Gilded Age*, 2nd ed. (Princeton: Princeton University Press, 2016).

39. Our study of the 2001 repeal of the estate tax buttresses these findings. See Michael J. Graetz and Ian Shapiro, *Death by a Thousand Cuts: The Fight over Taxing Inherited Wealth* (Princeton: Princeton University Press, 2005).

40. Pablo Illanes, Susan Lund, Mona Mourshed, Scott Rutherford, and Magnus Tyreman, "Retraining and Reskilling Workers in the Age of Automation," McKinsey Global Institute, January 2018, https://www.mckinsey.com/featured-insights/future-of -work/retraining-and-reskilling-workers-in-the-age-of-automation.

41. "Jamie Dimon, "Markets and the Microsoft Initiative," CNBC interview, September 24, 2018, https://www.youtube.com/watch?v=OPy9atrILCk; Catherine Clifford, "Billionaire Warren Buffett on Helping the Poor: 'A Rich Family Does Not Leave People Behind,'" CNBC, September 5, 2018, https://www.cnbc.com /2018/09/05/warren-buffett-on-why-rich-people-government-should-help-the -poor.html.

42. Jane Mayer, *Dark Money: The Hidden History of the Billionaires behind the Rise of the Radical Right* (New York: Anchor, 2017).

43. Dan Merica, "Mike Bloomberg Would Self-Fund Potential 2020 Campaign, Setting Up Clash with Other Democrats," CNN, January 12, 2019, https://edition .cnn.com/2019/01/11/politics/bloomberg-self-fund-campaign/index.html; Lisa Lerer, "Is Howard Schultz a Candidate without a Constituency?" *New York Times*, January 28, 2019; Maggie Fitzgerald, "Mark Cuban Leaves Open Possibility of Running for President as an Independent," CNBC, May 14, 2019, https://www .cnbc.com/2019/05/14/mark-cuban-leaves-open-possibility-of-running-for -president-as-an-independent.html.

44. "Day 1 Families Fund," Bezos Day One Fund, November 20, 2018, https://www.bezosdayonefund.org/day1familiesfund.

45. "Quality School Options," Michael and Susan Dell Foundation, 2019, https://www.msdf.org/initiatives/quality-school-options.

46. Rick Green, "Who Is Ray Dalio and Why Are He and His Wife Donating $100 Million to Help Low-Income Schools in Connecticut?" *Hartford Courant*, April 5, 2019, https://www.courant.com/politics/hc-pol-clb-who-is-ray-dalio -20190405-zcmypqoxtzdazg4txbaxcn5lri-story.html; Audra D. S. Burch, David Gelles, and Emily S. Rueb, "Morehouse College Graduates' Student Loans to Be Paid Off by Billionaire," *New York Times*, May 19, 2019.

47. Michael Bloomberg, "Why I'm Giving $1.8 Billion for College Financial Aid," *New York Times*, November 18, 2018.

48. Shirin Ghaffary, "San Francisco Has Passed a First-of-Its-Kind Tax on Big Businesses—Like Square and Stripe—to Help the Homeless," Vox, November 7, 2018, https://www.vox.com/2018/11/7/18065086/san-francisco-prop-c-marc -benioff-jack-dorsey.

49. See Marisa Kendall, "Tech Leaders Donate $20 Million to Fight Silicon Valley Housing Shortage," *Mercury News,* November 27, 2018, https://www .mercurynews.com/2018/11/27/bay-area-tech-leaders-pony-up-20-million-to-fight -housing-shortage; Hannah Norman, "Okta Joins Growing Number of San Francisco Tech Companies Donating to Fight Poverty," *San Francisco Business Times,* February 6, 2019, https://www.bizjournals.com/sanfrancisco/news/2019/02 /05/okta-for-good-tipping-point-homelessness-tech.html; Taylor Telford, "A Tech Billionaire Donated $30 Million to Try to Solve San Francisco's Homeless Problem," *Washington Post,* May 2, 2019. As chapter 8 relates, Google has also dedicated $100 billion to ease San Francisco's affordable housing shortage.

50. "CEOs Are Saying They Need to Be More Socially Minded. Will Anything Change?" PBS, August 20, 2019, https://www.pbs.org/newshour/show/ceos-are -saying-they-need-to-be-more-socially-minded-will-anything-change.

ACKNOWLEDGMENTS

We have had much help from many quarters while writing this book. For the better part of a decade we have been teaching seminars at both Columbia and Yale, where we hammered out many of the issues and controversies addressed here. Excellent, engaged students helped us hone and improve this book in those settings, surely more than they realize.

A number of colleagues, students, and former students have read drafts of the full manuscript and given us excellent comments and suggestions. These include: Ashraf Ahmed, Anne Alstott, Jonathan Coutinho, John Kane, Joseph LaPalombara, Jim Leitner, David Mayhew, Rick Pildes, Jedediah Purdy, Doug Rae, Alex Raskolnikov, Frances Rosenbluth, James Scott, and Peter Swenson. Sydney Graetz also read the entire manuscript with care and insight. We also benefitted from conversations with colleagues at the National Academy of Social Insurance.

Ian Malcom provided helpful feedback on several versions of the book proposal and edited the entire manuscript with his usual—but rare—skill and good judgment. He also commissioned three exceedingly helpful anonymous readers' reports for Harvard University Press. Simon Waxman, a talented editor who did the line edit for Harvard University Press, improved the clarity of our exposition and arguments. Our agent, Wendy Strothman, subjected the proposal to her usual—and also rare—critical scrutiny, sending us back to the drawing board several times to good effect. She also came up with the title.

We have had superb help from a series of research assistants: Lucas Entel, Perry Lumpkin, Hovik Minasyan, Leila Halley-Wright, and Charles Urban-Mead.

We have also been the fortunate beneficiaries of outstanding institutional support and research funds from Columbia Law School and Yale. We have had exceptional assistance with a myriad of tasks from Lourdes Haynes, Patricia Page, and John Christian White.

It would be an exaggeration to say that many hands make light work, as a good deal of heavy lifting by many people has gone into this book. But our task would have been immeasurably harder without all this support, and the end product notably more flawed. We are grateful to all who helped in so many different ways.

INDEX

moral commitments / arguments; moral hazard); proximate gains and, 49–58 (*see also* proximate goals); resistance to, 35; self-interest in, 44–45

divide-a-dollar game, 40–41, 44

Dodd-Frank regulation, 31

Doggett, Lloyd, 271

Dorsey, Jack, 278

Downey, Tom, 123

drug abuse, 18, 27, 29

du Pont, Alfred, 82

Duval, Zippy, 143

earmarked taxes, 256

Earned Income Tax Credit (EITC), 115, 121, 122–128, 169, 201, 212, 230; coalitions and, 127, 135, 136; effects of, 135; leaders / leadership and, 136; moral argument and, 124, 126, 135; political future of, 135–137; as redistribution, 126

economic growth: after World War II, 10–12, 85; need for, 81; slowing of, 14–15, 19; World War II and, 83. *See also* economy, US

economic mobility, 30. *See also* mobility, downward; mobility, upward

economy, US: composition of, 19–20 (*see also* manufacturing); trade liberalization and, 139; trade wars and, 142. *See also* economic growth; globalization; service industries; trade, international

Edsall, Mary, 14

Edsall, Thomas, 14

education: charter schools, 220–222; class segregation and, 219; coalitions and, 218; Coleman Report, 225; Elementary and Secondary Education Act (ESEA), 224–225; employment and, 20, 218–229; equity in, 223–224; Every Student Succeeds Act (ESSA), 227; funding of public schools, 219; impact of spending on, 226; income and, 31–32; job loss and, 22; in Newark, 220–221, 222, 225, 228;

No Child Left Behind (NCLB), 224, 226–227; political right, and, 219–220; productivity and, 167; Program for International Student Assessment, 218; public schools, 202; right to, 223; school choice, 219–222; school reform, 219–223, 226, 228; segregation in, 12, 54, 223, 224; taxes and, 223; technology and, 218; voucher systems, 219–222. *See also* child care / preschool

education, vocational, 233

egalitarian redistribution. *See* distribution of income / wealth

Eisenhower, Dwight, 102, 139

EITC (Earned Income Tax Credit). *See* Earned Income Tax Credit (EITC)

elderly, 52, 149, 206. *See also* AARP; Medicare; Social Security

election (2016): fear and, 30–31. *See also* Clinton, Hillary; presidential campaigns; Trump, Donald

elections, midterm (2018), 6

Elementary and Secondary Education Act (ESEA), 224–225

Emanuel, Rahm, 184, 221

Emerging Republican Majority, The (Phillips), 13–14

employment: automation and, 20 (*see also* technology / automation); creating, 230; education and, 20, 218–229; health insurance and, 203, 204; home ownership and, 80; infrastructure and, 172–200; limited private-sector opportunities, 170; long-term jobs, 114–115 (*see also* job security); movement for, 163–165, 230; need for college education and, 18; need for universal pre-K and, 216–217; paid family leave and, 217; private-sector, government finance of, 172 (*see also* infrastructure projects); right to, 170; Social Security's barriers to, 122; technology and, 20 (*see also* technology / automation); temporary, 151, 265, 266. *See also*

INDEX

George, Henry, 116
GI Bill, 10, 65
Gilens, Martin, 275
Gillibrand, Kirsten, 220–221
Gingrich, Newt, 48, 69, 242
Ginsburg, Ruth Bader, 92–93
Glaeser, Edward, 230
Glass-Steagall Act, 269
globalization: influence on income
    tax systems, 250–251; insecurity
    and, 79; job losses blamed on,
    20–21, 137–138; middle class and,
    64–68, 79; rise of, 19. *See also*
    economy, US; imports; out-
    sourcing / offshoring; trade,
    international
goals, proximate. *See* proximate goals
Goldman Sachs, 272
Goldstein, Dana, 222
Google, 236
GOP. *See* Republicans
Gordon Lasner, Matthew, 236
Gove, Michael, 272
Graham, Lindsey, 100
Gramm-Leach-Bliley bill, 269
Grant, Ulysses S., 54
Great Recession. *See* financial crises
Greenspan, Alan, 91, 243
Greenstein, Robert, 120, 124
Gross, Bill, 119
gross domestic product (GDP), 12, 139,
    243. *See also* economy, US

Hacker, Jacob, 207, 208
Hall, Marcia, 196
Harley-Davidson, 141
Harriman, Averell, 83
Harris, Fred, 118
Harris, Kamala: education and, 220; on
    infrastructure, 174
Harvard Business Review, 107–108
Hastert, Dennis, 178
Hastert rule, 178
Hayes, Greg, 148
health care legislation. *See* Affordable
    Care Act (ACA; Obamacare);
    health insurance; health insurance
    legislation

health expenditures, 102, 203–204. *See
    also* health insurance; health
    insurance legislation
health insurance: access to, 202; appeal
    of, 199; Children's Health Insurance
    Program, 202, 203; coalitions and,
    206–207; Democrats and, 208; for
    displaced workers, 161; employer-
    based coverage, 203, 204; federal
    subsidies for, 203; income and, 11,
    206, 207; Medicare-for-all, 3, 205,
    206; premiums, 204; provision of,
    11; single-payer national system,
    205–207; sources of, 202–203 (*see
    also* Affordable Care Act; Medicaid;
    Medicare)
health insurance legislation: business
    interests and, 101–105; effects of,
    34; moral argument for, 105; public
    option, 103. *See also* Affordable Care
    Act (ACA; Obamacare); Medicaid;
    Medicare
Henninger, Daniel, 47
Hensarling, Jeb, 271
Heritage Foundation, 59
Hickenlooper, John, 190
Hickory, North Carolina, 234–235
Hidden Welfare State, The (Howard), 119
highway system. *See* infrastructure
    projects
Highway Trust Fund, 181
Hirschman, Albert, 219, 222
Hochschild, Arlie, 4, 6, 26, 166,
    262–263
Hollande, François, 245
Home Affordable Modification
    Program, 74
home ownership, 64–80; appeal of to
    politicians, 72; Clinton's strategy for,
    64–67; cost of, 17, 29, 235–237;
    employment and, 80; enthusiasm
    for, 77; expansion policy, malign
    effects of, 76–80; Home Affordable
    Modification Program, 74; illusion
    of security and, 80; incomes and, 11,
    65; lower-income Americans and,
    67–80; minorities and, 67–80;
    moral agenda and, 79–80;

home ownership (*continued*)
National Housing Act of 1934, 65;
saving and, 77–78. *See also* mortgage
market
Homeownership and Opportunity for
People Everywhere (HOPE)
program, 65–66
Hoover, Herbert, 139, 270
Hope Scholarships, 39
housing, cost of, 11, 17, 29, 235–237.
See also home ownership
Housing and Urban Development,
Department of (HUD), 64, 65–66,
237
housing market crisis. *See* home
ownership; mortgage market
housing markets, 73. *See also* home
ownership; mortgage market
housing projects, 225
Howard, Christopher, 119, 126
Hufbauer, Gary, 139
human capital, 266. *See also* education;
skills

ideology. *See* individualism / bootstrapping; moral commitments /
arguments
immigrants, 6, 30, 33, 145, 149. *See also*
nativism; xenophobia
Immigration and Naturalization Act of
1965, 13
imports, 20–21. *See also* globalization;
outsourcing / offshoring; trade,
international
income: African Americans and, 32;
education and, 31–32; flattening of,
14; gender-based salary gap, 262;
health insurance and, 11, 206, 207;
home ownership and, 65;
race / gender and, 31–32, 262;
raising tax rates on, 248–249;
redistribution of. *See also* Earned
Income Tax Credit (EITC); income,
guaranteed; minimum wage; wages
income, guaranteed: Family Assistance
Plan (FAP), 116–117, 122; labor
unions and, 119; moral argument
and, 120; universal basic income,

115–121, 136, 201; work requirements and, 117, 118
individualism / bootstrapping, 11, 28,
152, 163–165, 265
inequality, 1, 4, 7, 37–38
inflation, 90, 241. *See also* stagflation
infrastructure projects, 172–200, 201;
airports, 186–187, 188–190; benefits
of, 172–173; business interests and,
177, 184; California's high-speed rail
project, 196; challenges to, 198–199;
Chicago's parking meters, 187–188;
coalitions and, 176–177, 184, 194,
196, 198; creating employment with,
230; debt financing of, 183–184,
191; degradation of, 173–174;
difficulty in improving, 176–179;
effects of, 192, 194; funding of,
179–183, 185–188, 191, 192–194,
197–200, 259; Gateway tunnel
project, 194–196; highway system,
180, 181; incentives to improve, 199;
leaders / leadership and, 174–176,
177–179, 184, 190, 194–196, 197,
198; Los Angeles transit project,
193–194; managing risks in funding
of, 185–188, 189, 197; mass transit,
181–182, 190–191, 193–194; moral
arguments and, 197; Port of Miami,
191–192; privatization of, 186–188,
189; proximate goals and, 198;
public financing of, 192–193;
public-private partnerships and, 175,
185–188, 190–192, 197–198;
rural-urban divide and, 176–177,
182, 197; Tappan Zee Bridge
replacement, 192–193; taxes and,
179, 182–183, 193–194, 242, 256;
tolls, 186, 193; Works Progress
Administration, 173, 198
inheritances, 248. *See also* estate tax
injustice, local, 262–263
international relations, 148, 274–275
interstates. *See* infrastructure projects
investment banks, 70–71. *See also*
financial institutions
investments, public, 258–259. *See also*
infrastructure projects

Nixon, Richard, 12, 41, 86; Child Development Act and, 210–211; FAP and, 116–117; health insurance legislation and, 102; Southern strategy, 13–14, 40, 41; steel industry and, 140; TAA and, 156

No Child Left Behind (NCLB), 224, 226–227

Norquist, Grover, 14, 242

North American Free Trade Agreement (NAFTA), 138, 139, 147, 158

NWRO (National Welfare Rights Organization), 117–118

Obama, Barack, 271, 274; climate change legislation and, 100; education and, 227; health insurance and, 199 (*see also* Affordable Care Act [ACA; Obamacare]); Home Affordable Modification Program, 74; infrastructure projects and, 174, 178–179, 182, 194, 197, 198, 199, 200; international trade and, 138; labor and, 92; on manufacturing, 18; minimum wage and, 132; public-private infrastructure partnerships and, 184; steel industry and, 140; taxes and, 243, 244, 246; Tea Party movement and, 50; on Trump, 53

Obamacare. *See* Affordable Care Act (ACA; Obamacare)

Ocasio-Cortez, Alexandria, 244–245, 246, 251

Occupy movement, 2, 5, 30; lack of coaltions in, 43; lack of resources, 59; lack of well-defined proximate goal, 50–51; obstacles to success of, 60–61

offshoring. *See* globalization; outsourcing / offshoring; trade, international

oil prices, 139–140

oil / energy crises, 14, 15, 86

Olson, Mancur, 45, 146

opioid crisis, 18, 27. *See also* drug abuse

opportunities, crises and, 198–199

opportunity zones, 231–232

organized labor. *See* labor unions

Orszag, Peter, 98

Our Kids (Putnam), 218

outsourcing / offshoring, 3, 20–21, 93, 95. *See also* globalization; imports; trade, international

overdoses, rates of, 27. *See also* drug abuse

PACs (political action committees), 86–87

Page, Benjamin, 275

Paine, Lynn, 107–108

Pareto distribution, 37–38

Patriotic Millionaires, 109

Patterson, James, 225

Pearl, Morris, 109–110, 111

Pearlstein, Steven, 278

Pence, Mike, 175

pensions, 11, 29, 77

Pepper, Claude, 130

Pepsi, 155

Perkins, Frances, 130

Peterson Institute for International Economics, 142

philanthropy, 277–278. *See also* Newark, New Jersey

Phillips, Kevin, 13–14, 31

Piketty, Thomas, 247, 260–261

place-based policies, 202, 228, 229–238; challenges of, 230; effectiveness of, 232–235, 236–237; housing costs, 235–237; Newark 2020, 232–233; opportunity zones, 231–232; skepticism about, 229–230

Plug Power, 141

Policy and Taxation Group, 58

political action committees (PACs), 86–87

political parties, 14. *See also* Democrats; Republicans; Southern strategy; *and individual politicians*

political realignment, 13–14, 40. *See also* conservatives; Democrats; liberals; presidential campaigns; Republicans; Southern strategy

Poor People's Campaign (1968), 112, 115